Surprising Significance
A Rhetoric with Readings

Surprising Significance
A Rhetoric with Readings

Roger Conner

Harold Washington College

Harcourt College Publishers

Fort Worth Philadelphia San Diego New York Orlando Austin San Antonio
Toronto Montreal London Sydney Tokyo

Publisher	Earl McPeek
Acquisitions Editor	Julie McBurney
Marketing Strategist	John Meyers
Project Manager	Angela Williams Urquhart

ISBN: 0-15-506977-2

Library of Congress Catalog Card Number: 00-111490

Address for Domestic Orders
Harcourt College Publishers, 6277 Sea Harbor Drive, Orlando, FL 32887-6777
800-782-4479

Address for International Orders
International Customer Service
Harcourt College Publishers, 6277 Sea Harbor Drive, Orlando, FL 32887-6777
407-345-3800
(fax) 407-345-4060
(e-mail) hbintl@harcourtbrace.com

Address for Editorial Correspondence
Harcourt College Publishers, 301 Commerce Street, Suite 3700, Fort Worth, TX 76102

Web Site Address
http://www.harcourtcollege.com

Harcourt College Publishers will provide complimentary supplements or supplement packages to those adopters qualified under our adoption policy. Please contact your sales representative to learn how you qualify. If as an adopter or potential user you receive supplements you do not need, please return them to your sales representative or send them to:
Attn: Returns Department, Troy Warehouse, 465 South Lincoln Drive, Troy, MO 63379.

Printed in the United States of America

0 1 2 3 4 5 6 7 8 9   039   9 8 7 6 5 4 3 2 1

Harcourt College Publishers

To
Margaret Rausch, the editor who taught me how to write
and
Jain Simmons, whose gentle joyous midwifery finally brought this book to light

I am not a scientist, not a naturalist, not a chef, not an expert, not the best or worst mother, but a writer only, a woman constantly surprised.

—Louise Erdrich

Preface:
To the Instructor

The Origins

The bug for this book bit me about 10 years ago when I realized that there might be a connection between my students' often lackluster writing and the discouraging fact that, too often, they were not enjoying the brilliance of their reading assignments. At the time, Roger Schank was teaching computers to read and summarize newspaper accounts. He did it by having his computers single out the unexpected element—whatever was outside the database of unusual details for that kind of story (the ambulance that, in responding to a heart attack, had an accident with fatalities, or the bank robbed by an octogenarian grandmother). The computer was trained to center its summary around the jarring element, leaving the typical elements to be filled in by readers' scripts of such situations. Surprise was the key to the stories' significance.

I decided to see whether the lessons of artificial intelligence could help sharpen human intelligence. So instead of asking students to find the main idea or thesis in their readings, I tried asking them to find the surprise, the anomaly, the curious quiddity that made the piece "newsworthy." I was nonplussed to find that students had almost a compulsion to ignore or explain away, rather than seize and enjoy, the surprises that the authors labored to dramatize. Could this be a major stumbling block in their writing, as well as their reading process?

The human mind seemed to have a natural surprise-avoidance strategy. The possibility that this resulted in inhibited writing was reinforced for me by an article in *CCC* by Betsy Hilbert titled, "It Was a Dark and Nasty Night It Was a Dark and You Would Not Believe

How Dark It Was a Hard Beginning" (Feb., 1992). She reported that having students create beginnings fraught with anticipation had succeeded in shaking them loose from their desperate reliance on what she called the safe AAA Triptik plan of thesis statement followed by a rigidly outlined development.

Thus sensitized, I began to notice references everywhere to the centrality of surprise as a liberating and organizing principle. Writers from novelists to scholars seemed to agree that surprise is the wellspring of effective writing. The novelist Louise Erdrich said, "I am . . . a writer only, a woman constantly surprised." The scholar Lee Odell titled an article "Strategy and Surprise in the Making of Meaning." In that article he said, "The notion of dissonance is central to work in rhetoric." And professors David Kaufer and Cheryl Geisler complained that "despite the attention paid to 'invention and inquiry' in writing instruction, novelty as a writing standard, much less strategy, is absent from our pedagogical traditions in composition. We find this situation curious."

So I tried just having students start their papers, not with a thesis nor an introduction nor a rambling narration, but directly with a dramatic shocker or a mystery building toward one. I was delighted to find that students who tried this produced essays that made a quantum leap ahead, both in interest and focus. But I found considerable resistance to my program since it cast student writers into uncharted territory without a road map. I clearly had an obligation to provide, if not a Triptik, at least some guidance gleaned from how professional authors proceeded after that "dark and nasty night" beginning. This sent me on a lengthy quest to reanalyze with a new eye those brilliant pieces we had been reading.

The best nonfiction writing seemed to follow, in broad outline, the trajectory our minds follow when we *encounter* an eye-opening anomaly. We immediately seek an *explanation* of that disjuncture hoping to find a *resolution* that will construct the significance of the original event. This rhetorical trajectory, I noticed, could be found in writing ranging from scientific articles in the *Smithsonian* to personal columns in the *San Francisco Chronicle.*

These writings, of course, did not follow the trajectory in a straight line. Instead, they seemed to follow a cyclical pattern, amassing conviction in the reader's mind by weaving a variety of strands around the basic encounter-explanation-resolution arch. The critically important strands seemed to fall into a few categories—*background, reasoning, search,* and *valuation*—reminiscent of the old modes of discourse.

But, while there was a definite shift of approach as the writing moved from one of these to another, it was not as if each section of a piece stood in fully developed isolation from the others. All were integrated into a dynamic process, which, after awakening readers with a surprise, ultimately satisfied them with its significance.

I decided to call these strands or modes of development *modalities*. I wanted a term that would be distinctive but that would reflect the truth contained in the idea of the modes—that to feel satisfied, readers need to experience a topic through a variety of approaches. And because each approach requires a different set of techniques, it seemed good to treat them separately, while still emphasizing the dynamic, recursive, interweaving processes that connected them into a unified whole.

Once I had marshaled enough material to put this initiative together as a textbook in beta form, I found myself faced with the same kind of anxiety that many students feel on the eve of handing in their first essay assignment. Would this fly? Could I really put "None" on the required text list for next semester and leave students and myself without any of those comfortable paradigms of the past—no (writer-centered) "process" exercises, no "writing with a purpose," no "introduction, body, and conclusion," no "thesis and development"?

When I did, some students went willingly into that dark and stormy night, others steadfastly refused to abandon the five-paragraph essay format. But my most intriguing successes occurred with students who, although listening attentively, resisted putting these techniques into practice until the last week of the term. Then for their final essay they went whole hog for the program and suddenly produced essays of near-professional caliber. It is my sincere hope that this book can help you do for your students what it has helped me do for many of mine: show them how to create writing of surprising significance.

The Result

Encouragement by Example

I have tried to build students' confidence in this new, dynamic, reader-centered approach by showing how I would shape surprising experiences of my own (see especially the "Opening the Topic" section at the beginning of Chapter 2, the section "Exploring the Topic: The Drama of Details" in Chapter 3, and "Protesting Purple Patriotism," Chapter 9). I have found that these self-revelatory examples do elicit a corresponding openness on the part of sometimes diffident or embarrassed students, giving them the sense that we are all apprentices in the stimulating craft of surprising significance from our life experience.

Of course there are other students who have no fear of writing but who have trouble structuring their energy into a coherent form. I have found that the writing of such students becomes much more unified when they envision the channel from surprising encounter through explanation to resolution as a guide. Every impulse can be evaluated and adjusted for its contribution to that central dynamic, reader-oriented trajectory.

Organization

The issues of confidence and coherence, along with the main trajectory and its justification, are mainly dealt with in Part I of the book, which after an introduction to the concept of modality cycles, contains chapters on *encounters, explanation,* and *resolution,* framed by chapters on *eye-openers* and *significance.* Part II demonstrates the role of the "satellite" modalities (*background, reasoning, search,* and *valuation*), concluding with a reprise of the first chapter on integrating the modalities. This division into parts allows for flexibility. If time runs short, it is certainly possible to pick and choose chapters from the second part, depending on what you feel would benefit your students most. I would, however, save time for the last chapter, "Integrating the Modalities," because it reinforces, with a substantial, analyzed example, the key point that switching through the various approaches to the subject is a dynamic, reader-centered process.

User-Friendly Style

I have used a style and tone aimed at directly engaging the college-age reader. I try to keep that reader engaged by putting the book's main principle into practice: the book itself is full of surprises—significant ones. Most important of these are certain selections that are printed with graphics and notes pushing into the text to drive home the point where it counts. (See "Demonstrations" in Chapters 1, 6, 9, and 11).

Readings on a Variety of Themes

Although the book is clearly a rhetoric with illustrative readings rather than a reader with some suggestions about rhetoric, the selections comprise enough variety that skillful readers may be challenged without the less skillful being turned off. And there is a loose thematic arrangement, with pieces on the art of writing in Chapters 1 and 2, pieces on the psychology of fear and cruelty in Chapters 3 and 4, love and marriage in 4 and 5, the family in 6 and 7, diversity in 10 and 11, and other social and political topics in Chapters 7 through 9. Although none of the pieces is of a specialized academic nature, readings deal with subjects from "across the curriculum" (written for a general educated audience) on natural science, sociology, psychology, and history.

Situated Writing

Just as the readings emphasize rhetorical strategies used by working writers, so the writing assignments encourage students to feel that they are colleagues of those writers. The most important technique for lifting the writing assignment out of the artificial venue of the classroom is one borrowed from the situated-writing movement. Starting with Chapter 4 most assignments are connected by the creation of a virtual-reality newspaper in a small city where the students are summer interns. Here the instructor can role-play editor to become more mentor than "teacher." The assignments—called "commissions" to further distance them from classroom drudgery—do, of course, emphasize the use of the modality demonstrated in the chapter, but they are such as an editor might actually have interns doing—writing a review of a poem (Chapter 4), creating an internal memo (Chapter 4), resolving an educational issue (Chapter 5), expounding the significance of social trends (Chapter 6), writing up a reporter's facts on a local dinosaur exhibit (Chapter 8), writing a mini research column on gender differences in math and science with a follow-up based on additional research of an "intern-conducted" survey (Chapter 9), analyzing the values in some of the virtual city's public symbols (Chapter 10).

Collaborative Writing

Collaborative writing is a fact of life in the contemporary business world and professional schools, and the fiction of the students being interns in a virtual newspaper office provides a natural setting for collaborative writing projects. In Chapter 4, "interns" cooperate in explaining one of a number of social problems; in Chapter 7 they use partners role-playing delegates to a convention of student government leaders to interview each other on cultural diversity; in Chapter

9 they collaborate on designing and conducting a survey; and in Chapter 10 they divide up tasks for mounting a public service ad campaign.

Structured Writing

To give students the sense that true authorship is not beyond their grasp, the book supplies the apprentice writer with plenty of concrete support. The situated writings are interspersed with "Writing Activities," which focus students' growing skills with structured practice. These activities offer an opportunity for specialized writing in a particular modality without sacrificing the holistic sense of its place in an entire essay. If the chapter is about discovering significant axes of similarity between events (as in Chapter 6), well-written descriptions are provided of the events between and around which the student is to craft connecting paragraphs. When the book talks about mapping issues representing different points of view (as in Chapter 7), acting out a talk show opens students' eyes to the variety of different points of view possible on an issue. If the point is to sort through a collection of facts logically and present them meaningfully to the reader (as in Chapter 8), the book provides the facts, sparing the student time-consuming library research.

Intuitively Persuasive Principles

In broad outlines, the approach of this text can easily be made persuasive to student writers. It grows from a widely acknowledged principle of effective writing: the centrality of surprise. If there is no novelty in what the writer has to say, after all, there is no point in saying anything. This is followed up by the intuitively reasonable sequence of explanation and resolution. The way professional writers make this sequence fully satisfying to a reader is by cycling through one or more of the following processes: filling in necessary background, deploying factual research, reasoning persuasively, and heightening emotional valuation. The organization of these elements may change from one genre to the next, but I hope by the end students will see that the principles presented here must inform nearly every successful piece of writing from abstruse scientific articles to humble office memos.

Contents

A Personal Note from the Author

OK. I'm here to sell you on the idea of giving up a significant part of your life, a portion that could otherwise be devoted to drinking, watching Jay Leno, flossing, or pet-sitting a rich old lady's cockatoo, to devote up to a couple of hours each day practicing something with a truly weird name.

I don't even want to tell you. Well, OK, it's "lubricity."

No, just kidding! Although that's a weird name, all right. But the thing I'm trying to sell you on is the study of **rhetoric.**

"Ah, yes," you say. "I've been looking forward to taking freshman rhetoric ever since old Miss Hellas taught us about the ancient Greeks in seventh grade. For a long time I thought she was talking about old geeks, and I was really interested because I had to deal with some of them trying to put the touch on me.

"Anyways," you say, "it must be a popular course, because all my cousins took it when they went to college. Even Cousin Joey that went to Harvard—the community college in Harvard, Illinois, that is."

Well, it is certainly a popular course with those administrators whose job it is to make students take certain courses—like social science and biology, which they think are necessary for every citizen—and discourage students from taking courses with clear benefits to everyone, like Movie Themes during the Flapper Era and Sex Lives of the Presid—. . . oops, I mean . . . of Anaerobic Bacteria.

Actually, rhetoric has been a required course (in European and American schools) for two thousand years—from way back, in other words, even before The Eagles and "Hotel California." Undergraduates in the Middle (or, as we used to say, "Dark") Ages had a core curriculum of rhetoric, grammar, and logic, with electives in beer drinking and sword fighting. But these were hand-me-downs from the lyceums of ancient Rome and Greece, where young men wrapped in white sheets reclined among tall pillars listening to Aristotle say things like "Rhetoric is the faculty of observing in any given case the available means of persuasion." This is hardly what you heard from old Miss Hellas; it's a far cry, too, from what I heard from the guy that taught my freshman rhetoric class at Northwestern. In fact, when you look at it, it's really kind of startling. It doesn't sound like composition at all. It's strategic, rather than tactical. It focuses on the ability to sum up a communication situation. It's like saying, "Skill in quarterbacking is the ability to size up the defense with the field position, the score, and the time, and to choose the best play from those that the team knows how to run."

Rhetoric, then, is like having a playbook that you can draw on to persuade your readers in a particular situation. And just as the football playbook is the product of years of experience watching films of previous games, the rhetoric playbook is the product of centuries of studying the writings of thousands of authors who ran good rhetorical plays that dazzled their readers. We will be assiduously reading samples from this rhetorical playbook in the essays selected for this course because they illustrate effective rhetoric that has been proven to interest and persuade a wide variety of readers.

The Greeks sometimes had to dazzle their listeners because, under the rules of the Athenians, who invented democracy, all laws were enacted at town meetings open to anybody—well, any citizen—well, any adult male citizen. Slaves and *barbaroi* (barbarians, or resident aliens) were excluded, and the women had to stay home with the kids. And, of course, a lot of the guys stayed home to watch Monday Night Discus Throwing. Still, out of 40,000 guys, 5,000 or so used to show up at the weekly town meetings to shout at each other about lowering taxes, raising the draft age, picking up garbage, and fixing the potholes. If you wanted a hearing, you had better get a rhetoric teacher, because it was a crowd only a little less tough than a condo committee.

Even scarier was the fact that legal proceedings were held the same way. If you drove your ox cart through somebody's cabbage patch, he could haul you into court where you would have to defend yourself in front of a jury of 200 to 1000 male citizens (too big to be fixed). And neither of you would get a lawyer, either. It was just his rhetoric against yours. If you had cut your rhetoric classes to run marathons while the cabbage patch owner was paying attention to Aristotle under the portico, you might end up owing a lot of drachmas.

Figure 0.1. Greek orator Demosthenes using rhetoric.

So rhetoric is important, and not just for lawyers and legislators. As Aristotle said, "All men make use, more or less, of [rhetoric]; for to a certain extent all men attempt to discuss statements and to maintain them, to defend themselves and to attack others. Ordinary people do this either at random or through practice and from acquired habit. Both ways being possible, the subject can plainly be handled systematically, for it is possible to inquire the reason why some speakers succeed through practice and others spontaneously; and every one will at once agree that such an inquiry is the function of an art."

So that's what we will do in this course: Systematically "inquire the reason why some" writers succeed. You will try to acquire, through practice, the art of choosing among the rhetorical moves we identify so that you can dazzle your readers. Today's writers are not reclining in their togas on the side of the Acropolis but are crammed into cubicles on the upper reaches of an office building, staring at word processing screens. But as you squeeze into your cubicle to become part of today's business world or rise to address a motion at a PTA meeting, your purpose will be the same as that of Aristotle's students: "to discuss statements and maintain them." The statements will not be about whether Macedonia should be attacked (unless Macedonia suddenly discovers a lot of oil under its territory, thus becoming part of our "vital interest").

Instead you will find yourself having to compose mission statements, to defend expenditures, to plead for new programs, and to admonish people to please put their soda cans in the recycling containers instead of leaving them hidden behind heating pipes. Someone has estimated—this is really true—that 70 percent of white-collar

work involves writing. So that's part of "how come this course": In your community, you will find you have the power to change how your children will be educated; in business, you will probably find your performance review is based largely on how persuasively you can write. And when you have to present that proposal in front of the school board or to defend that review in front of your boss, you may become aware of Aristotle in the corner surreptitiously monitoring your rhetoric!

Figure 0.2. Aristotle in the corner surreptitiously monitoring your rhetoric.

E-E-R

Encounter

Explain

Resolve

R-S-V-B

Reason

Search

Value

Background

PART I

The Core Modalities

E-E-R

Encounter

Explain

Resolve

R-S-V-B

Reason

Search

Value

Background

1

The Modalities Cycle

We begin a project relying on "spontaneous, routinized responses."
But almost inevitably we encounter some sort of surprise. . . .
Consequently we reflect on what we're doing.

—Lee Odell (citing Donald Schon)

Why This Book Is as It Is and Not Otherwise

"The Event of the Century!" (as it's being billed by the TV networks) is about to take place: The first human space mission to Mars.

Let's suppose that your English instructor has become very excited about this as a once-in-a-lifetime opportunity for a writing assignment. (You just *know* that is how we English teachers think, right?) So you are supposed to immerse yourself in the mission to Mars over the weekend and come up with "The Essay of the Century" by Friday.

So you put new batteries in the remote, get a bag of chips and a Pepsi, and prepare to let the warm surf of 250 channels wash over you. At first you flip aimlessly right up through the numbers, but you quickly find this confusing, leading nowhere. An essay based on this kind of channel hopping would be a disaster. You are going to have to become an active viewer hunting those "Aha!" moments that will impress your instructor.

You need a plan.

You go back to last Sunday's newspaper supplement, devoted to the upcoming event, and notice that individual channels have announced the particular kind of programming each has planned for its segment of the audience.

3

- ☐ CNN will be doing live, continuous coverage from Cape Canaveral and Houston of whatever they **encounter** that moves or talks.
- ☐ The major networks will be busy with their news analysts **explaining** the political infighting that led up to this galaxy-shaking event.
- ☐ PBS will be doing interviews with social scientists and political activists, most of whom will be **reasoning** about the social impact of the event and pointing out how the money could have been better spent on solving social problems here on earth.
- ☐ The Discovery Channel will be interviewing scientists and providing carefully re**search**ed information about the engineering principles and strategies that have enabled this light-payload breakthrough.
- ☐ Religion-oriented channels will be hosting debates among prelates and secular philosophers on the impact on human **values** of our expanding experience with the outer cosmos and of the possibility of extraterrestrial life.
- ☐ The History Channel will be giving **background** of human exploration from Asian and perhaps European sea voyages to this continent some 30,000 years ago up to the landing on the moon in the last century.
- ☐ All the channels, from their different perspectives, will be trying to help you, the viewer, **resolve** in your own mind your attitude toward the **significance** of this **eye-opening** rush to the stars.

This narrowed focus looks like the right stuff.

Now that you have a manageable number of channels, you no longer need to zip through them; you can stick with each one for a full segment. Your plan is, when they break for commercials, you will go to the next network until you have cycled through your whole agenda. Then you will pause and take some notes.

Once through the list, you are at a decision point. You ponder which channels are worth revisiting. Maybe you were surprised at the number of early failures in the moon rocket program, so you decide to go back to the History Channel. You didn't quite understand how earlier robot flights were managing to make fuel on Mars for the astronauts' return flight, so you revisit the Discovery Channel. Then you check in with CNN and ABC again to see how things are going, and you pause again to take some more notes as you begin to zero in on the particular line that interests you through this welter of information.

Of course, as the time for the blast off draws near, all channels switch to a common feed for the actual event. You hear the familiar ". . . 3 . . . 2 . . . 1 . . . We have ignition. . . . We have liftoff!" As the orange-headed trace fades away into the cerulean heavens, and after the soundless puff of the booster separation signals a successful launch attested by the cheering crowd of engineers in the control room, you return to your channel surfing, cycling through just those channels you feel you need to fill in gaps, get reactions, and shape your take on the whole scene. At last you switch off the tube and jot down your final notes.

As you look over what you've written, you are astonished to find that with just a few tweaks here and there your essay has practically written itself. It's not the way you have written essays before. Although there is a conclusion, there is certainly no introduction. You started right off with a tense, dramatic moment, seen on CNN, when the countdown had to be stopped because of a warning light indicating a potentially fatal fuel leak. You did not lay out the structure of the essay in advance, because you did not yet know what information you were going to find significant. Instead of following an artificially prescribed plan, your sections follow the path of psychological need that directed you from channel to channel through areas you might not have thought interesting before. These sections do not have topic sentences; they lead with surprises, twists, disagreements, ironies, problems. Your tour through media-land did not progress in a straight line; instead, you found yourself cycling back to summarize how each trip through the networks clarified and extended the point that you saw emerging.

Do you dare turn in an essay with this kind of structure? It doesn't sound like schoolwork exactly. But it does sound a lot like the columnists you sometimes read in the newspaper, and it seems to capture the drama of the event and the excitement shown by some of those commentators, historians, scientists, philosophers, and clergy that you saw on the programs. Yes, you decide, this will definitely make better reading than the kind of stuff you've written before, which tended to veer from the intensely-felt-but-hard-to-follow to the well-organized-but-deadly-dull.

OK, you decide, you're going to risk it. It may not be *the* essay of the twenty-first century, but it is going to be *an* essay of the twenty-first century.

This book is based on the observation that most modern nonfiction writing follows a strategic plan a lot like the one I just described.

To begin with, of course, the writer must have tripped over a surprise. It doesn't have to be as big a deal as the risky business of shooting a tin can filled with people on a year-long trip to a distant planet. It might just be a puzzling comment overheard at a mall. However, as the epigraph on the title page of this book suggests, writers are people who find surprises just about everywhere. That is the spark that sets off their search for significance. In pursuit of that search the writer takes the reader on a cyclical course through a number of different sections, as different in style, content, and approach as those different channels of the TV networks. All are tied together by the single-minded drive to explain the surprise and resolve it. ("Why does a nation expend such wealth and risk so much to conquer space? And should it?" might have been your thread through our space shot example.) And professional writers typically emphasize the unity of their quest by returning, after each cycle through the channels, to a repeated formulation of the gradually clarifying meaning.

Now, I think that the image of channel surfing is a good one for improving the rhetoric of your writing. If you find it useful as the course progresses, I hope you will hold onto it. But I'm going to shift from that concrete image to a made-up, abstract, neutral term for the balance of the book, because the TV channel analogy may not fit every person or every situation. And I have several other useful images that I want to introduce along the way that don't mesh well with this one.

The term I've picked to express the way professional writers shift rhetorical gears as they move from one kind of material to the next is *modalities*. It may take you a while to get used to this term, but I like it because it has a historical link to a venerable approach to rhetorical instruction called "writing in the modes." Under that system—still used in many textbooks—students practice for a while writing narratives, then for a while writing definitions, then for a while writing analysis, and so on. This recognizes the fact that the manner and technique of writing change as the purpose changes. The drawback with that nineteenth century system is that the modes seem static and isolated. There is no hint as to how to get them to work and play well together. Modalities, as I am presenting them here, emphasize the dynamic nature of the writing process, in which a writer shifts from one kind of material to another when a sense develops that the reader needs another kind of material. The word *modalities*, however, still recognizes that there are distinct, well-established ways of presenting each kind of material—ways that, as Aristotle observed, can be recognized, learned, and practiced.

The chapters of this book, then, are arranged according to these modalities, the names of which I slyly introduced as I described the specialties of each TV network. The first three form the core that parallels the mind's natural trajectory: We (1) **encounter** something that surprises, distresses, or puzzles us. We immediately begin a search for (2) an **explanation** that will lead to (3) a **resolution** that will provide an attitude or a program we can use to deal with that encounter, if not now, at least in the future. Think about that for a moment. Aren't those the steps we follow when something unusual happens to us?

In addition to these chapters on the essential modalities, the first part of this book also has two chapters on essential **qualities** of good writing—qualities without which the writing will not be remembered and may not even be read. These qualities are **surprise** and **significance.**

I think you will agree with me that no one is moved to write anything (other than a diary, a thank-you note, or a postcard) unless they have noticed something that strikes them as unusual, shocking, paradoxical, unbelievable, ironic, disjointed—in short, surprising. By the same token, readers expect surprise in writing, and, much more than in the past, there is a lot competing for their attention. In fact, good writers continue to feed the need for excitement by injecting surprising twists, mysteries, and jolts throughout a piece.

Surprise alone, though, can easily degenerate into sensationalism, as the papers at the supermarket checkout counters show. To be satisfying, writing must demonstrate how it impinges on the lives of its readers. Thus the writer has an obligation to make the experience and the investigation of that experience meaningful and helpful to the readers. This quality of **significance** is at once the moral and the social dimension of writing without which the entire activity is vain.

Because surprise is most important at the beginning and significance is most important at the end, I have bracketed the chapters on the three essential modalities with chapters on these essential qualities.

The second part of this book comprises the other modality channels, which may be used to varying extents, or even omitted, depending on the demands of the subject and the needs of the audience. Those modalities are

1. Background—facts and issues that the writer believes the audience may not be certain of

2. Search—generally doing research at the library, traveling for fieldwork, conducting surveys, or doing experiments, but also informally asking friends, combing one's memory, keeping one's eye peeled
3. Reasoning—logic, analysis, and argumentation
4. Valuation—use of symbolism, heightened language, or imagery designed to move the reader emotionally along the author's path to the resolution

Obviously these modalities overlap, and writing can be going on in more than one modality at the same time. There is, nevertheless, enough similarity of approach, tone, phraseology, and presentational technique within each of these—and enough difference between them—that a skilled reader immediately senses a change of modality, certainly from section to section, often from paragraph to paragraph, sometimes from sentence to sentence.

I invite you to take a quick peek back at those TV channels I listed earlier and use your imagination to sense how that "Essay of the Century" might have developed, cycling through some of these modalities, returning periodically to nail down your particular view of space exploration.

In this chapter, before we study them in detail, I am going to rely on your intuitive grasp of those channels, or modalities, as I try to give you an overall sense of how common and effective this cycle process is in the hands of professional writers.

INVITATION TO A READING

Let's start our inquiry into how some writers succeed by reading about the very first writing success of a student who went on to a distinguished career in journalism.

The Informal Essay
by Russell Baker

The notion of becoming a writer had flickered off and on in my head since the Belleville days, but it wasn't until my third year in high school that the possibility took hold. Until then I'd been bored by everything associated with English courses. I found English grammar dull and baffling. I hated the assignments to turn out "compositions," and went at them like heavy labor, turning out leaden, lackluster paragraphs that were agonies for teachers to read and for me to write. The classics thrust on me to read seemed as deadening as chloroform.

When our class was assigned to Mr. Fleagle for third-year English I anticipated another grim year in that dreariest of subjects. Mr. Fleagle was notorious among City students for dullness and inability to inspire. He was said to be stuffy, dull, and hopelessly out of date. To me he looked to be sixty or seventy and prim to a fault. He wore primly severe eyeglasses, his wavy hair was primly cut and primly combed. He wore prim vested suits with neckties blocked primly against the collar buttons of his primly starched white shirts. He had a primly pointed jaw, a primly straight nose, and a prim manner of speaking that was so correct, so gentlemanly, that he seemed a comic antique.

I anticipated a listless, unfruitful year with Mr. Fleagle and for a long time was not disappointed. We read *Macbeth.* Mr. Fleagle loved *Macbeth* and wanted us to love it too, but he lacked the gift of infecting others with his own passion. He tried to convey the murderous ferocity of Lady Macbeth one day by reading aloud the passage that concludes

> . . . I have given suck, and know
> How tender 'tis to love the babe that milks me.
> I would, while it was smiling in my face,
> Have plucked my nipple from his boneless gums. . . .

The idea of prim Mr. Fleagle plucking his nipple from boneless gums was too much for the class. We burst into gasps of irrepressible snickering. Mr. Fleagle stopped.

"There is nothing funny, boys, about giving suck to a babe. It is the—the very essence of motherhood, don't you see."

He constantly sprinkled his sentences with "don't you see." It wasn't a question but an exclamation of mild surprise at our ignorance. "Your pronoun needs an antecedent, don't you see," he would say, very primly. "The purpose of the Porter's scene, boys, is to provide comic relief from the horror, don't you see."

Late in the year we tackled the informal essay. "The essay, don't you see, is the. . . ." My mind went numb. Of all forms of writing, none seemed so boring as the essay. Naturally we would have to write informal essays. Mr. Fleagle distributed a homework sheet offering us a choice of topics. None was quite so simpleminded as "What I Did on My Summer Vacation," but most seemed to be almost as dull. I took the list home and dawdled until the night before the essay was due. Sprawled on the sofa, I finally faced up to the grim task, took the list out of my notebook, and scanned it. The topic on which my eye stopped was "The Art of Eating Spaghetti."

This title produced an extraordinary sequence of mental images. Surging up out of the depths of memory came a vivid recollection of a night in Belleville when all of us were seated around the supper table—I, Uncle Allen, my mother, Uncle Charlie, Doris, Uncle Hal—and Aunt Pat served spaghetti for supper. Spaghetti was an exotic treat in those days. Neither Doris nor I had ever eaten spaghetti, and none of the adults had enough experience to be good at it. All the good humor of Uncle Allen's house reawoke in my mind as I recalled the laughing arguments we had that night about the socially respectable method for moving spaghetti from plate to mouth.

Suddenly I wanted to write about that, about the warmth and good feeling of it, but I wanted to put it down simply for my own joy, not for Mr. Fleagle. It was a moment I wanted to recapture and hold for myself. I wanted to relive the pleasure of an evening at New Street. To write it as I wanted, however, would violate all the rules of formal composition I'd learned in school, and Mr. Fleagle would surely give it a failing grade. Never mind. I would write something else for Mr. Fleagle after I had written this thing for myself.

When I finished it the night was half gone and there was no time left to compose a proper, respectable essay for Mr. Fleagle. There was no choice next morning but to turn in my private reminiscence of Belleville. Two days passed before Mr. Fleagle returned the graded papers, and he returned everyone's but mine. I was bracing myself for a command to report to Mr. Fleagle immediately after school for discipline when I saw him lift my paper from his desk and rap for the class's attention.

"Now, boys," he said, "I want to read you an essay. This is titled 'The Art of Eating Spaghetti.' "

And he started to read. My words! He was reading my words out loud to the entire class. What's more, the entire class was listening. Listening attentively. Then somebody laughed, then the entire class was laughing, and not in contempt and ridicule, but with openhearted enjoyment. Even Mr. Fleagle stopped two or three times to repress a small prim smile.

I did my best to avoid showing pleasure but what I was feeling was pure ecstasy at this startling demonstration that my words had the power to make people laugh. In the eleventh grade, at the eleventh hour as it were, I had discovered a calling. It was the happiest moment of my entire school career. When Mr. Fleagle finished he put the final seal on my happiness by saying, "Now that, boys, is an essay, don't you see. It's—don't you see—it's of the very essence of the essay, don't you see. Congratulations, Mr. Baker."

For the first time, light shone on a possibility. It wasn't a very heartening possibility, to be sure. Writing couldn't lead to a job after high school, and it was hardly honest work, but Mr. Fleagle had opened a door for me. After that I ranked Mr. Fleagle among the finest teachers in the school.

CRITICAL READING

1. We are propelled through the story of Russell's struggle to write his essay by a question he plants in our minds: What is it?
2. Why did Russell think writing was not honest work?

DISCUSSION QUESTIONS

1. What do you think were some of the "rules" Russell feared he would be violating by capturing his fondly remembered feelings of that moment of his personal experience?
2. Are you surprised at Mr. Fleagle's reaction? Do you think your instructor would react as Mr. Fleagle did if you described an experience with the subject rather than addressing the subject directly?
3. Notice that the subject of this passage (the informal essay) isn't even mentioned until halfway through. How do you account for this?

PICKING UP POINTERS FROM THE PROS:
CYCLING WRITING MODALITIES

"What do English teachers want, anyway?" That question must certainly have been on the minds of some of Russell Baker's classmates when they got C's for following Mr. Fleagle's directions while Russell Baker got an A for coloring conspicuously outside the lines. The short answer to that question is "English teachers, like any readers, just want good writing." But, although we English teachers are expert readers and love to read good writing, the process of writing is so complex and the personalities and abilities of student writers so various that it is hard to know what advice will serve as a really helpful answer. It's probable that every kind of advice helps someone, and no single kind of advice helps everyone. For the Russell Bakers, the best advice is probably, "Just read a lot and write what gives you pleasure." Some of his less intuitive classmates, however, might have benefited more from being prescribed to write a five-paragraph essay that outlined three subtopics in the introductory paragraph and summarized them in the concluding one.

Your instructor has her or his valuable advice, born of witnessing the agonies and ecstasies of many students' creations. And, like every English teacher, I have developed my own set of advice with which to supplement that of your instructor. I am, of course, going to present that in this book, along with a selection of good professional writing from which you may well intuit more than I can teach. Our hope—your instructor's and mine—is that you will find a way, with our help or without it, to find joy in your increasing skill with words as the term progresses—the kind of delight Russell Baker found in his ability to affect others with his writing.

Russell had a fear that he was not writing what he vaguely felt was a "proper" essay. This vagueness, which occasionally gives rise to the plaintive question "What do you want, anyway?" may be the result of hearing us give varying advice—sometimes dogmatic—on how to produce good writing. Some "rules of composition" that you might have encountered are

- ☐ The formulaic approach of the five-paragraph essay noted earlier
- ☐ The process approach of journal writing, brainstorming, composing, and revising
- ☐ The central purpose approach of writing your way toward a predetermined purpose kept burning before you like a beacon
- ☐ The modes of discourse approach of first practicing discrete writing skills (narration, description, exposition, argument, comparison and contrast, explanation, definition, illustration, exemplification, analysis, classification, process analysis, and cause and effect) before combining them into full-blown essays

Each of these approaches has helped countless student writers to communicate more effectively, but each has frustrated countless others with its shortcomings.

For 35 years, I have tried to help students find the shortest path from the way their writing now proceeds to something approximating the shapes into which professional writers of short nonfiction might cast the same material. I have boiled that experience down to a somewhat cryptic three-word summary, which I will lay out briefly in the following section and follow up in more detail in succeeding chapters.

Opening the Topic: The Concept of Modalities

Henri Clozot asked, "But surely you agree, Monsieur Godard, that films should have a beginning, a middle part, and an end?" "Certainly," replied Jean-Luc Godard, "but not necessarily in that order."

—Cannes Film Festival, 1966

It often takes a surprise to wake us up to the significance of a situation. Let's suppose that you belonged to a popular clique in junior high. There was a girl, Filippa, who had just moved into the district at the beginning of the year. (I'm going to say "girls"; guys, you can translate.) The clique made fun of her for her strange name, for the clothes she wore, for her nerdishness. You felt a little sorry for her, but she was selfish and obnoxious, bragging about her superior academic ability, so you made fun of her along with the rest. One day, some of the girls in your clique decided to play a trick on Filippa. They convinced her that Pete, one of the most popular guys in the school, was interested in her, but was so intimidated by her scholastic ability that he was afraid to ask her for a date. They told her that they had it from Pete's best friend that she should just go up to him and ask him for a date. You felt this was going too far, so you didn't join in, but you didn't try to stop them or warn Filippa, either. She was suspicious, but the girls laid it on thick, and convinced her to try. Pete, not one of the princes of the world, just laughed at her and made her feel totally humiliated.

Surprising Significance through Modalities

You happened to see her afterward, sobbing in an empty room, and felt a pang of remorse. She screamed at you to get away, but you persisted and got her whole story. Her brother had died of leukemia when she was 11, throwing her mother into a depression. Shortly after that her father had left the family, and they had moved here because this was where her mother could find a job.

The energy created by the shock of witnessing her humiliating encounter with Pete and of the revelations about her background made the whole situation burn with significance. These pushed you to reason about why the clique existed, what its value was to you, and what you might do for Filippa. Feeling the need to find an explanation for the clique's actions, you searched out other friends, your sister, a peer counselor. You could not rest until you had resolved the disruption in your life caused by this surprising event.

A few years later you read a newspaper account of some alienated boys who came to school with guns to kill some of their classmates. You are reminded of the story of Filippa and decide to write about it, perhaps searching the news media for similar stories.

You might tell Filippa's story as a straight narrative, as I did just now, beginning at the beginning and carrying through to the end. But you may sense that such a pedestrian approach does not get across the intense feelings of her anguish and your remorse. Western writers since before the days of the Roman poet Horace have known to begin a story not at the beginning but, as he called it, in medias res—in the middle of things. Modern filmmakers know this too; hence Jean-Luc Godard is able (in the epigraph at the head of this section) to play with Aristotle's famous dictum that a piece of writing should have a beginning, a middle, and an end: "Certainly, but not necessarily in that order." Beginning this story where the girls are egging Filippa on to ask Pete for a date or even later, when you hear her sobbing in an empty classroom, would dramatize the surprise, electrifying the lines of significance that lead from the encounter through an explanation to an ultimate resolution.

You may have noticed that I used the modality terms in my description of the act of converting the Filippa story into writing: encounter, explanation, background, value, search, reasoning, resolution. My observation has been that significance emerges in the connections among those modalities, probably because the end of a particular modal segment becomes a decision point, calling for some reflection about the significance of what has gone before in order to know which modality needs to come next.

Setting down the Filippa story in a way that will be interesting and significant for the reader almost demands moving through some or all of those modalities. If you follow the advice of Horace and Godard and begin by jumping ahead to the encounter between her and the clique, you might increase the suspense by breaking off just as she is approaching Pete. Here you could fill in the now-expectant reader on the background of the situation, highlighting just those facts that are significant in explaining it. Then you might finish that first scene with Filippa running off in tears, leaving the reader anxious to learn what will happen to her.

At this point the reader expects you to turn in your writing, as you did in life, to **reasoning.** Let's say you decide to think logically about the **value** and **significance** of cliques. That could be made to lead naturally to your re**search** about the killings and other similar **encounters** with alienated youth that you have discovered in the news media. The similarities between your experience and the events on a national scale light up the **significance** of clique behavior.

At this point you might satisfy the reader's nagging curiosity about the Filippa story with your **encounter** in the empty room and your discovery of her personal **background.** Now, **significant** ties can be made between her and the kids in the newspaper accounts.

And the confluence of these stories could lead directly into the resolution expected by the reader. Here you might try to modify people's
attitudes toward cliques, or you might finish with what you did, or
what you wish you had done, in response to your experience with Filippa. Did you confront your clique members, try to get them to see
how they had hurt an already injured girl, quit the clique, become a
peer mediator? This could lead to resolution that calls for action from
the public. Either way, you have heightened your readers' awareness
of cliques as a **significant** phenomenon.

You will notice that this is not the kind of straight-line or mechan-
ically branching process often taught in text books. The skilled writer
plays with the readers' expectations, withholding information to create anticipation and portioning out conclusions and evaluations to
build consensus. The result is a weaving of significant strands back
and forth through **cycles of modalities,** which, if I diagramed one
cycle of it, might look something like this:

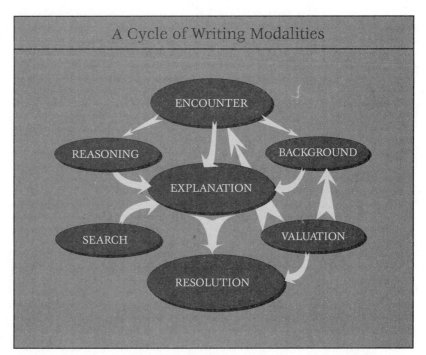

Figure 1.1. Good writing weaves repeated cycles of modalities to bind
together in the reader's mind an explanation of what the writer has
noticed, toward a way of thinking and acting in the future.

You will note that the main axis, almost universally expected, typically consists of the three central modalities **(e–e–r):**

1. A dissonance or surprise, often in an **encounter,** but often in another modality
2. An **explanation** of that dissonance
3. A **resolution** of the dissonance, in the form either of an attitude or a program

The other modalities **(r–s–v–b)**[1]

4. Reasoning
5. Search
6. Valuation
7. Background

are cycled through as needed. It is in the links between these—the reason you give your reader for moving from **reasoning,** say, to **search,** or from **background** to **valuation**—that you have an opportunity (and an obligation) to expose and expound on the **significance** of each.

In the Filippa story, for instance, when you move from her confession of her **background** to your media **search** for alienated youths who have committed violence, it is crucially important to tie these modalities together with sentences of **significance,** which I think of, not so much as modalities in themselves, but as the luminous strands carrying energy from the surprise of one modality to that of the next. In this case, it might need only a sentence or two, like: "Filippa's proudly hidden traumatic background—deprived as she had been within a year of brother, father, home—started a tragic cycle in which defensiveness provoked taunting that required still more aggressive defensiveness. It is likely that such a cycle, spiraling out of control, contributed to the mass killings committed by two students at Columbine High School in 1999."

This structure of significant modalities, possibly because it parallels the way our minds process all anomalies that we encounter, seems to be applicable to many kinds of writing. The boss who feels compelled to write a memo about being sure that all office doors are kept locked has certainly **encountered** shocked employees who have lost property and has **reasoned** about possible solutions. The

---

1. I put them in this order only as a mnemonic association with *rsvp (répondez s'il vous plaît*—"please reply")

scientist who has written a journal article on the mass of the neutrino has constructed **encounters** between cosmic rays and heavy
water and has **reasoned** about the surprising observations. In their
writings both will seek to **explain** why the surprising results
occurred and **resolve** the encounter with recommendations for
action or a readjustment of our attitudes based on that explanation.

In addition to just **reasoning** (on possible causes and explanations), the writing may involve a little or a lot of **search.** (The boss
may just walk the corridors testing doors; the scientist will have to
pour over hundreds of monographs and confer with colleagues at
conferences.) Each writer will have to consider how much and what
kind of **background** to provide for the audience, depending how
much they already know about the problem and whether there are
hostile camps—of employees, say, who hate the boss's micromanage-
ment style or physicists whose life work may be nullified by the discovery of neutrino mass. Of course, each must also constantly be
weighing the **value** of the **encounter** and its **resolution.** Need the
boss impress on employees that this is a major problem at the company, or can it be treated humorously with a light touch? Is the discovery of neutrino mass a major one that will require a radical revision of how we view matter, or is it just an interesting piece of the
ongoing puzzle?

Each of these genres of writing has its own rigid structural forms
that practitioners in those fields must learn and follow. But memos
written by bosses who are unaware of the effectiveness of the cycle
of modalities very often go unread. And some important scientific
discoveries have been delayed for years and even been wrongly
attributed because their first discoverers have been inarticulate.

Because this approach to writing follows the natural process of
the mind—seeking a **resolution** through **explanation** for a startling
encounter—it provides a comfortable way into the writing process,
especially if you are the kind of person who has always hated or
feared writing: Simply begin by describing an event that you find
memorable for some reason. Then, after highlighting the surprise of
that encounter (there must have been a surprise there somewhere,
or you wouldn't remember it), try to explain why it happened and
resolve your feelings about it by showing your readers what you and
they can learn from it. Backed by such a straightforward approach
you should not have to go through a panic attack whenever you have
to set fingers to keyboard. If you are already a budding Russell Baker,
this approach may give you some guidance in effectively channeling

your creativity to maximize your effectiveness with readers. I hope, in other words, that this book can provide you a way to avoid Russell Baker's late night anguish while enjoying the satisfaction he experienced in the power of his words to move other people.

WRITING COMMISSION: JOINERS AND LONERS

Cliques, fraternities, clubs—even barrios, ghettos, and reservations—depend on walling some people in and others out (to echo the famous lines from Robert Frost's poem "Mending Wall"). You have certainly had some experience either with the joy of being included or the pain of being excluded (although, to be sure, there is the pain of involuntary inclusion and the joy of the lone ranger).

Write about an experience with this, trying to use what you have picked up so far regarding the cycling of modalities in your writing. Right now we are just getting our feet wet with this, but at least avoid boring the reader with a general introduction and instead begin with a dramatic, surprising **encounter.** Be conscious of shifting channels when you start **explaining** why what happened happened. When you sense that your reader may need some **background** about the circumstances, it's time to switch channels and adopt a new tone and approach while focusing steadfastly on the same theme. You also will probably want to essay some **evaluation** of the practices you experienced. If you are inclined to do some **research,** feel free. Be constantly working toward a **resolution** that will give the reader some help in thinking about and perhaps acting on these social pressures.

INVITATION TO A READING

Before we start looking at the modalities separately in detail, I'd like, as I mentioned before, to give you an overall impression of how a professional column writer makes them all work together to produce a lively perceptive piece of the kind that I hope you will be able to write by the end of the course.

Read this next piece first for enjoyment. But then go back and read for awareness of the writer's technique in weaving her significance by shifting from one modality to the next.

Of course, good writers shift modalities smoothly, more like an automatic transmission than a double-clutching truck. So you may have to keep checking to notice where the shifts occur.

As you do this, notice the surprises that are contained in each shift and reflect on their significance. You will notice right away that the author begins with an encounter (with a potential boyfriend) that contains a surprise (they have no place to be alone together).

After you have had a chance to notice these things for yourself on a second reading, I will go through the essay with you and demonstrate what modality shifts I see in it.

Home Free?
by Joyce Caruso

Not too long ago, I met a real-estate broker—a nice Italian guy who'd married very young, had recently divorced and was now living with his parents. In New Jersey. Just until he found a place of his own, of course.

The relationship never went anywhere. Where would we have gone? The Holiday Inn? You see, I live at home, too. Back home, to be exact. Thanks to a head-on collision with the IRS last year—I won't bore you with the details—I found myself almost completely broke and tucked into my childhood bed. Mom still lives in the same house, in the same cozy, English style suburb of Manhattan where I grew up. It's about an hour from my job and any semblance of New York social life. In short, Toto and I are in Kansas again.

The last time I lived at home full-time, I was a chronically self-obsessed, navel-gazing high-schooler, surfacing only occasionally to read early F. Scott Fitzgerald, watch Mary Tyler Moore and indulge in some of my favorite extracurricular activities: a tennis player named Tom, dieting, discoing and warping my brother's Grateful Dead albums on the radiator.

Today, I'm a stat. I'm even a member of a new American subculture called "the boomerang set." (Get it? The post–baby boomers who've landed back at home with the parents.) According to the U.S. Census Bureau's 1992 statistics, 54 percent of 18- to 24-year-olds live under their parents' roof, while 12 percent of 25- to 34-year-olds do—more young adults, in fact, than at any time in the past. Experts have graciously allowed that we're not, by and large, a bunch of freeloaders, but rather casualties of the recession (and the 1992 9.5-percent unemployment rate among 20-somethings), the rising cost of living, college loans and fashionably delayed marriages. Meanwhile, in New York City, one-bedroom apartments in only occasionally "safe" parts of town often run over $1,000 a month. Rent is lower in other cities, but still well beyond the reach of many 18- to 24-year-olds.

Now, if you're of sound mind (i.e., you plan on growing up), you'll look at living with your parents as a temporary thing, a money-saving device. Still, it's hard not to feel like a dweeb sometimes, and this is probably because you feel like a grown-up playing a kid's part with your parents producing and directing the movie. They own the house; they call the shots.

Until you're directing your own life again, here are some snags you might run into.

- **Love life** Guys are weirded-out by your living with the Authorities, particularly if they've met Mom, she wasn't impressed, and it showed. Then they'll be afraid even to leave messages on the phone machine. My mother says she doesn't listen, but she isn't deaf. So, helloooo, young lovers, you can forget about lazy weekends in bed with the main man, or romantic dinners for two at your house. (What can you say? "Mom, take yourself to a movie tonight. Make it a long one. *Malcolm X* is worth seeing." Good luck.) If your boyfriend starts talking to you about your dependency issues, there's always his place. Well, actually, there isn't always his place, as I learned with the Italian real-estate agent. Here is a factoid worth filing. More young men than young women live at home (61 percent guys to 53 percent girls). One theory about why guys find the nest so attractive: Sons are asked to do even less around the house than daughters. Shocking, eh?
- **Shopaholism** Impulse buyers, beware: Come paycheck time, without a big rent to scrape together, you'll feel like Ms. Megabucks. I binged at Banana Republic my first two months at home. Set a new monthly budget and put your savings in the bank.
- **Leftovers** These are also an easy trap. Mom's fab cooking, which did such a number on your body in high school, can and will again.
- **The embarrassment factor** Some friends have given me a hard time about living at home, accusing me of being a superbrat, and taking my mom's side against me. My friend Joy frequently calls from L.A. to see how much housework I'm doing. Other friends are always asking whether I "miss my freedom," a sign, I suspect, of jealousy (they're all binge shoppers, too). I usually just smile and say, "Really, this blazer was marked down to nothing."

Nevertheless, the benefits of living at home outweigh the drawbacks for one simple reason: You may get the chance, as I did, to connect with the family. Talking to my mom (or anybody) about anything important never occurred to me as a teenager. (As you may have gathered, my mom and dad split up a while back. Dad lives alone in a smallish Greenwich Village apartment.) Now, though, Mom and I bond like crazy—in the morning, for example, when we're having coffee (espresso for me, the regular stuff for her), reading the papers and scrambling to get ready for work. Of course, it helps that we're on slightly staggered schedules and have different skin types, so we don't ever compete for the bathroom or covet each other's cosmetics. (In high school, I used up her best stuff shamelessly.)

We bond when she insists on driving me to the train instead of having me walk—it's not far, but in the opposite direction of her job. Formerly, every such ride would be preceded by a tantrum (mine), for I was always late for school, choir, fill in the blank. When we really bond is Sunday evenings, which are a nice occasion for us to spend real time together. We disagree on some things, of course—she'd risk hellfire rather than attend Mass with a woman priest on the altar—but arguing as an adult with someone who used to take credit for forming and nurturing all your beliefs and debating skills is, well, a trip.

Sunday is usually take-out night, and sometimes I'm struck by what my mom and I must look like sitting there in the living room in the blue glow of the TV. Two single, grown-up girls, crunching away on Chinese food, dissing some of the men we know and reminiscing about the family in the good old days.

At this writing, my debts are almost paid off, and I'm at last looking for a place in the city. Lately, I've been thinking about how I was in such a hurry to get out of the house as a teenager, dashing off my college applications and dreaming about the great escape I would make. This next escape will probably be the last one, and though I'm looking forward to it, I've also been thinking about that Carly Simon song—something about these being "the good old days."

CRITICAL READING

1. Why does Joyce Caruso put the phrase "In New Jersey" in a separate sentence?

2. How does the author generate interest in the statistics she presents? What is the surprise of those statistics? (Notice that there are two sets of statistics, distinct from just plain facts.)

3. What is surprising about the reaction of the writer's friends to her living at home? How does she explain this?

4. What item from early in the essay does the author pick up in starting her conclusion? Does it work to help tie the essay together? Remember this in your own writing!

5. The author's list of tips is specific advice for those, both parents and young people, who find themselves in this situation. What general lesson does she imply for anyone in the 18 to 34 age range and their parents?

DISCUSSION QUESTIONS

1. Do you think the statistics and facts in the essay help build a bridge from Caruso's personal experience to that of her audience? Explain.

2. This was written for *Mademoiselle* magazine. Do you think that Caruso's breezy tone, especially her sense of humor, is appropriate to the readership of that magazine? Give specific examples for your opinion. Are there any audiences who might not appreciate it?

3. Caruso's original article ends with a list of tips for young adults caught in this "boomerang" situation. Rather than reprint it here, I am going to let you suggest six lessons that you would have put in such a list. (Her original list can be found at the end of the demonstration that follows.)

DEMONSTRATION: HOME FREE

All right, here is my analysis of the cycles of modalities to be found in Caruso's essay. Citing suitable evidence, feel free to add to or disagree with these identifications in a class discussion. Comment also on whatever surprises you found.

Home Free?
by Joyce Caruso

Not too long ago, I met a real-estate broker—a nice Italian guy who'd married very young, had recently divorced and was now living with his parents. In New Jersey. Just until he found a place of his own, of course.

The relationship never went anywhere. Where would we have gone? The Holiday Inn? You see, I live at home, too. Back home, to be exact.

ENCOUNTER
An otherwise normal girl-meets-boy encounter contains the germ of mystery. Why couldn't they get anywhere?

Thanks to a head-on collision with the IRS last year—I won't bore you with the details—I found myself almost completely broke and tucked into my childhood bed. Mom still lives in the same house, in the same cozy, English style suburb of Manhattan where I grew up. It's about an hour from my job and any semblance of New York social life. In short, Toto and I are in Kansas again.

The last time I lived at home full-time, I was a chronically self-obsessed, navel-gazing high-schooler, surfacing only occasionally to read early F. Scott Fitzgerald, watch Mary Tyler Moore and indulge in some of my favorite extracurricular activities: a tennis player named Tom, dieting, discoing and warping my brother's Grateful Dead albums on the radiator.

Today, I'm a stat. I'm even a member of a new American subculture called "the boomerang set." (Get it? The post–baby boomers who've landed back at home with the parents.) According to the U.S. Census Bureau's 1992 statistics, 54 percent of 18- to 24-year-olds live under their parents' roof, while 12 percent of 25- to 34-year-olds do—more young adults, in fact, than at any time in the past. Experts have graciously allowed that we're not, by and large, a bunch of freeloaders, but rather casualties of the recession (and the 1992 9.5-percent unemployment rate among 20-somethings), the rising cost of living, college loans and fashionably delayed marriages.

Meanwhile, in New York City, one-bedroom apartments in only occasionally "safe" parts of town often run over $1,000 a month. Rent is lower in other cities, but still well beyond the reach of many 18- to 24-year-olds.

Now, if you're of sound mind (i.e., you plan on growing up), you'll look at living with your parents as a temporary thing, a money-saving device. Still, it's hard not to feel like a dweeb sometimes, and this is probably because you feel like a grown-up playing a kid's part with your parents producing and directing the movie. They own the house; they call the shots.

Until you're directing your own life again, here are some snags you might run into.

ENCOUNTER
Abbreviated, generalized encounters are often used as examples—in this case of the valuation that preceded them.

- **Love life** Guys are weirded-out by your living with the Authorities, particularly if they've met Mom, she wasn't impressed, and it showed. Then they'll be afraid even to leave messages on the phone machine. My mother says she doesn't listen, but she isn't deaf. So, helloooo, young lovers, you can forget about lazy weekends in bed with the main man, or romantic dinners for two at your house. (What can you say? "Mom, take yourself to a movie tonight. Make it a long one. *Malcolm X* is worth seeing." Good luck.) If your boyfriend starts talking to you about your dependency issues, there's always his place. Well, actually, there isn't always his place, as I learned with the Italian real-estate agent. Here is a factoid worth filing. More young men than young women live at home (61 percent guys to 53 percent girls). One theory about why guys find the nest so attractive: Sons are asked to do even less around the house than daughters. Shocking, eh?

RESOLUTION TIP
Like mountain climbers looking back to the valley where they started, a writer's looking back to the first encounter helps remind the readers of the track that the essay is pursuing toward the summit of **resolution**. Caruso does this adroitly here by reminding us of her Italian real-estate broker. It's an easy device. Use it regularly!

- **Shopaholism** Impulse buyers, beware: Come paycheck time, without a big rent to scrape together, you'll feel like Ms. Megabucks. I binged at Banana Republic my first two months at home. Set a new monthly budget and put your savings in the bank.
- **Leftovers** These are also an easy trap. Mom's fab cooking, which did such a number on your body in high school, can and will again.
- **The embarrassment factor** Some friends have given me a hard

RESOLUTION
Resolution is intended to suggest any insight arrived at during the cycles of other modalities. You may think of these as lessons you've learned expressed as help to your readers. Actually, most writers feel the need to restate their **resolutions**—often tentative or slowly building ones—several times to be sure the lesson or thesis or point sinks in. Here Caruso highlights some of the negatively **valued** lessons she has learned, illustrated by brief **encounters**.

time about living at home, accusing me of being a superbrat, and taking my mom's side against me. My friend Joy frequently calls from L.A. to see how much housework I'm doing. Other friends are always asking whether I "miss my freedom," a sign, I suspect, of jealousy (they're all binge shoppers, too). I usually just smile and say, "Really, this blazer was marked down to nothing."

VALUATION TIP
The word *nevertheless* (or a similar word like *but*) coming at the beginning of a paragraph usually is used to signal a major change in **valuation** and the move toward the final **resolution**.

Nevertheless, the benefits of living at home outweigh the drawbacks for one simple reason: You may get the chance, as I did, to connect with the family. Talking to my mom (or anybody) about anything important never occurred to me as a teenager. (As you may have gathered, my mom and dad split up a while back. Dad lives alone in a smallish Greenwich Village apartment.) Now, though, Mom and I bond like crazy— in the morning, for example, when we're having coffee (espresso for me, the regular stuff for her), reading the papers and scrambling to get ready for work. Of course, it helps that we're on slightly staggered schedules and have different skin types, so we don't ever compete for the bathroom or covet each other's cosmetics. (In high school, I used up her best stuff shamelessly.)

INCIDENTAL BACKGROUND
Expert writers do not begin with their life history. Instead, they insert only such background as is essential and only when it is clearly needed.

We bond when she insists on driving me to the train instead of having me walk—it's not far, but in the opposite direction of her job. Formerly, every such ride would be preceded by a tantrum (mine), for I was always late for school, choir, fill in the blank. When we really bond is Sunday evenings, which are a nice occasion for us to spend real time together. We disagree on some things, of course—she'd risk hellfire rather than attend Mass with a woman priest on the altar—but arguing as an adult with someone who used to take credit for forming and nurturing all your beliefs and debating skills is, well, a trip.

VALUATION WITH ENCOUNTERS
Here all the examples and even lessons learned to this point have been negative. Now we get the positive side, pointing us in the direction of the final resolution.

Sunday is usually take-out night, and sometimes I'm struck by what my mom and I must look like sitting there in the living room in the blue glow of the TV. Two single, grown-up girls, crunching away on Chinese food, dissing some of the men we know and reminiscing about the family in the good old days.

At this writing, my debts are almost paid off, and I'm at last looking for a place in the city. Lately, I've been thinking about how I was in such

VALUATION
Caruso weighs the values she had as a teenager in the light of her later experience, moving toward a **resolution** that will combine the best values of both.

a hurry to get out of the house as a teenager, dashing off my college applications and dreaming about the great escape I would make. This next escape will probably be the last one, and though I'm looking forward to it, I've also been thinking about that Carly Simon song—something about these being "the good old days."

RESOLUTION
The final **resolution** brings back hope for a mature, independent future with a newly mature view of her family past. This allows her readers of either generation and others in the society that might view the boomerang phenomenon with alarm or disgust to see a potential benefit that both parents and adult children can take advantage of.

Tips for a Stay-at-Home

Here's a to-do list designed to alleviate feelings that if he/she you're at/you fresh...

not only food but also a blackbond/princess/desdpest:

• Offer to pay your parents something—some token rent, however nominal, each month. You'll both feel better for it.

• Pitch in on Housework

• Pay for those luxury items you alone consume—in my case, raisin bagels. Philadelphia Life and Quaker Caramel Corn Cakes.

• Give parents their space. If they're having a party, take yourself to Malcolm X.

• Phone home if you'll be late—especially if it's three days late.

• Check your motivation level once in a while. A few experts on "boomerang" culture warn that excess parental attitude may reduce professional productivity in their offspring: Just thought I'd mention it···

Figure 1.2. Here is Caruso's original list of "Tips" promised in the questions above.

WRITING ACTIVITY: ENCOUNTERING YOUR FAMILY

You have seen two good examples of professional writers, each of whom probed a surprising event in the life of the parental home. Both felt that there was something significant to be found in the wake of that surprise. Engaging their readers in the search for an explanation helped these writers formulate and celebrate their own family encounters in a way that holds significance for almost any reader. As each encounter is made to blossom against a background of larger social movements (the Great Depression for Baker, a Generation X dilemma for Caruso), readers are drawn into a resolution of the experience. Of course, as with any good piece of writing, its significance may be somewhat different when seen through the prisms of different readers' experiences. But for me, both these writings show that strong family bonding is important in launching a young life toward successful adulthood, especially in difficult times.

Now it's your turn. Recall some meaningful encounter you have had with one or more immediate family members. If you remember the experience, it's almost certain you remember it because there was something unusual about it—a surprise, puzzle, disjointedness. Seek to explain why this surprising aspect occurred by considering how that experience would look to an audience either of your own age or of the older generation. Provide your readers with any necessary background so that the experience can become as meaningful to them as it was to you. Finally, resolve the essay in a way that comes to terms with the strangeness of your encounter and with similar experiences that your readers may have had.

Certainly write for your own joy or satisfaction or therapy, but remember that the seal on Russell Baker's experience with the informal essay was the class's reaction. So be mindful that you are also writing for your readers' joy or satisfaction or therapy.

Let's hope that, after having received due shaping and revising, your essay, too, will be held up by your instructor, who will turn to the class and say, "Now that is an essay, don't you see. It's—don't you see— it's of the very essence of the essay, don't you see. Congratulations!"

Points to Remember

- Rhetoric is the study of successful strategies for keeping people's attention and persuading them in any communication situation.
- Two qualities contribute hugely to success with readers: the writing needs to surprise people enough to get their attention, and it needs to show itself significant enough to keep that attention.
- Once a reader's expectations have been raised by dramatizing a surprising **encounter,** the reader expects an **explanation** and a **resolution.** This is a natural process of the mind in dealing with surprises; therefore, writing that follows that process has a good chance of succeeding.
- There are a number of distinctive ways of exposing the significance of the original dissonance and its subsequent explanation.

I am calling them *modalities* to suggest a more dynamic view of the traditional modes of discourse. These additional modalities, any or all of which may be found useful in persuading the readers of a particular piece of writing, are **reasoning, search, valuation,** and **background.**

↳ The end of each modal segment is a decision point prompting you to think about the significance of what you have just been saying. This should help you decide which modality is needed next.

↳ It may be helpful to you as you are writing to imagine shifting from one TV channel to another as you present different kinds of material in appropriate format and style.

↳ Professional writers weave complex cycles of these modalities, frequently returning to significant general statements of the explanation or resolution before looping out through another modality.

E-E-R

Encounter

Explain

Resolve

R-S-V-B

Reason

Search

Value

Background

2

The Eye-Opener

We feel dissonance in several different kinds of situations. There may be a conflict between us and our surroundings—a conflict, for example, between what we expect and what we encounter; between what we think (feel, perceive, remember, value) and what someone else thinks, feels, and so forth. Or the dissonance may arise within us—our thoughts about one

subject may be inconsistent with our actions; or we may realize that there is some gap in our understanding of the world. . . . In all cases, scholars such as Jean Piaget and Leon Festinger contend that an awareness of dissonance is the motivation for all human activity. . . . The notion of dissonance is central to work in rhetoric.

—Lee Odell, "Strategy and Surprise in the Making of Meaning"

Opening the Topic: Importance of Surprise

Life does not give us introductions. Neither nature nor an angel talked to me about death as I was walking home one cold February night. There was no abstract meditation on the psychology of grieving or the history of funerary customs or the philosophy of body and soul.

Instead I was just led to the edge of a deserted street and shown the body of my twelve-year-old son, his brown hood covering his head, which was face down in the gutter. His left leg twisted out from his lifeless body at an odd angle, broken by the now-vanished car that had killed him. "Here you are," my mind was told, "your dead son. Learn from this experience what you can."

This is the way life gets our attention.

We never forget.

Many writers today who write for the general public follow nature's plan. They get our attention immediately with the shock and mystery of reality. They wait until later in the composition to sit us in the lecture hall, lead us down the dusty aisles of libraries, or open the dictionary, the almanac, or the encyclopedia. They begin by taking us out onto the street of actual life experience and say, "Look. This is what happened."

It is not only writers who try to shape their communication so that there is a dramatic lead-in. Museum directors, interestingly enough, have come to recognize that there is a rhetoric of exhibitions. In 1998, the Field Museum in Chicago acquired the most nearly complete skeleton ever of a *Tyrannosaurus rex*. Having spent $8 million for this prize, the museum wanted to be sure to maximize its usefulness in furthering the museum's education mission. What Mr. Faron, the associate director of exhibit development, had to say about his plans might help us visualize, by analogy, what we need to do as writers to maximize the effectiveness of our material:

> I'm exploring ways to create theater around the skeleton. I'm the director, and the curators are the playwrights. You have to take an artifact and stage it, give it energy and motion and dynamics. You enter an exhibit like you would a theater, ideally. There should be anticipation and an unfolding for the visitor—for a story that should build toward some sort of conclusion—an Aha! moment. If you get people to that point, you are teaching them something.
>
> —*Quoted by William Mullen,* Chicago Tribune Magazine, *4/26/1998*

Try as you start writing to visualize your opening as the *T. rex* skeleton in this prospectus. Unenlightened writers might just present the bare bones of their encounters the same way they would tell it to friends—pretty much the way museums used to plop a skeleton, isolated, right in the middle of the floor. It's OK; it's interesting. But, as Faron points out, such a stark presentation lacks dynamic interest. It might help your writing to think of it as a process similar to leading your reader through a museum exhibit, an initial eye-opener pointing the way through a hall of eye-openers, each with its own explanation on a placard to be read after the exhibit has had its dramatic effect.

Figure 2.1. The $8 million *T. Rex* "Sue" gets visitors' attention at the Field Museum, Chicago. Does your opening have this impact?

Each stunning presentation should create anticipation for the next, weaving a story that builds to what Faron calls "an Aha! moment." Whether in film, in a museum, or in writing, it is the surprises, dramatically pointed from any of several modalities along an unfolding path toward a conclusion, that create significance for the visitor.

There are those who argue that the old stuffy museums were better—that by simply laying out what they had found in row after row of dusty cases, the museums let visitors discover their own surprises and create their own significances. Those people have a point, particularly in museums that have extraordinary collections—the equivalent, I suppose, of the diary and letters of a famous person or of scientific writing, where other researchers do not want findings colored by the prejudices and personalities of a particular practitioner.

Admittedly, dull writing, like dull life, has an appeal—it is safe. J. W. Saunders, writing back in 1964 in the book *The Profession of English Letters,* puts it well:

> No matter how much a man reads he expects every reading experience to provide something new, something he has not met before. He wants to read what he likes, certainly, but if the writer does nothing more than give him what he likes, he is quite ungratefully dissatisfied. Indeed, very often he cannot tell what he likes until he has been offered the something new which he finds he likes.

People think they only want writing that they are familiar with, writing that will be guaranteed not to bring them up short with a scene of horror at a deserted corner on a frigid February night. But then they are dissatisfied. If you want people to read and consider and remember your writing, it had better startle your reader the same way life startles us. For even those who admire dull writing rarely read it, as the following Dilbert cartoon by Scott Adams and the Russell Baker excerpt show.

Figure 2.2.

We have seen how Russell Baker learned the positive reward of writing that communicates its enjoyment to an audience. In the following selection from the same autobiography, he recounts learning the flip side of that lesson, the one that Scott Adams is trying to teach in the cartoon in Figure 2.2: Writing that does not somehow engage an audience is wasted effort, a futile exercise.

Cousin Edwin's Dull Writing
by Russell Baker

This is not a "right-between-the-eyes" eye-opener. But if you look up the average salaries of newspaper writers in an almanac and extrapolate that back to the era of this story (also available in the almanac), you will find a revealing little surprise in this **background**. This is followed by a jolt-awake joke in a revealing **background encounter**.

They also talked about Cousin Edwin who had made something of himself in a big way. "I hear Edwin's making $80,000 a year," Uncle Allen said one evening. "I always knew he'd amount to something. Edwin had sort of a way about him."

"Edwin was the worst tease I ever knew," my mother said. "And mean! He could say the meanest things to you."

"Edwin had plenty of nerve though," Uncle Allen said. "Did you ever hear how he got his first newspaper job? It was a paper in Pittsburgh, I think, and Edwin went in for an interview with the editor. The editor looked at him and said, 'Young man, how do I know you're not a damned fool?' And Edwin said, 'That's a chance we'll both have to take.' They gave him the job on the spot."

Edwin was their first cousin. Though he'd grown up near them in Virginia, they hadn't seen him in twenty years and didn't expect ever to see him again. He had achieved success on the monumental scale. "Edwin's no more going to visit his poor relatives than I'm going to walk on water," my mother said.

"You've got to realize, Lucy, Edwin's a big man," said Uncle Allen, who had no envy in him.

It's easy enough to explain the shock of Edwin's turning his back on this otherwise close-knit family by saying it's human nature. We need to let ourselves be surprised, however, to grasp Baker's implied **resolution** that his uncle was something of a humbug.

By New Street measures, Edwin was a big man indeed. Since 1932 he had been managing editor of the *New York Times.* I was only slightly impressed. I had seen the *New York Times.* Uncle Allen loyally bought it every Sunday because it was Edwin's paper. It was the dullest excuse for a newspaper I'd ever seen.

"Why doesn't it have any funny papers?" I asked one Sunday after declining Uncle Allen's offer to look at it.

"Because it's a real newspaper," he said. "All it prints is the news, and funny papers aren't news."

Cousin Edwin wrote a column on affairs of state which ran every Sunday in the *Times*. One Sunday Uncle Allen opened to Cousin Edwin's column and beckoned to me. "Look *here*," he said. "When you get your name printed there like your cousin Edwin, you'll be able to say you've made something of yourself."

There, over a mass of gray print I read that great name set down in large bold type: "By Edwin L. James." On Sunday afternoons, Edwin's column was a leaden family duty that filled the parlor. Aunt Pat, bustling in from the kitchen, would ask Uncle Allen, "Have you read Edwin's column yet, Dad?"

"Not yet. I gave it to Charlie." Uncle Charlie had always read it. My mother never had. "I'll get to it later. Let Hal read it," she said.

Uncle Hal, the sense of family obligation sitting strong upon him, would pick it up and after a paragraph or two say, "Edwin always had a good way of expressing himself," and lay it down casually and say, "I remember the time Aunt Sallie brought Edwin over to visit Mama and. . . ."

Then, interrupting his reminiscences he handed the paper to Aunt Pat, saying, "Here, Pat, take it out in the kitchen with you and read it while you're making dinner."

"Oh, you read it first, Lucy," Aunt Pat would say to my mother.

"I'm too busy right now," my mother would say, "but don't lose it."

In this way Cousin Edwin's column passed from hand to hand unread by all but Uncle Charlie, until, late in the afternoon, Uncle Allen settled himself in his favorite chair, opened the *Times* wide, and began to read. If Doris or I spoke too loudly Aunt Pat said, "Sh, dear, Uncle Allen's reading Edwin's column."

It was hard for me to see what Uncle Allen was doing behind the wall of newspaper, but I suspected there was little reading. One Sunday I watched the paper fall gently back over his face, then saw it rise and fall gently in rhythm with his breathing, and after a few moments heard a satisfied snore rumbling under the newsprint. Awakened by his own snoring, Uncle Allen let the paper fall to his lap and, seeing me grinning at him, gave me a small guilty smile.

"Edwin's a big man," he said, "but he sure can write some dull stuff."

Now comes the eye-opening irony of the main encounter. It is clear that, while protesting Edwin's greatness, the family shares Russell's **valuation** of Edwin's writing.

Startling statements can come in any of the modalities we have discussed. This admission on the part of Uncle Allen comes at the point of Baker's **resolution**: Being impressive is not enough; good writing has to be interesting.

CRITICAL READING

1. This section about Cousin Edwin opens with an encounter "one evening" that contains a couple of significant eye-openers. The first of these is Uncle Allen's estimate of Edwin's income. Do some research to find out what that would be in today's dollars. (You should be able to infer the approximate year of this conversation.) Also find out the actual salary of someone in his position. Why does Baker introduce Edwin in this way?
2. Why was Russell not as impressed with Edwin as the rest of the family? What criteria did the family judge success by? How were Russell's criteria different?
3. How can you reconcile the fact that the family considered Edwin a great newspaper man, even though all (except for Charlie) found his column too dull to read? Is it possible that a person chosen to be managing editor of the country's leading newspaper could have been a dull writer?

DISCUSSION QUESTIONS

1. Do you think Edwin's writing was probably as dull as the family thought it was?
2. Some people feel that in writing on less important subjects, it is all right to be interesting, but when you are writing about "affairs of state," being interesting should not concern you. What do you think?
3. Is writing on serious subjects automatically interesting (or dull), or can it be made one or the other by the skill of the writer? If it can be, should it be, or does manipulating the reader's interest somehow trivialize the subject?

WRITING COMMISSION: FINDING SOME EYE-OPENERS IN YOUR FAMILY

Recall a delightful (or contentious) experience from among your family's stories. Don't reveal too much at the beginning. Instead dramatize the surprise with mystery, details, and significant conversation. Once the story is moving, add any background you feel an outsider will need. The sense of what will surprise and create anticipation in a reader, as well as what background a reader will need, demands that you, as a writer, stand both inside and outside of your experience at the same time.

A few years ago, a young woman decided to mount a digital TV camera in her bedroom and display the image of whatever was going on there on her Web site. Imagine how you would feel visiting her. On the one hand, you would be directly involved in your encounter with her, but on the other hand, you would always be aware that hundreds of people were watching the scene. That is something like the writer's mentality in revisiting and exposing an experience from the past to readers.

The difference is that after each episode during which your readers have been watching your family encounter unfold, as a writer you turn directly to the camera, explain what just went on, and try to draw some conclusions about it that are relevant to your audience.

PICKING UP POINTERS FROM THE PROS:
How Dull Was Edwin's Writing?

Russell Baker did achieve the honor Uncle Allen projected for him of getting his name at the top of a column in the *New York Times*. The fact that he is one of the most widely anthologized nonfiction writers in America may indicate that he is enjoyed, as well as respected.

But what about his judgment of Cousin Edwin? Was the writing of Edwin L. James really as dull as Russell believed and Uncle Allen admitted, or were the comics really Russell's only criterion and the family's interests only sports and gossip?

Being curious about this myself, I went to the microfilm reader to find copies of Edwin James's column around 1935. It was an exciting time to be writing about foreign affairs, as the storm clouds of Hitler's Blitzkrieg were already darkening Europe. I picked a column written in response to an early thunderclap delivered by Hitler.

Some background is needed to dramatize how critical a juncture this moment was in the rush to the holocaust that was shortly to devour so many million lives. The harsh terms of the Treaty of Versailles demanded that Germany pay France, particularly, for all that World War I had cost that country and its allies. At the same time, one of the main industrial regions of Germany was transferred to France, leaving Germany with a financial catastrophe. It was largely Hitler's promise to ignore these humiliating and ultimately unworkable terms that made him popular with the German people. To make his refusal stick and to reassert the sovereignty of Germany as a nation, Hitler decided to increase the size of his army beyond the limits dictated by the treaty. The Allies met to consider a response to this dangerous violation. Their options were (1) attack Germany and force the dissolution of her army, (2) renegotiate the treaty to make the conditions more achievable and make Germany an ally, (3) ignore it, (4) impose further sanctions, or (5) continue to issue condemnations and ultimatums.

Consider whether James's way of writing conveys the exigency of the situation. Be ready to detail specific things he does or fails to do that do or do not get across the importance of that situation.

New York Times   Sunday, April 21, 1935

HITLER'S COOPERATION IS BECOMING DIFFICULT
On His Birthday the Fuehrer Rejects League Resolution of Censure in 'Most Resolute Manner'

PARIS AND MOSCOW HIT SNAG
BY EDWIN L. JAMES

On last Wednesday the Council of the League of Nations adopted a resolution condemning the German action of March 10 in establishing conscription in preparation for the building of a larger army in defiance of the Treaty of Versailles and set up a Committee of Thirteen to decide on economic and financial measures which might be taken in the future against any nation which might "endanger peace by unilateral repudiation of its international obligations."

Yesterday, on his forty-sixth birthday, Chancellor Hitler sent to the governments which participated in that action a note of less than 100 words attacking the effort to "judge" Germany and saying that Berlin rejects the resolution "in the most resolute manner." The Fuehrer said that later on Germany would make known her position on the issues discussed in the Geneva conventions.

In other words, Germany rejects the peace offer by which the former allies, acting through the League, agreed to pass over Hitler's action in announcing that Germany was to have a large air force and a bigger army with a declaration that he was wrong, and united to pro-

vide measures against his analogous steps with respect to other provisions of the treaty. It appears that the Nazis refuse to admit they were wrong in the past and refuse to agree they would be wrong in the future in tearing up what is left of the treaty.

Blow at Cooperation

It will probably be found that the Hitler note of yesterday is a blow at the British fostered plan for bringing Germany into a scheme of cooperation for the preservation of the peace of Europe. The Stresa conversations looked to such a development, Germany being invited to a Danubian conference to be held in Rome in May. The Franco-British note sent to Germany on Feb. 3 laid out a plan of cooperation, involving Germany's ultimate return to the League and an arms agreement which would be substituted for Part V of the Treaty of Versailles. It was while negotiations were in progress through diplomatic channels that Berlin announced its air and army plans. It was due to the insistence of the French that Paris, London and Rome agreed that, under the circumstances, the League resolution should state the position of the other European powers toward Germany's unilateral action before attempting further negotiations with the Reich.

It is apparent that the Hitler note replying to the League resolution complicates the situation; it certainly does not seem to bring Hitler any closer to the League, as was sought by London. Hitler finds it unpleasant to face the fact that a body has been created to deal with future German violations of her obligations. After all, there is still something left of the Treaty of Versailles. For example, there is the commitment of Germany to respect the independence of Austria. There is the acceptance by Germany of her eastern frontiers. There is the surrender by Germany of her colonies.

The Naval Question

Nor is all of Part V gone. The Germans are blamed in the League resolution for their action of March 16, which concerned the army. That was to have been condoned, however, and inasmuch as Britain and France were willing to make an air convention with Germany, it was presumed that her new air force was also condoned.

But Germany had made no public announcement concerning her navy, although she had said privately to Sir John Simon that she wanted a fleet as big as France. As matters stand, therefore, the measures proposed against future German disregard of the treaty would apply to plans to have a greater naval strength than the 150,000 tons allowed by Part V.

The British have announced that they will oppose any German effort to build up a navy of 500,000 tons as a measure which would overturn the calculations upon which are built present naval limitations and a measure which would disturb peace. If it is true, as it appears

to be, that all of the League powers stand ready to repress any German move to construct a new navy (including 100 submarines), it would seem that the British had put the proposed German navy in a hole. It would be no surprise if the naval situation proves to be one of the points with which Hitler will deal in his forthcoming elucidation of the German position on pending issues.

The Resolution Stands

On the other hand, Hitler can have an invitation to the coming naval conference if he wants it. In that connection it is worthwhile mentioning that the naval position of the United States might well be affected by a large German building program, since that would increase British naval needs, and the basis of our naval policy is parity with Britain.

Of course, the Hitler note of yesterday does not destroy the Geneva resolution. That represents the position of Britain, France, Italy and Russia, and it is set forth explicitly that its provisions apply even to a nation outside the League, should it threaten the peace. And whether or not the Germans join the air convention pledging the parties to it to come to the aid of any signatory nation victim of aggression, the air convention will be made nevertheless with its basic purpose of pooling the British and French air fleets against the German attack to the westward. Whether Germany attends the Rome convention or not the pledges made to support Austrian independence will stand.

Thus, while the week brought on the one hand the Stresa resolutions, which seemed to offer a probability of cooperation by Germany in a general peace scheme, it brought, on the other hand, the blaming of Germany at Geneva, which has resulted in the tart Hitler *fin de non-reçevoir.*

In addition, it brought another warning to Hitler. He summoned the British and Italian Ambassadors to ask them if they stood on their guarantee of the Treaty of Locarno, which pledges them to intervene on the side of Germany if she is attacked unjustly by France, as well as to intervene on the side of France if she is attacked by Germany. He received an affirmative answer. But he also received notification that London and Rome intended to insist on the preservation of the neutral zone running 50 kilometers east of the Rhine, which, under the Treaty of Locarno, is established as a fence between Germany and France which must not be violated by either country. That cuts off quite a slice from the Germany which Hitler may militarize and interferes seriously with any plan to place defenses along the famous river.

Difficulties for Berlin

Should Hitler follow up the truculent tone of his note the effect may well be to consolidate the opposition to the Reich. The French and their allies were willing to go along with the British plan for cooperation with Germany just so long as it did not interfere with their protective measures. But the British voted for the Geneva resolution, and German resentment, as expressed orally by the Wilhelmstrasse to Downing Street, is directed especially at London. It is not going to help the MacDonald-Simon plan for a general pact if Hitler shows no desire to do otherwise than to depend on his own resources.

Admittedly, it is not an easy situation. Germany withdraws from the League and finds the other countries using the League to try to make her behave. Germany considers that she has disposed of the Treaty of Versailles and finds out that powers with strong forces at their disposal are not willing to forget the treaty.

And, on top of that, there has grown up in the capitals of other European powers an idea that the Germans, after denying for so long that they had military equipment forbidden by the treaty, are now overestimating what they have. In other words, it is not believed that Germany now has an efficient air force equal to that of Britain. It is pointed out that the mere announcement of conscription which may at some future time give Germany a well-equipped army of 600,000 has not given Germany now any such force. In other terms, Germany's neighbors are not in so great a panic over Germany's present military strength. They have become more calm in their efforts to prepare to counteract a big German force when it does exist.

The Russians and French

In the meanwhile, one of the links in the chain being put around Germany has been slowed up in the forging. Litvinoff, the Russian Commissar for Foreign Affairs, was to have been in Paris over the week-end to initial a pact of mutual assistance in case of attack by Germany. Instead of going to Paris, Litvinoff went from Geneva back to Moscow. It is stated that the Russians would go too far for the French. They would provide that automatically either Russia or France would attack Germany if the Reich attacked either of them. It would appear that the French would reserve a certain elasticity or at least be given a chance to consider the issues before going to war. It is possible that Poland figures in the case. Russia might have to cross Poland to attack Germany, and it will be recalled that Poland, to the surprise of Germany, voted for the Geneva resolution.

The French insist that Laval's plans for a trip to Moscow have not been abandoned. If he goes, it will mean that Paris and Moscow have settled their differences.

GENERATIONAL DIFFERENCES

I'm sure your eyes began to glaze over after a few paragraphs. Yet James was obviously a respected journalist and news analyst in his day. Clearly many people must have read these columns, though one may be permitted to wonder if it was not more out of a leaden sense of duty than of delight.

What is missing, from my perspective a couple of generations later, is any attempt to dramatize the lapel-grabbing nature of these encounters. Indeed, Edwin James seems bent on suppressing the alarm that they might cause (and that, with the benefit of hindsight, we see **should** have caused). Partly this may be a result of the mind's natural impulse to explain away surprises; partly it may have been a result of the *New York Times* trying to elevate itself above the kind of sensational journalism that we can still see in papers like the *Enquirer.*

There are plenty of surprises there: Hitler's defiance of the vastly richer countries surrounding Germany; the Allies' concessions and their making resolutions without teeth in them; and England's new idea of trying to make an ally out of a former enemy. However, a reader must dig these out of the "mass of gray type" in which they are buried.

Aristocratic Usage

Edwin James's lack of rhetorical dynamics is matched by an equally soporific syntactical density. Look at the length of the sentences. The first sentence takes up a whole paragraph. The third paragraph has only two sentences, the first one of which is 62 words long. This is not to say that all long sentences are dull, but variety of length adds interest.

One trap that can catch the writer of long sentences is burying clauses within phrases within clauses. The first sentence contains a *which* clause nested inside another *which* clause:

> measures {which might be taken against any nation [which might endanger. . .]}

Another beauty of the same kind appears in this sentence:

> It was due to the insistence of the French {that Paris, London and Rome agreed [that, under the circumstances, the League resolution should state the position of the other European powers toward Germany's unilateral action (before attempting further negotiations with the Reich.)]}

Those who admired Edwin James's writing enough to make him an editor of the *New York Times* probably admired his elegance. There is a certain beauty to long, complex sentences, gracefully handled, as in this paragraph of balanced periods:

> Admittedly, it is not an easy situation. Germany withdraws from the League and finds the other countries using the League to try to make her behave. Germany considers that she has disposed of the Treaty of Versailles and finds out that powers with strong forces at their disposal are not willing to forget the treaty.

In writing, however, elegance can turn quickly into empty flourishes, decoration devoid of meaning, which distance readers from the content of the ideas and make them begin to yawn:

- ☐ . . . if Hitler shows no desire to do otherwise than to depend . . .
- ☐ . . . pledging the parties to it to come to the aid of any signatory victim . . .
- ☐ . . . to provide measures against his analogous steps with respect to . . .
- ☐ In that connection it is worthwhile mentioning . . .

Or it may simply tie itself up in knots:

> As matters stand, therefore, the measure proposed against future German disregard of the treaty would apply to plans to have a greater naval strength than the 150,000 tons allowed by Part V.

Perhaps the deadliest sin of all is James's overuse of the passive voice, which has the effect of holding the subject he is writing about, delicately pinched between thumb and forefinger, at arms length, like a smelly fish:

- ☐ there has grown up in the capitals . . . an idea that . . .
- ☐ In other words, it is not believed that . . .
- ☐ It is pointed out that . . .
- ☐ It is stated that . . .
- ☐ It would appear that . . .
- ☐ and it will be recalled that . . .

This nose-in-the-air elegance is a courtly virtue, appropriate to European palaces but out of place in the democratic realism of turn-of-the-century America. Our change in taste has probably come from the perception that it was the convoluted treaties, concocted by elegant, top-hatted diplomats and mustachioed, gold-braided and epauletted generals that brought about the poison-gassed trenches of World War I. The wars that finally put an end to the European colonial empires also left us with a distrust of elegant, dull writing.

Bureaucratic Usage

No sooner was courtly jargon ushered out the front door than business and legal jargon were welcomed in the back, the comforting companions of those who feel an inadequacy, perhaps, in their grasp of the subject. Check your own writing for the following common rhetorical stuffed shirts:

- [ ] Unwieldy uses of the passive voice—still a popular way to hide responsibility: "The project was unable to be completed in a timely manner."
- [ ] *In a timely manner* and *at this point in time* instead of *on time* and *now*
- [ ] *Due to* instead of *because*—also still epidemic
- [ ] *Stated* instead of *said* (note that James combines this with the passive: "It is stated that . . .")
- [ ] *And/or* instead of *or*
- [ ] *Etc.* instead of naming a few examples (or worse, *and etc.,* which is redundant)
- [ ] *Being that* instead of *since* or *because*
- [ ] *Consensus of opinion* instead of just *consensus*
- [ ] *Between* or *with you and I* instead of *between* or *with you and me*
- [ ] *Irregardless* instead of *regardless* (even the technically correct *irrespective of* sounds a little high-flown)
- [ ] Using *whom* or *whomever* incorrectly just because it sounds more formal (Not "I will assist whomever needs my services"; *whoever* is correct because it's the subject of *needs.*)

A similar problem occurs sometimes in the social sphere. In creating the character of Mistress Quickly—the tavern keeper, friend of Falstaff—Shakespeare had some fun with the type of person who tries to use big words to pretend to a more elevated station in life. Of course, she uses them wrongly. So she says "You cannot bear with another's *confirmities [infirmities].*" In trying to pacify Falstaff's rowdy companions she wants to say, "Mitigate your choler," but instead says "*Aggravate* your choler." Again, defending Falstaff against charges of lechery she says, " 'A did in some sort, indeed, handle women; but then he was *rheumatic,* and talked of the whore of Babylon"—by which perhaps she means that Falstaff was *romantic* and was morally outraged by the women whom he blamed for "seducing" him.

At the other extreme is the temptation to use clichés—the well-worn phrases that lubricate our social conversations ("She was always there for me, y'a know what I mean?"). In conversation, clichés make us feel comfortable that the person we are talking with will not shock us with a disturbing new idea. Interviews with sports stars and call-in shows about sports are replete with this kind of bonding talk ("We just have to play 'em one game at a time"; "It was a real team effort"). Perhaps the only social situation in which people are ridiculed for using clichés is that in which a man tries a standard pickup line on a woman: "What's your sign?" or "Don't I know you from somewhere?"

As writers we are not trying to cement a social relation with our readers; we are trying to wake them up to a new experience. Hence, although we certainly should avoid pretentious-sounding language, we should try at all times to sound original—more like the characters in *When Harry Met Sally* than like those in *As the World Turns.*
List some commonly used expressions that you find particularly fun to use—or irritating to hear. In fact, you are probably coming up with examples even as we speak!

Dynamic Usage

Good contemporary American writing, as most of us see it, has three characteristic qualities of American life—speed, diversity, and energy. Take a look at the following example of a modern column on the eve of another war—the Persian Gulf War—with nearly the same Allied countries facing a similar problem. Saddam Hussein had broken a treaty by invading Kuwait and was developing atomic weapons. Should the Allies risk a war of punishment if Hussein refused to accept the United Nations' directive, or should they try to use sanctions and persuasion to bring Iraq back into line with United Nations' demands?

Will Saddam Try to Duck the Punch?

by Tom Post   Newsweek: December 31, 1990

Get ready for a surprise from Saddam Hussein before the United Nations' Jan. 15 deadline for him to withdraw from Kuwait. So Secretary of State James Baker warned NATO foreign ministers last week. Baker urged the allies to beware an attempt "to undercut the collective will of the international community to use force." Translation: expect Saddam to pull a fast one.

What could the Iraqi leader do to duck the punch? The most likely scenarios:

- **Withdraw partially.** Pulling back to the northern part of Kuwait, Saddam would redraw the Iraqi border to give him control of the Rumaila oilfield and, with Warba and Bubiyan islands, direct access to the gulf. It's also a nimble way to undermine the international coalition, as members pummel one another over whether to settle for a halfway measure to avoid war. Bush administration officials worry that Iraq could announce a troop pullout without specifying the newly demarcated "Saddam Line." Dragging out the process might paralyze allied military action. "If Saddam is withdrawing, all the while saying, 'Wait and see,' it's going to be damn difficult for the president not to wait," concedes a senior U.S. official.

- **Start talking.** Saddam had willing listeners in Paris and Moscow. For all his tough rhetoric, President François Mitterand has strong reservations about the wisdom of a gulf war; Iraqi officials for their part are already trying to persuade French Foreign Minister Roland Dumas to intercede with Washington. A more cautious successor to Eduard Shevardnadze as Soviet Foreign minister will give Saddam another opening.

- **Defend Kuwait.** Defying so mighty and unified a force isn't as lunatic as it sounds: Saddam need only slaughter a few thousand Westerners to become the most successful Arab military leader since the 1956 Suez crisis. Standing up to a superpower—and surviving—could lend him the prestige to wring a deal from his nervous neighbors. The longer Iraq holds out in a conflict, the greater casualties it can inflict and the more likely U.S. public opinion is to turn against war. Even if chased out of

Kuwait, Saddam could gamble on being protected by Iraq's own border. The U.N. license to press beyond Kuwait is somewhat fuzzy; to do so could conceivably cost the Bush administration much of its international support.

- **Stall.** Saddam has good reason to put off the start of negotiations until Jan. 15. "Anything could happen during the next few weeks," says a Saudi official. "Mrs. Thatcher has already gone. Maybe the allied coalition will fall apart. Maybe Congress will block Bush. Saddam would see it as stupid to give up anything before he has to." The Bush administration may fret about timetables. But in the Mideast, explains a Western diplomat in Cairo, "a deadline is a starting line—and a very elastic one at that."

- **Attack Israel.** A trump card for Saddam in the event he faces defeat or overthrow at home, engagement with Israel could turn a Middle Eastern conflict into a holy war that had the support of many Arab nations. So far, at least, it's Iraq's opening move to make: Under U.S. pressure, Israeli officials have promised not to make a pre-emptive strike without notifying Bush. They have also agreed to key their responses to the nature of Iraqi attacks. If Baghdad fires conventional missiles causing limited damage, Israel will refrain from an all-out counter-attack, hitting only missile sites in western Iraq. Israel's sole pretext for drawing on its nuclear arsenal would be if Iraq's first strike causes massive damage through non-conventional weapons—a highly unlikely scenario.

- **Unleash terrorism.** Abu Abbas, notorious for the Achille Lauro hijacking in 1985, claims he has hit squads in the United

States and Europe poised to act if Iraq is attacked. Though such tactics could be self-defeating, Saddam can also threaten a Saudi refinery or city with chemical warfare, even bluff that a "doomsday" nuclear weapon had been installed in Kuwait.

Unlike Edwin James, Tom Post, writing 55 years later, does his best to keep us surprised, even starting with the sentence, "Get ready for a surprise." And some of the options that he shows for Saddam Hussein, like attacking Israel with nuclear or chemical weapons, or unleashing terrorist attacks in the United States, were shocking. Finally, in fact, Hussein chose what most people at the time considered the most unlikely option, what Tom Post calls a lunatic-sounding one: to defy and fight the united armies of over 30 countries, including the United States, Britain, France, and Italy. Surprise!

Modern writers are much more aware of the value of surprise in keeping the reader awake, as well as in pinpointing the most important aspects of what they are writing about.

I think you will notice right away that Post's sentences are shorter and less complex than those of Edwin James. Also, instead of telling **about** what people say, the author **presents** what they say in direct quotations. The actual words of a speaker always have more dramatic impact. When the quotations sound like diplomatic double-talk, he translates into punchy, idiomatic English:

> beware an attempt "to undercut the collective will of the international community to use force." Translation: expect Saddam to pull a fast one.

Notice the use of strong words, especially strong verbs:

duck the punch	pummel	paralyze	slaughter
chased	gamble	block	fret
fires	unleash	threaten	

Such words are appropriate to an article about war, of course, but strong verbs are always more interesting than the namby-pamby verbs used by James:

adopted	set up	might be taken	participated
make known	discussed	pass over	was to have
appears	would be	will be found	set forth
brought on	stood on	follow up	looked to

These stylistic and usage differences project a very different ethical persona of each author. Edwin James is cool. His manner of writing marks him as a man of the world, a sophisticated person who cannot be surprised by anything. This gives him a mantle of authority; we tend to believe what he says, because he can, like Germany's neighbors, contemplate war calmly, without being surprised. Of course, we now know that Germany's neighbors—Austria, Poland, The Netherlands, Denmark, and France—should have been surprised, should have been horrified by Germany's rearming.

It is possible that our culture's writers had their eyes opened by the monumental encounter of two world wars. And this may have had an influence on the contemporary determination to write in a more energetic, more pointed, and more surprising way.

WRITING ACTIVITY: FINDING AND EVALUATING EYE-OPENING TECHNIQUES

If we learn to talk by listening, we should learn to write by reading. To learn from reading, however, it must be critical reading. First we say, "I really liked Bob Greene's column in the paper yesterday," but then we must ask, "I wonder how he made it so interesting?"

Unless you are like Russell Baker and the idea of writing as a career has flickered on and off in your mind for years, you have probably been more concerned with **what** writers are saying than in **how** they said it. This exercise is designed to turn your perspective around. Here I'm going to ask you to find some nonfiction magazine writing that gets your interest immediately and then analyze how the writer turned that trick.

To do this, I'm asking you to find a stack of magazines, either in your library, your basement, or your dentist's office, and skim through them, reading just the first couple of paragraphs of each until you find five articles that immediately appeal to you.

There are a couple of rules. First, no news articles. We are not trying to learn news reporting, and it is a different genre. Second, cull your selections from at least two different magazines to insure some variety.

When you have made your selections, make a one-page photocopy of just the title and opening paragraphs of each article and bring it to class for a discussion of what makes an interesting start to a piece of writing. You may choose to cut the relevant parts of the articles out of your own magazines, but then please tape them onto full-size sheets of paper so that your instructor can handle them conveniently.

After the discussion, write a composition describing and comparing the techniques some of these writers used and evaluating their effectiveness. Be sure to focus on the **how** not the **what** of the articles. There are probably some subjects you are so interested in that you will read anything about them, no matter how boringly written. But we want to learn to write interestingly to people who may not be enthralled with our subjects. So try to reach some generalizations that you and your classmates can actually use to make an interesting start to **any** writing you may do.

In chapter 1 we looked at the column "Home Free" to get a general picture of how modality cycles work. Now we will take another general look at how eye-opening surprise energizes these modalities. The American poet Richard Wilbur caught the writer's trick of constantly reenergizing the piece with normalcy-defying surprises, as a performer juggling, first with one set of items, then with another— shifting modalities, as it were.

Juggler
by Richard Wilbur

A ball will bounce, but less and less. It's not
A light-hearted thing, resents its own resilience.
Falling is what it loves, and the earth falls
So in our hearts from brilliance,
Settles and is forgot.
It takes a sky-blue juggler with five red balls

To shake our gravity up. Whee, in the air
The balls roll round, wheel on his wheeling hands,
Learning the ways of lightness, alter to spheres
Grazing his finger ends,
Cling to their courses there,
Swinging a small heaven about his ears.

But a heaven is easier made of nothing at all
Than the earth regained, and still and sole within

The spin of worlds, with a gesture sure and noble
He reels that heaven in,
Landing it ball by ball,
And trades it all for a broom, a plate, a table.

Oh, on his toe the table is turning, the broom's
Balancing up on his nose, and the plate whirls
On the tip of the broom! Damn, what a show, we cry:
The boys stamp, and the girls
Shriek, and the drum booms
And all comes down, and he bows and says good-bye.

If the juggler is tired now, if the broom stands
In the dust again, if the table starts to drop
Through the daily dark again, and though the plate
Lies flat on the table top,
For him we batter our hands
Who has won for once over the world's weight.

What a great challenge for us as writers! We must really sweat to shake up the natural gravity of our readers, not just once during a performance, but again and again through cycles of different acts, until we are exhausted with the effort. Of course, as with all artists, the greatest trick of all is to "learn the ways of lightness" and not to let the effort show.

Here is a dazzling little juggling act by syndicated columnist Bob Greene. Let's see how he keeps the balls and plates and brooms in the air. Keep those surprises coming, folks!

The Colors of the World in Vivid Black and White
by Bob Greene

The idea of deliberately broadcasting a game in black and white is an obvious shocker!

The NBC television network, taking note of the huge national interest in the Bulls-Jazz NBA Finals series, has announced that as a service to viewers, Wednesday night's Game 4 will be telecast in black and white.

Well . . . not really. We're not at that point yet; Game 4 will be seen in color. But if you've been paying attention to what is considered desirable these days, you may have noticed that the concept of full color has gone decidedly out of favor. All of a sudden, for some reason, black and white is back.

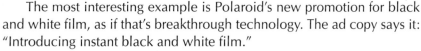

The most interesting example is Polaroid's new promotion for black and white film, as if that's breakthrough technology. The ad copy says it: "Introducing instant black and white film."

How can you "introduce" something old?

For those of you whose memories extend back to when Polaroid cameras were introduced, you know that the original Polaroid film was black and white—you couldn't buy the film in a color version. Your father would look at the second hand on his watch on Thanksgiving night as the film developed, would wait before peeling the covering back, careful not to get the goop on his fingers—and there would be the black and white image of the family gathered around the turkey. Quickly, the coating stick would be applied to preserve the picture.

Black and white Polaroid photos are as old as Polaroid itself. So why is Polaroid pushing black and white?

The "well," is the clue that even the writer is surprised to find that the color may not be better.

The ad slogan explains: "A way to make things look, well, better."

That seems to be the current thinking: The world looks better in black and white.

When Frank Sinatra died, national magazines all seemed to get the same idea: Put Sinatra on the cover, but in black and white.

Part of this was because Sinatra came to great fame in the black and white age—and part of it is that there's something black and white about the mind's picture of Sinatra: tuxedo, black bow tie, white shirt, black shoes. One of the most colorful entertainers in history was, at essence, a black and white guy.

It's surprising that suddenly it's a whole movement.

Sinatra notwithstanding, magazines for the last few years have turned to black and white any time they wanted to get across an impression of realism—as if color is false and black and white is true. The new issue of *Life* features on its cover a black and white photo of Dr. David Loxterkamp of Belfast, Maine, delivering a baby. The layout inside, showing Dr. Loxterkamp "practicing medicine the old-fashioned way," is entirely black and white.

The feature mirrors one of the most famous *Life* features ever, the 1948 story about a country doctor named Ernest Ceriani.[1] The Dr. Ceriani layout was in black and white, so half a century later it was sort of a nice decision to do Dr. Loxterkamp in black and white.

And it's everywhere: In beer commercials meant to show people who are supposedly authentic and gritty; on the American Movie Classics

---

[1] We will see some of that photo-essay in chapter 6.

Wow! **Really** everywhere!

Odd that kids find easy what adults still think of as challenging.

The **resolution** of the surprise is itself a surprising idea: that a black and white image, because it is more abstract, is also more idealized. This also **explains** the sudden rash of black and white in a disillusioned world.

channel in the old films our parents watched that are now coming into favor again; in promotions that are supposed to get our attention with the implied message: Because this is black and white, you can trust it.

Art directors seem to like it because . . . well, because any 5-year-old with a computer these days can come up with a dizzyingly vibrant palette of color images—color graphics are literally child's play. The world is turned around: Black and white means creative, color means predictable.

Yet the real meaning of this, if you examine it, is kind of funny. The black and white America—the America of 50 and 60 and 70 years ago, the America of RKO Pictures, of the old *Life* and *Look,* of the what's-black-and-white-and-read-all-over newspapers—is, in memory, the America in which our parents lived. That's one of the things that is so inviting about it.

But their America, of course, was just as colorful as ours is today. When they looked out their windows every morning, their streets and neighborhoods were filled with color. Only their movies, magazines, early television programs and other mass-market stimuli were black and white.

We never saw their world, so we imagine it in black and white. They saw their world daily. It was in living color. Their reflected world—the world the media of their day shined back at them—was the one that was black and white. It allowed them an alternate view of their reality, a bleached, darkened, yet idealized view—a view we gave up in the color age.

Discussion Questions

1. The same idea of a generational boundary between the black and white 1950s and the colorful now was used in the movie *Pleasantville,* which came out in 1998. If you haven't seen it, rent it! Then compare the valuation of color in it with that presented in Greene's article.

2. Can you think of another movie—famous classic—that uses the switch from black and white to color? What is the significance of the contrast in that film?

PICKING UP POINTERS FROM THE PROS:
SURPRISE BY PARADOX

Ron Grossman, in a *Chicago Tribune* article "A Short History of Hate," tells the following paradoxical story:

> A few years back . . . my father and my uncle were strolling through a California shopping mall that reverberated with a dozen and one different languages. Southeast Asian refugees were then pouring into this country. Turning to my uncle, my father said, "Gantsn tog, men hert nit ein vort English," which roughly translates from Yiddish as, "In a whole day, you wouldn't hear one word of English."
>
> When my father recounted the episode, I doubled over in laughter. It seemed deliciously funny to condemn others for not using the country's dominant language—and to do so in a foreign tongue. Yet my father could not see the humor. To his way of thinking, he hadn't been using a foreign language. Yiddish and English were equivalent in his mind. It was the "others"—those Thai, Hmong and Vietnamese shoppers—who needed to recognize that in America everyone ought to speak English.

This is paradox—the forced joining of two apparently contradictory ideas or facts to "deliciously" surprise readers and at the same time to wake them up to a deeper truth lying hidden beneath the surface contradiction. Paradox is a common device used by writers to shake the world's gravity up.

Grossman's purpose is to wake native-born, English-speaking Americans up to be more tolerant of first-generation and second-generation immigrants who may feel perfectly Americanized. The paradox points out the incongruous fact that immigrants who have become established here have often been the most eager to close the door through which they themselves entered the country.

Mathematicians enjoy paradoxes greatly. Statistics is a fertile field for mind-boggling seeming impossibilities that can be proven true. For example, there is about 1 chance in 100 that two strangers will have a friend in common. This might not seem overwhelming, but assuming that most people know about 1000 people, the chance that each stranger will know people who know each other rises to the almost certain probability of 99 in 100!

A study that showed that children with big feet could spell better than those with smaller feet certainly sounds paradoxical. Even though the explanation is simple—children with bigger feet are older and so generally spell better—stated this way the fact sounds absurd.

If you enjoy paradoxical puzzles like these, I recommend the book *Aha! Gotcha!* by Martin Gardner.

Philosophers also enjoy paradoxes. Here are some philosophical paradoxes from one of the founders of Taoism, Lao Tzu, quoted from the book *Vicious Circles and Infinity: An Anthology of Paradoxes*, by Patrick Hughes and George Brecht:

> Thirty spokes share one hub. Adapt the nothing therein to the purpose in hand, and you will have the use of the cart. Knead clay in order to make a vessel. Adapt the nothing therein to the purpose in hand, and you will have the use of the vessel. Cut out doors and windows in order to make a room. Adapt the nothing therein to the purpose in hand, and you will have the use of the room. Thus what we gain is Something, yet it is by virtue of Nothing that this can be put to use.

Explain what is contradictory in these paradoxes. Can you discern a philosophical wisdom behind them?

Taoist philosophy teaches that paradoxes seem insoluble because the human mind constructs polar oppositions and erroneously treats one of the poles as good and the other bad. This philosophy has a modern reincarnation in deconstructionism. Its founder, the French philosopher Jacques Derrida, blamed polar opposite thinking specifically on Western logical constructions.

Paradox is one technique of deconstructionist analysis that seeks to wake us up to our unconscious acceptance of exclusionary thinking. The technique is to take a commonly accepted pair of opposites (for example, truth/falsehood) and deconstruct the opposition, either by paradoxically reversing the usual value, making the second of the pair the better of the two, or by denying that there is any opposition. One might in this case say that lying is sometimes better than truth-telling because it may spare people's feelings, and, further, in the form of hypocrisy, it can improve society by getting people to at least profess what they cannot always practice. One might also say, with jesting Pilate, "What is truth?" That is, the truth is really indeterminate, and people say just what they feel they need to say in any situation with the conviction that it is true.

The women's movement has found the deconstruction of two-term oppositions a particularly powerful tool in trying to overturn the cultural bias evident in preferring the first, masculine item in pairs like active/passive, breadwinner/homemaker, command/obey, rational/emotional, realistic/sentimental, resolute/lenient. The argument is that until society can accept that a person can be paradoxically both **objective** and **subjective** at the same time, for example, society will continue to treat feminine virtues as less valuable than masculine ones. (*Virtue,* ironically, is derived from the Latin words for "man" and "manly.")

Paradoxes are good eye-openers, and Greene, whose very title poses the first paradox, employs them freely in the previous column.

CRITICAL READING

1. I count about a half-dozen paradoxes in Greene's column. Find as many as you can and discuss them with your classmates. They propel us through the essay because we expect that he will ultimately reveal the hidden truth behind them. And we are not disappointed. Discuss the last paragraph. Do you agree with the explanation that Greene gives there?

2. As I pointed out in chapter 1, writers typically run through the modality cycle from **encounter** through **explanation** to **resolution** a few times in the course of a column. Greene rounds out a two-paragraph minicycle with a general statement that concludes his opening joke and sets the stage for the rest of the piece. What phrase does he use specifically to motivate the reader to read on? Do you think it works? Why?

3. Greene offers Polaroid's ad slogan as the explanation for their surprising reintroduction of black and white film. In the following paragraph he restates the same idea, but it now has a different rhetorical effect. What is there in the way the idea is reformulated that lifts it to the status of **resolution** in this paragraph?

4. Greene has reached the end of a full modality cycle with that one-sentence paragraph: "That seems to be the current thinking. . . ." Then he is faced with a decision point. I'm sure you are familiar with such moments—sometimes long, frustrating "moments"—from your own experiences in the writing process. It's too soon to end the piece. Readers are not satisfied with a 266 word column. It would be like paying $8.75 for a 45-minute movie. Because they

expect a minimum of 600 words for a column (this one is about 750), you are at the point the juggler was when he reeled in the first set of balls and had to reenergize his performance with a new trick. In writing, the next trick is another cycle of modalities, which can start with another **encounter** (first or second hand); re**search** into dates, facts, statistics; **reasoning** about the significance of the phenomenon or issues involved; further **background,** especially if controversial issues are involved, or **valuation**. Greene chooses another encounter. He goes through perhaps three more modality cycles before "all comes down, and he bows and says good-bye." Find those decision points and explain what Greene seems to expect to accomplish by choosing the next cycle.

WRITING COMMISSION: DRAMATIZING A CHANGE IN SOCIAL BEHAVIOR

Notice some eye-catching change in social behavior or some paradox that you observe in social behavior. (The change or paradox does not have to be a profound one, and your tone does not have to be serious, although it certainly can be if the topic warrants it.) Dramatize it in an eye-opening way, probably with a personal **encounter.** Wrap up the first modality cycle with an **explanation** of the change. At this decision point begin a new cycle, probably using other encounters or paradoxes as examples that might offer a similar explanation of why this change is taking place.

After writing a first draft go back and rewrite it. Think of it as a series of startling museum exhibits. Put your most spectacular skeleton first. After describing it, put a placard on it to explain it. Add a sign to direct the browser to the next exhibit. Describe it, and add another placard. Repeat the cycle.

Triumph over the world's weight with your dexterous verbal skill! Create something that will make your readers shout, "Damn, what a show!"

Points to Remember

- Think of organizing your writing like a good museum exhibit. Deliberately put an attention-getter at the beginning, and plan the placement of eye-opening encounters at strategic points throughout to keep the reader moving.

- Unless your writing is interesting, people who don't have to won't read it, and you will have wasted whatever effort you have put into it.

- Interest-making energy comes not only from what you say but from how you say it. Avoid clichés, exercise your whole range of vocabulary, inject energetic verbs, use a variety of sentence lengths and structure.

- Try applying rhetorical techniques used in other media—movies, advertising, museum displays, poetry, music—to keep the reader surprised and interested.

- When you feel you have reached the end of a passage, think of this as a decision point. Energize the new direction with a new paragraph, a shift in modality, and a fresh eye-opener.

E-E-R

Encounter

Explain

Resolve

R-S-V-B

Reason

Search

Value

Background

3

Encounters

"Oh, the novel. I dashed it off at odd moments. It doesn't take long to write things of which you know nothing. When you write of actual things, it takes longer because you have to live them first."

[Said by 14-year-old Francie, imagining what she would say to her critical English teacher when she came back to see her after having become a successful novelist.]

—from *A Tree Grows in Brooklyn* by Betty Smith

Opening the Topic

We all know that Newton was supposed to have been awakened to the idea of gravity by an encounter with a falling apple. Prior to this it had been accepted not that bodies were attracted to each others' masses but just that things tended to go down. It was also accepted by educated Europeans that horses had the number of teeth specified by Aristotle two thousand years earlier. Only with the great change in thought of the scientific revolution in the 1600s did someone think to get the actual number from the horse's mouth. The authority, Aristotle, was proven wrong by a direct encounter.

In the Middle Ages, the world of experience had been thought transitory and undependable. (After all, they would argue, the horse whose mouth you looked in may have neglected to floss and lost some teeth.) In the Renaissance, the intellectual world began scrambling to catch up with the past—the distant past before the fall of the Roman Empire. Readers were only convinced by writings that could cite ancient, honorable authorities. From the scientific revolution on, societies based on Western culture have come increasingly to distrust the voice of authority and the rhetoric of abstract ideas.

One problem is that language is inherently abstract. Words are the mind's shorthand for rough-and-ready grouping of experiences, meant not for accuracy but for giving us a way to cut a swift and safe path through what the philosopher William James called "the humming-buzzing confusion" of the world. The confusion of the senses and the safe, clear stability of ideas was what led Plato to the conclusion that ideas must be more real than things. However, as Francie implies in the epigraph at the beginning of this chapter, it is all too easy to be led astray by the captivating ease and pure beauty of manipulating ideas. Karl Marx, for example, thought he could prove by ideas alone that capitalism had to fail, but 50 years of concerted effort to embody his ideas in the humming-buzzing confusion of Russia proved vain. Perhaps because of this failure and because of the horrifying ideal of Fascism's pure Aryan race—an idea that obliterated so many millions of lives during World War II—people now tend to mistrust writing that exists primarily in the exalted Platonic realm of ideas. Instead, readers now look for writing that is substantiated by first-hand experience. This is the rhetoric of the **encounter.**

(By the way, do you believe that story of Aristotle and the horse's teeth? I only passed it along on the authority of a philosophy professor

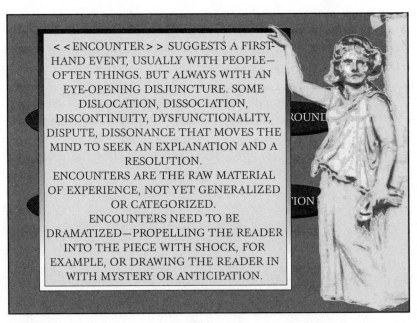

Figure 3.1. Every bead on that string of remembrances we call our life is an **encounter**.

I had as an undergraduate. The modern danger of accepting facts from an authority can be seen from the trust some people put in what they read on the Internet. In a celebrated case, Pierre Salinger, onetime press secretary to President Kennedy, announced that the explosion that downed TWA Flight 800 in 1996 had been caused by friendly fire from one of our own military missiles. It soon became apparent that he had gotten this disinformation from the Internet, and he had to retract and apologize.)

Dramatizing Experiences

Of course, we describe our encounters all day long to people who are interested in us personally and will listen no matter how we tell them, short or long, backward or forward or mixed up, interestingly or dully. When we write, however, we are writing to strangers. To get and keep their interest we have to reshape our stories in a dramatic form.

Let me demonstrate what I mean.

When I was a teenager, just after World War II, families were able to get new cars and gasoline for the first time since the war had started. We could travel! And color slide film was now available, so every family brought back cartons full of slides from their vacations. Inviting your friends over for an evening of vacation slides became a national pastime. It didn't take long for this practice to become a national joke, however, because, no matter how good a friend you were, it was impossible to keep from falling asleep during two hours of watching "Here's Mildred at the Laundromat in Provo. Now that orange blob is Frank behind the ranger's campfire at Bryce Canyon. And here, can you see those little specks? Those are wapiti on the road to the North Rim of the Grand Canyon. We always called them 'elk,' but the ranger taught us that they're really wapiti."

It's not hard to see why the drama of television doomed this plodding, if sociable, form of entertainment. Many apprentice writers, even those who have learned that **presenting** a verbal slide show of their encounters is far more colorful and immediate than just telling **about** them, still have a hard time moving from slide-show writing to the dynamism of TV presentation.

Encounters, even interesting ones, need to be dramatized to realize their full effectiveness. How can we learn to dramatize our encounters so that we can keep our audiences awake? Dramatists have, over a few millennia, been figuring out ways to do this. Maybe we, as prose writers, can pick up some pointers from them.

In dramatizing an encounter, writers of soap operas, for example, do not just lay things out the way they happened, as my parents did with roll number one of their slides. Instead they find a way to bring the story to an excruciatingly emotional point and then break for a commercial. They know we will sit through the commercial to find out what happens next. In prose writing, that "commercial" is the message, the idea, the call to action that we want to convey.

It is instinctive for all of us to reshape the stories of our happenings a little. We learn by many retellings what can be left out, what people laugh at or cry over, what creates stimulating controversy, what should be saved for the punch line. That degree of shaping is a natural process. However, it doesn't amount to much more than sorting your slides and throwing out those accidental shots when you pushed the button while pointing the camera at your feet. To become dramatic requires a radical reorganization that will pump excitement, mystery, shock, anticipation into the story to drive the reader through it. That is what dramatists have to do and what we can learn to do.

INVITATION TO A READING

You have probably seen the classic film *The African Queen* with Humphrey Bogart and Katherine Hepburn. The principal author of the screenplay was the well-regarded film critic James Agee. The following excerpt is from the autobiography of his son, who was transplanted first to Mexico and then to Communist East Germany by his mother and her second husband, Bodo Uhse, a well-known novelist there.

Growing up in a home where literary art was a staple of conversation and where authors were regularly entertained, Joel Agee imbibed an ambition to become a writer himself. Although Joel was only four the last time he saw his famous American father, he was certainly aware of his reputation in the world of film. Joel's stepfather thought enough of Joel's artistic abilities to ask him to assist in his attempt to write a screenplay.

The following excerpt from Agee's autobiography shows much of that author's flair for dramatic writing. I have sprinkled notes along the way to show where and how he has used some of those dramatizing techniques. The numbers on each of the notes refer to a summary list of techniques at the end. You may want to keep checking that list as you read to familiarize yourself with the terminology.

Cruelty
by Joel Agee

The next day, Jochen[1] led me to a hill where children were sledding, on the other side of the lake. He told them I was an American, and new here, and asked them to speak slowly and in *Hochdeutsch,* and, generally, to be nice to me. A few of the older boys ostentatiously rejected Jochen's authority by dashing down the hill on their sleds before he had finished talking. But the others listened and gaped at me in disbelief.

*(2) The older boys' reaction gives us a **hint** of coming trouble.*

"Bist du wirklich 'n Ami?" one girl asked. I looked to Jochen for a translation into High German. "She wants to know if you're really an American," he said. *"Ami* means American." *"Ja,"* I said. *"Ich bin ein Ami."* They laughed then, Jochen too, and there was a little malice in some of the laughter, but mostly it was friendly—so I laughed, too. With my nationality established to nearly

*(3) Direct **quotation**—like concrete description—shows the reader the exact tone of the situation. In the theater, the words of the characters are the dramatist's most important tool.*

everyone's satisfaction, the kids resumed their sledding, and, prompted and coached by Jochen, I joined them. After a while Jochen left, reminding me to come home when it started getting dark. No sooner was he out of sight than I became the center of a vortex of peering eyes, questions, and comments.

*(7) Conflict is the essence of drama, so showing people with **conflicting values** communicates tension. Here it's the difference in cultures, in educational level, and in class that creates animosity.*

"Ick gloobe Jochen spinnt. Jochen's got to be crazy, there aren't any Amis around here."

"Maybe he's a Russki."

"No, he's an Ami, just listen to the way he talks. Go ahead, boy, say it again: *Ich bin ein Ami."*

"Ich bin ein Ami." Again there was laughter, and I heard some imitations of my Mexican-American accent. Three little girls about my age stood up for me: "Stop laughing at him, how would you feel." That only encouraged the two or three mockers to step up their taunting: *"Guck dir mal die Dinger da an,"* said one, referring to my earmuffs.

"Typisch Ami," said another.

"Lasst ihn in Ruhe," said one of the girls. "Leave him alone or I'll tell Jochen. Come," she said to me then, pulling me by the sleeve, "don't listen to them, they're stupid," and her friends translated by tapping their forehead with their index finger, a gesture I hadn't seen before: in Mexico

---

[1]The chauffeur supplied to this exemplary Communist family by the East German government.

(8) Along with dialogue, **gesture** is what creates drama in the theater. Here the finger tapping for "crazy" unlocks a new level of complexity of the threat.

they made corkscrew motions by the side of the temple. In any case, I assumed it must be as dangerous here as it was there to associate with weak people who cast aspersions on the intelligence of people with muscles; so I carefully avoided giving any sign of complicity. But no one seemed out to hurt me.

When one of the big boys inspected the runners on my sled, I feared for a moment that he would take it away from me, but then he asked if he could ride it. Of course I let him, and after him all the others. It seemed I was okay now; my sled was of superior quality and I was willing to share it. When it was time to leave, the three girls who had defended me offered to pull their brand-new Ami home on his sled, an offer which I did not refuse, even though it caused them some difficulty, since they had sleds of their own to pull.

(5) **Partial revelations** as a technique is familiar from movies: A threat is raised, but relief follows. However, we **know** that the respite is only temporary. Darth Vader **will** return. Here, because the fear is mentioned, we know the boys are only temporarily appeased by Joel's letting them use his sled.

I went to that hill every day. The three girls were absent more often than not. That was unfortunate, since no one else was quite so friendly. I remained a stranger among those tough boys, mystified (to this day) by the wild combative excitement that broke out each time someone reached the foot of the hill (neither speed nor distance seemed to be the object of whatever contest it was); mystified, too, by their incomprehensible jokes, by their occasional fights, which never came to blows but were waged with insults and staring bouts and some pushing, quarrels the origin and dissolution of which were completely hidden from my understanding by the quick choppy dialect my tutor in Babelsberg had failed to teach me.

It wasn't long before my value as a curiosity wore off and the bare fact of my foreignness remained as an irritant. I could feel it coming, one day, a tentatively encircling menace of looks, sneers, and distances. It occurred to me that I should leave before being made to leave, but I stayed, as if paralyzed, or fascinated. I'd been through this before, in Mexico: in the midst of a band of children playing American-style *futból*—not soccer, the usual *futból*, which I could deal with, but a violent game with arcane rules everyone but I seemed acquainted with. On top of that, I was the only gringo. The same subtle network of tentative malice, cruel half-hidden jibes sent not at me so much as into the air, as a test, as a probe, and the confirming snicker, and the ritual repetition and variation upon the joke, increasingly deliberate and momentous, until

(1) An atmosphere of **anxiety** can be created in many ways. Here it is the half-repressed violence that could spill over any time.

someone delivers the catalytic stroke of brutality—a humiliating kick in the behind that time, a fistful of snow stuffed down my collar now. Mercifully, just a few badly aimed snowballs were added for good measure; back in Mexico, the kids chased me, or probably, since I wasn't caught, pretended to chase me, all the way home: "Get him! Pull down his pants!"

> (6) The thread of a new story (Mexico) is woven into the ending of the first story (snowballs). I call this **crocheting.** Like a soap opera, it gets the reader curious about the next episode before ending the last one.

It's strange, the way memories cluster and illuminate one another, or even blend, as if whatever agency handles the punctilious business of storing up the past had at some point lapsed into reverie and become more mindful of meaning than accuracy. In the background behind the shouting of those Mexican boys, in place of what should be their footsteps, panting, and laughter, I seem to remember music, and it's the same music that accompanies another memory (which dates back to about the same time, my seventh year, when we were living in Mexico City), of Alma explaining to me how and why Mussolini was lynched. It's a terrible music that sounds like something living being slowly torn to death, a shrieking and blaring and rending that goes on and on. Mussolini is a fat and very bad king who has been thrown in a pond and is being stoned. Of course, Alma must have told me something akin to the facts—that Mussolini was shot and subsequently hung upside down at a gas station in Milan. But I see him bobbing up and down in the water and stones bouncing off his round red head with a sickening, dull, thudding sound, and the music envelops and fills and explodes the scene. Mussolini puts his hands on the edge of the pond, and people step on his fingers, which are pink and very slender.

> (8) **Emotionally charged** words ("torn to death, a shrieking and blaring and rending") and imaginative comparisons (Mussolini like a rat king but also victimized).

> (6) The dream **crochets** the next two episodes. We will directly see a rat being stoned in a pond, but we continue to wonder why the image of the fascist Mussolini is here.

But most of that's drawn from another memory, a translation of it, so to speak. I was playing marbles with a band of children—some of the same children who later threatened to pull down my pants—when someone called out from a side street in great excitement: "Un ratón! Un ratón!" A moment later everyone was rushing to where the rat had been trapped, in a deep and wide puddle that had developed where workmen had broken up the pavement, damaged a water main, and, I guess, left in perplexity.

Figure 3.2. Mussolini and mistress after assassination.

The rat was trapped because all around the puddle was a thick forest of legs—naked legs, legs in rags, legs sheathed in pressed cotton
slacks. I remember I was one of the few kids with shoes. The rat swam in
slow circles, drawing a line in the water with its long, pink tail. The boys
threw stones at it, big stones and little stones. Some stones splashed into
the water, and some hit the rat with a thud, and often the rat would
squeal when it was hit. The boys kept running off to collect stones and
stuff their pockets with them, but there were always enough boys around
the puddle to keep the rat inside. One of the richer boys had a slingshot
and he was a smart shot and got a lot of applause. He was using marbles, an impressive gesture because they were worth something, and he

hit the rat with terrible accuracy and force, you could see its little head snap back, and for a moment it seemed, and I hoped, that it was dead. But then it started swimming again. It was bleeding from the mouth and one eye was smashed, everyone pointed that out. The rat came up to the sidewalk where I was standing, rose on its hind legs, and curled its incredibly delicate pink fingers around the edge of the curb; its mouth was open, I could see its pink tongue, its whiskers, the smashed eye; and the other, myopically blinking eye seemed to be looking up at our faces.

(3) The torture of the rat is told with graphic **details** that intensify the drama.

Someone took me firmly by the elbow, and only then did I realize that I had bent over a little and started reaching out to the rat. It was an older boy who stopped me, almost a man. He shook his head and went ts-ts-ts in a big-brotherly way, and then he put his hand on my shoulder, filling me with a kind of astonished pride. "Rats are poisonous," he said, "you mustn't touch them. They kill babies." Then he stretched out his leg and carefully stepped on the rat's fingertips with the tip of his sandal. The rat fell back into the water and started swimming in circles again. The big boy took his hand off my shoulder, pulled a stone out of his pocket, and handed it to me. "Throw it," he said. I threw it, and missed. "Try again." I kept throwing and missing, and the boy kept giving me stones. Finally I hit the rat in the side; there was a cheer. I looked up at the boy, he was smiling but he didn't look at me. He didn't hand me any more stones either, he kept them for himself.

A woman called from a window above us, she was waving an arm: "Step aside! Step aside! I'm going to pour hot water on it!" Everyone moved away. Now was the rat's chance to escape. But it didn't know. The woman heaved a large potful of steaming water into the puddle. It came down with a huge hiss and splash. Most of it missed the rat, but some of it didn't. The rat screamed. Still, it kept swimming in circles. Later the rat was let out of the puddle. By now it could hardly walk. Peo-

(3) **Detailed description**—analogous to a close-up in a movie—is one of the most potent dramatic tools in a writer's repertory. Dredging up all those details of the rat's destruction cost Agee extra "special effects" effort, but you'll agree it was worth it.

ple were kicking it. A truck came along, plowing aside the crowd of shouting and laughing people—some adults had joined in by then—and the truck ran over the rat, bump with a front wheel, bump with a back wheel. The driver leaned out of the window to make sure he didn't miss. Everyone cheered and applauded, including the woman in the window. Now the rat's belly was split open, its guts were oozing out. A boy took the rat by the tail and started swinging it around. Everyone started moving away fast then. I ran home to tell Alma and Bodo about it. I remember the look of disturbance in Alma's eyes, and the look of shy gravity and sadness in Bodo's expression when I had finished my story. . . .

I was ten or eleven—I'm not sure—when I went down to Bodo's Laube in search of something to read and found a book full of facsimiles of Nazi documents and photographs taken in concentration camps. I already knew about the cattle cars and the gas chambers and the mountains of shoes and hair and the lampshades made of human skin. I also knew that children just like me had been hanged, burned, asphyxiated. Nevertheless, I was not prepared for that book. No, not the book, just one picture, one among dozens. All the others I've forgotten, but this one photograph I remember clearly. It shows a skeletally thin man standing inside a swimming pool, his hands gripping the stone edge. The water looks dark and opaque. It reaches up to the man's chest. On his face is a look of mortal anguish and exhaustion, and also of supplication. There are two other men in the picture. Both are comfortably seated in chairs by the side of the pool. One of them has a uniform on, the other is wearing a suit. The uniformed man has one booted leg crossed over the other, and he is holding a stopwatch in his palm. The man in the suit is taking notes on a pad in his lap. There seems to be a smile on the face of the man with the stopwatch. He is looking down at the man in the pool, and the man in the pool is looking up at him. The caption beneath the photo identifies the two seated men and explains that they are measuring the human body's tolerance to extreme temperatures.

(4) When a writer starts a completely new encounter without a crocheted link to the previous one, we are challenged as by a puzzle to anticipate where this story will connect with the others. I call this **triangulation**. As we see the directions the story lines are taking, we begin to sense the significant point at which they will intersect. Here the rat has already been linked to the fascist Mussolini; now Agee starts something about the German fascists. We can sense that the horrors of the concentration camps will eventually triangulate to a resolution point with the horrors of the other stories.

(3) Photographic realism of commonplace **details** dramatizes the easy acceptance of horrible cruelty.

Coming upon this picture was like discovering a door through which I could step directly into hell. No one reckons with such a door until it appears, and once opened, it can never be closed again. I could turn away, of course, I could close the book. But I don't know how many times over the years, at troubled and unguarded moments—sitting by the lake fishing, or just before falling asleep—I have returned to that glance exchanged between those two men—the suffering man begging for mercy and the smiling man in the uniform of cruelty. The enormousness of it. The wrongness, unfathomable. And that this moment, which should never have been, was given a bland unalterable duration by a finger pressed on a shutter. And by myself.

(9) As the drama nears the end, writers try to **link** up all the episodes. It can be explicit, but it's even more effective when done with concrete tokens or symbols. We remember his mention of Mussolini, an ally of Hitler, when Joel is reminded of the cruelty of the German Nazi regime, and the (presumably) Jewish victim in the pool recalls the helpless rat.

CRITICAL READING

1. How many encounters do you see in this excerpt from Agee's autobiography? Describe them: Who is encountering whom or what?
2. Describe as many similarities as you can among the encounters.
3. What background did Agee feel his readers might have needed about Mussolini and about the Nazi concentration camps? How does he provide that background? Do you agree that today it is still about the right amount?
4. What is the significance of the last two sentences? What happened earlier that justifies Agee's identification with the photographer?

DISCUSSION QUESTIONS

1. Describe the conflicting feelings in Joel as he is persuaded to throw a rock at the rat. Why does he do so? Why is he not given another rock once he has succeeded?
2. There are many surprises—not to say shocks—in this excerpt. Name the ones you find most interesting and explain why.
3. If we construct a scale of 0 to 5 where 0 is "clinically objective" and 5 is "strongly value-oriented propaganda," where would you place this piece? Why? How does the author achieve this particular mix of objectivity/valuation?
4. Joel's dream is of Mussolini as a victimized rat. The Italian people who, along with other Western countries, had hailed Mussolini as the savior of Italy in the 1920s, turned against him when he joined with Hitler, enacted anti-Jewish laws, and led Italy unprepared

into World War II. Yet Joel obviously felt pity for the rat that Mussolini's image replaces in the dream. Is it possible that Agee has pity for Mussolini, or is there some other explanation for his connecting these images?

5. Plato believed that democracy could not succeed because people in groups do not follow their best individual values but succumb to mass hysteria and tyrannical leaders, as in Agee's examples. Do you agree that this is a danger in a democracy? If not, why not? If so, is there some way the danger can be avoided?

PICKING UP POINTERS FROM THE PROS:
TECHNIQUES OF DRAMATIZING

Here is a summary of the dramatic techniques we have been observing our author working into his story as he converted the slide show of his memories into a TV docudrama. I have simply compiled this list from the marginal comments I made throughout the text.

1. Creating fear, anxiety
2. Making hints, raising suspicions, creating anticipation
3. Using detailed, selective description and direct quotation to heighten emotion
4. **Triangulating** apparently unrelated elements toward a significant connection
5. Withholding information to feed the reader a succession of partial revelations
6. **Crocheting** a chain of puzzles—introducing the thread of a second story as the first is ending
7. Showing people with strongly conflicting values
8. Using heightened, emotional language; describing gesture
9. Linking elements gradually together to propel drama toward the end

Think of some favorite movies and see how many of these techniques you recognize.

I suggest that you put a sticky-note tab on this page so that you can return to it every time you write. These techniques work just as well in nonfiction writing as they do in drama. See how many you can apply as you craft each essay toward a final draft through the two or three revisions you will undoubtedly want to make.

Exploring the Topic: The Drama of Details

"God is in the details," the author of *Madame Bovary*, Gustave Flaubert, is supposed to have said. It is also a saying that the architect Mies van der Rohe said he made the touchstone of his art. We should learn from these influential experts just how important is number 3 in the list just given.

As I mentioned in the "Opening the Topic" section, writers must fight the abstract nature of language by constantly searching out the concrete exemplary detail. It is not surprising that inexperienced writers have a tendency to generalize details. Such a writer describing Joel Agee's experience in Mexico might have said, "A young man made me throw stones at the rat until I hit it." This brief general description would miss Joel's moral dilemma. Or, describing the picture at the end, the novice writer might have said, "Two Nazis are observing the effect of cold water on a prisoner." You can see that this misses the cruel effect of the clinically detailed description rendered in short, choppy sentences.

One reason that some student writers avoid specific details may be that once you begin with details, it's hard to know where to stop. Indeed, some student writers go to the opposite extreme and produce writing that is nothing but a pastiche of details. The writer of an effectively dramatized encounter needs to have a principle of selection. It's easy to see that the details of Agee's dream are chosen to create a strong nightmare quality. Besides the visual ones—the fat king with slender pink fingers, vulnerable to being stepped on—he emphasizes auditory details—the dull thudding sound of the stones hitting Mussolini's head, the blaring music that finally fills and explodes the scene. (Notice in this last description how much Agee's description sounds like a movie.)

A careful selection of details can make connections between stories on an emotional level that cannot be reached by generalized description. Notice how the detail of the **legs** of the boys surrounding the rat's pool (something one might not think to emphasize) are echoed later by the booted **leg** of the Nazi officer above the man in his pool. Again the detail of the fingers gripping the edge of a pool tie together the stories of the rat, the dream of Mussolini, and the Nazi's victim. These repeated tokens or motifs build the reader's emotional intensity and underline the theme of mass cruelty that is the ultimate vertex of Agee's triangulation.

Figure 3.3. Details of encounters are necessary to sustain interest, but they must be in line with others pointing ahead to the resolution.

Another way to grasp the way a writer must manipulate details in an encounter to dramatize them is to think of how a photographer composes a picture. Books to help amateur photographers take better pictures always include a section on techniques for highlighting and foregrounding the main subject and eliminating or de-emphasizing the distracting clutter of unimportant details. My son wanted to capture the surprise he felt watching his younger sister doing her stretching exercises for ballet. So he took a series of pictures to show the amazing extension of her legs. Figure 3.4 is the first.

You may notice that it is hard to find the focal point of the picture. Your eye has difficulty getting past the bright bookcase in the right foreground. Then it may be drawn to the bright radiator that seems to be sitting on top of the subject's head, and there is all that distracting clutter on the left. Finally, some of the drama of the dancer's extension is lost because the foreground wall cuts off her left foot.

Notice the big improvement achieved in a later photo in the series (Figure 3.5).

By moving closer to the subject, my son eliminated the foreground clutter and made the gym shoes—amusing footwear for a dancer, echoing the humor of the long-fingered gesture—prominent. The lower angle makes the person clearly the dominant focal point of the picture and fortuitously changes the exposure so that irrelevant

Figure 3.4.

Figure 3.5.

(but unavoidable) details are cast into outer darkness. This lowered perspective also places the radiator in a less prominent position, clearly behind the subject, and I further reduced its distracting presence by darkening it electronically on my computer. The result is, I think you'll agree, an altogether more entertaining picture, and the significance of what first surprised my son—his sister's long, loose lankiness—becomes dramatically clarified.

How can this lesson be applied to writing? To illustrate, I'm going to give you two descriptions of a dramatic accident that happened to me a few years ago.

Version A

The other night I took the family down to the Goodman Theater to see the new production of *Death of a Salesman*. Even though it wasn't raining, it was kind of a chilly night, so I dropped everybody else off at the theater and went to park the car in the underground lot at Monroe Street. As I came up the stairs at Columbus Drive, I turned left to cross Monroe because the light had just turned green in that direction. Because it was cold, it was a clear night and the lights of the skyline created an effervescent backdrop for what promised to be a memorable evening.

You know that's a big intersection there. Both streets are three or four lanes wide, and it takes quite a while to get across. When I'd gone a little over half way, just past the center line, I suddenly heard what sounded like a car turning toward me. Then I saw the reflection of the headlights on the far curb, and I knew I was in for trouble. I couldn't depend on my ears for evasive action, so I turned to face the oncoming vehicle. Sure enough, there, just a few feet away was a car headed right for me and apparently not about to stop. My only chance was to jump on the hood, so I did. (Luckily there wasn't any hood ornament!) Actually, I had seen this done a few times in chase scenes in cop movies, so I guess I was kind of ready for it. Anyway, I ended up flat on my stomach looking at the driver, who turned out to be a teenage girl. She stopped, of course, when she realized what had happened. She must have been pretty startled. I slid off the hood and didn't seem hurt. But I could hardly believe that, so I went over to the curb to check myself out.

The girl got out of one side of the car, and her friend got out of the other. Can you believe it? They were laughing. I was pretty upset at that, especially when, after I asked her for her insurance information, it turned out she didn't have any. Here they were, two teenage girls, driving all the way down to Chicago from Wisconsin, apparently in the car of the parents of one of them, because, although I didn't notice the make, it was a nice new car—and driving all that way without insurance. She did have a license, however—that's how I found out she was from Wisconsin—and I took down her information in case it turned out that an injury became apparent later, as often happens. Actually, my knee got nicked just a little. I guess I jumped a small fraction of a second too late. Anyway, they drove off and I went on to the theater and actually had some fun telling about my narrow escape.

I think you can see how this description corresponds to the photograph in Figure 3.4. That picture was taken on the spur of the moment, responding instantaneously to what suddenly struck my son as a funny scene. My first telling of my near accident is an unreflective, unorganized outpouring of the story just as it happened, without any attempt to shape it so as to bring out elements that coalesce into a whole. It took about five minutes to write it. Just as my son was not satisfied with his first shot of his sister, however, I find this account unsatisfying, and I know my readers will be even less enthusiastic.

Here begins the important process of revision. With photographers, it is a matter of moving lights, changing camera position, giving instructions to the model, and snapping the shutter another time—all according to principles, built on centuries of experimentation by painters, and codified in numerous books on the art of photographic composition. With writers, likewise, it involves re-creating the piece completely, using the same elements but reorganized to build the readers' reactions, reinvigorated with punchier words and images to keep the readers' interest, and realigned to link with broader issues to establish the significance of the event to the readers' lives.

Version B

The other night I was downtown, crossing that big intersection at Monroe and Columbus Drive. I was crossing with the light, which may have been my mistake. I maintain that sometimes it is safer to cross against the light because then you know who your enemies are. There were a lot of lanes to cross, but the "Don't Walk" signal hadn't started yet, so I seemed to still be OK. But there was still a ways to go, and, as always in the city, I was alert to the sounds of cars coming up behind me, thrumming along with me, and whooshing past me across Monroe street.

I had just passed the center line of Monroe Street, when out of the thrumming and whooshing I became aware of a car slowing and sounding a little louder. At the same time I saw headlights begin to sweep the distant curb, and I realized a car from behind me was turning left into my path. There were three lanes for the car to choose from, so my first reaction was, "Well, there's plenty of room and it's a brightly lighted street; he'll just slow up a little and pull around behind me." But a split-second triangulation of the rate of sweep of the headlights coupled with the now quite audible sound of the approaching vehicle led me to realize that the driver was not slowing at all and was continuing to pursue a path that would exactly flatten me.

Since I didn't know whether to jump forward or back, I had to spin and face the oncoming car. Sure enough, like a Star Destroyer locking its powerful tractor beam onto a Rebel Fighter the glaring headlights of the car were beamed straight at me and the car was no more than three yards away and closing fast. There wasn't time for evasive action.

Actually, I had been preparing myself for this moment for years, ever since I saw the first cop chase sequence where a car was bearing down on a victim trapped between narrow brick alley walls. I crouched. At the last moment I did what I had seen the undercover cop do: I sprang forward, spread-eagled onto the hood of the oncoming car. Fortunately there was no hood ornament, and I found myself briefly face to face with my assailant—a teenage girl—through the windshield of the car.

This got her attention from whatever conversation had been distracting her, and she stopped the car, allowing me to slide back to a standing position on the pavement. I walked to the curb, trying out all of my joints, hardly able to believe that my vicarious training had enabled me to walk away unscathed like a lucky toreador, tossed by a mechanical bull. The girl—who was of course uninsured—pulled over and, with her friend, got out of the car. Between gasps of laughter she asked if I was all right. It took me a few days to see the humor of the situation from the other side of the windshield as she saw a man suddenly flying toward her with open arms. It must have seemed like a movie to her, too. I am not much of a movie-goer, but I felt strangely proud that, with the help of those outrageously violent fantasies, I was better equipped to negotiate the violent realities of urban life as it begins to approximate cinematic art.

I hope you found this a better read, because it took me about two-and-a-half hours to write and polish. Just as the photographer took more time for the second shot, changing his perspective to eliminate a lot of irrelevant detail, you may notice that I zoomed in on just the incident itself, omitting the clutter of why I was there or what I did afterward. And just as the photographer had a purpose in changing his perspective, so did I. He became aware as he looked at the scene through his view finder that what intrigued him were the unusually long legs, arms, and fingers that seemed comical, especially with the clunky gym shoes—in such contrast to the graceful dancer he had seen on the stage. So he chose an angle and lighting that would emphasize the **significant** details—the legs stretching from one side of the picture frame to the other, the fingers highlighted against the dark background in the middle of the frame, the gym shoes with their conspicuous white trademark and soles.

As I played with the material of the accident, I, too, became aware of a line of significance that I wanted to emphasize—the movie-like quality of the entire event; the sense that I was a victim being hunted down in a violent urban fantasy. So I chose details and arranged them in a way that I hoped would reproduce in the reader a sense of watching such a movie, and I reinforced this with statements to that effect, and even a bit of figurative language about the Star Destroyer.

Finally, although I had intended to stop with just the encounter, I found I couldn't. The emotional inertia that had developed during the description literally propelled me into a **resolution. I had** to tie the significant strands together. I simply **couldn't** abandon this project until I had left the reader with what I had learned from the experience—that one really does need to train for the dangers of urban life as for battle and that the fantasies of movie makers actually can make good training films.

It is this kind of process that writers are thinking of when they use the word *revision.* It is not just a matter of checking spelling and correcting grammar (though that certainly should happen during revision). It is a matter of consciously reshaping the material with specific rhetorical principles in mind. It is applying craft with proven effectiveness to reshape the original draft so that it will have greater impact and significance for the reader.

In revising an **encounter** specifically, then, it is helpful to make use of techniques familiar to us from the world of photography, theater, and movie making so that the reader will feel as the famous English poet John Keats felt when he first read the *Iliad* of Homer in a translation by George Chapman.

On First Looking into Chapman's Homer

Much have I traveled in the realms of gold,
And many goodly states and kingdoms seen;

Round many western islands have I been
Which bards in fealty to Apollo hold.
Oft of one wide expanse had I been told
That deep-browed Homer ruled as his demesne;
Yet did I never breathe its pure serene
Till I heard Chapman speak out loud and bold:
Then felt I like some watcher of the skies
When a new planet swims into his ken;
Or like stout Cortez when with eagle eyes
He stared at the Pacific—and all his men
Looked at each other with a wild surmise—
Silent, upon a peak in Darien.

That is a wonderful, highly pictorial image for us to keep projecting before us as we write. We want to treat the life and world around us as discoverers do, writing about what widens our eagle eyes so that, hearing our stories, our audience will turn and look "at each other with a wild surmise."

WRITING ACTIVITY: REVISING AN ENCOUNTER FOR DRAMA

I'd like you to practice the kind of revision that I demonstrated in the preceding section. Think of an important encounter that you were either part of or a witness to. Find a willing listener who hasn't heard the story before and tell it to him or her while recording it on a tape recorder. Then transcribe what you said.[2] This is Version A of your story. It may seem awkward and time consuming, but I think you will learn some important lessons from it about what must be changed when we dramatize an event in written form.

Now reorganize the story to make the arrangement more dramatic, add some details and shed others to focus the event toward some resolution, some idea that the incident suggests to you. Substitute powerful verbs and dramatic language to heighten the emotional effect. In fact, use any of the nine dramatic techniques listed at the end of "Cruelty."

Depending on your personality you may be the bare essentials type of writer or the luxuriant overflow type. If you are the bare essentials type, like Agnes in the cartoon in Figure 3.3, you probably figure that any intelligent reader can supply the details if you just

---

[2]If you have access to IBM's ViaVoice™ or similar dictation program, this can be easy.

give the necessary signposts. Well, maybe they **can,** but they don't **want** to. If this is the way you work, then you will have to revise by adding details. But don't add them as Agnes did just to satisfy a teacher; select them carefully to amplify the dramatic tone you are trying to achieve. If you are the luxuriant overflow type, then you are like Annie Dillard, author of "God in the Doorway," which follows. You might want to read the invitation to that reading now to get a taste of revising by cutting back to just those details that point to the resolution you are aiming at.

If you really cannot come up with a suitable incident of your own, you may, if you wish, adopt one of the following as your Version A. You will notice that these versions are much longer than the Version A in the previous "Exploring the Topic" section. These are written in the luxuriant overflow style of first drafts to provide you with plenty of material. They will need to be cut back as well as rearranged to concentrate the energy of the drama. Of course, if you can think of better details than those I provide, you are welcome to invent them.

(These are all things that happened to me, but I have put them in the third person to make them easier for you to handle. You may leave them in the third person or put yourself in the scene as any one of the participants.)

Story 1

The Franklin family was headed out west on a vacation. Well, not the whole family, because Mrs. Franklin was staying home with a newborn baby sister named Louise. But the father, Michael, and their two sons, Bill and Pete, were driving out to the Grand Teton National Park in Wyoming. Bill was ten and Pete was eight at the time. They stayed the first night in Lincoln, Nebraska, in a motel, although they planned to camp when they got to Wyoming. They had been driving across Nebraska all morning when they came to the first thing that looked almost like a mountain. It was Chimney Rock, near Scott's Bluff National Monument. Standing several hundred feet high, this rock formation was a famous marker guiding pioneers west on the Oregon Trail. In fact, at Scott's Bluff you can still see the ruts made by the wheels of the old Conestoga wagons over a hundred years ago.

Anyway, they stopped to explore Scott's Bluff. They saw the wagon trails and then proceeded to drive up to a lookout point from where they were supposed to be able to see the vast expanse of prairie to the east. Before they got to the top, though, they drove through a tunnel and came to a turnout where there was a trail that led to the bottom of the bluff. The three of them walked down the trail a way, and, even though the trail was supposed to be about three quarters of a mile long, they could see what looked like most of it where it led from the bottom of the bluff to the bottom of the road that they had just come up.

The boys had been hiking in the mountains in years past, so Mr. Franklin decided that it might be fun for them to hike on their own down this short trail and he would meet them at the bottom. The trail was made out of asphalt, so it looked safe enough, and anyway, as I said, he could see what seemed like almost all of it and there didn't seem to be any problem.

The boys, of course, were enthusiastic, so they set off down the trail, and Mr. Franklin turned the car around and drove back through the tunnel to the point where the trail crossed the road. The boys, of course, had not arrived by the time he got there. So he got out of the car to wait. While he was waiting, he looked up the side of the bluff and realized that he could see the whole trail from top to bottom. But as he scanned it, he realized that he couldn't see his two sons anywhere. He began to panic, fearing that somehow they had slipped off the trail.

He decided to walk—well, more like run—up the trail, figuring he would have to find them either on the trail or, as he feared, down at the bottom of the bluff. There certainly seemed to be only one trail, so he would have to encounter them somewhere along it. But as he rushed up the trail, he saw no sign of the boys. He continued to worry, but at least he could see every inch of the bluff below, and there were no bodies down there.

Mr. Franklin had decided that they must have gone back to the top, but he had a sinking feeling they would not be there. And sure enough, when he got to the parking turnout, it was empty. He was frantic. How could two boys simply have vanished. He asked another couple there if they had seen two boys, but they hadn't. Just at that moment, a ranger's truck drove up, and the ranger asked if the kids he had in the truck were his.

What a relief! The ranger had picked them up as they were walking down the road just before they got to the tunnel. He pointed out that that was really dangerous, because the tunnel was narrow, and if they had met a car there, the driver might not have been able to see them.

Mr. Franklin thanked him, and he quizzed the boys about what had happened. As they walked back down the trail together, the boys pointed out where the trail seemed to go out on a promontory where people had walked to get a better view. As they had followed that path, it seemed to get dangerously narrow, so they had turned back. They had not noticed that the main trail had made a hairpin turn at that point and the asphalt part had continued.

When they reached the level prairie near the car, they saw a very unusual banded snake which the rangers at the headquarters were unable to identify. They were all very relieved to have gotten down safely and to be able to continue their trip.

Story 2

Michael Franklin went out to Des Moines, Iowa, one summer to visit his aging parents. His mother, Judith, was still in good health, but she was not strong enough to take care of his father, Tom. Tom had been a star football player in college—six feet tall at that time but now somewhat stooped and shorter. Furthermore, although he had lost some weight from his peak of over two hundred pounds, he was still pretty heavy, and Judith was unable to help him maneuver when he had trouble getting in and out of bed, for example. She was not small, but she wasn't strong either, and they were both in their upper eighties.

Michael's father slept most of the time and didn't have much opportunity to get outside since Judith was unable to go through the difficult process needed to get her husband into and out of a car. It was a rather long trip for Michael to get to Des Moines, but he made it a few times a year. When he was there he liked to help his father get out and see things.

Looking around for things to do on this trip, Michael noticed that Madison County with its bridges made famous by the book (it had not at that point been made into a movie) was not far from Des Moines. So he suggested that they all take a trip to see them. Tom was glad to have a chance to get out for a while, and his wife was pleased by the idea also.

Tom stayed in a wheelchair most of the time he was up, but he could walk for short distances, although he always looked very unsteady. He refused to use a cane or a walker, which would have helped. But today he seemed to be able to walk short distances all right. And the weather was beautiful. So Michael wheeled his old father to the car which he had brought up to the door, helped Tom out of the wheelchair, and stood by ready to support him as he slowly turned his body and backed carefully into the seat of the car. Then Tom lifted one leg at a time into the car, and they were ready to go.

Michael had gotten the idea for the trip from an article which had been published in the *Des Moines Register*. This article had a map locating all the covered bridges in Madison County, so they were able to find them easily.

They stopped at each bridge and Michael got out of the car and usually his mother also, but since it was such a struggle for his father to move, he just sat in the front seat of the car and watched. When it came to be lunch time, Michael felt that his father might be able to walk as far as a table in a fast food restaurant. When he saw a Pizza Hut, he asked his father if he wanted to try it, and his father said yes. So they parked next to the door (they had acquired a handicapped license by this time), and Michael helped his father out of the car. He reflected that his father's training as an athlete certainly helped him know how to balance and position his body to make the best use of his failing strength.

Michael had already learned that a major problem in taking care of old people was tending to their bathroom needs. He knew too that his father often did not become aware of his need to go until the last minute, so he suggested a trip to the bathroom before lunch. Tom agreed, and Michael supported him while his father did what was necessary to use the urinal. Michael was really pleased that his father was able to do most of this by himself, even though laboriously. He reflected that women are much less embarrassed at helping the elderly with these bodily functions, perhaps because most of them have done it for their babies.

Anyway, they finally got out of the bathroom and had their pizza. Tom ate his with obvious relish. He really liked pepperoni. When it was time to leave, Michael suggested another bathroom visit to his father. It reminded him of the regular routine he always used with his kids. But Tom said he didn't need to go, so Michael let his father walk by himself to the car, although he stayed next to him because it looked as if he could fall with any misstep.

They saw another bridge close by, and that was almost the last one. But there was one that was farther out several miles on a gravel road. However, it was back in the general direction of home, so Michael decided they could see it on the way. When they had gone a few miles through the corn fields, Tom began making signs of discomfort. Michael's mother, from the back seat, said that those signs meant that he had to go to the bathroom. Michael asked his father if that was true, and his father said yes. Michael asked if he could hold it for a while, but it quickly became obvious from his father's distress that he could not. There was nothing to do but to stop—as he had often done with his kids—and let his father go by the side of the road. There was no embarrassment factor since the road was perfectly deserted. So Michael stopped the car and told his father to wait for him to help him. His mother remained immobilized in the back seat. Michael got out of the car as quickly as he could, but it was obvious that the urgency of nature's call was not going to permit his father to wait for him. Michael asked him if it was number one or number two, and, as he had feared, it was number two.

When Michael was out of the car and had closed the door, he took a quick look through the window and saw his father's figure framed in the window on the other side of the car. He yelled to his father to wait for him, but even as he was watching through the window, he could tell by his bending forward that his father was already dropping his pants and starting to squat. Michael froze, realizing that he would be too late to help and just hoping that his father's old athletic balance would preserve his stability, when he saw his father's head and shoulders lurch a couple of times and then arc forward as if in slow motion down out of the frame of the window.

His father had obviously taken a step or two to keep his balance, but then had been tripped by the pants around his ankle. Had it not been for his father's age, the scene he had glimpsed through the window with its obvious implications as to what was happening on the other side of the car would have been comic. But the implications for such an old man to take a fall like that—full out on the gravel pavement—were horrifying. He was bound to be hurt, possibly unconscious, probably with something broken, and Michael was alone on a deserted country road with no one to help him. There would be no way for him to get his father's inert body back in the car, and this was in the days before cell phones.

He rushed to the other side of the car expecting the worst. His father was down on his side bent in a fetal position. But his eyes were open. When he asked him if he was hurt, his father shook his head and kind of smiled. Michael couldn't believe it. Apparently the old football instincts had served this eighty-five-year-old man well. He had fallen just as he had hundreds of times when he had been tackled holding the ball. There was a slight abrasion on his forehead, but it wasn't bleeding. He was a little disoriented, but with all his faculties. The bottom part of his body and his underwear were a mess, but that was a minor point.

Michael told his father to lie still until he could get him cleaned up. When he looked up for help, he realized that his mother had not moved from the back seat of the car. Even now, she did not offer to help. He couldn't believe it, but he did get her to find some tissues, and he cleaned his father up as well as he could. There remained the problem of getting the old man back into the car. Amazingly, though, with help, he was able to roll on his hip to a sitting position, and then, using the slope of the road's shoulder, roll forward and up. Michael got his father's pants back up and managed to ease him into the car seat. As they drove back to the nursing facility, Michael anxiously checked for signs of concussion, but saw none. His father responded to questions and continued smiling as if he, too, appreciated the comic element of what, now all was well, probably reminded him of an old vaudeville schtick.

Story 3

It was a Saturday night in January when Bill Franklin, a high school junior, informed his parents that he was going to a party with some friends. He didn't really ask for permission, but his father, Michael, quizzed him about the nature of the party. Who was going? Where was it? He found out that one of Bill's friends was a member of a yacht club and so he could take his friends there for a party. A yacht club? In the middle of winter? Well, yes, why not? It was just a building by the river. Michael had supposed any yacht club would be on the lake, but then realized that since the river connected with the lake, people could probably moor their boats there more cheaply than the expensive moorings on the lake. OK, but who was driving? Well, the kid himself. He had his own car. Hmmm. But there was snow predicted for that night. It really wasn't a good time to go there. And where was it exactly?

Michael found out that it was miles away, over on the east side of the city. He became alarmed. He did not think this was a good idea at all. What if they got stuck in the snow? Well, there were five guys, they certainly could handle any problem that arose. Michael watched his son go out the door with misgivings, but it seemed overly protective on his part to forbid a strong sixteen-year-old kid to adventure out with his buddies.

It kept on snowing. This was way back in the days before accurate weather forecasting, so Michael really had no idea if this was going to be a bad storm or not or when it might end. The hours dragged on. It got to be after midnight, but Michael kept telling himself that all those guys together would be able to deal with any problems. He remembered his father talking about driving his college's basketball team from one small South Dakota town to another when the drifts were five feet deep. They often couldn't see the road and just set off cross-country. When they got stuck, four guys would jump out and lift the Model T out of the drift.

Anyway, at some point the telephone rang. Michael's heart jumped in his throat. Sure enough, it was his son. They were still at the club because his friend's car wouldn't start. Bill told his dad that he was going to have to come after them. Michael felt a wave of panic. He looked out at the street. The snow was a foot deep and there had been no plows. They wouldn't be plowing, of course, because the wind would just fill the streets back in.

Michael asked his son if there weren't any of the other parents who would come for them. No, his son assured him. They all had balked. Couldn't they just stay at the club all night? No. The club was going to close at 2:00 A.M.

OK. Michael had no choice. Bill seemed quite confident that his father could do it. But Michael was frankly terrified. His son snug inside the club could have no idea what a wasteland the storm had created over the city.

Of course, this was a time before cell phones, too, so there was no way to call for help if he got stuck.

Then Michael had an idea. His neighbor had a son, a strong young man, Peter. If he could get Peter to ride with him, Peter could push the car if they got stuck. Peter was asleep when Michael called, and he was certainly not enthusiastic, but he finally agreed to go—for pay. Armed with shovels, they set out. Fortunately, because of the light traffic, the snow gave good traction. Even though it was deep, it hadn't been packed to ice. On the expressway, one lane was kept passable by the few people who were foolish or desperate enough to be out driving on such a night.

But when Michael finally had to leave the expressway, he was appalled to see no tracks on the exit ramp. He told himself to just keep going steadily and stop for nothing. Years ago he had stopped in a similar situation when he realized he was off the road, and he had had to shovel all the way back to it. Now again he had to judge by the light poles where the road should be, and he finally made it to the street and at last to the club.

What a relief it was when his son and four more guys piled into the car. The weight gave them traction, and the combined muscle made it certain that, if he could avoid an outright wreck, they would get home OK. When he dropped the last kid off, he was positively joyful. What had been a nightmare now became just another one of the wild family stories of bizarre adventure.

Strangely, Michael never got even a "thank-you" from the parents of any of the other boys.

INVITATION TO A READING

The joke about starting the school year by having to write an essay on "What I Did on My Summer Vacation" (mentioned by Russell Baker in chapter 1) reflects the essential truth that personal encounters are the easiest things to write about. This is why most freshman rhetoric courses—including this one—begin with such assignments.

Another reason for starting here is that most other kinds of writing, even outside the ivy-covered confines of the classroom, gain authenticity and energy by including personal encounters.

Although this may seem like the easiest kind of writing, Agee showed us that shaping an encounter well so that it will be interesting and significant to a reader is by no means straightforward and requires some crafty application of dramatic art.

It is not a big step from writing an encounter for an autobiography to using an encounter as the basis for an essay or column, but there are additional constraints. An essay is short, so the encounters must be described economically, still using details and direct quotations, but just the most telling ones. Additionally, readers expect it to make a point, explicitly stated or strongly implied. So the encounters must be tightly triangulated toward a final resolution.

Again unlike autobiography, the topic is often given. For students, it may be given by the instructor, as was Baker's topic "The Art of Eating Spaghetti"; for columnists, it may be dictated by the issues of the day. There seems to be an instinct to start writing with generalities, especially if the topic is phrased as a generality. The author of the following essay wrote it in response to a request from a magazine editor to describe Christmas memories. The assignment was to write about encounters. Dillard has said, however, in an essay about how she composed this piece, that she still started her first draft abstractly:

> "Like everyone in his right mind, I feared Santa Claus. Maybe this is the beginning of every child's wisdom. Of course I thought he was God. He was unseen but real and somehow omnipresent." . . .
>
> Reading this over I saw how appalling boring it was. Who would want to read something that practically begins with the word "omnipresent"? Who would want to read something so vague and drippy it uses the word "somehow"? Where are we, anyhow? What, if anything is happening? So I chucked all this and began with the scene: it's Christmas Eve, some time ago, in a living room.

She goes on to describe how easily she was led off the point she was trying to make by interesting extraneous details and side issues. So even experienced writers have to go through several major revisions of their encounters to shape them into something surprising and significant.

Again in this piece, I have sprinkled questions along the way that ask you to identify the dramatizing techniques used by Dillard. The list of nine techniques is repeated for you in question 1 following the essay.

God in the Doorway
by Annie Dillard

One cold Christmas Eve I was up unnaturally late because we had all gone out to dinner—my parents, my baby sister, and I. We had come home to a warm living room, and

a. The normal word here would be "unusually." Why does Dillard choose "unnaturally late" instead?

Christmas Eve. Our stockings dropped from the mantel; beside them, a special table bore a bottle of ginger ale and a plate of cookies.

I had taken off my fancy winter coat and was standing on the heat register to bake my shoe soles and warm my bare legs. There was a commotion at the front door; it opened, and cold wind blew around my dress.

b. Notice the particular details of the heat register and the wind whipping her dress around her bare legs. How is this better than just saying, "The door opened?"

Everyone was calling me. "Look who's here! Look who's here!" It was Santa Claus. Whom I never—ever—wanted to

c. What is the effect of repeating "Look who's here!" after the girl's reaction is described?

d. What is the effect of the word *looming*?

meet. Santa Claus was looming in the doorway and looking around for me. My mother's voice was thrilled: "Look who's here!" I ran upstairs.

Like everyone in his right mind, I feared Santa Claus, thinking he was God. I was still thoughtless and brute, reactive. I knew right from wrong, but had barely tested the possibility of shaping my own behavior, and then only from fear, and not yet from love. Santa Claus was an old man whom you never saw, but who nevertheless saw you; he knew when you'd been bad or good. He knew when you'd been bad or good! And I had been bad.

My mother called and called, enthusiastic, pleading; I wouldn't come down. My father encouraged me; my sister howled. I wouldn't come down, but I could bend over the stairwell and see: Santa Claus stood in the doorway with night over his shoulder, letting in all the cold air of the sky; Santa Claus stood in the doorway monstrous and bright, powerless, ringing a loud

e. Isn't *powerless* a rather unexpected word here?

bell and repeating Merry Christmas, Merry Christmas. I never came down. I don't know who ate the cookies.

For so many years now I have known that this Santa Claus was actually a rigged-up Miss White, who lived across the street, that I confuse the *dramatis personae* in my mind, making of Santa Claus, God, and Miss White an awesome, vulnerable trinity. This is really a story about Miss White.

f. What do you make of the contrary pairs of words—"enthusiastic/pleading" "monstrous/bright" and later "awesome/vulnerable"?

Miss White was old; she lived alone in the big house across the street. She liked having me around; she plied me with cookies, taught me things about the world, and tried to interest me in finger painting, in which she herself took great pleasure. She would set up easels in her kitchen, tack enormous slick soaking papers to their frames, and paint undulating undersea scenes: horizontal smears of color sparked by occasional vertical streaks which were understood to be fixed kelp. I liked her. She meant no harm on earth, and yet half a year after her failed visit as Santa Claus, I ran from her again.

g. It is certainly surprising not to find out until better than halfway through what the story is really about (Miss White). Why does Dillard do this?

h. With the mention of a new inexplicable event ("half a year later . . . I ran from her again") Dillard crochets it to the earlier one. This is a deliberate technique to keep us reading. How does it work?

That day, a day of the following summer, Miss White and I knelt in her yard while she showed me a magnifying glass. It was a large, strong hand lens. She lifted my hand and, holding it very still, focused a dab of sunshine on my palm. The glowing crescent wobbled, spread, and finally contracted to a point. It burned; I was burned; I ripped my hand away and ran home crying. Miss White called after me, sorry, explaining, but I didn't look back.

i. Of course, we know what is going to happen with the magnifying glass. So how does the author build suspense?

Even now I wonder: if I meet God, will he take and hold my bare hand in his, and focus his eye on my palm, and kindle that spot and let me burn!

But no. It is I who misunderstood everything and let everybody down. Miss White, God, I am sorry I ran from you. I am still running, running from that knowledge, that eye, that love from which there is no refuge. For you meant only love, and love, and I felt only fear, and pain. So once in Israel love came to us incarnate, stood in the doorway between two worlds, and we were all afraid.

j. How can Dillard justify blending Miss White and God?

CRITICAL READING

1. The direction of an encounter becomes much clearer when it is linked to another encounter. Just as, in geometry, it takes two points to determine the direction of a line, so the lines of similarity that run through two encounters triangulate to a single significant point of intersection. See if you can remember a movie that uses triangulation—the sudden starting of a new story, apparently unrelated to the first one—for suspense or propelling puzzlement.

2. Think of making a movie of Dillard's life in which these encounters occupy a couple of scenes. Would the significance of the point she is making come across through dialogue and gesture alone? What other cinematic elements might you, as a director, use to make those points?

DISCUSSION QUESTIONS

1. Here again is the list of dramatic techniques we saw Agee use in the selection "Cruelty."
   1. Creating fear, anxiety
   2. Making hints, raising suspicions, creating anticipation
   3. Using detailed, selective description and direct quotation to heighten emotion
   4. **Triangulating** apparently unrelated elements toward a significant connection
   5. Withholding information to feed the reader a succession of partial revelations
   6. Crocheting a chain of puzzles—introducing the thread of a second story as the first is ending
   7. Showing people with strongly conflicting values
   8. Using heightened, emotional language; describing gesture
   9. Linking elements gradually together to propel drama toward the end

   You will notice that I have given a letter to the marginal boxes through the essay where I point out special ways that Dillard dramatized her encounters. Match each lettered marginal note with one or two of the techniques from this list and justify each choice.

2. It is understandable that a child might fear a magical Santa Claus that could see her badness, but Dillard says she is still running. Can you explain why?

3. The young man who cannot commit to marriage is a stock comic figure these days. Might Dillard's experience shed light on his problem? If so, how?

WRITING COMMISSION: CREATING MYSTERY BY TRIANGULATION

Recall two dramatic experiences you have encountered that are linked in some way. Tell the first story, consciously using some of the dramatic techniques enumerated previously (especially that of selected, concrete details). Partially reveal the significance of this story early, but try to leave the reader anticipating a fuller explanation. Then start the second story without at first letting the reader in on the connection. Finally make clear the connection between the stories and the full significance that the triangulation of the two brings into focus.

This technique takes careful crafting, and probably a lot of reworking. But it's fun—a little like constructing a puzzle, and your readers will get equal enjoyment out of seeing how the puzzle works out.

Points to Remember

- The most trusted ideas are those that originate in actual encounters—things perceived or measured by direct observation.
- Significant encounters are those that contain some surprising dissonance.
- The telling of an encounter requires artful dramatization by withholding information to create anticipation or mystery, heightening conflicts by using emotional language and concrete details, triangulating two or three encounters that point to a similar resolution, and by crocheting—developing a new puzzle as the first is being solved.
- Details are a crucial element in dramatizing an encounter for a reader.
- Details must be selected and composed much as a photographer selects and composes elements in his picture to highlight what is significant.

- It commonly requires major revision of the first telling of an encounter to dramatize it enough to maintain reader interest and focus its significance.
- Depending on your personality, revising may mean, in addition to rearranging material, adding effective details or ruthlessly trimming those that lead away from the main dramatic line.

E-E-R

Encounter

Explain

Resolve

R-S-V-B

Reason

Search

Value

Background

4

Explanation

*It is true that Poets, after having spoken of a memorable event,
neglect it for a while in order to keep the reader in suspense. . . . But
the theme must not be abandoned for too long, so the reader should
not become lost among too many other, parallel actions.*

—Umberto Eco, *The Island of the Day Before*

Opening the Topic

In real life when we meet with something puzzling or unexpected,
our minds leap almost compulsively for an explanation.

1. It seems strange that Betsy asked me if I'd seen Rob today.
2. Our campaign seemed to be going so well. How could our candi-
    date have lost?
3. I've noticed that there are only a few places in the woods where
    there is a wide variety of spring wildflowers. You'd think they'd
    be almost everywhere in the same forest.
4. Why didn't I get a precipitate in my chemistry experiment?
5. I've tried three times to call my sister today. We're supposed to go
    shopping. I'm worried that something happened to her.
6. How come this little red light on the dashboard keeps coming on?

The dynamic of almost any piece of writing is the same, except
that in the course of pursuing the explanation for your personal
puzzle, you realize that other people probably have similar vexing
encounters and would benefit from your assiduous efforts to find an
answer.

1. Betsy was trying to break up my relationship with Rob. I think she's angry at her father's leaving the family and tries to prove there aren't any dependable men. This probably happens a lot.

2. I realize that when I was talking to friends and going to rallies I saw only our supporters. Other candidates had more friends and bigger rallies that I never saw. I suppose to get a realistic political perspective we should all talk to people outside our little circles.

3. Apparently plants are very sensitive to microclimates, and the heat, moisture, and soil content vary greatly depending on the slope and direction of the land. I suppose if you're gardening it's really important to choose different plants for different locations in your yard—how close to a reflecting wall, how exposed to cold wind, and so on.

4. Oops. The instructions said to add solution B to solution A. I just assumed I should add A to B. I think people get tired of reading instructions because so many directions are simple minded.

5. This guy had wanted Sis to go shopping with him, but they'd had to go to a second mall. She wanted to call, but she didn't have any change and her cell phone battery was dead. It's amazing how quickly we become dependent on fragile technology and how much faith we mistakenly place in it.

6. My friends said it was probably just a defective switch on the idiot light, but I took my car in anyway. It turned out that the alternator belt was loose and my battery was discharging. I guess you should always check out warning signals, even if you think nothing could be wrong.

When we encounter an eye-opener, we start looking everywhere we can think of for an explanation. The places we look are reflected in the modalities that we will study in detail in later chapters of this book. We think back on our own experiences to see if we can remember similar **encounters,** or we use **reasoning** to figure out causal relationships. We use **search** by asking friends for an explanation or by going to the library or bookstore to get **background.** The purpose of all this is to reach a **resolution** about the significance of the experience.

To this point, the writer's mind does what every mind does: It seeks an explanation for an out-of-the-ordinary, eye-opening **encounter.** But the writer's mind goes one step farther. Writers are impelled (or required) to see this personal encounter as part of a significant pattern that affects other people as well. One great reward of

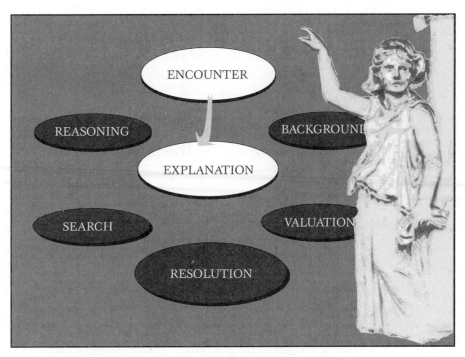

Figure 4.1. The mind demands an explanation of every surprising **encounter**.

writing comes in being able to forge explanations of such general significance that a large circle of readers will find them valuable.

INVITATION TO A READING

Every night listeners to talk-radio host Art Bell expound explanations for what they see as disturbing coincidences or encounters—often "close encounters of the third kind." And millions of people listen—some 9 million a week. Some are disturbed by the jet contrails that they see in the sky and explain them as a secret military mission that sprays poison chemicals over the country. Others see strange atmospheric phenomena and attribute them to alien space ships. Much of the hysteria that existed about the end of the last millennium (the Y2K fear) was generated and spread through this radio talk show. Some callers have been visited by angels, and others can hear messages from the dead. Some calls are hoaxes, but many are sincere.

It may be that we live in an age of heightened anxiety and mistrust when many people feel that their experience cannot be adequately explained by either religion or science. Such people look for evidence of extraterrestrial or conspiratorial activity to explain and share their fears.

Others go to the movies.

Why We Crave Horror Movies
by Stephen King

I think that we're all mentally ill; those of us outside the asylums only hide it a little better—and maybe not all that much better, after all. We've all known people who talk to themselves, people who sometimes squinch their faces into horrible grimaces when they believe no one is watching, people who have some hysterical fear—of snakes, the dark, the tight place, the long drop . . . and, of course, those final worms and grubs that are waiting so patiently underground.

When we pay our four or five bucks and seat ourselves at tenth-row center in a theater showing a horror movie, we are daring the nightmare.

Why? Some of the reasons are simple and obvious. To show that we can, that we are not afraid, that we can ride this roller coaster. Which is not to say that a really good horror movie may not surprise a scream out of us at some point, the way we may scream when the roller coaster twists through a complete 360 or plows through a lake at the bottom of the drop. And horror movies, like roller coasters, have always been the special province of the young; by the time one turns 40 or 50, one's appetite for double twists or 360-degree loops may be considerably depleted.

We also go to re-establish our feelings of essential normality; the horror movie is innately conservative, even reactionary. Freda Jackson as the horrible melting woman in *Die, Monster; Die!* confirms for us that no matter how far we may be removed from the beauty of a Robert Redford or a Diana Ross, we are still light-years from true ugliness.

And we go to have fun.

Ah, but this is where the ground starts to slope away, isn't it? Because this is a very peculiar sort of fun indeed. The fun comes from seeing others menaced—sometimes killed. One critic has suggested that if pro football has become the voyeur's version of combat, then the horror film has become the modern version of the public lynching.

It is true that the mythic, "fairytale" horror film intends to take away the shades of gray. . . . It urges us to put away our more civilized and adult penchant for analysis and to become children again, seeing things in pure blacks and whites. It may be that horror movies provide psychic relief on this level because this invitation to lapse into simplicity, irrationality and even outright madness is extended so rarely. We are told we may allow our emotions a free rein . . . or no rein at all.

If we are all insane, then sanity becomes a matter of degree. If your insanity leads you to carve up women like Jack the Ripper or the Cleveland Torso Murderer, we clap you away in the funny farm (but neither of those two amateur-night surgeons was ever caught, heh-heh-heh); if, on the other hand your insanity leads you only to talk to yourself when you're under stress or to pick your nose on the morning bus, then you are left alone to go about your business . . . though it is doubtful that you will ever be invited to the best parties.

The potential lyncher is in almost all of us (excluding saints, past and present; but then, most saints have been crazy in their own ways), and every now and then, he has to be let loose to scream and roll around in the grass. Our emotions and our fears form their own body, and we recognize that it demands its own exercise to maintain proper muscle tone. Certain of these emotional muscles are accepted—even exalted—in civilized society; they are, of course, the emotions that tend to maintain the status quo of civilization itself. Love, friendship, loyalty, kindness—these are all the emotions that we applaud, emotions that have been immortalized in the couplets of Hallmark cards and in the verses (I don't dare call it poetry) of Leonard Nimoy.[1]

When we exhibit these emotions, society showers us with positive reinforcement; we learn this even before we get out of diapers. When, as children, we hug our rotten little puke of a sister and give her a kiss, all the aunts and uncles smile and twit and cry, "Isn't he the sweetest little thing?" Such coveted treats as chocolate-covered graham crackers often follow. But if we deliberately slam the rotten little puke of a sister's fingers in the door, sanctions follow—angry remonstrance from parents, aunts and uncles; instead of a chocolate-covered graham cracker, a spanking.

But anticivilization emotions don't go away, and they demand periodic exercise. We have such "sick" jokes as, "What's the difference between a truckload of bowling balls and a truckload of dead babies?" (You can't unload a truckload of bowling balls with a pitchfork . . . a joke, by the way, that I heard originally from a ten-year-old.) Such a joke

---

[1] You may know this successful actor as the character Spock in *Star Trek*. He has also written several books of poetry.

may surprise a laugh or a grin out of us even as we recoil, a possibility that confirms the thesis: If we share a brotherhood of man, then we also share an insanity of man. None of which is intended as a defense of either the sick joke or insanity but merely as an explanation of why the best horror films, like the best fairy tales, manage to be reactionary, anarchistic, and revolutionary all at the same time.

The mythic horror movie, like the sick joke, has a dirty job to do. It deliberately appeals to all that is worst in us. It is morbidity unchained, our most base instincts let free, our nastiest fantasies realized . . . and it all happens, fittingly enough, in the dark. For those reasons, good liberals often shy away from horror films. For myself, I like to see the most aggressive of them—*Dawn of the Dead,* for instance—as lifting a trap door in the civilized forebrain and throwing a basket of raw meat to the hungry alligators swimming around in that subterranean river beneath.

Why bother? Because it keeps them from getting out, man. It keeps them down there and me up here. It was Lennon and McCartney who said that all you need is love, and I would agree with that.

As long as you keep the gators fed.

CRITICAL READING

1. The author probably expects his readers to recoil from the shock of his eye-opening statement "We are all mentally ill," so he mentions some common encounters that he thinks will justify the shock. Explain why you think he is or is not successful. Find a couple of other common **encounters** that King uses later to illustrate our common insanity.

2. King uses the one-sentence paragraph of weak explanation—"And we go to have fun"—followed by "Ah, but . . ." as a gear-shifting device to move us to a deeper level of explanation. What earlier sentence acts as a signpost setting the reader's expectation for this transition? Notice, for the benefit of your own writing, that this structuring means King had decided on a layout for this essay before making the final draft, and he thought up a way of making that layout clear to his readers without using intrusive section markers.

3. Explain King's statement that the best horror films are (a) reactionary, (b) anarchistic, (c) revolutionary. Do you think King's explanations of each of these terms are adequate? Explain.

4. Why do you think liberals might "shy away from horror films"? Can you think of evidence either for or against this statement?

DISCUSSION QUESTIONS

1. King's explanation of how society is able to function when its members are all insane follows the model of Sigmund Freud. King's "gators" correspond to Freud's "id"; the "trapdoor" is the "superego" internalized from society's graham crackers and spankings; and King's "I" is the socially functional "ego" of Freud. Like King, Freud also believed that keeping the trapdoor shut too tightly caused antisocial insanity. But he felt that those gators should be let out, not to roll on the grass or be exercised but to be tamed in the controlled settings of dreams and the psychoanalyst's couch. There are many critics of violence in movies who would argue that exercising the gators in public just stimulates the insanity of people with weak trapdoors and encourages them to commit violence. In other words, tasting red meat, the gators, instead of being satisfied, just want more. What do you think?

2. Mark Edmundson, another analyst of the popularity of horror movies, has written a whole book on the subject called *A Nightmare on Main Street.* He believes that the taste for gothic horror is the flip side of the New Age belief in easy fixes and happy endings through spiritualism, diet, guardian angels. Both, he believes, are a result of the culture's general loss of a deep religious belief that demands discipline and sacrifice in return for a sure sense that human life has an absolute, meaningful foundation. According to Edmundson, New Age spiritualism pulls down the blinds when the heightened fears and anxieties of our age appear at the window. But this haunting terror, barred at the window, comes in through the door, taking wildly grotesque forms and nightmarish power because there is no firm mental, cultural, or spiritual counterpoise to it. Do Edmundson's views overlap King's? Which explanation do you find better for people's love of horror films? Why? Looking inside yourself at your own reactions, can you find other reasons for their popularity?

3. It is not only horror story writers who use the subconscious to engage their readers. If you remember Russell Baker's story of his inspiration for the essay on spaghetti that he wrote for Mr. Fleagle (chapter 1), you will remember that the topic "produced an extraordinary sequence of mental images [s]urging up out of the depths of memory." In this case the gators under the trapdoor are warm and friendly, and most students rightly find this a liberating example of how to approach the task of writing. But if you

tried just letting the creatures of your memory out of the pit to roll around on the grass wherever they felt like it, you would probably find your reader simply baffled and confused rather than moved. What is the function of rhetoric in shaping an effective piece of nonfiction (or a screenplay) out of the energized fragments that surge up out of the subconscious mind?

PICKING UP POINTERS FROM THE PROS: HUMOR

Bad humor fails more obviously than other kinds of bad writing, but good humor is probably no harder to write than other forms of good writing. Unfortunately, most student writers seem to think humor has no place in school writing assignments. But when explanations might prove unpalatable, humor acts as a sugar coating, and it certainly adds much interest to many subjects because it always contains a surprise.

☐ Groucho Marx **owned** the surprising twist that delivers the punch in the genre we call *one-liners.*

Behind every great man stands a woman, and behind her stands his wife.

The secret of life is honesty and fair dealing. . . . If you can fake that, you've got it made.

In these gags, as in much humor, the eye-opener depends on the contrast between the standard world of expected behavior ("Behind every great man stands a woman" and "The secret of life is honesty and fair dealing") and a contrasting world of cynical reality (many great men have been inspired by their mistresses and watched jealously by their wives; many people who appear honest and fair are hypocrites).

☐ We pick up a picture of the writer's linguistic world in a few paragraphs. Words that belong particularly to one world or another often are labeled *formal, technical, jargon, colloquial, regional, slang,* or *vulgar* by dictionary makers. One way to get a laugh is by unexpectedly dropping in a word from a world totally different from the kind of normal, informal one you have established— something slangy like *puke* or *twit,* regional like *gators,* or out-of-the-way like *squinch.*

Find another example where King suddenly drops into slang from his established tone to give a laugh.

☐ Of course, it can work the other way, as when King uses "this invitation . . . is extended"—a rather formally polite phrase—to apply to "madness," suggesting a world very far from formal and polite.

Find another example where King juxtaposes the formally polite world with a coarser world for humorous effect.

☐ The sick joke represents a common form of humor in which humans are treated as objects. One of the most famous of these is the James Thurber cartoon that shows a woman crouched on top of a bookcase like a large predatory animal while the husband introduces her/it as his **former** wife.

☐ We've all heard and used sarcasm. In this essay King humorously shows his frustration with social norms by sarcastically mimicking the uncles and aunts twittering the clichéd phrase "Isn't he the cutest little thing."

☐ Metaphors are a rich and sometimes profound source of humor. The power of metaphor is making a connection between the thing being described—the human psyche in this case—and a picture evoked by subconscious suggestion. In this case, King's imagination suggested, for human raw feelings, a picture of alligators controlled by an occasional feeding through a trapdoor.

Find another metaphor in this essay.

There are many other kinds of humor.

☐ Wild exaggeration, for example, is a Dave Barry trademark. When describing his vacation in Paris he noted the parking problem thus:

Paris has only one vacant parking space, which is currently under heavy police guard in the Louvre museum. This means that thousands of frustrated motorists have been driving around the city since the reign of King Maurice XVII looking for a space, and the way they relieve their frustrations is by aiming at pedestrians, whom they will follow onto the sidewalk if necessary. Often the only way to escape them is to duck into one of Paris' historic cathedrals, which fortunately are located about every 25 feet (or 83.13 liters).

☐ Playing with words is another form. Many jokes are puns, words where we expect one meaning but where a second thought reveals a surprisingly appropriate different one, as in these bumper stickers: "My Mother Is a Travel Agent for Guilt Trips"; "Veni, Vedi, Visa: I Came, I Saw, I Did a Little Shopping."

Sometimes puns are phrasal:

A scientist cloned himself, but the experiment created a duplicate who used very foul language. The scientist couldn't stand this nasty image of himself and finally pushed it out the window. It fell to its death, still uttering filthy imprecations. Later, the scientist was arrested for making an obscene clone fall.

Mahatma Gandhi, as you know, walked barefoot most of the time, which produced an impressive set of calluses on his feet. He also ate very little, which made him rather frail, and with his odd diet, he suffered from bad breath. This made him what?—A super-callused fragile mystic plagued with halitosis.

Although many people consider puns a silly form of humor, honored authors from Shakespeare to James Joyce have loved them.

Bring a couple of your favorite jokes to class. With the class analyze what technique is used to create their humor.

Don't be afraid to try humor in some of your writing. After all, the worst that could happen would be that your instructor would project a fourteen foot image of your paper on a screen in front of the whole class and say, "So you think this is FUNNY, do you Mr. (or Ms.) [your name]? Come class, let's all laugh at this pathetic attempt at humor by our class clown. Hee-haw!"

Just shrug it off. I'm sure next time you'll have the whole class rolling in the aisles!

INVITATION TO A READING

Experiences that bother us deeply are often pursued in poetry.

What happens when you encounter a bug in your ear? Once, camping on a sandbar beside the Colorado River at the bottom of the Grand Canyon, I was awakened in the middle of the pitch-dark night by the sensation of a bug—no, a couple of bugs—no, a bunch of bugs—sharing my sleeping bag and exploring the contours of my skin. Fighting panic, I took inventory of the situation. They were not biting or stinging; to get rid of them, I would have to crawl out of my bag, turn it inside out; then I'd crawl back in and . . . what? Lie awake anxiously awaiting their return?

What a theme for a horror movie—*The Intrusion of the Sleeping Bag Bugs!* "No," I said to myself, "they're not doing me any harm. Let's coexist as friends. If I quietly go back to sleep, they will probably do the same. After all, even without these bugs, the entire surface of my skin is a battleground between bacteria and fungi; the only difference is I can't usually feel them except when the fungi win in the spaces between my toes." So I more or less calmly went back to sleep. And when I awoke in the morning, I found they had all left my bag and were contentedly taking their breakfast on the flowering shrub, next to which, with poor judgment, I had dossed down.

The revulsion and panic most of us feel when we encounter grubs, spiders, snakes, or wasps is a reaction far in excess of any rational danger that we are in. What is the **explanation** for this feeling? How should we resolve it? We cannot pause each time we encounter an irritating bug. We cannot, each time, stop to consider our relation to all other life with which we share this planet—to wrestle with the problem of whether to kill the bug, with how to kill it, and with whether it feels the kind of agonies we would feel being tortured. Poetry is the kind of writing that deals most directly with the disturbing flotsam and jetsam from our unconscious. So we read a poem like the following one to cut through our stereotypes and let a writer in intimate contact with her feelings reawaken in us the surprises of the commonplace and explore the gator pit for us thoroughly, once and for all.

Ignorance
by Sarah Duffy

I just killed a bug.
I just killed a bug because
It was racing across the dark
Cement I happened to be sitting on
And did not care to share.
Maybe if the breeze wasn't quite so
Subtle, and the lunar sun of dark
Hadn't slipped behind the clouds for
That moment I would have been distracted
And not seen that bug.
But I saw it and I killed it.
I didn't ease the heel of my shoe
On it and let it die a smothered
Death.
I didn't drop a rock in its path so it
Could be crushed under the heavy boulder
Forever.
Instead I found a stick and tapped the
Black creature until it deliriously ran in circles.
Then I tapped it harder until it staggered

In crooked spirals.
As I watched this black shiny creature's
Drunken dawdle, the anger within my mind,
Within the blood that travels through vessels
To every inch of my flesh, boiled until the hate
And the torment inside me were thousands of
   these creatures
Winding through those same blood vessels.
I grabbed a larger stick and in the midst
Of its devilish, cursly saunter I
Sliced it into two, three,
Four different parts. And as
The twitching of the last antennae
Slowed to a quiver of
Nothing,
I flattened the creature and made
It part of the darkened cement I sat
Upon.
And only then realized I shared what I dared
   not share before.

After experiencing her encounter, we may or may not resolve to change our routine encounters with bugs. But the author has heightened the significance of our commonplace ideas about nature by dramatizing an encounter. This is the service that all of us writers owe our audience. Many of my students respond to Sarah Duffy's poem "Ignorance" by brushing her off as "wacko." But as we saw in King's essay, we all may be a little mentally ill. The poet, as much as the horror movie writer, gives us a look into our own gator pit—if we can stand it.

One difference between the two is that, unlike the horror movie, the poem moves entirely in shades of gray. There is no sense of the ego being in control of the id. But poetry allows the writer to exercise our sometimes monstrous reactions on the controlled leash of the tight structure of language.

This is not the same as understanding or explaining those reactions. Explanation—the subject of this chapter—is the job of prose writers. The man who gave his name to the Freudian slip was the first to explain the disturbing labyrinth of causes behind some of our ordinary but often inappropriate actions in a book called *The Psychopathology of Everyday Life*. Here he describes a simple but somewhat puzzling almost-accident that, he discovered, had a cluster of deep, almost sinister explanations.

> I once undertook to improve the marriage relations of a very intelligent man, whose differences with his tenderly attached young wife could surely be traced to real causes, but as he himself admitted could not be altogether explained through them. He continually occupied himself with the thought of a separation, which he repeatedly rejected because he dearly loved his two small children. In spite of this he always returned to that resolution and sought no means to make the situation bearable to himself. Such an unsettlement of a conflict served to prove to me that there were unconscious and repressed motives which enforced the conflicting conscious thoughts, and in such cases I always undertake to end the conflict by psychic analysis.
>
> One day the man related to me a slight occurrence which had extremely frightened him. He was sporting with the older child, by far his favourite. He tossed it high in the air and repeated this tossing till finally he thrust it so high that its head almost struck the massive gas chandelier. Almost, but not quite, or say "just about!" Nothing happened to the child except that it became dizzy from fright. The father stood transfixed with the

child in his arms, while the mother merged into an hysterical attack. The particular facility of this careless movement, with the violent reaction in the parents, suggested to me to look upon this accident as a symbolic action which gave expression to an evil intention toward the beloved child.

I could remove the contradiction of the actual tenderness of this father for his child by referring the impulse to injure it to the time when it was the only one, and so small that as yet the father had no occasion for tender interest in it. Then it was easy to assume that this man, so little pleased with his wife at that time, might have thought: "If this small being for whom I have no regard whatever should die, I would be free and could separate from my wife." The wish for the death of this much loved being must therefore have continued unconsciously. From here it was easy to find the way to the unconscious fixation of this wish.

There was indeed a powerful determinant in a memory from the patient's childhood: it referred to the death of a little brother, which the mother laid to his father's negligence, and which led to serious quarrels with threats of separation between the parents. The continued course of my patient's life, as well as the therapeutic success confirmed my analysis.

—*from* The Psychopathology of Everyday Life *by Sigmund Freud*

(**An aside:** If you have never read Freud, you may have been as surprised as I was at how good a writer he is—far more interesting than most of his commentators or summarizers. The lively energy, the sense of expectancy and discovery is hardly what one expects of scientific, academic writing. And that perception is too bad, I think, because the search for explanations that scientists and other academicians pursue is truly exciting. How does Freud's writing capture this? If you look at this selection from the point of view of the principles of this text, you will see many of the elements that we are talking about. There is a **surprising encounter,** filled in with enough **background** to make it **significant.** The writer then looks for other **encounters** with the same client and **reasons** about them in order to **explain** the **significance** of this puzzling action and reaction. The general **resolution**—that internal rage from earlier, unassociated events may lie "hidden behind apparently accidental awkwardness and motor insufficiency . . . which seriously endanger the life and health of others"—appears in some form between each of the encounters he describes.)

WRITING COMMISSION: EXPLAINING A POEM

From this point on in this book I'd like to make some of your writing assignments less like "assignments" and more like real-life professional writing commissions, in which you must satisfy an editor who, in turn, is looking for your work to satisfy a real audience. For these, I'm going to ask you to turn your classroom into a virtual-reality newspaper office.

Imaginatively situate yourself as a summer intern for this weekly newspaper, which has a circulation among youngish, well-educated people, some working in the town's businesses, some for the city and county governments, some for the college. There is, of course, a mix of singles, couples, and families.

In this virtual-reality world, your instructor becomes your editor. As editor working with an intern, your instructor will be anxious to make the craft of writing an attractive possible career choice for you and do everything needful to improve your skills. But the editor has a paper to put out and an audience to entertain and inform. You are now part of a team to accomplish that. If you can transcend the teacher-student role and rise to the editor-intern role in which your instructor is striving to help you produce writing that will attract and keep an audience, I believe you will find the writing in this course at once more challenging, more fun, and more satisfying.

All right; let's try it.

Your editor has just received a review copy of a collection of poetry of high-school students and has selected Duffy's poem "Ignorance" as one that she (or he) thinks is an outstanding example. He (or she) has given it to you to review. "What does that mean?" you ask. "What am I supposed to do?"

"Just what you always do with all your writing," is the reply. "Describe what happened . . ." (Ah, the **encounter**, you think to yourself) ". . . then write a full explanation that does justice to the complexity of Duffy's reactions. In order to do that, you'll probably want to link this up to a personal experience of your own so that the readers don't just think Sarah Duffy is some wacko sadistic nut."

"But I really don't understand much about this. Like, why did she feel she had to do anything about the bug in the first place? And what does that lunar disk have to do with making her notice the bug? Then she just tapped at it. OK, but why did the bug's dazed wanderings drive her into a rage that made her so brutal? And it wasn't enough to just cut it till it stopped twitching? She had to grind it into the cement. Why?"

"Good!" your editor replies. "Those are exactly the questions that make it such an interesting poem! And they are the ones your readers will want you, as a reviewer, to try to explain. Now, run along. We both have work to do."

"One more question," you persist. "How should I end this review? I feel that if I just stop after explaining it, my piece won't be complete."

"Right," your editor replies. "If the poem is good, rather than just kind of interesting, it is because it speaks to a whole lot of people. The significance of any experience lies in the links you can make between it and other experiences. So in this case, what this poem can mean to other people should be found in the link you made between it and that experience of yours that I spoke of a moment ago. From there you should be able to generalize to something about how "ignorant" (don't forget the title!) we are of the connectedness of life on the planet."

"OK, gotcha."

Then someone else asks, "Do we have to use this poem? How about using another one from the collection?"

Your editor agrees that would be OK.

[In the "real life" of the classroom, this means selecting a poem from your own high school or college collection of student writing.]

"The caveat," your editor adds, "is that the poem have an equivalent subconscious depth that needs explaining and a wide enough significance that our audience can relate to it."

Exploring the Topic: Conscious Explanations

When people's eye-opening behavior needs explaining, the id is probably the place to look. But we like to think of our egos being in control of those gators under the trapdoor, so most nonfiction prose writing concentrates on trying to find conscious, rational explanations for the event, idea, or finding that startled us into beginning a verbal quest.

We are a nation of news junkies. Major TV stations broadcast hours of news each day, and many radio stations broadcast nothing but news. As a result, most column writers get their material from

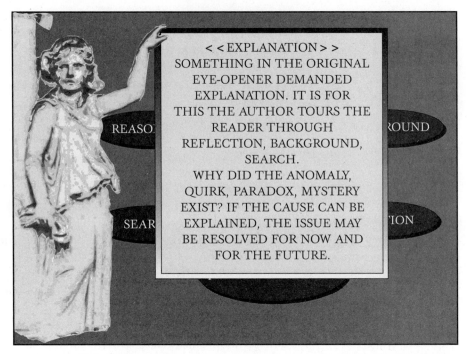

Figure 4.2. After an eye-opening **encounter** our minds immediately start looking for an **explanation** that will head us in the direction of a **resolution.**

shockers they find in the daily diet of news. Their jobs, as they see them, is to analyze those shockers for explanations.

WRITING COMMISSION: EXPLAINING SOCIAL PROBLEMS

Your editor has decided to devote space for a series on social issues in the news. He (she) wants to explore alternative solutions, so the decision has been made that this will be a collaborative writing project in which groups of three of you interns will either choose or be assigned to a single problem.

"The three or four of you on a team can meet to come up with a variety of explanations and brainstorm some possible resolutions to the problem, if there is a problem, or possible attitudes toward the trend, if there is a trend.

"My picture for these issues is to get a variety of viewpoints, maybe create a little controversy to stimulate our readership. So I want each of you to do your own miniarticle, each with a different explanation or call for action or change of attitude."

"Is this supposed to be totally objective?" someone asks.

"I don't know that I've ever seen writing that is totally objective," your editor responds. "But no. Your own experience with the issue adds a human interest dimension that our readers appreciate. Definitely show how you or someone you know is connected with it. I've sketched out a list of topics that I think would work. But, of course, if your team comes up with another social situation that needs explaining, be my guest."

---

1. What are the causes of poor performance of kids in inner-city schools?
2. Pick any current fad or cultural change among young people (I'm too out of it to suggest any) and explain its causes.
3. Is violence on TV, in video games, and in movies an explanation of violence in some kids' behavior? Are there other explanations?
4. Find and explain causes of job dissatisfaction among office workers.
5. What are some explanations for the differences between generations and some of the hostility that seems to exist between them?
6. Explain why many people are turning to alternative medicine practices like acupuncture, Ayurveda, chiropractic, herbal medicine, homeopathy, massage, meditation, naturopathy, prayer, shamanism, therapeutic touch, and yoga in an age of rapid progress in conventional medicine.
7. Examine the reasons some people display hostile reactions to immigrants.
8. Why do some people love to hunt? How is it possible for such people to be environmentalists?
9. How do you explain the popularity of e-mail even between people who can call or visit each other easily?

INVITATION TO A READING

Now take a look at how a group of professional writers (like your group in the preceding Writing Commission) might have handled another social problem that is much in the news—divorce.

Advice columns and books of advice on how to handle personal relations in this era are an industry unto themselves. Many young men and women have started approaching marriage, for example, as they would a loveable porcupine—not eager to embrace it in the first place and ready to drop it at the first sign of bristling. At least that's one explanation of some statistics that appeared as part of a news release by the National Marriage Project, claiming that marriage is a dying institution. Many in the media found this so startling that columns trying to explain—or explain away—those findings scattered like so many porcupine quills over op-ed pages across the country and continued to pop up as a news item in other papers over a period of six months.

Following are three write-ups from different newspapers of the same report on the state of marriage. Some differences are attributable to the fact that the three writers perform in different roles. The first two articles are by regular columnists, and the third by a professor. Each author encountered the same facts, but notice the differences in eye-openers, explanations, and resolutions.

Reflections on the State of the Unions
by Sandy Banks

It was the sort of conversation that makes me put aside my single-mom blues and, for a moment, feel lucky that I'm no longer married: Two men, behind me in line at the bagel shop, were comparing notes on their exercise routine.

The short guy complained that his legs had been aching, so he'd spent extra time stretching that morning. But that set him back, cut into his schedule.

And spurred his wife to launch World War III.

"Again?" asked his buddy, chuckling. "What was it this time?" Well, he'd started on the treadmill late so he wasn't finished when it was Carol's turn. Before he was even at 15 minutes, she was badgering him about taking so long.

"Get off. . . . Aren't you off yet?" He mimicked her whine, her caustic tone. "For chrissakes, now I'm gonna be late. It is my turn; you are out of time!" So he cut it short, but that wasn't enough.

"She started pointing to these drops of sweat on the treadmill, complaining that I didn't wipe it down." And when he did, she yelled because it was with her good towel. And he missed a spot. And he took too long. And why was he always so sloppy, so slow? . . . "So I said,

'Nothing I ever do pleases you . . . I get the feeling I can't do anything right.' " And that really made her blow.

His friend nodded sympathetically. "That's why I never say anything, no matter what she complains. They just want to fight. They start looking for conversation, and that leads to trouble.

"So I just get out of the house as quickly as possible . . . and try to stay away." They both laughed, and the conversation shifted . . . to interest rates and EBay[2] and whether they'd booked time on the links this weekend.

And I wondered if Carol was still fuming, what she was telling her friends, and what they would say.

     * * *

Looking back at 17 years of marriage, I can remember plenty of those conversations: You did. I did not. You don't care. I'm sick of listening to you complain. You're selfish. You drive me crazy. If it wasn't for the children. . . .

They often had little to do with the topic at hand—the sweat-smeared treadmill, the untrained dog, the unexplained charge on the Visa bill—but reflected the inner angst and outside pressures that could turn partners into competitors and make marriage feel like a battlefield.

In fact, a new study by the Rutgers-based National Marriage Project suggests that married couples today are less likely to be happy than ever before. Twenty-five years ago, more than half of all married people said they were "very happy" in their marriages. Today, only about one-third feel that way. In fact, the study suggests that after 10 years of marriage, only about 25% of marriages can be considered "successful" . . . that is intact and happy.

"Americans haven't given up on marriage as a cherished ideal or a personal life goal," the study says. "But the quest for a good marriage is becoming more difficult and uncertain" as the role of marriage in society changes.

The importance of marriage as an institution is declining, the study's authors say. Witness the increase in single-parent families, the acceptance of unmarried cohabitation, the fact that more people marry later (or not at all) and divorce more often and easily.

That has forced a redefinition of marriage and made us more apt to enter marriage looking not for economic security, social ties or moral grounding, but for fulfillment of our sexual and emotional needs . . . and thus more likely to be disappointed.

---

[2] eBay is an e-commerce Web site where people can buy or sell items to each other electronically by computer.

"Our standards and expectations for marriage have risen to a much higher level than in earlier decades," says Rutgers professor David Popenoe, one of the study's authors. "Fewer marriages can meet these standards." In other words, happiness in marriage is not measured these days by whether we are raising healthy children, climbing the economic ladder, contributing to our community's well-being. But by whether we're meeting each other's sexual and emotional needs.

Or by whether we finish our workout on time. And whether we leave the treadmill clean.

    * * *

Back in bagel shops across America, the conversation continues: "Now, why would you say that? I never said you couldn't do anything right! I'm just tired, because your dog kept me up all night."

"All night? I took him out before I went to bed so we wouldn't have a problem."

"Well, we had a problem. He started barking at 3 AM, but you didn't hear him. You never stopped snoring. And I never got back to sleep the whole night." And on and on. . . .

Surviving Marital Miseries
by Kathleen Parker

You know the script. A young couple jubilantly announces their plans to marry and you call your bookie. Two years, tops. Then you drop by the bridal shop for a piece of everyday china. Save the good stuff for Round 2.

Sad, but not surprising, marriage is at a 40-year low, according to a recent report by the National Marriage Project. Some demographers are predicting that 85 percent of young Americans will never marry.

Why? Because they're afraid they won't be "happy." In fact, fewer people today are happy with marriage than just 30 years ago. In the early 1970s, 53 percent of people in their first marriages were "very happy." By 1996, only 37.8 percent were.

Such is cause for concern. As Utah Gov. Michael O. Leavitt said at a recent meeting of marriage researchers: "If the institution of marriage ever falls from grace, our society will fall as well because there is no institution that can take its place."

In response to these troubling figures, researchers are building seminars on conflict-resolution, intimacy, infidelity and children, while marriage advocates are urging Congress to eliminate marriage penalties in the tax codes.

Well and good, but aren't we overlooking the obvious? I'm talking about the word "happy." We need to rid it from our adult vocabulary. "Happy marriage" belongs in the Dictionary of Oxymorons next to "deliciously low-fat."

Blame it on the Constitution and the American ideal of the pursuit of happiness, but happiness can never be an expectation in any endeavor involving other human beings. Especially not in marriage, which is the toughest human arrangement ever conceived.

That's not to say you won't experience happiness in marriage. Many do. But you won't find it like a pearl in an oyster. Happiness isn't bestowed. You don't wake up on your 10th anniversary, examine the respiring mound beneath the covers next to you and exclaim, "Dadgum I'm happy!" If you do, I want your prescription and your doctor's phone number.

Like most things of value, marital happiness is earned, mostly through hard work and self-sacrifice. The rule in marriage shouldn't be: I want to be happy in my marriage. Rather, the rule should be: I want to make my spouse happy in our marriage. What a concept.

Yet nowhere, at no time, are we told this. A lucky few witness it growing up within their own families. Most learn early that nothing lasts, not even families, and that the solution to problems lies just beyond the exit.

Leavitt, speaking at a recent Smart Marriages, Happy Families conference in Crystal City, Va., was exactly right when he said, "We need more straight talk about the value of marriage."

We might begin by teaching our children as much about marriage and family as we do about sex. We need straight talk about why we marry, the purpose of marriage and family in a stable society, the importance of sticking out the tough times in spite of occasional "unhappiness."

The secret to marriage, we need to tell them, is understanding that sometimes you have bad days or bad weeks. Sometimes you have bad months. In the absence of abuse, there is value to keeping your mouth shut and weathering the inevitable storms. There is value to giving more than you receive. There is value to placing the marriage—the family, the common good, the higher goal—above one's individual wants or wishes.

Given such lessons early in life, we might see not only fewer divorces and broken families, but also a more civil society. The rules for family and society are really the same. Whither goes the family, so goes the other.

Asking More from Matrimony
by Douglas J. Besharov,
assisted by Andrew R. West

In 1986, a much-discussed study contended that a woman over 40 had a less than 1 percent chance of getting married—or, in the words of *Newsweek,* she was more likely to be "killed by a terrorist."

It was a vivid phrase but an inaccurate one, it turned out. Other researchers quickly corrected the study. Women were getting married, they were just getting married later.

Now comes a new study from the National Marriage Project at Rutgers University claiming that the marriage rate has declined by roughly 43 percent since 1960. According to this report, the marriage rate of single women 15 years old and older declined to 49.7 per thousand in 1996, from 87.5 per thousand in 1960.

Once again, the demise of marriage is being exaggerated. How? Age 15 is the wrong cut-off for comparing marriage rates in 1960 and 1996, because people now just don't wed at such an early age. Since 1960, the median age of women getting married for the first time has increased by four and a half years, to 24.8 from 20.3.

To measure marriage rates accurately, most demographers today calculate the percentage of women who are "ever married." Assuming that one should not count teen-agers because so few marry, in 1960 the proportion of women 20 and older who had ever been married was 90 percent. Thirty-six years later the proportion of women who were then or had at one time been married stood at 83 percent—only about 8 percent lower.

That's the statistic for women who get married. What about staying married? Here, the situation has worsened. Divorce rates rose sharply through the 60's and 70's. Although divorce is down slightly since its 1980 peak, about 1 marriage in 3 still fails. Moreover, remarriage after divorce or a spouse's death is way down, partly because the stigma attached to cohabitation has been substantially reduced and partly because more women can survive financially on their own.

To measure these combined trends, demographers calculate the percentage of women "currently married." Here, by my calculations, we can see a big change. If one accounts for later marriages and longer life spans by counting only those Americans between the ages of 20 and 74 (after age 74, too many husbands are dying to get a fair count of marriage), only 64 percent of women were currently married as of 1996, versus 76 percent in 1960.

Yes, marriage bonds are weaker than ever. And people now divorce for what, to many, seem like insubstantial reasons.

Out-of-wedlock birth rates remain high, and cohabitation rates continue to climb. But this does not mean that young people have rejected marriage. If anything, they want more from marriage than ever before.

These days, young people tend to marry later, after they have completed their education and have a better idea of who they are. Because they have seen so much divorce, many want to be very sure before making such a big decision. Studies show they want marriage to be a partnership, with equality between men and women, and to be emotionally satisfying in ways never dreamed of by their parents, let alone grandparents.

And they think that a bad marriage is worse than no marriage—so they are more willing to divorce even if they have young children. Young women are also less willing to wed just because they are pregnant.

One does not have to sympathize with all these lofty aspirations (or ignore their inconsistencies) to recognize that young people aren't giving up on marriage; they are just modernizing it.

So, instead of exaggerating the death of marriage, and instead of making obsolete assumptions about when young people should marry, we should try to understand this seismic change in their behavior and attitudes.

CRITICAL READING

1. Describe the explanations given by each of the authors for the shocking conclusion of the National Marriage Council's study that the institution of marriage is failing.

2. Thinking back to King's explanation of why some people crave horror movies, which of these three writers do you think would be most likely to find that going to a horror movie might help them deal with their life problems? Explain.

3. Describe the techniques each of the authors uses to add spice to her or his title.

4. Banks in "Surviving Marital Miseries" describes the term *deliciously low-fat* as an *oxymoron*—that is, two terms that seem to be exact opposites yoked together to surprise the reader into searching for a deeper meaning. (If you remember our discussion of *paradox* after Greene's column "The Colors of the World" [in chapter 2], you may notice that an oxymoron is a special, more intense case of paradox.) Explain why *deliciously low-fat* is an oxymoron.

Banks also claims that *happy marriage* is an oxymoron. Here there is an additional twist: We do not normally think of *happy marriage* as self-contradictory. How does the shock of this assertion drive the reader to look for a deeper explanation?

DISCUSSION QUESTIONS

1. Comparing the three articles, which way of explaining the statistics seems most satisfactory to you? Why?

2. Our political labels (used by King in his essay on horror movies) *anarchist, revolutionary, liberal, conservative* suggest people who look for the explanation of social problems in different places. Anarchists blame government for social problems and believe that people would function better without it. Revolutionaries see the present ruling establishment as causing problems for everyone else; if the establishment is overthrown, the rest of society would be able to arrange a fairer system of government that would reduce social problems. Liberals believe that people are basically rational and that they will accept and can be helped by intelligent government programs that address social problems. Conservatives believe that social problems arise because there is some inherent evil in all of us. Fortunately the good in people generally outweighs the bad, which is held in check by the socializing power of all our institutions. Discuss (a) how accurate you think these descriptions are, (b) which label best fits each of the three authors, and (c) what there is in each essay that justifies your classification.

WRITING COMMISSION: COMPARING THREE APPROACHES TO THE WRITING TASK

Your editor has just been tapped by a friend of hers (his) who owns a small publishing house to edit a balanced anthology of essays, articles, and columns on the issues of marriage and divorce. As part of your internship, and to help with the mountain of material to be gone through, she (he) gives you the three preceding articles and tells you to write a carefully considered report recommending one to include in the anthology.

You will need to adjust your audience sights a little for this piece of writing. It is in the form of an internal memo, so, instead of a title, you will head it with the usual memo heading:

To: Elma Hackett
From: Roger Conner
Subject: Recommendations on National Marriage Project
          Columns
Date: 11/16/01

More important, you now have a specific audience of one, very critical reader on whose recommendations your immediate employment prospects may depend! But that person is a reader like any other and will appreciate your best efforts to make this memo lively and entertaining, as well as insightful and incisive. In other words, everything you have been learning up to this point applies to this kind of workplace writing just as it applies to writing for the public. After a long morning of reading, your editor will certainly appreciate an **eye-opening** surprise. The **encounter,** of course, is just those three columns that you have read. Because your editor will not have read them, it is up to you to create a vivid mental picture of what is contained in each of them, dramatized by at least a couple of quotations. Be sure to pick details that add up to a strong, unique impression of each piece as it relates to your editor's and publisher's purpose and audience.

The key element that your editor will be looking for is your **explanation** of why the piece you chose is best for the anthology's purpose. You will find yourself pushed to use other modalities that we have not yet practiced intensively, but that's OK. Writing is a dynamic, holistic process. It is unrealistic to practice individual skills entirely in isolation. But as you are **reasoning** about the suitability of the piece for the intended audience or filling in **background** of the National Marriage Project or e**valuating** the quality of the writing in the several pieces, focus on the purpose—an **explanation** of why this or that piece is better than another. Once that explanation is made clear, it is a short step to finishing the piece with a **resolution,** which in this case is nothing more than your recommending one of the pieces to be included in the anthology. It is a short step, but a very necessary one. It is a surprisingly common failing of people making a request or a proposal to feel that what they want is so strongly implied in the explanation of why it is deserved or desirable that they stop short of actually stating in so many words what exactly they are requesting or proposing. In the end, you must be clear. Be definite. Don't be mealymouthed!

Enjoy every aspect of your work on this commission and your editor will appreciate the zest of your performance!

Points to Remember

- Good writing follows the natural mental process of looking for an explanation of the surprises, puzzles, mysteries, and unsettling aspects of our encounters.

- The ultimate goal is, through explanation (aided by reasoning, search, valuation, and background), to lead readers to a resolution of those surprises that they will find significant for their own lives.

- Humor, which can be an effective way to make even serious points, usually turns on a surprising disjuncture, as between social or linguistic worlds, between reality and imagination, between conventional surface and cynical reality, and between disparate meanings of the same words.

- The explanation core, lying between the surprising encounter and a resolution that will be significant for the readers, is a flexible zone, the outcome of which depends on the writer's use of the other modalities we will study: reasoning, search, valuation, and background.

5

Resolution

E-E-R

Encounter

Explain

Resolve

R-S-V-B

Reason

Search

Value

Background

The road to resolution lies by doubt;
The next way home's the farthest way about.

—Thomas Quarles, "Emblems" (1635)

Opening the Topic:
Why "Resolution" not "Conclusion"?

The concept of "conclusion" derives from that traditional idea alluded to in the epigraph in chapter 1, in which Jean-Luc Godard was asked if a work should not have a beginning, a middle, and an end as Aristotle had prescribed. If you remember, the famous filmmaker replied, "Certainly, but not necessarily in that order." This jest reveals one problem with the word *conclusion*. Something called a conclusion sounds as if it must come at the end. But in every kind of writing of any length, the main idea toward which the writing tends must be tried and retried, doubted (as the epigraph to this chapter suggests) and revised, repeated several times, usually incrementally, to impress itself on the mind of the reader. And often, especially in scientific writing, it is desirable to give the reader at the beginning a general idea of how the pieces of the puzzle are going to fit together. The word *resolving* seems to capture that idea of fitting together.

The second problem with the word *conclusion* is that it indicates a place on the page rather than a process in the mind. It is more natural to speak of mysteries and issues being resolved rather than concluded. And writing is the process of wrestling that original surprise into a position comfortable to the mind of your readers.

Finally, the word *resolution* has a sense of looking to the future, whereas *conclusion* has the sense of wrapping up the past. The mind, when it has **explained** one puzzling **encounter,** hopes to learn a lesson that will **resolve** the problematic aspects of it for the future. And that writing works best that follows the natural workings of the brain.

INVITATION TO A READING

In chapter 4 we looked at three newspaper columns that reached differing explanations of the sociological phenomenon of declining marriage rates. We also noticed that by negotiating the explanation process differently, the three authors came up with three different proposals for addressing this disturbing social change. You may remember that Kathleen Parker ("Surviving Marital Miseries") reached a **resolution** that advocated a **program:** people should teach their children that marriage is about family, not personal happiness. On the other hand, Douglas Besharov ("Asking More from Matrimony") reached a **resolution** in which he pleaded for people to change their **attitude** toward those who were exploring alternatives to traditional marriage. And Sandy Banks seemed to end with an **attitude** of resignation.

I think you will find that no matter what kind of public writing you do, your ultimate purpose—the one toward which your writing tends and which should appear clearly in the conclusion—will be one or the other—a program or an attitude (or some combination of the two). In chapter 1 I took first the hypothetical case of a boss writing a memo, the **resolution** of which was a **program** of getting employees to lock their doors. The second case was a scientist who made discoveries about the mass of the neutrino and wrote a paper, the **resolution** of which was an attempt to get other scientists to change their **attitude** about the structure of matter. Of course, to some degree the boss hopes his employees will change their attitude toward security and the scientist hopes his discoveries will launch a program of further investigation. But when writing it helps to be clear about which purpose is uppermost in your thinking.

In the following essay a well-known columnist addresses the sociological problem of endemic poverty. In the course of her column, Anna Quindlen weighs the relative effectiveness of enacting **programs** for this purpose against that of changing **attitudes.**

To Defray Expenses
by Anna Quindlen

> They are the children who fall out of their perambulators when the nurse is looking the other way. If they are not claimed in seven days they are sent far away to the Neverland to defray expenses.

The Lost Boys made news. The television crews and the newspaper reporters went to that Neverland called East New York to take note of the fact that one of them, aged fifteen, had allegedly shot and killed two others in a high school hallway in what classmates called a "beef." This means a disagreement.

It could have been Bushwick or the South Bronx or any of the other New York neighborhoods that are shorthand for going nowhere. It could have been Chicago or L.A. or any one of dozens of other cities. The Lost Boys are everywhere. Most especially in prison. By then, unlike the children Peter Pan described, they have grown up.

We reporters won't stay long. The Lost Boys claim public attention for only a short time, and many of us are loath to walk in their neighborhoods, which makes us no different from the poor people who live in them. The mayor was at the high school the day of the killings. He came to tell the students that they, too, could build a future. For many of them, the future is that short period of time between today and the moment when they shoot or get shot.

Homicide is the leading cause of death for black teenagers in America.

There is a lot of talk now about metal detectors and gun control. Both are good things. But they are no more a solution than forks and spoons are a solution to world hunger. Kids, particularly kids who live amid crack houses and abandoned buildings, have a right to think of their school as a safe haven. But it's important to remember that a kid can get himself a box cutter and wait outside until the last bell rings. With a metal detector, you can keep the homicide out of the hallways. Perhaps with something more, you can keep the homicide out of the heart.

"These boys die like it's nothing," said Angela Burton, whose boyfriend was one of the two killed in East New York.

The problem is that when we look into this abyss, it goes so deep that we get dizzy and pull back from the edge. Teenage mothers. Child abuse. Crowded schools. Homes without fathers. Projects lousy with drugs, vermin, crime. And, always, the smell of urine in the elevator. I have never been in a project that hasn't had that odor, and I have never smelled it without wondering, If your home smells like a bathroom, what does that tell you about yourself?

One of the ways to motivate kids is to say that if you do this bad thing now, you won't be able to do this good thing tomorrow. That doesn't work with the Lost Boys. They stopped believing in tomorrow a long time ago. The impulse control of an adolescent, the conviction that sooner or later you'll end up dead or in jail anyhow, and a handgun you can buy on the corner easier than getting yourself a pair of new Nikes: the end result is preordained.

"If you don't got a gun, you got to get one," said one teenager hanging with his friends at the corner of East New York and Pennsylvania Avenues.

If news is sometimes defined as aberration, as Man Bites Dog, it's the successes we should be rushing out to cover in these neighborhoods, the kids who graduate, who get jobs, who stay clean. Dr. Alwyn Cohall, a pediatrician who runs four school-based clinics in New York, remembers the day he was giving one of those kids a college physical, which is the happiest thing he ever does, when from outside he heard the sound. Pow. Pow. One moment he was filling out the forms for a future, the next giving CPR to another teenager with a gunshot wound blossoming in his chest. The kid died on the cement.

"He never even made the papers next day," the doctor recalled.

The story in East New York will likely end with the funerals. A fifteen-year-old killer is not that unusual; many city emergency rooms provide coloring books on gun safety. Dr. Cohall says that when the students at his schools come back after the long hot summer, they are routinely asked by the clinic staff how many of their friends were shot over vacation. The good doctor knows that it is possible to reclaim some of the Lost Boys, but it requires money, dedication, and, above all, the will to do it. Or we can continue to let them go. To defray expenses.

CRITICAL READING

1. What are the two specific encounters contained in the column? What is the significant relation between the second and the first?
2. How do you explain the quotation from J. M. Barrie at the beginning of the article and the connection Quindlen makes to it?
3. Explain specifically the bitterly ironic explanation of why Lost Boys are sent to Neverland. What is the parallel Quindlen finds in modern America to the situation that Barrie was criticizing in Britain a hundred years ago?

4. Quindlen leads with a statement she believes is surprising: "The Lost Boys made news." Not everyone would find that immediately surprising, so she explains the surprise of it later. Why does she find it surprising?

5. To what extent does Quindlen seem to be proposing a **program** and to what extent urging a change of **attitude**? Cite specifics from the column to support your view.

DISCUSSION QUESTIONS

1. The author lists a number of possible explanations for the nearly hopeless state of the Lost Boys of New York. Think of some other, perhaps very different ones. Which of your explanations might Quindlen accept as significant, which might she reject? Why?

2. What actions does Quindlen urge us to take to alleviate the social dislocation that distresses her? How successful do you think they would be? Why?

3. Quindlen calls metal detectors and gun control the "forks and spoons" of a resolution of the problem of teen violence. What does she mean by this metaphorical analogy? Recount any experiences you have had with guns—owning them, seeing people with guns, using or seeing them used. Based on those experiences, how useful do you think gun control laws and metal detectors are in limiting violence in schools?

PICKING UP POINTERS FROM THE PROS:
CROCHETING THE ENDING

In chapter 3 I talked about Joel Agee's dramatic technique of crocheting earlier material into the current scene. There we saw it as a dramatizing technique, raising anticipation of the next event before the last one had been fully resolved. But the end of a piece of writing also is best knotted off by pulling an important strand from somewhere earlier, usually from the beginning.

Notice how Quindlen handles the strand of Peter Pan's Lost Boys. She establishes it firmly in the beginning three paragraphs. Then she reminds us of it again about halfway through. And finally ties the knot with it in the last paragraph. Even more effective, perhaps, is her way of using the phrase that contains the sordid reason for losing the boys—"to defray expenses." It is mentioned only at the very beginning and the very end, where it hits us like a slap in the face.

This trick is so slick and so easy that you should never end an essay without at least trying it. It has two very solid benefits. First, it reminds the readers of where the essay started and gives them a satisfying sense of completion. Second, it reminds **you** of where you started and forces you to see if you are still on track.

INVITATION TO A READING

In chapter 4 we looked at several attempts to explain the erosion of marital commitment. In the following column, Ellen Goodman, Pulitzer Prize–winning columnist and author of an early book on feminism, takes a look at the children who are products of the changed attitudes toward marriage and reaches a complex resolution toward some unanticipated consequences of those changes.

In Love Fornow
by Ellen Goodman

They are in their twenties and in love. Not in love forever. In love fornow.

They haven't said this exactly. But as a certified FOF (friend of the family) I have heard it in their silence. Certain words don't come up when we talk. Words like our future or even next year.

They are sharing their plans with me. But these are not shared plans. She has applied to East Coast graduate schools, he has been interviewing for West Coast jobs. They tell me this casually, their limbs familiarly entwined on the sofa in the position they adopted a year ago to tell everyone they were in love.

As an FOF, I quietly take in this scene. Have my young friends mastered the ability to love in the now? I ask myself. Or are they missing the romantic glue of futurism? I wonder if this is what it's like to be young lovers today.

Sitting with them, I am reminded of my reading trip through this year's Valentine's Day cards. I flipped through dozens of messages. The poetic pledges of forever love were almost all marketed for old lovers. The mush quota was highest for the cards marked: To Grandma.

But the Valentines for young lovers were, by and large, careful, cool. Some risqué, some even raunchy, but not emotionally risky. The Valentines I read carried no promises that would last longer than flowers or chocolate. They were about love fornow.

The woman who had dubbed me the Friend of this Family stands beside me. At her son's age, she had been married for two years. She was the example they didn't want her two children to follow. Married at 22, divorced ten years later.

"We were too young." How many times had she said so to the two children of this marriage and divorce? Children who had watched her start a career at 32. Children who had watched their father start another family at 40. My friend had told her sons, "Wait a while. Get to know several people, including yourself."

This young man had listened. His whole college generation had listened to some variation on that parental or societal advice. They had learned to put reason over romance. This young couple were like the graduate in that Dow Chemical ad last year. They were able to say—"I am going to miss you next year" and accept parting as the given at their stage of life.

"So what," I ask my friend when we retreat to privacy, "do you think of this reasonableness now? Is it not just what you wanted?"

"Yes," she says, but slowly, and goes on. "I think they are doing the right thing. There are too many changes ahead for them. They are too young to limit their options—jobs, schools, cities—for each other." Then she adds quietly, "But what about the option to have each other?"

We sit quietly with each other, thinking about the dramatic reversal of life patterns in two decades. The young people we know have a passion for finding the right work. And caution about finding the right relationship. Those in their twenties pursue careers wholeheartedly. And embrace love halfheartedly. The half that is missing may be the part that pulses with the idea of a future, the desire for forever.

My friend and I, FOFs for a dozen or more young people, figure that on average these began their first love affairs between 18 and 20. If our small statistical sample holds up, they are likely to be single until 28 or 30. The time lapse between intimacy and commitment, between first love and marriage, has expanded enormously from our twenties to theirs.

In the interim these young people may become very good at conditional love, love "until," love fornow. But it seems to us that it is hard to love fully in a limited time zone. Love without a belief in a future is like a chocolate heart made of skim milk and Sweet 'n Low.

The timing of our revisionist notion is probably lousy. This is the Love Carefully era. A balanced life is more prized than a sudden disorienting fall into love. On campuses, this Valentine's Day is celebrated by distributing condoms, not commitments.

Yet my friend and I, harbingers of realism, proponents of caution, survivors of one or more disasters, have, to our great surprise, discovered that we are more romantic than the young lovers in the next room. We wish them wholeheartedness and the rich flavor of forever.

CRITICAL READING

1. Goodman describes some experiences in which love just in the present has replaced love with a commitment to the future—love fornow having replaced love forever. Five times she makes a general statement of her evolving resolution. Find these five sentences.

2. We have seen that the statement of a general **resolution** usually grows out of an experience by way of an explanation. See if you can find an explanation leading up to each of the lesson statements that you have found.

3. Goodman applies the technique of crocheting the ending to the rest of the piece with a couple or three strands from earlier in the essay. What are they?

4. Why is the word *fornow* spelled as one word in the title like the word *forever*?

5. What other contrasts between "forever" and just "fornow" do you see in this article?

6. Goodman employs several rhetorical devices that I am sure you are familiar with:

   (a) **Balanced constructions**—repeating the same grammatical structure with different but related words. Here are some examples. Find others. See if you can write some.
   - Sharing/shared (Goodman balances active and passive voices here to point up a surprising contrast. What is it?)
   - Children who had watched. . . . Children who had watched. . . .
   - . . . pursue careers wholeheartedly. And embrace love half-heartedly.

   (b) **Alliteration**—beginning two or more words in a sequence with the same letter or sound. Here are some examples. Find others.
   - Friend of the family
   - Careful, cool

   (c) **Paradox**—an apparent contradiction (which we discussed in chapter 2 with reference to Bob Greene's column "The Colors of the World").
   - Conditional love
   - Love fully in a limited time zone

Explain how these rhetorical devices create enjoyable surprises that push us toward a complex, qualified resolution.

DISCUSSION QUESTIONS

---

1. Skillful writers often express their **resolutions** with a subtlety befitting the complexity of their subjects. If you go back to your answers to Critical Reading question 1, you may notice that four of the five sentences suggesting a resolution are cast in the form of images and the fifth is a question. (Of course, I'm talking about the ones I identified as resolution statements. You may not agree, but for the purposes of this question you can check the ones I'm talking about in Figure 5.1.) Unwrap the literal meaning and emotional vector of each metaphor—that is, what is being imaginatively compared with what? And how does Goodman expect the reader to feel about it?
2. Rephrase each sentence as a clear resolution statement in straightforward prose.
3. Compare your resolution statements with those of your classmates. What are some of the advantages Goodman enjoys by her metaphorical expressions over the more straightforward statements? Which do you prefer for this essay? Why?

Exploring the Topic

Repeating the Resolution

Here is the opening scene from the play *Ghost on Fire* by Michael Weller, the author who wrote the screenplay for the movie version of the musical *Hair*. Read it carefully, because I will ask you two surprising questions when you finish. Don't peek!

---

1. Or are they missing the romantic glue of intuition?
2. The half that is missing may be the part that buzzes with the idea of a future: the desire for forever.
3. Love without a belief in a future is like a chocolate heart made of skim milk and Sweet 'N Low.
4. We wish them wholeheartedness and the rich travel of forever.

And the question that is NOT a metaphor:

5. But what about the option to have each other?

Figure 5.1. The **resolution** sentences of "In Love Fornow" (question 1).

A married college professor is talking to a student with whom he has recently had a love affair. They are discussing a screenplay she has written that describes a love affair like theirs. But in her story the wife and the husband are both killed in separate accidents.

PROF: Don't you think it's just the teeniest bit arbitrary, killing off two of your main characters for no reason at all?

STUDENT: There's plenty of reason. . . . It's my screenplay, I can do what I want with it.

PROF: Laurel . . . fiction has to reflect life, and life is never arbitrary; if you want to make stories, you have to find a unifying order beneath events so they unfold in a way that feels . . . well, true.

STUDENT: Okay. Then why did Ken leave Alexis? Tell me, Dan. After all the incredible times they had together? After he told her she was the only one he'd ever been able to really talk to? Why do you think he'd just call it off one day, no explanation, nothing?

PROF: I'm not here to write your screenplay.

STUDENT: How long are you going to pretend you don't know what this movie is about?

PROF: This is classroom time.

STUDENT: Why did you walk away? Don't I even deserve an explanation?

PROF: (beat): Well, for one thing, my wife is not dead.

STUDENT: She would be if I had anything to do with it.

PROF: I assure you the feeling is mutual.

STUDENT: She knows?

PROF: That it happened, yes. Who it was, no.

STUDENT: So you talk to her but you won't talk to me.

PROF: There's no point, Laurel. Please.

STUDENT (tries new tactic): You've been daydreaming in class. They think maybe you're losing interest. I think it's something else that we could talk about.

PROF: No, Laurel. It's just me losing interest.

STUDENT: Oh, how smart and cool and above it all. Nothing gets to you, does it! Was I the first?

PROF: The first what? Affair? Student? Student this year?

Now the questions. Can you remember the name of the student without looking back? Yes? I think you probably can. Can you remember the name of the professor without looking back? My guess is that you cannot. Why? Look back at the scene and see if you can see the difference between the mentions of the professor's name and the student's name. You will see that the student's name is mentioned three times, the professor's only once.

"How many times do I have to tell you to brush your teeth before you go to bed?" the mother yells at her son—again. "How often do I have to remind you how much it means to me for you to remember our wedding anniversary?" the wife nags her husband. How many times do we, as writers, have to repeat something to be sure the reader notices and remembers? Writers of plays, like Michael Weller, traditionally follow the Rule of Three. The Rule of Three says that, if you introduce a character in your play, you must repeat his or her name three times to be sure the audience notices and remembers it.

The same Rule of Three (or Four or Five!) applies to getting the reader to notice and remember the evolving **resolution.** Many beginning writers feel it is somehow insulting to the reader to state the lesson of the essay clearly and repeat it and repeat it again. But, like all of us, readers can be inattentive and forgetful. General ideas, which are less surprising and often less interesting than experiences, are especially forgettable. So readers must be gently reminded of what it is you are talking about. By gently, I mean with the same kind of subtlety that we saw Goodman use five times in her column. The lesson should be rephrased each time to avoid saying it in the same words. And it certainly should **not** be announced, as in: "Again, I'd like to say . . ."; "So, to sum up again . . ."; "As I mentioned above. . . ." **No**! Don't be clunky. But **do** repeat important ideas.

Equally important, repeating the resolution three or four or five times during the process of your writing is useful in reminding yourself where you are going and how you are getting there. It is common for a writer, finishing up a section of the piece, to pause and wonder how to proceed. This usually signals time for a modality change, and the later chapters of this book are there to help you with how to make that change. But before you go on from a decision point, you should look back at your title and your opening and make a summary statement of what has been learned so far. It may help you to recognize what is yet unsaid, and it will help your readers catch their breath and feel ready to plunge ahead.

Not "Whatever"!

In high school you very likely read a story by Frank Stockton called "The Lady or the Tiger." If you didn't, here is a summary: A handsome young commoner in a barbaric land is able to attract the love of the king's daughter. As punishment for his daring he is put in an arena with two doors. Behind one is a beautiful young woman for his wife, behind the other, a hungry tiger. The princess learns which door is which, and on the day signals her lover to open the door on the right, which he does. But the story ends with a question: Which came out of the door, the lady or the tiger?

It is easy to explain either resolution. If the princess loved the young man with an unselfish love, she would presumably yield him to another woman to save his life. But if she loved him jealously, she might well yield him to the tiger to avoid seeing another woman marry him.

It was an amazingly successful trick ending, which Stockton originally envisioned as a parlor game to create a lively discussion among his guests. But it's been done. Don't do it again! As a rule readers feel cheated if the author evades his or her responsibility of bringing the essay to a satisfactory resolution based on the carefully crafted explanation of the original surprise.

There is a cultural climate that leads some people to say, "What-EV-er! It's true for me." You may feel that in this climate it is rude to express a definite conclusion lest your readers feel that another conclusion is true **for them.** Truth is usually indeterminate or provisional. You should expect that a substantial portion of your audience may disagree with you about the significance of your experience. That's OK. You are not a hypnotist; you do not have to worry about influencing someone against their will! If you succeed in influencing your readers at all, you will prove yourself a supremely able writer.

Nevertheless, your readers really want to know how you feel after you have labored over your subject for so long. Do not frustrate them by leaving the choice of the lady or the tiger up to them!

Two other words of caution. First, there is no need to label your conclusion by beginning it with a phrase like "In conclusion." There is some justification for this in speeches as a signal for the audience to wake up and start gathering up their belongings. But in a piece of writing, the reader can see that this is your last paragraph. A second overly mechanical and graceless formula is to recapitulate all of the points you have made during the course of the essay. Those should all add up to a single (perhaps complex and carefully qualified) resolution. If they don't, then your essay is not unified; that is, it has not followed a direct line from the surprise of the encounter through an explanation of the surprise to the resolution. You need to go back and cast out the material extraneous to that path.

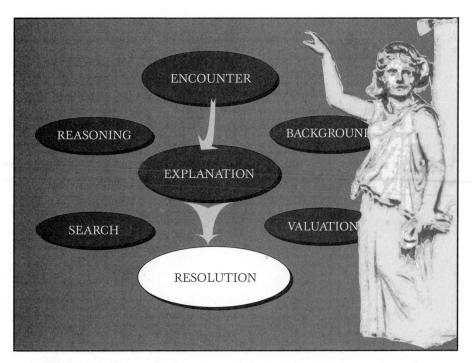

Figure 5.2. The main line of needed modality elements moves from an explanation of the surprise to a resolution that will be significant to all readers.

WRITING ACTIVITY: CHOOSE YOUR OWN IDEA ADVENTURE AND COOK IT AS SHISH KEBAB

As a kid you may have enjoyed those story books that at certain crucial points allowed you to choose how the adventure would continue. If you wanted Pete to decide to go alone into the cave, you turned to page 23; if you wanted Pete to peek in the window of the suspect's home instead, you turned to page 42. Here, instead of the plot turnings of a mystery story, you have the opportunity to chart the turnings of ideas in an essay on the issue of immigration.

I will provide you with a choice of encounters, background, and research, which you can use as part of your essay with some adaptation. My reason for doing this is to free you up to concentrate on explanations and, especially, **resolutions.** The encounters and background research material has already been selected and shaped for dramatic effect. Your job is to find a significant path through enough of this material to be informative and persuasive to an audience. Be aware that your audience may include a range of opinions about immigrants as people and about the policy of admitting more. To find a meaningful axis you will want to familiarize yourself with the sometimes complex facts, statistics, and trends presented here. You will find that some could be used to support liberal policies, others, restrictive policies; some augur well for immigrants themselves and for native residents, others auger ill. Then review these facts in the light of your own experience to reach a tentative target resolution to the issue—an anchor for that axis of significance along which you will arrange clumps of facts and encounters.

Think of it as making shish kebab.

The spit is the line of significance that you evolve as you chop up and examine the ingredients available. I have grouped these ingredients into three categories—encounters, facts, and statistics—to aid you in proceeding modally—that is, shish kebab fashion. First, skewer the best eye-opener you can find that suits your purpose. It will probably be one of the encounters (changed, if necessary, from first to third person.) Of course, if you have an experience of your own, that might be even better. Then you will stick on a piece of meat—an explanation of the eye-opener that at least suggests the

Figure 5.3.

flavor of the resolution. Following that, another item from the cutting board—a group of dramatic facts or an encounter—that will fit on the same straight line toward the resolution and will blend well with the meat preceding it. Then repeat the process—a meaty piece of explanation/resolution; another piece of statistics/facts. Finally (although this is not the practice with real shish kebabs), the juiciest piece of meat you have—the ultimate resolution—goes on the end of the spit, summing up all the rest. This should be clearly along the lines of the previous resolutions but with a wider perspective.

Be sure as you skewer your choice of related items together that they proceed along a line leading to a clear resolution, with the meat of your own insights interspersed between them.

Now cook it. That is, let it simmer for a few hours until all the juices of the various elements flow together in your mind. In practice, this means preparing to revise your whole essay into an organic whole by looking carefully at those junction points between the meat and the onions or zucchini to be sure that when the reader bites into one after having chewed the other there will be a noticeable carry-over of flavor. There should be actual sentences—usually called transition sentences—or at least phrases at the beginning of each modality shift that look backward to the previous section, and there should be actual sentences at the end of each modality section that look way ahead to the culminating resolution.

Reread the entire essay; then take a step back and consider the long-term implications for the society. What do you want your readers to carry away from this or how do you want your readers to carry on from this (attitude or program)? (Dropping the shish kebab image for a moment, remember to crochet a strand from earlier in the essay to tie the whole into this paragraph.)

OK, now it's done. *Bon appétit!*

ENCOUNTERS
A.

Once again my 17-year-old daughter comes home from a foreign-language fair at her high school and accusingly tells me about the pluses of being able to speak two languages. Speaker after speaker has extolled the virtues of becoming fluent in another language. My daughter is frustrated by the fact that I'm bilingual and have purposely declined to teach her to speak Spanish, my native tongue. . . .

In 1972 I fell in love and married an American who had been living in Peru for a number of years. Our first son was born there, but when he was 6 months old, we came back to the States. My husband was going to get his doctorate at a university in Texas.

It was in Texas that, for the first time, I lived in a community with many Hispanics in the United States. I encountered them at the grocery store, the laundry, the mall, church. I also began to see how the Anglos in the community treated them. Of course, I don't mean all, but enough to make me feel uncomfortable. Because I'm dark and have dark eyes and hair, I personally experienced that look, that unspoken and spoken word expressing prejudice. If I entered a department store, one of two things was likely to happen. Either I was ignored, or I was followed closely by the salesperson. The garments I took into the changing room were carefully counted. My check at the grocery store took more scrutiny than an Anglo's. My children were complimented on how "clean" they were instead of how cute. Somehow, all Hispanics seemed to be lumped into the category of illegal immigrants, notwithstanding that many Hispanic families have lived for generations in Texas and other Southwestern states.

To be fair, I also noticed that the Latinos lived in their own enclaves, attended their own churches, and many of them spoke English with an accent. And with their roots firmly established in the United States, their Spanish was not perfect either.

It was the fact that they spoke neither language well and the prejudice I experienced that prompted my husband and me to decide that English, and English only, would be spoken in our house. . . .

When our eldest daughter was born in 1980, we were living in southeast Missouri. Again, we decided on an English-only policy. If our children were going to live in the United States, then their English should be beyond reproach. Of course, by eliminating Spanish we have also eliminated part of their heritage. Am I sorry? About the culture, yes; about the language, no. In the Missouri Legislature, there are bills pending for some sort of English-only law. I recently read an article in a national magazine about the Ozarks where some of the townspeople are concerned about the numbers of Hispanics who have come to work in poultry plants there. It seemed to me that their "concerns" were actually prejudice. There is a definite creeping in of anti-Hispanic sentiment in this country. Even my daughter, yes, the one who is upset over not being bilingual, admits to hearing "Hispanic jokes" said in front of her at school. You see, many don't realize, despite her looks, that she's a minority. I want to believe that her flawless English is a contributing factor.

Last summer I took my 10-year-old daughter to visit my brother, who is working in Mexico City. She picked up a few phrases and words with the facility that only the very young can. I just might teach her Spanish. You see, she is fair with light brown hair and blue eyes.

—Gabriela Kuntz,
"My Spanish Standoff," "My Turn," *Newsweek* 5/4/98

B.

Yu Li says she cried for nearly a year after she was brought over to find a better life. She paid gangsters to get out of China three years ago to join her husband, who had illegally entered the U.S. in 1991. She paid the snake-heads money her husband had borrowed and sent over. Almost immediately after reaching New York, she began working 17-hr. days, seven days a week, at a local garment factory. But because she was new and the factory paid piece rate, she made only $1 an hour. "Sometimes we had nothing for ourselves. I made less than $100 a week." She and her husband made so little money they couldn't afford to live together. He continued to sleep on the floor of the restaurant that employed him. She slept in a basement owned by relatives. Her husband would ask angrily, "Why don't you work harder?" "But," says Yu, "I couldn't work any harder."

Yet the couple again dealt with the snakeheads in order to be reunited with the three children they left behind. The price: $132,000. It was a harrowing journey. Their 14-year-old son was separated from his sisters shortly after the journey began, abandoned in Cambodia when war broke out and stuck in a Vietnam jail until he bribed his way out with $500 he had stashed away. Relatives helped pay off the snake-heads, but each month Yu has to pay $3,000 on the debt. "It is hard. We have nothing." Now they have fettered their children to their fate. "The hardest thing," she says, "is that I have had to make the children work. They should be in school, but we need the money they bring home." She sighs. "It was never this hard in China."

—Edward Barnes, "Slaves of New York," *Time,* 11/2/98

C.

Marcelo Salaises, 30, misses Mexico but says the living is good in Dalton. On $10.60 an hour with benefits and profit sharing at Durkan Patterned Carpet, where he's in quality control, he and his wife bought a nice three-bedroom house for $49,000. And Thomas Durkan III, he says, orchestrated the donation of private land and helped raise $1 million for the construction of a soccer complex used primarily by Mexican families.

Dalia Martinez, 29, and all but one of her fellow teachers recruited from Mexico intend to return next school year. "When we arrived, they had banners welcoming us. At the apartments, they had food in the refrigerators for us. It's been very warm, and we've been able to make a difference for the children."

So many Hispanics have moved to Whitfield County in the past several years, it's standing room only at St. Joseph's. Carl Bouckaert, a parishioner and the owner of Beaulieu of America carpets, could not help noticing. Thirty percent of his work force of 7,500 (soon to be expanded to 10,000) is Hispanic.

"It was clear they were going to have to build a new church, and to do that for a lot of people costs a lot of money. My wife and I came to the conclusion we should do something major. It was a chance to give back to a community that's been good to us."

So they wrote a check for $1 million.

—Thomas England, from "America's Secret Capitals," <*Time.com*>,

7/13/98

D.

I was no more than seven when my family migrated from Arkansas. But I remember the time as if it were yesterday. Poultry processing companies such as Tyson Foods and Case Farms were a major source of employment opportunities for unskilled blacks. I remember drivers picking up loads of black laborers. On many days, the backs of these trucks were so full of workers that there was no room for others to climb aboard. And these workers would endure daily rituals including a four- to five-hour ride to Fayetteville, then on to Rogers and Bentonville to "pick" chickens, as it was called.

At least three of my brothers were among those laborers who began their daily journey around 2 AM, returning home every night around 9 or 10 PM. reeking of chicken excrement. They would sleep less than four hours before beginning their journey again. They provided 85 percent of the labor force for companies like Case Farms for generations.

However, over the years, the number of trucks scouting the South, picking up black laborers has steadily declined. Now, the trucks aren't around any more. Those trucks are now transporting undocumented workers who provide cheaper labor.

—Karen Huff, from a letter to the *San Diego Union-Tribune*, 12/10/97

FACTS

A.

There have been two major shifts in immigration policy in this century. In the twenties the United States began to limit the number of immigrants admitted and established the national-origins quota system, an allocation scheme that awarded entry visas mainly on the basis of national origin and that favored Germany and the United Kingdom. This system was repealed in 1965, and family reunification became the central goal of immigration policy, with entry visas being awarded mainly to applicants who had relatives already residing in the United States.

The number of immigrants began to rise rapidly. As recently as the 1950s only about 250,000 immigrants entered the country annually; by the 1990s the United States was admitting more than 800,000 legal immigrants a year, and some 300,000 aliens entered and stayed in the country illegally. . . . Although people of European origin dominated the immigrant flow from the country's founding until the 1950s, only about 10 percent of those admitted in the 1980s were of European origin. It is now estimated that non-Hispanic whites may form a minority of the population soon after 2050.

—George Borjas, from "The New Economics of Immigration,"
The Atlantic Monthly, November 1996

B.

- The relative skills of successive immigrant waves have declined over much of the postwar period. In 1970, for example, the latest immigrant arrivals on average had 0.4 fewer years of schooling and earned 17 percent less than natives. By 1990 the most recently arrived immigrants had 1.3 fewer years of schooling and earned 32 percent less than natives.

- Because the newest immigrant waves start out at such an economic disadvantage, and because the rate of economic assimilation is not very rapid, the earnings of the newest arrivals may never reach parity with the earnings of natives. Recent arrivals will probably earn 20 percent less than natives throughout much of their working lives.

- The large-scale migration of less-skilled workers has done harm to the economic opportunities of less-skilled natives. Immigration may account for perhaps a third of the recent decline in the relative wages of less-educated native workers.

- There are economic benefits to be gained from immigration. These arise because certain skills that immigrants bring into the country complement those of the native population. However, these economic benefits are small—perhaps on the order of $7 billion annually.

—George Borjas, from "The New Economics of Immigration,"
The Atlantic Monthly, November 1996

C.

The immigration surplus has to be balanced against the cost of providing services to the immigrant population. Immigrants have high rates of welfare recipiency. Estimates of the fiscal impact of immigration (that is, of the difference between the taxes paid by immigrants and the cost of services provided to them) vary widely. Some studies claim that immigrants pay $25–$30 billion more in taxes than they take out of the system, while other studies blame them for a fiscal burden of more than $40 billion on natives.

—George Borjas, from "The New Economics of Immigration,"
The Atlantic Monthly, November 1996

D.

The welfare reform act of 1996 limited the time anyone could receive welfare and required adults to seek work and teenage mothers to live at home and stay in school. The original provision to deny food stamps and SSI to legal immigrants was effectively dropped in 1998.

E.

Many of our famous contributors to American society have been immigrants—Alexander Graham Bell, Andrew Carnegie (steel magnate and philanthropist), Albert Einstein, Enrico Fermi (leader in development of atomic energy), Wernher von Braun (rocket scientist, leader of the U.S. space exploration), Henry Kissinger.

STATISTICS

A.

Table 5.1 shows how much of the population growth during 5-year and 10-year periods can be attributed to immigration.

B.

Table 5.2 shows the number of immigrants as a fraction of the total population.

Table 5.1.

Period	Population Growth (in %)	Period	Population Growth (in %)
1901–10	39.6	1950–54	10.6
1911–20	17.7	1955–59	10.7
1921–30	15	1960–64	12.5
1931–34	−0.1	1965–69	19.7
1935–39	3.2	1970–80	19.4
1940–44	7.4	1981–90	32.8
1945–49	10.2	1991–96	47.1

Table 5.2.

Period	Total Immigrants	U.S. Population Rate (per 1,000)	Period	Total Immigrants	U.S. Population Rate (per 1,000)
1820–30	151,824	1.2	1911–20	5,735,811	5.7
1831–40	599,125	3.9	1921–30	4,107,209	3.5
1841–50	1,713,251	8.4	1931–40	528,431	0.4
1851–60	2,598,214	9.3	1941–50	1,035,039	0.7
1861–70	2,314,824	6.4	1951–60	2,515,479	1.5
1871–80	2,812,191	6.2	1961–70	3,321,677	1.7
1881–90	5,246,613	9.2	1971–80	4,493,314	2.1
1891–1900	3,687,564	5.3	1981–90	7,338,062	2.9
1901–10	8,795,386	10.4	1991–96	6,146,213	2.3

C.

Donald Huddle of Rice University, in the 1993 book *The Cost of Immigrants,* estimated that, primarily because of the need for human services, immigrants end up costing the United States $43 billion. On the other hand, the Urban Institute, in the 1994 book *How Much Do Immigrants Cost?,* estimated that, primarily because of the productivity that immigrants create working long hours at low-paying jobs, they end up benefiting the economy to the tune of $27 billion.

D.

- Before the new welfare laws took effect, 1.7 percent of the native population was receiving Aid for Dependent Children, compared to 3.1 percent of the immigrants.
- 43 percent of immigrants are judged to have acquired a reasonably good command of English, 57 percent not.
- Although only 57 percent of the foreign born adults have graduated from high school, compared with 83 percent of native born adults, almost the same percentage of both groups (21 percent) have graduated from college and 7 percent have advanced degrees.

PICKING UP POINTERS FROM THE PROS:
CLOSING THE RING

I'm sure that, even if you've never seen a single opera, you at least know of the famous Ring Cycle of four lengthy operas by Richard Wagner and have undoubtedly heard some of its famous music, like the *Ride of the Valkyries.* The name *Ring Cycle* refers to a magic gold ring stolen at the beginning from maidens who guard it at the bottom of the Rhine River. Wotan, chief of the gods (after whom our "Wednesday" is named), pays for the construction of his palace, Valhalla, with the stolen and now accursed ring. Love, jealousy, honor, marital infidelity, and greed move the plot toward its end—the death of all the gods and the burning of Valhalla.

The use of the word *ring* in the title of this cycle of music dramas has a meaning in addition to the physical one made out of Rhine gold, a meaning important for our more humble kinds of writing—the cyclical nature of human experience. This point is well made in a very funny routine (available on CD from Sony Masterworks) performed by the singer Anna Russell. In this she does a twenty-minute

Figure 5.4. Anna Russell as Brunhilde from the Anna Russell Album CD cover.

summary of the entire twenty-**hour** opera cycle, having knowledge-able and loving fun with many of its conventions. At the end, when Brunhilde has immolated herself on Siegfried's funeral pyre and burned Valhalla, the Rhine River overflows its banks and covers the ashes. Anna Russell asks, "Remember the Rhine? And who do you think turns up next? The Rhine Maidens. So they take their . . . ring . . . and put it back where it came from. And after sitting through this whole operation, what do you hear?" Anna Russell now sings the beautiful motif that identified the Rhine Maidens when they first appeared, swimming in innocent pleasure before their gold treasure had been stolen. And she concludes, "You're exactly where you started twenty hours ago!"

But, as the audience knows, you are **not** just where you were at the beginning. The return to a beginning motif to **close the ring** is a powerful rhetorical strategy, because now the beginning, full of sur-prise, mystery, and promise, returns laden with the **significance** of all the *sturm und drang,* the turmoil and tragedy, the humor and pathos that has happened in between.

We have already seen some examples of writing that makes use of the power of **closing the ring.** In chapter 1, Joyce Caruso, in "Home Free?" reminded us near the end of the Italian real-estate boyfriend and her trouble with the IRS, which she had mentioned in the first two paragraphs.

In chapter 4, Sandy Banks in "Reflections on the State of the Unions" begins with a conversation overheard in a bagel shop. She ends "Back in bagel shops across America the conversation contin-ues," illustrating the hopeless repetitiveness of couples' typical bick-ering fights.

Douglas Besharov starts with an overhyped, inaccurate study from 1986 about older women's chances of getting married. He ends by a plea not to exaggerate the death of marriage from similarly flawed statistics.

In this chapter, Anna Quindlen starts with a reference to the Lost Boys of *Peter Pan,* and she ends with another reference to them. And Ellen Goodman starts with a play on the words *forever* and *fornow* and ends reminding us of that, and also by referring to her other earlier wordplay on the weak flavor of chocolate hearts made from skim milk and Sweet 'n Low.

Beginning a conclusion (or the wrap-up of any section of your piece of writing) with a reference to the beginning is an easy way to give readers the sense that you are an author with a plan, that you have your material under control, that you knew all along where you were headed, and that you have achieved closure.

If this was not altogether true (and it probably wasn't!), then this is a good chance for you to look back at the beginning and revise the parts in between to **make** it true. Then close the ring!

WRITING COMMISSION: RESOLVING EDUCATIONAL ISSUES

Controversial public issues are the subjects that most clearly demand a **resolution,** most often in the form of a call to enact a **program.** But of course, a call for action will go unheeded by opponents unless it is accompanied by some persuasive **attitude** adjustments—the other kind of **resolution.**

To practice this, let's go back to that newspaper office where you are interning.

Imagine that you are nearing the end of your summer intern program. Your editor has decided that it would be good to have the whole group of interns (your class) do pieces for the traditional back-to-school issue. And who better to do these pieces than people for whom the back-to-school experience is still fresh: you interns! The editor lays before you a number of national issues regarding schools that are bound to be appearing in the national papers and magazines during the next couple of weeks and challenges you to come up with some answers:

1. School safety: What can be done about gang violence and crazed vengeance seekers?
2. Teen pregnancy: Do schools have a responsibility, and if so what?
3. School girls with babies: Should schools provide day care or alternative programs?
4. Home schooling: It's on the rise; is it wise?
5. Government vouchers for private schools: Would competition improve public school quality?
6. Racial integration: It's on the wane; is it sane?
7. Religion in public schools: Should we tolerate private expression and religion-based public holidays?
8. Education for character: Should it be a required subject or a personal decision?
9. Sex education and condom distribution: Are these best left to church and home?
10. [Your choice!]: [Your question]?

The editor wants you to pick one of these issues (or provide your own) with which you have had some direct experience. Start with an **eye-opener,** probably a dramatized description of your **encounter** with the issue. Search your memory for other similar encounters, either experienced directly or heard about, supplemented by a little digging in the library or on the Internet to turn up relevant facts and statistics. Weave all this material together to create a pattern of **explanation** that will lead to your **resolution.**

"I'd like to get as much variety as I can," your editor points out. "Maybe you can consult with each other so that we don't have 15 people writing on one issue and end up with 5 issues not covered. If you have some experience with one of the more unusual ones, I hope you'll pick that.

"Just a reminder or two about organization," your editor adds. "Don't be dogmatic. Make it seem as if your ultimate conclusion is evolving. You can do that by arriving by stages. Some trial balloons floated at strategic junctures through the piece will help guide your readers along toward your final resolution. And don't be afraid to spread yourself a little at the end. These are national issues, and your experience provides a soapbox to stand on. Take advantage of it!"

"I'm ready for this one!" you answer gamely.

Points to Remember

- A **resolution** is a general summary that evolves from the **explanations** of the surprise, puzzle, or mystery that motivated the writing. It is repeated in an evolving way several times throughout a piece of writing, often revealing successive facets of the topic.
- **Resolutions** are attempts to wrestle the opening surprise into a position comfortable to the mind of the reader.
- **Resolutions,** as well as summing up, try to show how situations similar to those in the essay can or should be thought of or dealt with in the future.
- **Resolutions** seem to fall into two broad categories: attempts to change or clarify readers' **attitudes,** or **programs** to change people's actions. Or, of course, both.
- As a writer moving from one modality to another you will be faced with several decision points during your composing process. At each of these, you should construct a carefully

worded general statement of the evolving resolution that repeats but upgrades previous ones and points the reader in the direction of the final one.

- The reader does not expect a simplistic, clichéd answer to difficult problems but does expect the author to provide as definitive an answer as the case allows while preserving the complexity that has been demonstrated.

- It is an effective device to include in any resolution a detail, word, or other reference from an earlier encounter. It gives a sense of **closing the ring.** This gives both author and reader a chance to reflect on the course of the essay up to that point and provides an effective sense of completion at the end.

E-E-R

Encounter

Explain

Resolve

R-S-V-B

Reason

Search

Value

Background

6

Significance

Opening the Topic: Connecting Significantly

Significance often follows in the wake of a surprising event. The significance of the Civil War, for example, became clear only after it was half over, when Lincoln made his Emancipation Proclamation. It was late in the Vietnam War before the devastating costs of America's compulsive prosecution of the cold war emerged as its leading significance.

We have watched professional writers dramatize their **encounters** so that their readers would feel compelled to follow them in their search for **explanations** and **resolutions.** And just as the quality of **surprise** is necessary throughout to keep the items of the writers' juggling acts in the air, the quality of **significance** must be constantly reemphasized to keep the readers feeling that they are not wasting their time. Recall these examples that we have seen:

1. Standing against a culture filled with formula writing where potential is judged on past economic performance, Russell Baker finds meaning in the success of writing that sustains readers' interest.
2. Joyce Caruso as an adult discovers new meaning in renewing her relationship with her mother.
3. Bob Greene's noticing the reemergence of black and white photos leads to the realization that, in a world overfull of distracting images, the significance of simplified black and white becomes dignity and seriousness.

4. Joel Agee sees a deep and disturbing universal cruelty lying significantly behind acts that we tend to write off as children's horseplay or historical aberrations.
5. Stephen King believes that the significance of horror films in our society is the releasing in a harmless way of that subconscious cruelty that Agee identified.
6. Sandy Banks, looking at the somewhat shocking statistics on the number of unhappy marriages, sees in them the reflection of a stressful and competitive society.
7. Kathleen Parker, looking at the same statistics, sees them as signifying a generation self-absorbed in pursuing their own happiness at the expense of more fundamental values.
8. Douglas Besharov, again looking at the same statistics, sees them as being less significant than did the doomsayers who promulgated them, indicating nothing more than a normal evolutionary change.
9. To Anna Quindlen, the tragedy of teenage homicide means that society is not doing enough to provide opportunities and encouragement to poor young people.

I have not classified **significance** as a separate modality because I do not sense the same kind of shift in gears that tells me that **now** the author is going to concentrate on the significance of the events or explanations in the piece. Just as eye-opening surprises can pop up anywhere, so significance emerges everywhere.

I talked about **dramatizing** as the technique by which an author makes surprises work. **Significance,** I believe, emerges from the author's forging **connections,** connections between encounters, between encounters and their explanations, between differing explanations, between any of these and resolutions, or even between attempts at different resolutions. Looking back at the list of examples just given, I find that the **significances** cited are born out of connections like the following:

1. Baker contrasts the resolutions arrived at by the adults at home and school with the experience of watching their reactions as they read.
2. Caruso contrasts her memories of childhood with her present experiences with her mother in the light of explanatory statistics.
3. Greene finds an underlying similarity when he compares Polaroid's announcement with ads and other images he has encountered recently.

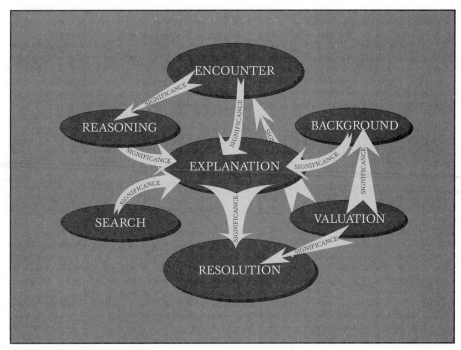

Figure 6.1. Significance is made apparent in the linkages we forge between modalities.

4. Agee lets his subconscious connect a number of experiences and images of cruelty to plumb its pervasiveness.

5. King compares three common explanations of the popularity of horror movies. Finding none of them adequate, he is pushed to accept their Freudian significance.

6. Banks gets at the significance of some facts she has read by connecting them with an overheard conversation and remembrances of her own unhappy marriage.

7. Parker gets us to see a different significance from those facts by connecting them with explanations from an expert and her own generalized observations.

8. Besherov is able to come up with yet another meaning from those facts by contrasting them with a wide range of facts from other sources.

9. Quindlen's mind offers up a remembered literary allusion that suggests a more pervasive social commentary on two encounters she has had as a reporter.

WRITING ACTIVITY: LEARNING FROM THE PHOTO AND CAPTION ESSAY

It may take a thousand words to duplicate a picture, but it usually takes less than twenty to supply the caption. For most kinds of writing, the image of picture and caption is a useful one to follow: *Picture* equals **encounter,** framed to emphasize dramatic detail (as we saw in the pictures of my ballerina daughter in the "Drama of Details Exploration" in chapter 3); *caption* equals **significance.**

You may find this analogy helpful in the following ways:

1. The picture comes before the caption. You remember from grade school that it's "Show and Tell" not "Tell and Show." Your kindergarten classmates crowded around to see the black widow spider you'd brought in the paper bag, but they probably didn't pay much attention to your telling where you'd gotten it. The reader must see your surprise first to be at all interested in what it means or where it came from. This is why professional writers of short pieces rarely begin with introductions. They begin with an eye-opener.
2. The picture is much bigger than the caption. Writing an encounter with all its conversation and descriptive detail takes many more lines than summing up its significance in a few general sentences.
3. A picture without a caption is interesting but meaningless; a caption without a picture is ungrounded, vapid, tiresome. Apprentice writers tend to be good at one and slight the other. They tell good stories but then stop and just smile, leaving their readers to wonder why they told them. Or they reiterate their opinions forcefully at length, leaving yawning readers to question their credibility.

In the following activity the content of the **encounter** has been visually supplied for you with a series of photographs from a classic *Life* magazine photo essay from 1948. This is really quite appropriate because it seems likely that our modern column and essay style, which begins with an enigmatic or jarring event and gradually opens up its full significance through successive related examples, derives partly from the photojournalism that was hugely popular in the first part of the twentieth century.[1]

---

[1] For another example of a photo essay, you might want to look at the famous study of the Great Depression by James Agee (whose son wrote the piece "Cruelty" that we read in chapter 3) and Walker Evans, *Let Us Now Praise Famous Men*. If you go to the *Time* Web site < www.time.com > you will find a contemporary selection of photo essays, although they are more thematically grouped photos than true essays.

Figure 6.2. What is the significance of dramatizing these elements as the photographer did? The gathering clouds. The man's apparent look of dejection or weariness. The contrast between his rather formal dress and the rural setting. The neglected fence and yard. The black bag.

Figure 6.2 was the lead picture of the article. Such a picture standing at the head of an essay largely takes the place of an opening encounter described in words. The still photographer was undoubtedly influenced by film photography. We can certainly imagine this scene at the beginning of a movie, with the credits rolling over it. The scene suggests a man in a somewhat incongruous setting, seemingly bent on a mission, possibly commercial or medical, with a storm threatening. I think you will find you might be able to write several different captions for this picture. Try it, and compare yours with those of your classmates. There is no right answer; the point is to see how many axes of significance might be drawn through a single encounter. (But just for fun, you can see the one that the *Life* editors actually used on page 151.)

The actual readers of the article would have seen the title "Country Doctor" above that picture by W. Eugene Smith, and that would have given them some help interpreting this first encounter. But what significance are we, as readers, supposed to pick out of this? Toward what **resolution** are the authors going to direct our **reasoning** on this subject? If you were one of the staff writers on this project who had just received several hundred pictures from Smith, and it was the staff's job to turn these into a photo essay, how would you proceed?

The first job would be to sort through the pictures and decide on an editorial line—an axis of significance through the confusing mass of images supplied by the photographer. The photographs are really a record of the photographer's encounter with the doctor, an encounter that probably extended for a few days, sharing and recording his experiences. Someone has to find a significant link that will meaningfully sort out the details to move the reader toward a single explanation and ultimate resolution of the enigma contained in the opening picture. Let us suppose that your senior editor has done that and organized Smith's pictures into several groups of encounters, one of which comprises a typical day starting in the doctor's office in a small hospital built by the Colorado town where he lives and works.

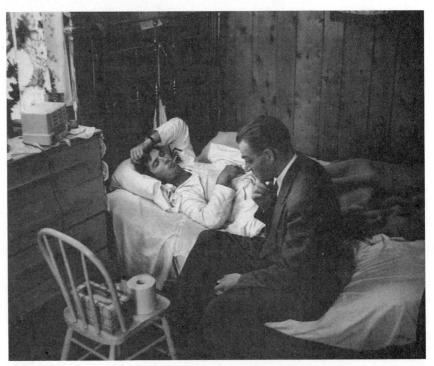

Figure 6.3. Picture 1.

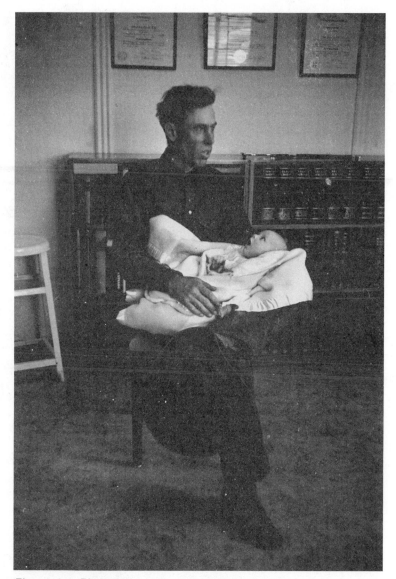

Figure 6.4. Picture 2.

The **significance** of what W. Eugene Smith and your senior editor **encountered** here was a whole way of life that surprised them because it was so different from their own. The doctor, presumably, does not see his way of living as extraordinary, though he has to be aware that, by choosing to be a rural practitioner, he has set himself apart from the vast majority of doctors attracted to the rewards of

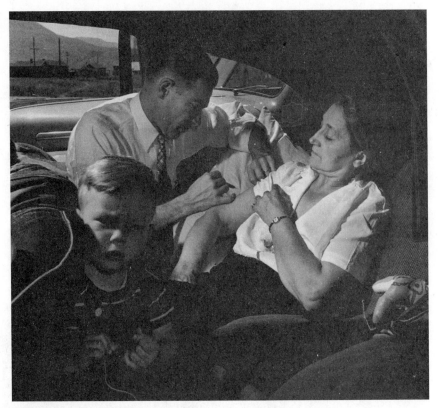

Figure 6.5. Picture 3.

suburban specialization. And certainly his practice is full of surprises, as any doctor's must be. But if we were to have asked the doctor to list the cases that stood out in his memory, they would probably not be the ones selected by the *Life* authors. From their perspective, it is just his ordinary experiences that are extraordinary because his life is set at an angle so sharply deviant from their own and that of their readership. So they find **surprising significance** in his commonplaces. The focus of that is in the title "Country Doctor." Implied by that title: "Let's see what the significant differences are between the life and work of a country doctor and the life of the doctors most of us know."

Try your hand at creating significant captions for these pictures.[2] First, make a caption for each of them. As you are doing

[2] This is a real-life job, by the way. I myself spent several months writing captions for a heavily illustrated textbook. It was a lot of fun, especially when I had no hard information about the pictures. I had to finesse their actual content and focus on the significance of each picture to the editorial purpose.

Figure 6.6. Picture 4.

this, tie them together with a single channel of significance, trying at the same time to bring out what may surprise your readers, most of whom are city dwellers. (These can be extended captions. The original captions from the Life *article consisted of a title of several words followed by a few sentences of explanation averaging 50 words. There are no wrong answers here, but you may enjoy comparing your captions with those of the original article. They are printed on page 152.) Finally, write a caption that makes a point that applies to this entire group of pictures. Compare yours with others in the class and discuss.*

THROUGH WEEDS GROWING RANK in an unkempt dooryard, Dr. Ernest Ceriani of Kremmling makes his way to call on a patient.

Figure 6.7. The original caption for the lead picture.

The general caption for all pictures was "He must specialize in a dozen fields."

Here are the specific captions for each picture. Note the reflection each contains on the general topic of how a country doctor's practice is different from that of an urban specialist.

(1) HOME CALL at 8:30 a.m. starts Ceriani's day. He prefers to treat patients during office hours at the hospital, but because this patient had a fever and symptoms of influenza, Ceriani thought it would be unwise for him to get up and make the trip.

(2) THE DAY'S FIRST OFFICE CALL is made by a tourist guide and his baby, who've come to Kremmling from an outlying ranch. Ceriani's patients are of all ages and incomes and come from doctorless areas as far as 50 mi. away.

(3) MINOR EMERGENCY disturbs Ceriani's office routine. A 60-year-old tourist, suffering from heart disturbance aggravated by a trip through an 11,000-foot pass in the Rockies, came to the hospital to get an injection of morphine.

(4) ANOTHER HOME CALL turns up a feverish 4-year-old suffering from acute tonsillitis. Although a large proportion of patients are children, Dr. Ceriani is still inexperienced in pediatrics and studies it whenever he has an opportunity.

Figure 6.8. The actual captions that appeared in the *Life* article.

INVITATION TO A READING

Now we will see how the photo-caption idea can be applied to a writer's pursuit of significance.

As we saw with the photographs, any experience is so rich in details of varying and unrelated significance that nothing stands out of the "humming-buzzing confusion" to give the whole experience shape and meaning. To find an axis of significance through the confusion, we need at least one other point of reference, just as a surveyor needs a second point to draw a straight line over broken ground. The first thing we try to do is to find a second experience that reminds us of the first. Then we let the similarities and contrasts of the two experiences throw the significant points into high relief.

Linking an experience to similar ones from our past to discover their **significance** is a natural reaction. In the following excerpt by a nurse who has taken care of two dying patients, we see how this works in the most personal mode of composition—diary writing.

As you read, take note of the striking similarities and equally striking differences between the two patients. Notice how having the two experiences to compare makes the significant features of both stand out. Consider what the significance of those features might have been to the author, Rachael de Vries, and what they might mean to you.

Two Dying Patients

by Rachael de Vries

Taking care of Jennie reminds me of Michael. Jennie is 51, an English professor: a wife: a mother. She is dying of multiple myeloma at home. She lies, day after day, on a hospital bed in the room that used to be her dining room. Michael was 18 months old when I took care of him in 1969. He was dying of leukemia, his baby's skin aged with petechiae.

This morning when I walked into the dining room, Bill was helping Jennie with her breakfast. He cooks for her every day now; he calls her Mommy and she calls him Daddy. Later in the morning, after I bathed Jennie, I got her from bed, with Bill's help, in the Hoyer lift. After we had the sling in place and began to hoist her from bed, she started to whine, "Daddy, Daddy, don't let me fall." Bill kept saying, "I won't, Mommy, I won't." They touch each other all the time, little pats on the face, or they brush their cheeks together.

In the afternoon, after I poured her meds, after lunch and nap, I put Jennie through range-of-motion exercises. She tells me about the tumor resting on her spine, how it has paralyzed her legs. I lift each leg, counting twenty times: then flex each knee and lift again. I get tired from these exercises, the heavy, solid, immobile weight of her legs on my forearms. But this is when Jennie likes to talk. She loves John Gardner, asks me if I'd read *The Sunlight Dialogues.* She talks about teaching, about her kids, and how Bill helped her all these years. Today is June 14: their wedding anniversary—the thirtieth—is the thirtieth of June. She won't live till then. Today she is weaker, more anxious than even two days ago.

Michael died in June. Three weeks before he died, his father carried him up to the pediatric unit, tears streaming down his cheeks. Michael had been in and out of the hospital in the months before. But this time he was dying. The methotrexate had caused tiny, multiple brain hemorrhages; he was unconscious, his small face too white, too still. On another admission I'd pulled him around, during my night shifts, in a wagon. He watched me pour meds, flush IVs, change dressings. During a lull in the night, I'd read to him. He used to sometimes fall asleep on my chest. When he was dying in that hospital crib I specialed him, 16 hours straight duty, monitoring his vital signs, repositioning him, putting his arms and legs through those same range-of-motion exercises. His little legs were so light, so small, I can still feel their lightness resting on my arms.

CRITICAL READING

1. Find five similarities between de Vries's experience with Michael and her experience with Jennie.
2. Find three striking differences between their situations.
3. Point out some poignant ironies in these comparisons.

DISCUSSION QUESTIONS

1. How do you think de Vries felt about her intense experiences with these patients?
2. What features of the death experience are highlighted by the similarities and differences of these two cases?
3. Do you have a sense of what the author's view of death might be from this brief diary entry? How does it seem to differ from your own? Has your view of death been influenced by any direct experience?

WRITING ACTIVITY: GENERALIZING THE SIGNIFICANCE

We can imagine that de Vries came home upset after what must have been a difficult day acting as a private nurse for Jennie. She did what people often do to help themselves through difficult emotional experiences: She wrote about it.

This textbook is mostly about leading readers through a process that will help them resolve a bothersome kind of experience, but it is clear that writing also helps the author, as Claudia Kalb reports in an article in *Newsweek* (4/26/99):

> Since the mid-1980s, studies have found that people who write about their most upsetting experiences not only feel better but visit doctors less often and even have stronger immune responses. Last week, scientists reported findings that make the link even clearer. A study published in *The Journal of the American Medical Association* (JAMA) showed that writing exercises can help alleviate symptoms of asthma and rheumatoid arthritis. "It's hard to believe," says James Pennebaker, a psychology professor at the University of Texas at Austin and a pioneer in the field of expressive writing, but "being able to put experiences into words is good for your physical health."

In sorting out the trauma of dealing with Jennie's imminent death, de Vries did what we have seen our minds are built to do: She searched her memory for another experience with **significant** links to this one. And then she recorded both **encounters** with moving skill, filling them with just those specific details that dramatize her feelings and push the significant links into high relief.

Much writing starts with this exact process. But if de Vries were to turn these personally connected experiences from diary entries into an essay for the general public, she would need to add captions to her photo vignettes. She would be looking to find a way to make explicit their **significance.**

And that is what I am going to ask you to do for her. Your job in this assignment is to role-play de Vries as she takes the material of her diary and turns it into a tiny gem of an essay. Writing as if you were she, you will provide a significant link between the two experiences, very much in the form of extended captions. It is an excellent exercise in that it allows you to concentrate on this one very important step without having to come up with a topic and remember details.

All you have to do is create two short paragraphs, one between de Vries's existing paragraphs and one after them providing the meat of the shish kebab. Based on your answers to the Critical Reading questions for de Vries's entries, select **one** axis of similarity or difference that seems **significant** to you. Write a transition sentence from the actual Jennie paragraph (just as written) to a few carefully crafted sentences that express what I called in chapter 1 "the luminous strands carrying energy" between the two experiences. Then write another transition sentence that will turn the reader's focus to the Michael paragraph. Last, construct a final paragraph based on the **same** significant connection that helps the general reader **resolve** some of his or her feelings about the loss of someone they know well.

Beware of the simple bromide[3] remedy. Do not resort to trite overgeneralization like "Death is sad." Examine the significance of the one link you have chosen and let the energy of your thought flow back and forth along that conduit until you have come up with something genuinely significant that fits the depth of your and de Vries's feelings and that you confidently believe will elevate your readers' attitudes toward death in a helpful way.

---

[3] A *cliché,* so called because bromides were sedatives and clichés tend to put readers to sleep.

Exploring the Topic: Using Significant Axes of Similarity and Difference to Explain an Encounter

As the previous exercises demonstrate, the first way we try to understand the significance of an eye-opening encounter is to pair it with a similar one that we remember. Let's see how this works in the case of Frank, who has just had yet another startling experience in his stormy relationship with his wife, Pat:

> Frank had been out all day entertaining his mother and father, who were visiting from Fargo. He took them shopping, lunching at the Berghoff, and visiting the art museum. All this time his wife stayed home cleaning up the house, which their three young children did their best to turn into a fantasy playground, making a fort from the couch cushions, using the pots and pans as vehicles, and stacking books to make obstacle courses to chase each other around. When Frank and his parents got home, the house was nearly straight, the table was set, and a steaming dinner of pot roast and mashed potatoes was cooking on the stove.
>
> "Actually, I'm not too hungry," Frank's father told his daughter-in-law, Pat. "We had a big dinner at the Berghoff."
>
> During dinner, Tommy, the six-year-old tried to snatch his spoon back from Danny, the eight-year-old who had dropped his. In doing so, he upset his milk.
>
> Frank's mother said to Pat, "I really think you should teach your children better table manners."
>
> Frank said, "Yes, she really lets them get away with murder."
>
> After dinner, Frank and his parents went into the living room to watch TV while Pat began cleaning up. Frank went out to the kitchen and told Pat, who was carrying a stack of dirty plates to the sink, that his mother wanted to go see a movie. He said, "Do you want to come?"
>
> At that, Pat took the stack of plates and, without a word, dashed them all on the floor. Frank was stunned. "What's wrong?" he asked. Without saying a word, Pat stalked to the front hall closet, grabbed her coat, and slammed out the front door.
>
> Frank stood in the kitchen, scratching his head, wondering what this burst of violence from his wife signified.

It's pretty easy for us, as outsiders, to see why Pat blew her stack. But, immersed in the situation, Frank's mind has had to shift into high gear to pick out **significant** elements of the event that might help him **explain** the nasty surprise his wife has thrown into his smooth-running day. Eons of evolution have conditioned our brains to do just that—explain any surprises so that, in the future, **significant** elements in a new situation can warn us to avoid a similar problem. One way our brains produce such **explanations** is to remember other situations that have produced similar surprises and see links of **significance** between them. With enough of these remembered experiences we may be able to answer that nagging question: "Why does this keep happening to me?" Here are some earlier events that Frank was reminded of:

A. Pat got mad at Frank when he forgot to get her a gift last Mothers' Day.
B. She was upset when Frank's parents insisted on taking them out to eat the very evening she had prepared a big dinner of roast lamb.
C. The last time report cards came home, Frank had accused Pat of not making the children do their homework. Pat then threw a cereal bowl in his direction.
D. Another time, when his parents were visiting, Frank had agreed with his mother that the dress Pat had chosen to wear to a Sunday afternoon concert was really too formal. Pat then refused to go at all.
E. Shortly after their youngest child was born, Frank went on a weeklong cruise sponsored by his company. When he came home, he found that Pat was staying with her mother.
F. On weekends, Frank likes to take the children to museums, on picnics, or out bicycling. He says it gives Pat time to clean the house and do the gardening. She never seems grateful for this relief.

But just remembering these earlier experiences is not enough. Frank needs to use the axis of connection between them to learn a lesson. That connection acts like a searchlight beam to pick out and highlight the **significant** elements from among that "blooming-buzzing confusion" that usually clouds our understanding of the experiences we are living through. If you have ever lived through a newsworthy event—marched in a demonstration, participated in a play, played in a sports event, hunkered down through a tornado or hurricane—and then read about it in the newspaper later, you know that it reads very differently than it was lived. Reporters standing above the fray are able to spotlight those elements that your particular march or performance or game or storm shares with others and thereby evaluate its **significance**—its differences, its notable points, its quality—from a broader perspective.

Formulating a significant lesson from a surprising experience by relating it to earlier ones and by comparing notes with other people is a primary function of our minds. But it is normally an unconscious process. Making the process conscious is central to learning to live and write better. How is it accomplished? How do we use the juxtaposition of two experiences to make manifest **significances** that may surprise even ourselves?

In the past Frank has just shrugged his shoulders when these things happen and repeated some trite saying like "It sure is hard for married partners to get along" or, "I guess I'll never understand women." But if Frank is going to save his marriage, he is going to have to look at these experiences more critically to explain precisely what is going wrong and what can be done about it. To do this, Frank needs to find an axis of significant similarity running from each remembered experience to the latest debacle.

Take some time now to do this for Frank. Take each of the earlier experiences in the list A through F and match them with a specific event in the current uproar that is similar to it.

If Frank focuses specifically on the **significance** of each of these axes, he should be able to pinpoint some surprisingly accurate **resolutions** that will enable him to make real progress and that might, if he decided to write about these experiences, help other husbands as well.

Here is a list of lessons that Frank came up with. Can you see how he did it? Match each of these lessons with one of the remembered experiences in the previous list:

1. He shouldn't criticize the way his wife handles their children.
2. He must be careful not to gang up with his parents against her, making her feel isolated and unsupported.
3. He should counsel his parents to avoid unintentional rudeness when they are guests.
4. He must realize that Pat sometimes feels overwhelmed and trapped by having all the work and responsibilities dumped on her.

5. He has to be more considerate of Pat's need to feel appreciated.
6. He's got to avoid going off to have fun while leaving Pat at home like Cinderella to do the domestic chores.

Even student writers who possess or have acquired the ability to describe experiences graphically sometimes shortchange this crucial step of searching out the precise significance of the link that joins the particular experiences. Avoid Frank's mistake of just shrugging your shoulders and taking the closest bromide off the shelf. The generalization of **significance** should be medicine custom compounded to target the discomfort of these experiences specifically. Take time to become conscious of this natural mental process, because it will form the basis for expounding and supporting more abstract ideas later on.

INVITATION TO A READING

The examples we have seen so far involve making **significant** links between personally experienced encounters. But connections are often between direct experience and some other modality, like **background** issues and **research.** In the next piece, columnist Shana Alexander discovers significance in her observation of a California beach by connecting her encounter with some statistics she has read. In chapter 1 we talked about the effectiveness of cycling through the modalities. In chapter 4 we talked about the dramatist's Rule of Three—the need to repeat any information several times in order for it to stick in the readers' minds. There we saw the effectiveness of repeating the resolution shish kebab–style several times, usually at each decision point between modalities. As you read this column, look for those gear-shift points and notice how Alexander each time restates the general **significance** of whatever observation or facts she has just described.

Motherliness

by Shana Alexander

"Motherly" to most of us, means gentle, open, warm, uncritical, and adoring. By these lights, some of the most motherly people I know are fathers.

Take a look at any beach in summertime. Here the motherly fathers are out in force. They help build the sand castles, they rub on the sun creme, go for the ice cream, and carry the toddlers into the surf. For this is the height of America's custody season and these are the week-end fathers.

The bright summer sunshine reveals all the new patterns in part-time parenthood which our soaring divorce rate has forced us to devise. About a third of all American marriages now end in divorce. In some communities, like Southern California, the divorce rate has passed 120 per cent, which means that the mythical "average citizen" has been divorced one and one-fifth times. Divorce, here, is considered a normal part of marriage, much the same as death is accepted as a part of life.

But what of the children? What does a man do with a four-, or a six- or an eight-year-old child, or perhaps all three of them, when "Daddy's Day" rolls around? Visits with the new wife or girl friend are difficult; Disneyland is expensive. Every spare cent Daddy has already goes for alimony and child-support. So it comes down to a choice of the beach—or visiting your children in your ex-wife's living room.

One stretch of California coastline has become so chockablock with weekend fathers and their offspring, it is known as Alimony Beach. The regulars here do not greet each other by name, but by number—"two-two-five," or "three-five-oh," according to the amount the divorce is costing them per month, in cash.

One day across the sand lurched a lone man festooned with beach towels, umbrella, hamper, and thermos jug, and followed by five small children. "That's seven-five-oh!" someone whispered. I watched seven-five-oh all the long day—finding lost sneakers, settling fights, and brushing sand out of the peanut butter—and I have never seen a more gentle, more patient, and—well—more motherly parent.

That qualities like "motherliness" or "fatherliness" are not inborn, nor God-given, but are really states of mind, is something men and women both must remember as drastic changes in patterns of marriage and family life tug at the fabric of our society.

CRITICAL READING

1. What is the surprise in the first paragraph?
2. What surprises Alexander when she looks at the beach?
3. What is the significance of this surprise as a social trend?
4. There are many telling and amusing photo vignettes. But, like a good photographer, once Alexander has decided on the axis of significance, she screens out all the details that don't contribute to the significance she is highlighting. Make a list of details that a beginning writer might be tempted to include that Alexander ignores.
5. What sentences can you identify that act as captions for Alexander's pictures?

DISCUSSION QUESTIONS

1. How is the issue of divorce significant in an essay on motherliness? What do you think her views are on this subject?

2. Is it possible that Alexander's reading about divorce statistics and custody problems sensitized her so that, when she saw the crowd at the beach, that information acted like a spotlight to pick out the number of fathers on the beach? Or do you think it more likely that she noticed the preponderance of motherly fathers first and then looked up the information?

3. Do you agree with Alexander's list of motherly qualities? Do you agree that fathers can develop them? Explain and give examples from your own experience.

4. Give some examples of Alexander's use of humor. What techniques does she use to make us smile? Decide in each case whether the surprise of the humor emphasizes the main lesson of the article as a whole.

5. Does the lesson in the last paragraph of the essay grow organically out of the explanation of the surprises? Could you come up with a different social significance for this essay?

DEMONSTRATION: TOLLING THE BELL OF SIGNIFICANCE

In Table 6.1, I try to demonstrate how Alexander connected the modalities in her essay so that they illuminate each other's **significance.** The modalities of **reasoning, search,** and **background** will be taken up in detail in later chapters, but I'm sure you have an intuitive grasp of their meaning. I have put a bell next to the right-hand column of **resolution/significance** to suggest how, almost like a clock tolling the hour, the process repeats, ringing the bell of significance as regularly as caption follows picture.

I hope that this map of the modality cycles in Alexander's column helps you visualize how nimbly professional writers move from one modality to another and how they return again and again to restatements or elaborations of the general **significance** of the piece.

There are a number of interesting things to notice about this map.

☐ Most of the modality sections are quite short—one paragraph or less.

☐ The distribution is fairly even—two occurrences of each modality—but the connecting bell of significance is rung five times as a caption, once after almost every modal shift.

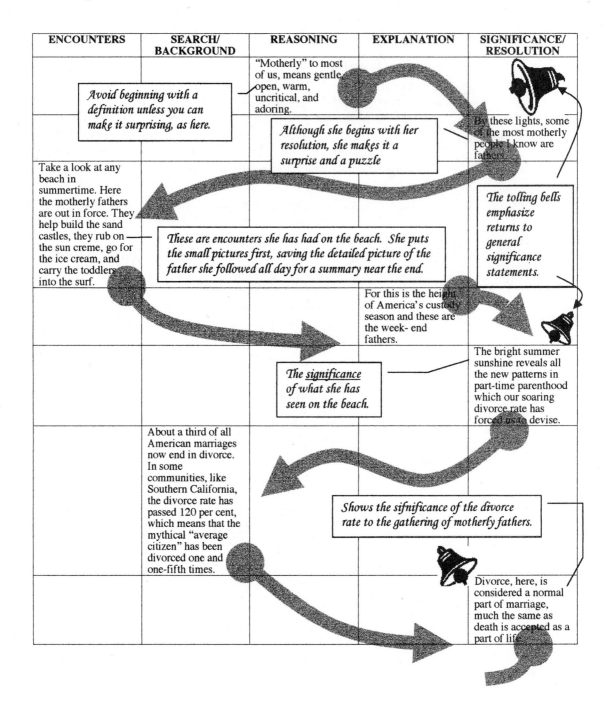

ENCOUNTERS	SEARCH/ BACKGROUND	REASONING	EXPLANATION	SIGNIFICANCE/ RESOLUTION

Table 6.1. Modality Cycling in "Motherliness."

ENCOUNTERS	SEARCH/BKGND	REASONING	EXPLANATION	SIGNIFICANCE
	Reasoning aimed at finding the significance of the new pattern children with fathers on the beach.	But what of the children? What does a man do with a four-, or a six-, or an eight-year-old child, or perhaps all three of them, when "Daddy's Day" rolls around? Visits with the new wife or girl friend are difficult; Disneyland is expensive. Every spare cent Daddy has already goes for alimony and child-support.		
			So it comes down to a choice of the beach—or visiting your children in your ex-wife's living room.	
	One stretch of California coastline has become so chockablock with weekend fathers and their offspring, it is known as Alimony Beach. The regulars here do not greet each other by name, but by number— "two-two-five," or "three-five-oh," according to the amount the divorce is costing them per month, in cash.			
One day across the sand lurched a lone man festooned with beach towels, um-brella, hamper, and thermos jug, and followed by five small children. "That's seven-five-oh!" someone whis-pered. I watched seven-five-oh all the long day—finding lost sneakers, settling fights, and brushing sand out of the peanut butter.	*The main detailed encounter.*			

Table 6.1. (*Continued*)

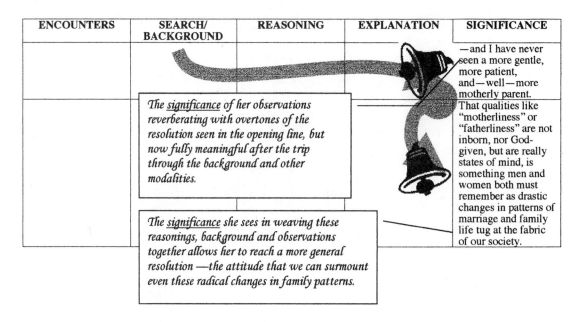

ENCOUNTERS	SEARCH/ BACKGROUND	REASONING	EXPLANATION	SIGNIFICANCE
				—and I have never seen a more gentle, more patient, and—well—more motherly parent.
	The significance of her observations reverberating with overtones of the resolution seen in the opening line, but now fully meaningful after the trip through the background and other modalities.			That qualities like "motherliness" or "fatherliness" are not inborn, nor God-given, but are really states of mind, is something men and women both must remember as drastic changes in patterns of marriage and family life tug at the fabric of our society.
	The significance she sees in weaving these reasonings, background and observations together allows her to reach a more general resolution —the attitude that we can surmount even these radical changes in family patterns.			

Table 6.1. (Continued)

☐ The pictures of the main encounter with "Seven-five-oh," is longer than any of the captions of significance, corroborating my earlier statement that verbal pictures take more words than their captions.

WRITING COMMISSION: APPLYING SIGNIFICANT CAPTIONS TO TREND IMAGES

We're back at the newspaper office, and your editor has a great idea for all you interns.

"A substantial number of our readers are middle-aged and older," she (he) says. "I know from the letters we get that quite a few are mystified by the trends and fads among young people today. 'What does it all mean?' they say constantly. Well, heck, I don't know what it all means, or if it means anything! But most of you guys are young enough that you probably can make some good guesses.

"What I want each of you to do is pick one of these that you've noticed and that you think might be a bit puzzling or even disturbing to older folks and try to evaluate its social significance for them. You might start with a personal anecdote and you might dig around in news magazines for some other stories or even statistics to show how significant it really is.

"As always, be vivid. When you describe the kids wearing or doing whatever, make it like a picture. And after each one, put, like, a caption. Remember, the folks have seen the picture, but they still want to know what it all means.

"Oh, and don't be squeamish about hammering the point home. Us older folks tend to nod off while we're reading, so keep ringing the bell to wake us up!"

"Can we be funny?" someone asks.

"You can be as funny as chocolate-covered ice cream on a stick."

"Hunh? . . . Oh!, I get it!"

"Yeah. If you can write **good** humor, go for it."

"That was **bad!**"

Points to Remember

- **Significance** is a quality that should permeate your writing, emerging periodically as you show links between **encounters, explanations,** and **resolution** statements.
- The quality of **surprise** is necessary throughout a piece to keep the reader's interest alive, but the quality of **significance** is equally necessary throughout to keep alive the sense in the reader that this is something worthwhile and rewarding.
- Old experiences may grow in significance and new ones acquire significance by linking one with the other. Use this psychological fact in your writing by deliberately energizing this synergy.
- The reason links clarify the **significance** of events is that they light up axes of similarity and differences. Considering these axes helps you as a writer to know which aspects and details of an issue, a person, a cultural item, or an **encounter** to emphasize and which to ignore.
- Whenever you reach a juncture in your writing—that is, a point where you have finished one modality section and are searching for another—formulate a general statement of the **significance** of your axis to serve as a caption for the picture you have just presented and toll the bell of significance.

E-E-R

Encounter

Explain

Resolve

R-S-V-B

Reason

Search

Value

Background

PART II

The Satellite Modalities

E-E-R

Encounter

Explain

Resolve

R-S-V-B

Reason

Search

Value

Background

7

Background

To learn a culture is natural to human beings. Children can express individuality only in relation to the traditions of their society, which they have to learn. The greatest human individuality is developed in response to a tradition, not in response to disorderly, uncertain and fragmented education.

—E. D. Hirsch Jr., *Cultural Literacy*

Disingenuous rhetoric, visceral distrust, maximal posturing, minimal progress. Political debates escape this kind of dead end when . . . leaders emerge with fresh ways of framing the issues.

—Matthew Miller, "A Bold Experiment to Fix City Schools"

Opening the Topic

You may have been in one of these trick houses (shown in Figure 7.1); they are scattered across the country as tourist attractions. The man is not being held up with wires; he is standing normally. What is **not** normal is the house that serves as the **background.** (The solution is shown in Figure 7.2.)

It is hardly too much to say that the **significance** of an event cannot be made clear without knowing the relevant context in which it occurs. We cannot understand how the man is made to lean until we understand how the house is constructed.

The importance of the **background** modality does not, however, mean that background should come first in a piece of writing. On the contrary, if I had explained this picture before showing it, all the surprise value would be lost. Background does not make interesting

Figure 7.1. How does he do it?

reading in its own right. It becomes interesting only when something puzzles us enough that we need to understand it. That is why "Background" is chapter 7 in this textbook rather than chapter 1.

When *Star Wars: Episode I—The Phantom Menace* came out, *Time* magazine's reviewer, Richard Corliss, complained that the opening background text was talky.

"Turmoil has engulfed the Galactic Republic," the now familiar trapezoidal text-crawl tells us. "The taxation of trade routes to outlying star systems is in dispute." Immediately one is perplexed. A summary made sense in the earlier films; they were episodes IV, V and VI in the grand fable, and as continuations of an initially untold saga, they required some elucidation. But what's the need for back-story text in a tale that is just beginning? Can it be that Lucas was unable to dramatize these events, so he put them in the crawl? That would explain the gobs of dry exposition, devoted to blustering, filibustering debates on taxation and elections. It's all very edifying. Like . . . school.

You yourself may remember having had an almost irresistible tendency to launch into **background** at the beginning of a piece of writing.

Resist it!

Unless there is something inherently surprising or mysterious or otherwise interesting about it, **background** is much better left until the need for it has become clear. The need, when it arises, will also **structure** the **background,** showing you, the writer, what you have to include and, perhaps more important, what you should leave out. Writing a background introduction is popular with amateur writers because it seems like the easiest way to get the subject started. But what is easiest for the writer is not normally best for the reader. You do not need a college course to find the **easiest** way to write something; you need it to find the **best** way—a way that will get and hold your readers' attention while you raise their consciousness.

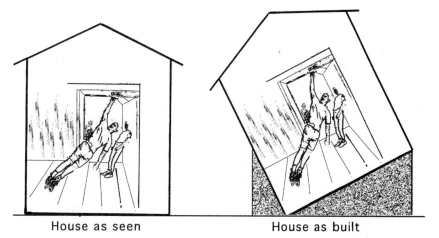

House as seen   House as built

Figure 7.2. Here is the solution to the leaning man at the beginning of the chapter. If the tipped house is viewed as vertical, the man appears tipped.

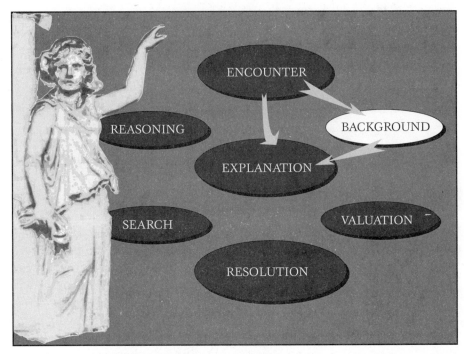

Figure 7.3. **Background** following **encounter** highlights the surprise by contextual contrast and creates a map of the intellectual terrain on which its **significance** becomes clear.

Exploring the Topic

Background and Workplace Miscommunication

"I just ordered a reconditioned monitor from your company about a week ago, and it doesn't work," I said, pleasantly enough, to the Customer Service Representative (call him "Cuss").

"You mean a 'refurbished' monitor," said Cuss.

"OK, reconditioned, refurbished, whatever. It didn't work, right out of the box," I said, after a brief pause to wonder why he felt it necessary to lecture me about using the company's preferred term.

"What would you like to do?" said Cuss.

"Well, I'd like to return it."

"I'm sorry, you can't return anything after seven days."

"Well, it has been about seven days since I got it."

"Seven days from the date it is shipped," said Cuss.

"What!" I said, with a little edge to my voice. "That doesn't leave any time to receive it, unpack it, and try it out!"

"That's why you should pay the $78 to have it FedEx'd," Cuss said, with what sounded to me like a note of "gotcha" in his voice. "There is a 90-day warrantee period during which you can have it repaired."

"OK, well, if that's the best you can do. . . ."

"No, I can't do that. I would advise you to call tech support."

"Well, OK. Can you transfer me?"

"They will need the shipment number. Do you have the shipment number that is packed with every order?"

"Just a second. I saved every scrap of paper that came with it in case this happened. . . . No, there is a packing list, the warrantee, a little gizmo to test the color, but, no, no shipment number."

"Ninety percent of our customers say that the number was not shipped with their order, but it always turns out that they find it."

I began to get really hot. "Now, listen here. I saved every shred of paper. It's not here. Surely it's possible that your shipping department could have made a mistake."

"The number is packed with every order. They will need it."

"Look, I'm getting really [bleep]!" I shouted. "You're telling me I have a warrantee, but that there is no way for me to get the [bleep] monitor repaired!"

"No, I'm not saying that. What I am trying to tell you is—"

"—is that you won't give me the [bleep] phone number without the [bleep] packing number which I never got."

"I am trying to give it to you, but you are cursing at me."

"If you are **trying**, as you say, to give me the [bleep] number, then why haven't I heard it?"

"I'm trying, but you keep shouting and cursing."

Eventually Cuss did give me the number, and when I called it the woman who answered, call her Grace, was very helpful. None of the things that Cuss said I would have to have were needed. She just looked the order up on the computer and gave me the necessary case number, saying that, since it was still well within the 90-day warrantee period, there would be no problem.

After my blood pressure subsided to something under 220/102, I felt a little sorry for Cuss. I realized that his day was probably hell if he had to handle many calls like mine. But then, contrasting his behavior with that of the woman at tech support, I also realized that he had brought his bad day on himself by being unable to see the situation from his customer's point of view. His problem, it seemed to me, had been brought on by not visualizing the background of the communication situation in which he was working and the place of his customer in it. If only he had had the English class you are taking, his life at that company would have been happier—and probably longer. If his call was monitored for quality control, he was headed for trouble.

He certainly should have been able to see that a customer has a right to be upset if a product does not work when it is first plugged in, and, though he could not change company policy, there would have been nothing wrong with his having apologized for the problem. Then, since he knew that the shipping number was often and easily discarded by customers, he should have seen that requiring it might look like a deliberate attempt on the part of the company to get out of paying repair costs. Finally, instead of focusing on how bad the customer was making him feel, his communication should have focused on why the customer was irritated and what he could do to short-circuit that irritation. This he could have done by emphasizing what **could** be done rather than what could **not** be done.

A lack of awareness of what background scenery the reader may be bringing to what you have to say costs big money in the workplace. I will certainly never again buy a reconditioned—oops! **refurbished**—product from that company. And bad communication within companies causes sometimes monumental foul-ups and delays daily. The ability of employees to picture the reader/listener's mental map is something that many companies are now taking account of when they hire.

As a further example, instructions are an apparently simple form of writing that can really turn and bite the hapless hack who writes without clear background awareness of the situation in which the reader will be operating. The following collection of (putatively) actual instructions and warnings seen on products came to me (unattributed) via e-mail off the internet.

Absurd Instructions

Here are some object lessons in why you should stand in the reader's background when you revise your writing.

1. On Sears hairdryer:
    Do not use while sleeping.
2. On a bag of Fritos:
    You could be a winner! No purchase necessary. Details inside.

3. On a bar of Dial soap:
   Directions: Use like regular soap.
4. On some Swanson frozen dinners:
   Serving suggestion: Defrost.
5. On a hotel-provided shower cap in a box:
   Fits one head.
6. On Tesco's Tiramisu dessert (printed on bottom of the box):
   Do not turn upside down.
7. On Marks & Spencer Bread Pudding:
   Product will be hot after heating.
8. On packaging for a Rowenta iron:
   Do not iron clothes on body.
9. On Boot's Children's cough medicine:
   Do not drive car or operate machinery.
10. On Nytol sleep aid:
    Warning: May cause drowsiness.
11. On a Korean kitchen knife:
    Warning: Keep out of children.
12. On a string of Chinese-made Christmas lights:
    For indoor or outdoor use only.
13. On a Japanese food processor:
    Not to be used for the other use.
14. On Sainsbury's peanuts:
    Warning: Contains nuts.
15. On an American Airlines packet of nuts:
    Instructions: Open packet, eat nuts.
16. On a child's Superman costume:
    Wearing of this garment does not enable you to fly.

This kind of embarrassing imbecility, which reflects badly on the entire company, can be avoided by standing where the reader stands when using the product and assessing carefully what the reader's needs are given the background from which he or she is approaching the product.

INVITATION TO A READING

It has been estimated that white-collar and professional workers spend 75 percent of their working day writing. I happen to have two sons in managerial positions in business who attest to the truth of that statistic. They complain about the incomprehensibly bad writing produced by college-graduate employees. Too many graduates, it would seem, return to the college what they have learned about good writing along with their rented cap and gown. One of the main causes of bad writing in the workplace is the apparent inability of the writers to correctly assess the **background** knowledge of the intended readers. As a result they either insult their readers by treating them like nincompoops or baffle them by sailing over their heads. Sometimes both.

In the following column from *Forbes* magazine, a noted economist turns his attention to the subject of readers' frustration when a writer, ignoring the readers' **background** perspective, provides too little or the wrong kind of instructions.

Instructions That Do Not Instruct
by Thomas Sowell

No one seems to be more in need of instructions than the people who write instructions for computers and computer software.

It is, of course, only an assumption that these are people. They could be aliens from outer space—and the instructions themselves suggest that this possibility should not be dismissed out of hand.

The first instruction for those who write computer instructions should be: Never start at Step Two, since whatever you say will be lost on people who do not know what Step One is.

For example, the ironically titled "Help" file on a well-known backup software begins by saying what you are to do after the "Restore" screen appears. It says nothing about how you get that screen to appear in the first place. Nor is there anything on the opening screen to offer a clue.

Instruction writers should remember that, no matter how simple or sophisticated the computer or software might be, in the end the user is going to have to push some keys on the keyboard, click a mouse or perform some other specific act, if only smashing the computer in frustration.

Too many computer instructions do not specify what act you are to perform. Instead, they characterize what you are to do, such as "access the backup files." If the user knew how to do that, he would not have to suffer through such instructions.

While such statements are called instructions, they could more accurately be called reminders. If you already know how to do these things, they remind you when to do it.

How the user is going to learn to perform these operations the first time is something that seems to be of little concern to the computer instruction writers. Maybe they think we will just blunder into it by guess and by golly. Often they are right. Some users have in fact learned the hard way that trial and error is sometimes faster than trying to figure out what the instructions are saying.

The first time I installed chess software in my computer, I made it a point to ignore the instructions completely. Only months later did my curiosity cause me to take a look at these instructions. If I had relied on the manual, I would still be waiting to make my opening move.

Simplifying instructions does not mean adding a lot more words. Words that specify what act you are to perform need not be any more numerous than words which characterize these same acts. Specific words are just more helpful.

As it is, computer instructions are needlessly wordy. Too often they rhapsodize about all the wonderful options and variations available for doing what you want to do and engage in advertising puffery about the glories of the product. Since you have already bought the product, or you would not have the instruction book, all of this could be eliminated.

In many cases, you would never have bought the product if you had read the instruction book beforehand and realized what an impenetrable jungle it is.

Too many computer and software producers seem to think that being condescending to the user is the same as simplifying. My backup software, for example, opens up with a screen showing a guy with a vacuous smile on his face, saying "It is now time to start a new backup job. . . ." No kidding! Why do you suppose I turned on the backup software? At the end, he offers gratuitous advice on how I should number the cartridges I use.

In between, there is only the unhelpful "Help" to turn to.

Probably the main reason for instructions that do not instruct is that the writers cannot or will not put themselves in the position of the users. Instead, these writers—notice that I still will not tip my hand as to whether or not I believe they are people—seem far more interested in all the fancy features that may be used 3% of the time than with all the boring stuff that is used the other 97% of the time.

Perhaps computer companies and software companies should hire some low-tech people to try to follow the instructions written by their high-tech writers. The better manuals that could result from this process might let some users think that they really are valued customers, as they are told repeatedly by recordings while waiting to talk to someone in technical support.

PICKING UP POINTERS FROM THE PROS:
Modalities in Workaday Writing

The methods of writing well that we are establishing here are as valid on the corporate campus as they are on the academic one.

Let us start with the **eye-opener.** Thomas Sowell complains that his "backup software, for example, opens up with a screen showing a guy with a vacuous smile on his face, saying 'It is now time to start a new backup job. . . .' No kidding!"—that is, no surprise. The eye-opener must focus on what will be novel to the reader—specifically in the case of instructions, what the users will confront that they are likely not to understand.

Sowell emphasizes that instructions should center around an **encounter:** "Instruction writers should remember that, no matter how simple or sophisticated the computer or software might be, in the end the user is going to have to push some keys on the keyboard, click a mouse or perform some other specific act, if only smashing the computer in frustration." Notice particularly Sowell's advice not to **characterize** experiences but to **specify.** This means, for example, that describing the specific experience of one day and letting it stand for other similar experiences is better than making a general statement that characterizes all of them.

But above all notice this warning:

> **Bad writers "cannot or will not put themselves in the position of the users."**

This is the "thou shalt not" from which all the other commandments of good writing may derive. What will be an **eye-opener** for your specified audience? What will that audience need **explained** to them? What can that audience learn from the **resolution** to your encounter? And, in this case particularly, how much **background** can you assume that your readers have?

This reaction is particularly interesting: "Too many computer and software producers seem to think that being condescending to the user is the same as simplifying." These writers omit **background** needed by the readers who are not conversant with the material. This is a trap that experts in a field often fall into when writing to lay people. An equally dangerous pitfall is not giving enough background for fear of seeming condescending.

Writing is doing something for a reader. True, the act of writing often results in an exciting experience of self-discovery for the writer.

But that wouldn't happen if the writer weren't trying to reenvision his or her experience from the perspective of someone with a different background. Remember the lesson Sowell is teaching in this column when you revise your writing: Read your writing through the user's eyes.

WRITING ACTIVITY: Writing Instructions

Computer-generated presentation slides have become an almost universal crutch for speakers. Write an essay titled "Power Point for Dummies" that shows technophobe users how to use this tool to enhance a presentation, with some tips for avoiding boredom. You can also write instructions for some other technological device or application that lay persons may have to deal with: using the advanced features of a digital camera or camcorder, for example.

This should be a much better piece of writing than the instructions that came with the product. If you have been frustrated, as Sowell was, with a particular set of instructions, you can try your hand at rewriting them. In that case, your instructor might like to see a copy of the original to appreciate your success.

For pointers, you might take a look at any of the many computer books with titles like *DOS for Dummies* to get an idea how good professional writers of instructions focus on the surprise of the readers' encounter with the product and how they maintain a light, lively, and entertaining style. Most of these publications do very well at giving basic instructions in a way that will neither embarrass nor overwhelm the reader who has inadequate background knowledge.

INVITATION TO A READING

In 1980 Alvin Toffler published a blockbuster follow-up to his already highly successful vision of *Future Shock,* which warned of the disorienting hyperspeed social changes we would be experiencing in the next decades. In the later book (from which the following selection is taken), the changes he sees happening are those made possible (and indeed forced on us) primarily by the revolution in electronics, which makes possible the massive assembling and lightning-fast dissemination of information worldwide to everyone. Most people have easily and eagerly adapted to the changes insofar as cell phones, e-mail, word processors, and the Internet make their lives more flexible and convenient, but other aspects can create wrenching changes.

Terrorist attacks, family disintegration, loneliness, child porn, loss of privacy, political revolution, obliteration of cultural roots—all these become more common if not downright inevitable.

Toffler likens this electronic information revolution we are going through to a massive wave—the third such wave in history. To understand it, of course, we must understand the **background** of those earlier massive technological waves that humans have been swamped by—the agricultural revolution and the industrial revolution. In the following selection, Toffler identifies ways in which the needs of the factory forced a synchronization on nearly every aspect of public and private life. Lockstep behavior has become so much a part of our unconscious background mentality that we often follow the old customs even after the information age has, in advanced countries, eliminated the need for it. Understanding this background is a necessary step toward adopting productive programs and attitudes in the transition period that we are living through.

from *The Third Wave*
by Alvin Toffler

In January 1950, just as the second half of the twentieth century opened, a gangling twenty-two-year-old with a newly minted university diploma took a long bus ride through the night into what he regarded as the central reality of our time. With his girl friend at his side and a pasteboard suitcase filled with books under the belt, he watched a gunmetal dawn come up as the factories of the American Midwest slid endlessly past the rain-swept window.

America was the heartland of the world. The region ringing the Great Lakes was the industrial heartland of America. And the factory was the throbbing core of this heart of hearts: steel mills, aluminum foundries, tool and die shops, oil refineries, auto plants, mile after mile of dingy buildings vibrating with huge machines for stamping, punching, drilling, bending, welding, forging, and casting metal. The factory was the symbol of the entire industrial era, and, to a boy raised in a semi-comfortable lower-middle-class home, after four years of Plato and T. S. Eliot, of art history and abstract social theory, the world it represented was as exotic as Tashkent or Tierra del Fuego.

I spent five years in those factories, not as a clerk or personnel assistant, but as an assembly hand, a millwright, a welder, a forklift driver, a punch press operator—stamping out fans, fixing machines in a foundry, building giant dust control machines for African mines, finishing the metal on light trucks as they sped clattering and screeching past on the assembly line. I learned firsthand how factory workers struggled to earn a living in the industrial age.

I swallowed the dust, the sweat and smoke of the foundry. My ears were split by the hiss of steam, the clank of chains, the roar of pug mills. I felt the heat as the white-hot steel poured. Acetylene sparks left burn marks on my legs. I turned out thousands of pieces a shift on a press, repeating identical movements until my mind and muscles shrieked. I watched the managers who kept the workers in their place, whiteshirted men themselves endlessly pursued and harried by higher-ups. I helped lift a sixty-five-year-old woman out of the bloody machine that had just torn four fingers off her hand, and I still hear her cries—"Jesus and Mary, I won't be able to work again!"

The factory. Long live the factory! Today, even as new factories are being built, the civilization that made the factory into a cathedral is dying. And somewhere, right now, other young men and women are driving through the night into the heart of the emergent Third Wave civilization. . . .

[A new civilization is emerging in our lives. . . . This new civilization brings with it new family styles, changed ways of working, loving, and living, a new economy, new political conflicts, and beyond all this an altered consciousness as well.

Humanity faces a quantum leap forward. It faces the deepest social upheaval and creative restructuring of all time. Without clearly recognizing it, we are engaged in building a remarkable new civilization from the ground up. This is the meaning of the Third Wave.

Until now the human race has undergone two great waves of change, each one largely obliterating earlier cultures or civilizations and replacing them with ways of life inconceivable to those who came before. The First Wave of change—the agricultural revolution—took thousands of years to play itself out. The Second Wave—the rise of industrial civilization—took a mere three hundred years. Today history is even more accelerative, and it is likely that the Third Wave will sweep across history and complete itself in a few decades. Those of us who happen to share the planet at this explosive moment will therefore feel the full impact of the Third Wave in our own lifetimes.

The Third Wave brings with it a genuinely new way of life based on diversified, renewable energy sources; on methods of production that make most factory assembly lines obsolete; on new, non-nuclear families; on a novel institution that might be called the "electronic cottage;" and on radically changed schools and corporations of the future. The emergent civilization writes a new code of behavior for us and carries us beyond standardization, synchronization and centralization, beyond the concentration of energy, money and power][1].

Synchronization

[One] principle of [Second Wave] industrial civilization [was] synchronization.

Even in the earliest societies work had to be carefully organized in time. Warriors often had to work in unison to trap their prey. Fishermen had to coordinate their efforts in rowing or hauling in the nets. George Thomson, many years ago, showed how various work songs reflected the requirements of labor. For the oarsmen, time was marked by a simple two-syllable sound like O—op! The second syllable indicated the moment of maximum exertion while the first was the time for preparation. Hauling a boat, he noted, was heavier work than rowing, "so the moments of exertion are spaced in longer intervals," and we see, as in the Irish hauling cry Ho-li-ho-hup!, a longer preparation for the final effort.

Until the Second Wave brought in machinery and silenced the songs of the worker, most such synchronization of effort was organic or natural. It flowed from the rhythm of the seasons and from biological processes, from the earth's rotation and the beat of the heart. Second Wave societies, by contrast, moved to the beat of the machine.

As factory production spread, the high cost of machinery and the close interdependence of labor required a much more refined synchronization. If one group of workers in a plant was late in completing a task, others down the line would be further delayed. Thus punctuality, never very important in agricultural communities, became a social necessity, and clocks and watches began to proliferate. By the 1790's they were already becoming commonplace in Britain. Their diffusion came, in the words of British historian E. P. Thompson, "at the exact moment when the industrial revolution demanded a greater synchronization of labor."

Not by coincidence, children in industrial cultures were taught to tell time at an early age. Pupils were conditioned to arrive at school when the bell rang so that later on they would arrive reliably at the factory or office when the whistle blew. Jobs were timed and split into sequences measured in fractions of a second. "Nine-to-five" formed the temporal frame for millions of workers.

Nor was it only working life that was synchronized. In all Second Wave societies, regardless of profit or political considerations, social

---

[1] These four paragraphs are interpolated from *Creating a New Civilization* by Alvin and Heidi Toffler (Turner Publishing, 1995) pp. 19–20.

life, too, became clock-driven and adapted to machine requirements. Certain hours were set aside for leisure. Standard-length vacations, holidays, or coffee breaks were interspersed with the work schedules.

Children began and ended the school year at uniform times. Hospitals woke all their patients for breakfast simultaneously. Transport systems staggered under rush hours. Broadcasters fitted entertainment into special time slots—"prime time," for example. Every business had its own peak hours or seasons, synchronized with those of its suppliers and distributors. Specialists in synchronization arose—from factory expediters and schedulers to traffic police and time-study men.

By contrast, some people resisted the new industrial time system. And here again sexual differences arose. Those who participated in Second Wave work—chiefly men—became the most conditioned to clock-time.

Second Wave husbands continually complained that their wives kept them waiting, that they had no regard for time, that it took them forever to dress, that they were always late for appointments. Women, primarily engaged in noninterdependent housework, worked to less mechanical rhythms. For similar reasons urban populations tended to look down upon rural folk as slow and unreliable. "They don't show up on time! You never know whether they'll keep an appointment." Such complaints could be traced directly to the difference between Second Wave work based on heightened interdependence and the First Wave work centered in the field and the home. . . .

Once the Second Wave became dominant even the most intimate routines of life were locked into the industrial pacing system. In the United States and the Soviet Union, in Singapore and Sweden, in France and Denmark, Germany and Japan, families arose as one, ate at the same time, commuted, worked, returned home, went to bed, slept, and even made love more or less in unison as the entire civilization, in addition to standardization and specialization, applied the principle of synchronization. . . .

It is hardly any wonder that parents—still mainly tied to the industrial-era code book—find themselves in conflict with children who, aware of the growing irrelevance of the old rules, are uncertain, if not blindly ignorant, of the new ones. They and we alike are caught between a dying Second Wave order and the Third Wave civilization of tomorrow. . . .

Second Wave civilization synchronized daily life, tying the rhythms of sleep and wakefulness, of work and play, to the underlying throb of machines. Raised in this civilization, the parents take for granted that work must be synchronized, that everyone must arrive and work at the same time, that rush-hour traffic is unavoidable, that meal times must be fixed, and that children must, at an early age, be indoctrinated with time-consciousness and punctuality. They cannot understand why their offspring seem so annoyingly casual about keeping appointments and why, if the nine-to-five job (or other fixed-schedule job) was good enough in the past, it should suddenly be regarded as intolerable by their children. . . .

The reason is that the Third Wave, as it sweeps in, carries with it a completely different sense of time. If the Second Wave tied life to the tempo of the machine, the Third Wave challenges this mechanical synchronization, alters our most basic social rhythms, and in so doing frees us from the machine. . . .

During Second Wave civilization machines were clumsily synchronized to one another, and people on the assembly line were then synchronized to the machines, with all the many social consequences that flowed from this fact. Today, machine synchronization has reached such exquisitely high levels, and the pace of even the fastest human workers is so ridiculously slow by comparison, that full advantage of the technology can be derived not by coupling workers to the machine but only by decoupling them from it.

Put differently, during Second Wave civilization, machine synchronization shackled the human to the machine's capabilities and imprisoned all of social life in a common frame. It did so in capitalist and socialist societies alike. Now, as machine synchronization grows more precise, humans, instead of being imprisoned, are progressively freed. . . .

In short, as the Third Wave moves in, challenging the old industrial way of doing things, it changes the relationship of the entire civilization to time. The old mechanical synchronization that destroyed so much of the spontaneity and joy of life and virtually symbolized the Second Wave is on its way out. The young people who reject the nine-to-five regime, who are indifferent to classical punctuality, may not understand why they behave as they do. But time itself has changed in the "real world," and along with it we have changed the ground rules that once governed us.

CRITICAL READING

1. Certain aspects of family life, work life, entertainment, and education are rooted in the demands of the factory-dominated past. Explain how the knowledge of this background can be liberating for people today.

2. Why did the young Toffler find his **encounter** with "the heart-land of the world" so strange and exotic—such an **eye-opener,** in other words?

3. Toffler found the words of the woman who had been mangled by the machine so deeply shocking that he vividly remembered them 15 years later. Trace the line of significance that probably exists in the author's mind between her reaction and the generational conflict that he hints at when he says, "It is hardly any wonder that parents—still mainly tied to the industrial-era code book—find themselves in conflict with children who [are] aware of the growing irrelevance of the old rules. . . ." How might today's victim of such an industrial accident react?

4. Give examples of how the increased speed and precision of Third-Wave machines free workers.

DISCUSSION QUESTIONS

1. In their book *Creating a New Civilization,* Alvin and Heidi Toffler give a brief guide for sorting out the things that are happening around us to see which are dead-end Second Wave projects and which initiatives point to the Third Wave future. Here is one of their rules of thumb:

> The factory became the central symbol of industrial society. It became, in fact, a model for most other Second Wave institutions. Yet the factory as we have known it is fading into the past. Factories embody such principles as standardization, centralization, maximization, concentration and bureaucratization. Third Wave production is post-factory production based on new principles. It occurs in facilities that bear little resemblance to factories. In fact, an increasing amount is done in homes and offices, cars and planes.

> The easiest and quickest way to spot a Second Wave proposal, whether in Congress or in a corporation, is to see whether it is still, consciously or not, based on the factory model.

> America's schools, for example, still operate like factories. They subject the raw material (children) to standardized instruction and routine inspection. An important question to ask of any proposed educational innovation is simply this: is it intended to make the factory run more efficiently, or is it

designed, as it should be, to get rid of the factory model altogether and replace it with individualized, customized education? A similar question could be asked of health legislation,
welfare legislation and of every proposal to reorganize the
federal bureaucracy. America needs new institutions built
on post-bureaucratic, post-factory models.

If a proposal merely seeks to improve factory-style operations or to create a new factory, it may be a lot of things. The
one thing it is not is Third Wave.

Apply this rule to aspects of your home, work, school, interper-
sonal relations, entertainment. Where do you see elements of
Second-Wave and Third-Wave patterns?

2.   Although this is a small selection from a large book rather than a
single unit column or essay, I found it interesting that this futurol-
ogist chose to open one of his central chapters with the **encounter**
that you see at the beginning of this selection. It is, of course,
simultaneously personal **background** about himself. Compare
that way of beginning with the following strictly **background**-
modality opening of another chapter from the book:

Three hundred years ago, give or take a half-century, an
explosion was heard that sent concussive shock waves racing
across the earth, demolishing ancient societies and creating a
wholly new civilization. This explosion was, of course, the
industrial revolution. And the giant tidal force it set loose on
the world—the Second Wave—collided with all the institutions of the past and changed the way of life of millions.

Which do you think makes the better opening? Why?

3.   In growing up did you ever experience an elementary or high
school with Third Wave characteristics? If so, describe them and
explain their unique characteristics. If not, imagine what such a
school might be like.

INVITATION TO A READING

Misjudging differing background needs can be, as we have seen,
expensive in business, but in human relations it is often anguishing.
In a society as pluralistic as ours, a miscalculation of the need for
articulating cultural background can easily result in disputes, disaf-
fection, or divorce.

When, in the eighteenth century, Samuel Johnson determined to stop the centrifugal breaking apart of this polyglot English language of ours by writing the first comprehensive dictionary, he faced a tough choice: Should the spellings he was going to establish follow sound or follow history? He chose history. And generations of school kids—if they knew who was to blame—would probably make of Johnson's name a hissing and a byword for condemning them to years of learning spelling demons.

But Johnson was trying to build into the heart of our common culture the recognition that its strength is in its diversity. English started off as the forcible union of two complete languages, the Germanic language of Hägar the Horrible and his crew of Anglo Saxons and the French of William the Conqueror. This openness to foreign influence paved the way for the founders of modern science to lard the language with technical terms made up from ancient Latin and Greek words and for the Brits of the sun-never-sets-on-it empire to bring back words like *shampoo* from India and *gnu* from southern Africa. (That *g,* by the way, represents a unique clicking sound that is part of the language of the Bushmen in the area where the animal is found.)

E pluribus unum proclaims this nation's motto on every coin of the realm. And this background of one culture from many cultures is the unique strength of Western civilization. "The mongrel civilization par excellence" is what Jacques Barzun calls Western civilization in his lively and compendious history *From Dawn to Decadence.* Even the rebelliousness of those who want to reject parts of it is a prized element of a tradition that goes back to the diverse nonconformist martyrdoms of Socrates and Jesus. Religions from the Middle East; geometry and early medical investigation from Egypt; an alphabet from the Etruscans; a number system and spices from India by way of the Arabs; democracy, art, and early science from Greece; engineering and law from ancient Rome; gunpowder and tea from China; popular music from sub-Saharan Africa; and coffee (thank you very much) from Ethiopia, again by way of Arabia. *Diversity* is a current catchword for a value that has continued to drive Western culture profitably past the parochialism and bigotry of individuals and groups for 2500 years.

We are all painfully aware, though, that the assimilation of ideas and customs from outside the culture, however beneficial to the society as a whole, often carries a price, paid by the individuals through whom the change comes. Marriage across traditional ethnic cultures is the ultimate end of assimilation. When that gulf is widened by differing religious or racial backgrounds, the price can be that much higher. But when the amalgamation of background is made to work, it can initiate a small renaissance—a rebirth of the energy that originally informed those cultures. The result may not be that of a melting pot, as the older image of diversity had it, leveling the differences into an indistinguishable mass, but a powerful transmutation—an alchemist's alembic, creating new gold out of the old dross.

The following column shows some of the ironic twisting that may occur from such chemistry.

She Converted and Now Wants to Be a Rabbi. He's a Jew Who Wants to Sleep Late on Saturdays.
by David Brooks

I can't say I wasn't warned. For centuries the Jewish sages have been admonishing their young men not to marry outside the faith. But I've never paid much attention to their teaching, and 11 years ago I married a Unitarian. Two years after that I got my just deserts; my wife converted to Judaism. Really converted. Now she is studying in hopes of becoming a rabbi. This just shows you God must exist. Only he would go to such extraordinary lengths to get me dragged to synagogue on Saturday mornings. But it also makes my family something of a case study. America is a country divided between the secular and the devout, and suddenly the frictions between the two are replicated right in my own home.

My wife and I are perpetually negotiating the level of our family's religious observance. My idea that the kids would enjoy having a Christmas tree was among the first notions to go. Then pork products were banished from the house. Every few weeks my wife will suggest another step toward full observance, and what is striking at these moments is how weak the arguments are on my secular side. Her faith is a resolute force, my secularism is a marshmallowy object.

It wasn't always this way. For most of the past two centuries the secularists have been the assertive and ascendant ones. The French revolutionaries dismissed religion as mere superstition that clouds the mind. The Marxists saw it as the opiate of the people. These people would have had a hundred reasons to give my wife on why we shouldn't allow religious ritual to spread in our home. But today their antireligious claims seem vainglorious. The armies of progress set up a series of secular creeds—socialism, Freudianism, rationalism, New Ageism—that promised to pierce the mysteries of life. All of them now lie in ruins. We secularists are suffering a crisis of confidence while the ranks of the religiously devout unexpectedly increase. For the first time in 200 years, the number of Orthodox Jews is growing.

Secularists used to scoff at people who in the age of scientific progress needed the religious "crutch." But even secularism is now infused with spiritualism, albeit of a cloudy sort. You can't fall down in a bookstore these days without bumping your head on a book with the word "soul" in the title. A trip to the mall has suddenly become a spiritual StairMaster session: by selecting the right organic coffee, the Shaker-inspired cabinet and the environmentally attuned cosmetic, we firm up our metaphysical selves. Whenever I eat some Rain Forest Crunch I realize my ice cream has a cleaner conscience than I do.

Baby-boomer spiritualism is always aflight, never settling anywhere. Too often, it is a sentimental vagueness that never requires something of a person he wouldn't want to do anyway, that sidesteps the really tough issues, like death and evil. With this sort of spiritualism of the great-hearted self, nonobservant America acknowledged the reality of the transcendent realm. We're playing on organized religion's turf. But our well-meaning intuitions are really no match when confronted with an organized religion that places God outside the self, that has a complex and authoritative theology, that makes demands. My wife comes at me with the Torah and the long tradition of Jewish law admonishing us not to shop on the Sabbath. What am I supposed to say, that as long as I buy only natural fibers our souls will remain pristine?

The one vibrant secular creed is the creed of diversity. The ideal today is that we should lead our lives amid diverse cultures and people. But religious observance inevitably involves some sectarianism. In order to get away from the vulgarity of popular culture, millions of evangelical Christians have constructed their own separate culture. The Jewish school we send our kids to is aggressively antiracist, but it is not diverse. The strongest argument against organized religion is that it limits you; many Jews gave up religious observance precisely so they could integrate with the American mainstream.

For the devout, diversity and pluralism may be important, but other things are more important. One of them is fulfilling the covenant with God, obeying the injunction in Deuteronomy to diligently pass the covenant on to the children. And you can't do that if Judaism is reduced to a smorgasbord helping as part of some multicultural approach to life. To explore in depth you have to sacrifice breadth. To build community you have to accept boundaries.

Some writers believe that America is experiencing another Great Awakening. If so, we may be in for more religion than anyone now predicts. Religion is certainly playing a bigger role in my home than I ever would have expected, and so far I can't say it's for the worse. Anyway I'm looking on the bright side. If my son grows up and marries a shiksa, I hope at least he marries one who wants to be a rabbi.

CRITICAL READING

1. Describe all the eye-opening ironies you can find in the first paragraph.
2. Writers sometimes sense that what they find surprising may not seem so immediately to others. So they often explain **why** something is surprising before moving to **explain** the surprise. What surprise in the second paragraph does David Brooks feel called on to illuminate?
3. Brooks is writing for a well-educated audience and freely makes use of allusions to Western intellectual history that he expects all readers to recognize. If these references are new or fuzzy to you, here is a chance to bone up on some **background** information that will make some of your later courses in college more **significant.** Do whatever research you need to answer these questions.
   (a) Who were the leading philosophers of the French Revolution? Outline some of their major beliefs.
   (b) What were the major beliefs of Karl Marx? Why did he see religion as a political threat to his views?
   (c) When and what was the Great Awakening?
4. Explain the point Brooks is making humorously with his trips to the bookstore and the mall and eating cereal.
5. What do you think Mrs. Brooks hopes to accomplish for their children by establishing in their consciousness a **background** of rules and rites of Judaism? Has this new background had an effect on Brooks also? Explain.
6. Give examples of the vibrant "creed of diversity" as it is practiced today.

DISCUSSION QUESTIONS

1. Do you agree that Freudianism, socialism, rationalism, and New-Ageism all lie in ruins? Again, do whatever research you need to gain sufficient background for this question. Give some evidence

for your opinion or describe where and how you might find evidence. It's OK to split research on this topic into teams.

2. Reconstruct some of the reasons the French revolutionaries and Marxists might have given Brooks's wife for not letting religion into her home.

3. Do you agree that secular spiritualism as seen in today's culture is centered in the self? Give examples either way.

DEMONSTRATION: BACKGROUND MAP FOR "SHE CONVERTED"

Figure 7.4 is a very sketchy background map of the intellectual-spiritual issues in Western thought over the last 400 years, showing roughly where Brooks's allusions fit in as the pendulum has swung between the devout and the secular. Now that you have researched some of these people and names, locate their territories on this map and try to get a feel for why people living their lives out against the background of one set of beliefs and traditions might have felt the need to change in a different direction.

I do not pretend that this map has scholarly exactitude; it is based only on my own long-ago courses in philosophy, psychology, art, music, and literature, added to by scattered reading since. But as such it represents a common educated view that, in broad outlines, Brooks expects his readers share with him.

Of course, I was educated before "The Great Disruption" started in about 1960. This phenomenon, which Professor Francis Fukuyama, like Toffler, identifies as a seismic change caused by the transition from the industrial age to the information age, liberated women from home-bondage, sex from reproductive function, and students from standard curricular requirements. In the Universities, by 1987 the issue of whether the common historical culture of ideas (a part of which I diagrammed in Figure 7.4) was worth trying to salvage came to a head. In that year Alan Bloom published *The Closing of the American Mind*, decrying the loss of that culture, and E. D. Hirsch published *Cultural Literacy: What Every American Needs to Know*, showing what would be needed to carry it on. Arrayed against Bloom and Hirsch in the universities—possibly part of the Great Disruption—were the women's movement and the multicultural movement, which saw the Western canon of shared culture as unduly dominated by "dead white males."

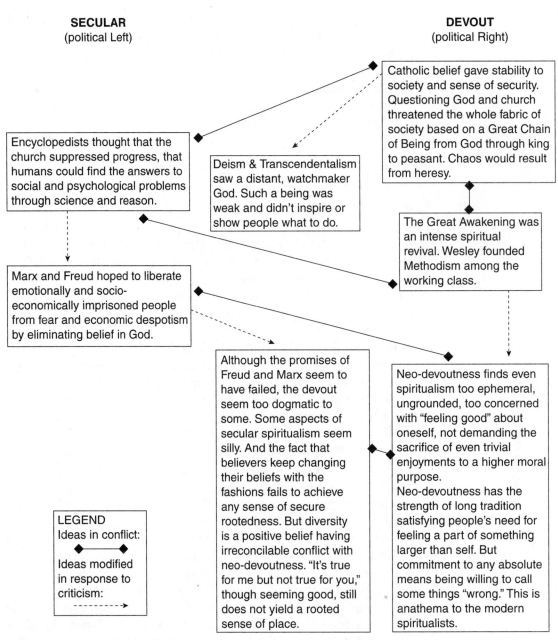

SECULAR
(political Left)

DEVOUT
(political Right)

Catholic belief gave stability to society and sense of security. Questioning God and church threatened the whole fabric of society based on a Great Chain of Being from God through king to peasant. Chaos would result from heresy.

Encyclopedists thought that the church suppressed progress, that humans could find the answers to social and psychological problems through science and reason.

Deism & Transcendentalism saw a distant, watchmaker God. Such a being was weak and didn't inspire or show people what to do.

The Great Awakening was an intense spiritual revival. Wesley founded Methodism among the working class.

Marx and Freud hoped to liberate emotionally and socio-economically imprisoned people from fear and economic despotism by eliminating belief in God.

Although the promises of Freud and Marx seem to have failed, the devout seem too dogmatic to some. Some aspects of secular spiritualism seem silly. And the fact that believers keep changing their beliefs with the fashions fails to achieve any sense of secure rootedness. But diversity is a positive belief having irreconcilable conflict with neo-devoutness. "It's true for me but not true for you," though seeming good, still does not yield a rooted sense of place.

Neo-devoutness finds even spiritualism too ephemeral, ungrounded, too concerned with "feeling good" about oneself, not demanding the sacrifice of even trivial enjoyments to a higher moral purpose.
Neo-devoutness has the strength of long tradition satisfying people's need for feeling a part of something larger than self. But commitment to any absolute means being willing to call some things "wrong." This is anathema to the modern spiritualists.

LEGEND
Ideas in conflict:

Ideas modified in response to criticism:

Figure 7.4. Movement and Countermovement in Western Thought.

Writing in the year 2000, J. Bottum notes:

> Hirsch's mistake lay in forgetting that the old cultural knowledge was not meaningful because it was shared; it was shared because it was meaningful. It all fit into a frame, a generally accepted public system of belief about the way God and history and the world work. And when that frame at last broke, the old knowledge drifted out of public awareness, like the carefully organized contents of filing cabinets dumped in a pile and left to blow away sheet by sheet.

Because we all feel a strong need for a shared culture, what has rushed in to fill the gap, Bottum goes on to say, is thousands of well-known lines from songs, movies, and commercials.

In a time of such rapidly changing value systems it becomes more difficult, and hence more important, to judge accurately the extent and the kind of background needed by your intended audience.

WRITING COMMISSION:
INTERVIEWING FOR CULTURAL DIVERSITY

In my comments on writing **resolutions** I mentioned that the-lady-or-the-tiger ending was a cop-out. But I also noted the attraction of that ending because of today's "what-**ev-**er" approach to differences that arise from people's differing cultural backgrounds.

Find a partner in the class who has some significant cultural differences from you. These do not have to be racial or ethnic—they can be age (teen/young adult/middle/elderly); musical (classical/popular); entertainment (theater/sports); economic (wealthy/struggling); regional (southern/east-coastal/west-coastal/midwestern/western); setting (rural/urban/suburban/town). These differences are going to be the basis for this writing commission.

Again in your role as intern for a newspaper, imagine that there is going to be a national convention of student government leaders here. Your editor decides that this is a ready-made opportunity for you interns. Who could better cover a convention of college students than other college students?

Because "diversity" is a hot item these days (and sure to have come up in discussions by any student government), your editor wants to use the problem of diversity versus community as the slant for the paper's issue covering the convention. Therefore, each of you is to write up an interview with another student, digging for experiences that involve a difference of cultural backgrounds, either constructive or destructive, lighthearted or serious, cosmic or personal. For this, one of you will role-play the paper's intern while the other plays the part of a delegate to the convention from some other part of the country.

"There's an issue out there that I'd like to shape this edition around," says your editor. "The issue is: How do we find community in diversity? Or is that important? Is it better to find community within 'your own kind'? When you do your interview, be a reporter. Don't stop with superficial answers. Probe for contradictions."

"Can we use our own experiences as a kind of sounding board to highlight significant issues?" someone asks.

"Sure, but find a common theme to skewer them into a single column."

Exploring the Topic: Mapping Issues

"Where does the Republican Party stand on the issue of racism?" was essentially the question asked of Jack Kemp in one of the vice presidential debates in 1996. It was a tough question because in the battle for the hearts and minds of African American voters, the Democrats (i.e., liberals) are perceived as holding the high ground. Whatever Kemp might say about racism would be seen by his hearers against the premapped background of American race politics. Kemp knew that if he were to win any points in this debate, he would have to fight from a different location on the battlefield, where the lines of the issue were not fixed to his disadvantage. He had, in other words, to change the mental issue map that his audience carried in their heads.

As a writer it is clear enough that you must fill your audience in on background they are unfamiliar with. But where we are dealing with issues, the audience usually has quite a bit of background information. It then becomes crucial to repaint the background for your readers so that your experience and ideas will not be distorted by their preconceived perception of how the land lies. As Matthew Miller tells us in the epigraph at the beginning of this chapter, old arguments need "fresh ways of framing the issues" if the usual gridlock of discussion is to be transcended.

Jack Kemp shifted the question from race to economics. The welfare system, he said, was really a socialist dependency state operating as a separate economic system within big cities. He proposed giving economic support to business ventures in the inner cities so as to provide jobs for those residents (understood to be mostly African American and Hispanic). By thus shifting the issue map, he was able to make affirmative action and welfare—the usual Democratic answers to the problem of racism—look like programs that were really holding back the people they were designed to help.

If we are fully to understand an issue, we must understand other viewpoints—even those we violently disagree with—so well that we could argue **for** them. There is probably no more important principle of persuasive rhetoric than this: to persuade people you must show you understand both their emotional and intellectual **background.** This principle was the cornerstone of the highly successful client-centered counseling pioneered by psychologist Carl Rogers. A confrontational stance on an issue is fun and even has a function in boosting the morale of true-blue believers, but it will certainly stiffen the opposition rather than soften it and is likely to knock fence-sitters off into the other camp's compound.

Giving careful attention to how to draw the **background issue map** requires considerable **reasoning** on the author's part. But it forms the board on which the rest of the game is going to be played, so it is effort well spent when writing on a controversial topic. To produce an effective **issue map,** you must have or get sufficient **background** on the issue so that you could act as a lawyer even for the people who obstinately disagree with you.

You may need to get some of that background by re**search.** But much of it can be supplied by just using your imagination to put yourself in other people's situations. Consider the issue of whether young mothers should go out of the home to work. You may already have strong feelings about this, and you may feel, at first blush, that there are only two sides to the issue. But there are many subissues and crosscurrents in this vexed question. A good exercise to get yourself aware of the complex **map** of such an **issue** might be to visualize a talk show on the topic and try to imagine a motley collection of people kicking this ball around, sometimes into each others' teeth.

DISCUSSION: MAPPING AN ISSUE

I'm going to pick a controversial topic and let you, with your class-mates, try mapping it by enacting a talk show with your instructor as whichever host she or he would like to play.

The issue you are to map is: **Should mothers with young children stay home with them rather than work outside the home?**

Obviously the issue is complex, involving a number of subtopics, each of which is itself controversial. These subtopics are like the regions of a war zone, each with its own particular firefight that must be accommodated in the battle plan of the entire issue. Only against that total map can we assess the **significance** of individual contentions about this **issue**.

I am going to list five of these subissues. To prepare yourself for participating in the talk show, please fill in this outline with as many arguments as you can, both pro and con (that is, for **and** against mothers working when they have young children), for each one. Then meet with a small group of your classmates and compile as detailed a map as you can of all the possible arguments for each subissue.

1. Money
2. Proper care
3. Morals and supervision
4. Bonding—emotional attachment
5. Parental roles

You can also add a category or maybe two if you think those I gave don't cover the ground. But be careful not to divide the map too finely. What we want, if we are organizing an issue map in an essay, are categories broad enough to make clear the significance of particular statements in the context of the whole topic.

Now let the games begin! Have about a half-dozen volunteers form a panel with the rest of the class acting as a participatory audience, moderated by the Magister(tra) Ludi, your instructor. Each of the panelists should either have or create the background of a particular persona with appropriate views on this topic. For example, one student might imagine that she was running a day care center in her home. Another might role-play someone who has been raised by a mother on welfare. Another might have had a full-time mother and felt that she had saved him from gang influence. Still another might put himself in the position of a father who is working three jobs to support his wife and children. And, of course, one might be a young single mother struggling to survive, while another might be a mother who, although married to a husband with a high income, feels that she is not realizing her full potential staying at home 24/7.

However sensational most talk shows may be, the image of the talk show is a good one for us to keep in mind as we writers try to visualize the diversity of our audience. It forces us to become aware of how and why our views may surprise others. I once watched a talk show provocatively titled "Take That Job and Shove It," during which the participants came up with an amazing 32 different positions on this issue of whether mothers with young children should take jobs outside the home.

You may find in going all out to present your views in a talk show free-for-all that you are acting like a field commander who may take a particular hill with brilliant tactics but then be surrounded and captured by an opposing general who has full understanding of the deployment of all the forces in the battle. Having clever arguments and whole armories of facts is not enough to convince people who don't agree with you. You must grasp not only their positions but the entire dynamic of forces struggling over the entire terrain of the issue in order to convince them of the weakness of the particular ridge that they are holding.

The fact that there can be 32 different points of view expressed on the same topic is an excellent illustration of how many opposing fronts there can be on a map of the entire war of a major issue. Talk shows are revealing about how views that seem triumphantly self-evident to one person are diminished in **significance** to another who is operating from an equally small map of a different part of the field.

If you made a tape of your class's talk show, you might go back and review the variety of arguments made by the participants. See if you can fit them into the five categories I outlined at the beginning of this "Discussion." If not, what other categories need to be added? Once you have done this, you should be a veritable Napoleon of the young-mothers-working-issue terrain.

I have been describing writing on a controversial topic as a battle, and it sometimes is. But the best salesperson is not the high-pressure, sell-you-the-product-whether-it's-what-you-need-or-not type but the type who carefully listens to your needs and tries to find a solution to your problem using, if possible, one of his or her products. So the best writer on a controversial subject is the one who tries to help the reader to a better understanding of the issue map and, if possible, to get the disagreeing reader to change somewhat. Your map of the issue will be a help to any reader, creating, through careful reasoning, a background against which the reader can better define her or his own views.

WRITING COMMISSION: WORKING MOTHERS

Now it is time to put all you have learned about this topic into practice by writing an entire piece that primarily lays out the background map of this complex issue of working mothers. Although the **background** will be the most important modality of this essay, the backbone of **encounter, explanation,** and **resolution** are still needed, as in any piece of writing. And **surprise** and **significance** must provide the ever necessary dynamic to drive your reader through the piece. So begin with a personal encounter, if you have a relevant one, and dramatize the surprise. If in your case you think a personal experience is not the best opener, find some other **eye-opener** to launch it. Then do your darndest to draw an **issue map** that will show to all your classmates the relative **significance** of their particular concerns against the **background** of our current culture.

If you can come up with a brilliant new perspective on this issue—wonderful! You should think about publishing your work! But at least show how your issue map provides an **explanation** for your opening and for others' problems in the area of working moms. In this kind of essay, the clear drawing of the issue boundaries is the main reader benefit. But you will not want to leave it without your own imprint—a suggested **attitude** or **program** as a **resolution.**

Points to Remember

- ✹ Don't start with **background.** Fill in specific background as necessary after the reader becomes aware of a need for it.
- ✹ Acquiring background knowledge is a lifelong process. The more you have, the more people you can relate to.
- ✹ On the subject of your writing, you must either have or get more background knowledge than your readers; then you can judge how much and what kind they will need.
- ✹ As a writer you must fight against the natural tendency of background to sound encyclopedic (i.e., boring). This means using creative rhetorical tricks to enliven paragraphs written in **background** modality.
- ✹ Readers who have considerable background knowledge are delighted by writers who make allusions to that knowledge—specific, detailed Trivial Pursuit–type references that only someone with the requisite background knowledge would understand.

Recognizing allusions gives the reader a satisfying sense of being an insider—a member of a valuable community.

ᒫ Because one of the pleasures of reading nonfiction is the sense of shared background with the author, as a writer, you must be careful not to insult your readers by assuming they need background that, in fact, they already know.

ᒫ Any topic that has a history of disagreement benefits from a sympathetic laying out of all sides of the issues.

ᒫ A writer cannot hope to persuade readers without demonstrating a full and sympathetic understanding of their various points of view.

ᒫ Issue mapping allows a writer the opportunity to break out of the gridlock of former arguments on a tired topic by remapping it from a new perspective and perhaps reaching a resolution that conflicting parties can unite in.

ᒫ In workplace writing, or other communication with a practical purpose, it is first crucial to fully understand the **background** of the communication as a social situation—what purpose brings you and the reader together and what the reader needs or expects to get from your communication.

ᒫ When you have a constrained audience that has to understand your communication, it is even more important to be able imaginatively to stand in the readers' background and visualize how your approach will look to them. You need consciously to adjust the **background** in your communication to bridge the gap between your power or expertise and theirs.

ᒫ Each person's personal map of his or her cultural background is built up piece by piece, largely through academic and journalistic reading. It is these maps that enable us to make coherent sense out of the cultural experiences we have—hearing family or "tribal" stories, reading literature or original science, listening to music, looking at images, traveling. Most of the writing you are doing for this course has a cultural context. Your readers will understand and appreciate you more if you sketch your view of that cultural map and show how your experience helps fill in some blank spaces or change or confirm some cultural boundaries.

E-E-R

Encounter

Explain

Resolve

R-S-V-B

Reason

Search

Value

Background

8
Reasoning

Imagination abandoned by Reason produces impossible monsters; united with her, she is the mother of the arts and the source of their wonders.

—Francisco de Goya,
text for an engraving in his satirical collection *Los Caprichos*

Opening the Topic:
Reasoning—Flowcharting the Ideas

Encounters by themselves cannot explain why they happened. Suppose I suddenly have sores in my mouth. Is it an STD or not? Is it herpes or canker sores? Is it thrush or chlamydia? Was it caused by something I did or by too many antibiotics or by a depressed immune system? Could it be AIDS? Laboratory tests are not conclusive.

We depend on the reasoning of doctors, but the fact that they often disagree demonstrates that the facts do not speak for themselves. Doctors can run through diagnostic if-then programs that are, in fact, just like branching computer flowcharts. Does your throat hurt all the time or just when you swallow? If just when you swallow, the diagnosis is shunted down one branch of the program. There the next question is, Do you cough? If you cough, do you cough up mucus? If you do, then is it clear? And so on until the program gets to the root of the tree and resolves that your problem is an allergy.

But each doctor is going from her or his gestalt picture of me—my age, my lifestyle, my medical history, the aura I present of mental and physical health. All these are plugged into that practitioner's mental computer to be compared with a data base of memorized facts

201

and directly experienced encounters. I wait anxiously for the explanation of first this doctor, then that one. And when they disagree, I am left with my own reasoning from which I must make my resolutions about how to proceed with my life.

Depending on the explanation of the mechanism of these sores, they might punctuate my life's previous equilibrium and force it into a whole new pattern. Or maybe their ambiguity will permit me to proceed as before, with only incremental modifications of my behavior. I had better use well all the powers of careful reasoning that I have learned, hadn't I?

In chapter 6, to demonstrate the importance of **background,** we looked at the optical illusion of the leaning man to see how tilting the background fools the mind into thinking that a vertical man is leaning. The mind's tendency to complete patterns from whatever information is available gives rise to another set of illusions like the one in Figure 8.2. Whether you first see a woman's face or a sax player may depend on your mind-set.

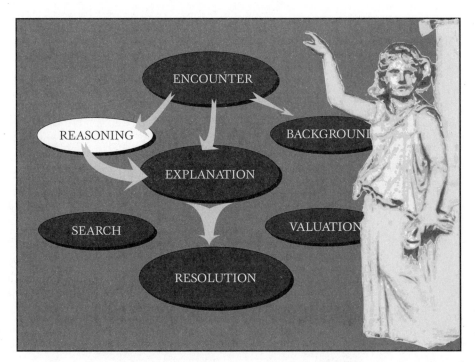

Figure 8.1. Careful **reasoning** about the **encounter** produces a mental extension guiding the reader toward **explanation** and, finally, **resolution.**

Figure 8.2. What do you see?

The mind does similar things with ideas, filling in the blanks to make a complete picture in order to grasp the significance of sketchy information.[1] But in doing so, the brain tends to create the picture it wants to see and may ignore other pictures that explain the incomplete facts equally well. So each doctor in my previous example puts the facts of a few tests into a pattern that seems to fit the overall pattern of behavior and past health history. It is the same mechanism that allows us to spot a friend, even at a distance, in a crowd of people, even when we catch only a glimpse from the side. Of course, if it's a very close friend whom we are hoping against hope will unexpectedly be in the crowd, our overzealous, illusion-making brain may pick a total stranger with embarrassing results. So this compulsion of the brain sometimes enhances and sometimes interferes with communication.

Again, if we are trying to converse in a noisy restaurant, we count on the brain's ability to fill in the blanks when every fourth or fifth word gets drowned out. We all know the feeling of tight friendship that comes from someone's being able to complete our thoughts correctly before we finish speaking. Of course, we all know the opposite feeling of anger when someone verbally tries to follow out our thought and gets it wrong.

[1] This phenomenon is studied thoroughly in Gestalt psychology.

"Do you know what this check number 2201 was for and how much?" I ask my wife.

She responds, "When was it? You know we've had a lot of expenses this month and they certainly weren't for me!"

She gets angry assuming that I was thinking "Why are you spending so much money?" whereas I was really just trying to figure out how much we had left in the bank. Then I get angry because she hasn't given me the information I need.

Or, I say to my wife, "The rehearsal of our musical group is going to run pretty late tonight."

She replies, "Go ahead; have a good time. I'll probably be in bed when you get back."

I get angry and come back with, "Oh, come on. Don't start up with that again," assuming that she is responding with jealousy of the time I spend (and perhaps the personnel I meet) at these rehearsals. Then she gets angry because actually she was just trying to release me from any sense of guilt at spending a night out without her.

Think of some specific conversations you have had or heard where you have talked at cross purposes with someone else. If they are not too personal, describe one of them to the class.

For all the potential dangers of extending cantilevers of **reasoning** over a gaping abyss of the unknown, the ability of our minds to do so is the foundation of science and technology. Deciding whether you see a sax player or a face in Figure 8.2 is a subconscious function of the brain. But the conscious mind has an analogous extension— logic—by which it can build bridges from discovery to scientific theory.

Logic works basically because the brain slams the door on ambiguous ideas. That picture must be either a woman's face or a sax player. It can't be both or something in-between. By proceeding by strict on-or-off logic, science and technology have achieved their astounding successes. As a result, critical readers demand this kind of thought precision. The widespread use of computers has trained us in the discipline of rigorous logic. Because computers have no human automatic picture-completion program, they do only and exactly what you instruct them to do. If your instructions are even minutely imperfect, you will not get the result you anticipate.

Trying a little programming logic will help make clear how necessary it is to scrutinize each step of the thought process if one is to carry the reader convincingly beyond the immediate **encounter** to a dependable **resolution** through **reasoning**.

The basic tools of computer programming are (1) getting needed information, (2) making choices on the basis of that information, (3) processing the information through searches and repetitive loops, and (4) outputting resulting information.

Programs are often mapped by flowcharts that show the order and direction of these steps using conventional symbols, the most important of which are identified in the flowchart in Figure 8.3. This flowchart is designed to total all the checks someone has written in any specified category, such as "books," "rent," "movies," or "food." It assumes that the user has a file of checks recorded by number,

Use of shapes

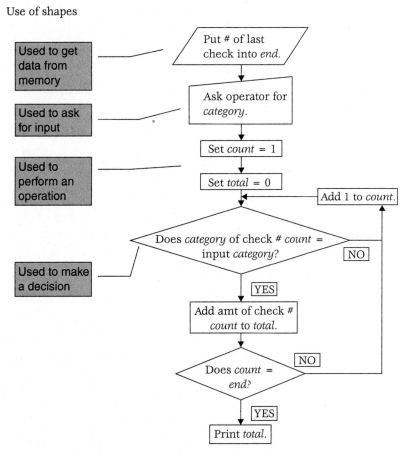

Figure 8.3. Flowchart to total checks in a specified category.

amount, and category. The program then asks the user to specify the category she or he wants to total and prints out the result. The flow-chart shows each step a computer would have to be instructed to perform to do this.

CRITICAL READING

1. What would happen if we left out the step "Add 1 to *count*"?
2. What would happen if we left out the step "Set *total* to 0"?
3. What would happen if we left out the decision step "Does *category* of check # *count* = input *category*?"
4. What would happen if we left out the decision step "Does *count* = end?
5. There is a bug in this program. Sometimes it will work, sometimes it will go into an endless loop and the computer will freeze. Can you find the bug? How would you fix it?

Again meet in small teams. Each team can draw a flowchart for the following situation.

Photos can now be delivered to you via e-mail with one file containing a whole roll of 24 pictures. Write a program to view a roll of these pictures in this way: ·

Have the program go through the roll in order. When the file name for each picture comes up, give the viewer the option of (1) looking at it on the screen, (2) printing it directly without viewing, or (3) skipping it. If the viewer decides to view it on the screen, give her or him the options of (1) going to the next file name, (2) printing it, (3) erasing it to save disk space.

Once all the groups have made their flowcharts, display or copy them for the whole class to critique. If there are differences, decide which programs would work. If two different programs would both work, which would work better?

INVITATION TO A READING

An on-or-off question that has tantalized and exasperated people for at least the last 150 years is the question why plants and animals come in discrete species.

Why, for example, do we have just dogs and cats? Why not dags or cogs or dats?

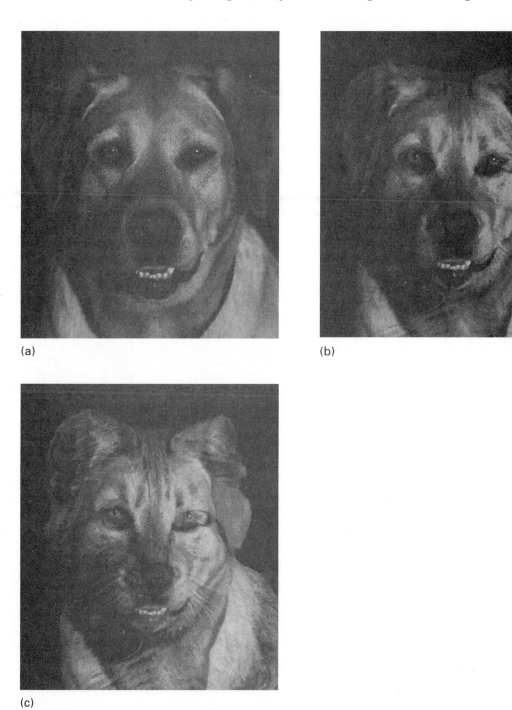

(a)

(b)

(c)

Figure 8.4.

(d)   (e)

Figure 8.4. (Continued)

I'm sure you remember Aristotle from my discussion of rhetoric in my personal note at the beginning of this book. As he followed his pupil Alexander the Great on the latter's conquests, he sent many strange animals back to Greece. When he got back to study them, he noticed that he could classify them according to similarities and differences, thus inventing the whole idea of genus and species that we still use. But he had gotten the idea of breaks between species from his teacher, Plato. In his writings, Plato, famous for his ability to expose inconsistencies in people's reasoning, portrays his teacher, Socrates, reducing students' casual arguments to rubble. If we could get in a time machine and confront Plato with our particular question of species formation, he might say, "Listen. Everybody knows what a dog should look like and what a cat should look like. The fact is that we see many different kinds of cats but still have only one basic picture of 'cat.' That proves that somewhere, in a universe only our minds can perceive, there is a changeless and perfect cat-idea. And for the same reason, there is a changeless and perfect dog-idea. The dogs and cats of this very imperfect and constantly changing world—the ones we can see and smell—are produced from these eternal patterns. But they come out weird, just as, when you try to mold your ideal cat in clay, the clay seems to resist and you come out with something different than you pictured—maybe one of those 'cags' you showed me. By experience we learn to recognize an animal as a cat or a dog even when it varies from our ideal picture. But we know," Plato continues, "that those fake morphed pictures that you stuck in between the dog and the cat are neither fish nor fowl, as it were. There cannot possibly be dags or cogs or what have you, because, if there were, we would perceive the idea of them with our minds."

"OK, Mr. Plato," you respond, "but why do we have just the animals we have and not a plethora of others like these (see Figure 8.5)?

(a)

Figure 8.5.

(b)   (c)

Figure 8.5. (Continued)

"Mr. Lucas could imagine these freaks vividly enough to put them into his movie *Star Wars;* why shouldn't nature produce them?"

"Did they have names?" responds Plato.

"Well, not that I know of in the movie," you are forced to admit.

"And even if your Mr. Lucas gave them imaginary names, those names are not recognized by others, so they cannot be true idea forms. Furthermore, just to show you the power of those forms, if you look closely, you can name them yourself. They're not really that different—just an exaggerated snake, elephant, and pig. So you see, even your creative movie maker cannot imagine animals without looking with his mind at that eternal zoo of fixed forms!"

Plato's idea was that the bewildering variety of individuals that we see can be reduced to a few permanent types. This sat well with the Biblical version of the creation of animals, which said that a fixed number of species were created by God and named by Adam.

In the nineteenth century, as scientists dug through earlier and earlier layers of fossil-rich rock, they again began to make some headway on the problem of where species come from. It became clear to most paleontologists that species have evolved over time from simpler to more complex forms. We are so in the habit of thinking that Darwinism is the only pattern that explains evolution that it is hard to realize that creative scientists could and did come up with pictures quite different from Darwin's that seemed equally plausible at the time.

One theory proposed that all the animal forms had existed **potentially** from the beginning, either in nature or the mind of the Creator, and came into being over time as conditions became favorable.

Plato would have been proud!

Another picture was that each species evolved into a higher one—moved up the ladder, as it were—while new simple species continued to form from the muck at the bottom to occupy the niches left by the evolved forms' climb to the next rung. It was thought that simple species were created by "spontaneous generation" out of decaying organic material.

Isn't the mind wonderful? It just keeps on spinning out those bridges!

What was lacking in these explanations was a description of the mechanism for any new evolving species. Darwin is now famous because he found a mechanism. He saw that random variations might produce features in individuals that would improve their chances to survive, mate, and pass those new features on to their offspring. Over a long time, those variations might lead so far from the original ancestors that a boundary would be crossed and a new species would have evolved. This view of gradual change was opposed by those who saw sudden breaks in the fossil record, with tons of trilobites in one layer of rock and none in the next, a few inches above it. To their mind, the only explanation that logically meshed with those observations was a catastrophist view: something big, bad, and sudden must have happened to the earth—worldwide volcanic eruptions, collision with an asteroid—that made the environment hostile to trilobites.

It took Darwin's gradualist theory almost a century to tip the balance against the catastrophists. One reason was that the catastrophist view seemed to fit better the Biblical creation idea that God suddenly created new species. At the same time, gradualists covered up large flaws in Darwin's theory because they did not want to give aid and comfort to what they saw as the superstitions of religious belief.

So, as long as ambiguity remains, even scientists are capable of bridging the missing pieces in such a way as to create the picture they want. And the debate between the gradualists and the catastrophists is still hotly contested, as the following article by J. Madeleine Nash shows.

I have provided this little lecture on evolution because I thought you might find the background helpful in reading this rather technical article. And, yes, it is rather technical. But it did appear in *Time* magazine, whose editors clearly believed that educated Americans could understand and could be made interested in its material.

For our purpose it is, I think, instructive to see how a skillful writer dramatizes the significance of abstract ideas.

from *When Life Exploded*
by J. Madeleine Nash

> For billions of years, simple creatures like plankton, bacteria and algae ruled the earth. Then, suddenly, life got very complicated.

An hour later and he might not have noticed the rock, much less stooped to pick it up. But the early morning sunlight slanting across the Namibian desert in southwestern Africa happened to illuminate momentarily some strange squiggles on a chunk of sandstone. At first Douglas Erwin, a paleobiologist at the Smithsonian Institution in Washington, wondered if the meandering markings might be dried-up curls of prehistoric sea mud. But no, he decided after studying the patterns for a while, these were burrows carved by a small, wormlike creature that arose in long-vanished subtropical seas—an archaic organism that, as Erwin later confirmed, lived about 550 million years ago, just before the geological period known as the Cambrian.

Figure 8.6. A rock similar to the one Douglas Erwin found.

As such, the innocuous-seeming creature and its curvy spoor mark the threshold of a critical interlude in the history of life. For the Cambrian is a period distinguished by the abrupt appearance of an astonishing array of multicelled animals—animals that are the ancestors of virtually all the creatures that now swim, fly and crawl through the visible world.

Indeed, while most people cling to the notion that evolution works its magic over millions of years, scientists are realizing that biological change often occurs in sudden fits and starts. And none of those fitful starts was more dramatic, more productive or more mysterious than the one that occurred shortly after Erwin's wormlike creature slithered through the primordial seas. All around the world, in layers of rock just slightly younger than that Erwin discovered, scientists have found the mineralized remains of organisms that represent the emergence of nearly every major branch in the zoological tree. Among them: bristle worms and roundworms, lamp shells and mollusks, sea cucumbers and jellyfish, not to mention an endless parade of arthropods, those spindly legged, hard-shelled ancient cousins of crabs and lobsters, spiders and flies. There are even occasional glimpses—in rock laid down not long after Erwin's Namibian sandstone—of small, ribbony swimmers with a rodlike spine that are unprepossessing progenitors of the chordate line, which leads to fish, to amphibians and eventually to humans.

Where did this extraordinary bestiary come from, and why did it emerge so quickly? In recent years, no question has stirred the imagination of more evolutionary experts, spawned more novel theories or spurred more far-flung expeditions. Life has occupied the planet for nearly 4 billion of its 4.5 billion years. But until about 600 million years ago, there were no organisms more complex than bacteria, multicelled algae and single-celled plankton. The first hint of biological ferment was a plethora of mysterious palm-shape, frondlike creatures that vanished as inexplicably as they appeared. Then, 543 million years ago, in the early Cambrian, within the span of no more than 10 million years, creatures with teeth and tentacles and claws and jaws materialized with the suddenness of apparitions. In a burst of creativity like nothing before or since, nature appears to have sketched out the blueprints for virtually the whole of the animal kingdom. This explosion of biological diversity is described by scientists as biology's Big Bang.

Over the decades, evolutionary theorists beginning with Charles Darwin have tried to argue that the appearance of multicelled animals during the Cambrian merely seemed sudden, and in fact had been preceded by a lengthy period of evolution for which the geological record was missing. But this explanation, while it patched over a hole in an otherwise masterly theory, now seems increasingly unsatisfactory. Since 1987, discoveries of major fossil beds in Greenland, in China, in Siberia, and now in Namibia have shown that the period of biological innovation occurred at virtually the same instant in geologic time all around the world.

What could possibly have powered such a radical advance? Was it something in the organisms themselves or the environment in which they lived? Today an unprecedented effort to answer these questions is under way. Geologists and geochemists are reconstructing the Precambrian planet, looking for changes in the atmosphere and ocean that might have put evolution into sudden overdrive. Developmental biologists are teasing apart the genetic toolbox needed to assemble animals as disparate as worms and flies, mice and fish. And paleontologists are exploring deeper reaches of the fossil record, searching for organisms that might have primed the evolutionary pump. "We're getting data," says Harvard University paleontologist Andrew Knoll, "almost faster than we can digest it." . . .

Evolving at Supersonic Speed

Scientists used to think that the evolution of phyla took place over a period of 75 million years, and even that seemed impossibly short. Then two years ago, a group of researchers led by [John] Grotzinger, Samuel Bowring from M.I.T. and Harvard's Knoll took this long-standing problem and escalated it into a crisis. First they recalibrated the geological clock, chopping the Cambrian period to about half its former length. Then they announced that the interval of major evolutionary innovation did not span the entire 30 million years, but rather was concentrated in the first third. "Fast," Harvard's [Stephen Jay] Gould observes, "is now a lot faster than we thought, and that's extraordinarily interesting."

What Knoll, Grotzinger and colleagues had done was travel to a remote region of northeastern Siberia where millenniums of relentless erosion had uncovered a dramatic ledger of rock more than half a mile thick. In ancient seabeds near the mouth of the Lena River, they spotted numerous small, shelly fossils characteristic of the early Cambrian. Even better, they found cobbles of volcanic ash containing minuscule crystals of a mineral known as zircon, possibly the most sensitive timepiece nature has yet invented.

Zircon dating, which calculates a fossil's age by measuring the relative amounts of uranium and lead within the crystals, had been whittling away at the Cambrian for some time. By 1990, for example, new dates obtained from early Cambrian sites around the world were telescoping the start of biology's Big Bang from 600 million years ago to less than 560 million years ago. Now, with information based on the lead content of zircons from Siberia, virtually everyone agrees that the Cambrian started almost exactly 543 million years ago and, even more startling, that all but one of the phyla in the fossil record appeared within the first 5 million to 10 million years. "We now know how fast fast is," grins Bowring. "And what I like to ask my biologist friends is, How fast can evolution get before they start feeling uncomfortable?"

Freaks or Ancestors?

The key to the Cambrian explosion, researchers are now convinced, lies in the Vendian, the geological period that immediately preceded it. But because of the frustrating gap in the fossil record, efforts to explore this critical time interval have been hampered. For this reason, no one knows quite what to make of the singular frond-shape organisms that appeared tens of millions of years before the beginning of the Cambrian, then seemingly died out. Are these puzzling life-forms—which Yale University paleobiologist Adolf Seilacher dubbed the "vendobionts"—

Figure 8.7. Fossil of a soft vendobiont.

linked somehow to the creatures that appeared later on, or do they represent a totally separate chapter in the history of life?

Seilacher has energetically championed the latter explanation, speculating that the vendobionts represent a radically different architectural solution to the problem of growing large. These "creatures"—which reached an adult size of 3 ft. or more across—did not divide their bodies into cells, believes Seilacher, but into compartments so plumped with protoplasm that they resembled air mattresses. They appear to have had no predators, says Seilacher, and led a placid existence on the ocean floor, absorbing nutrients from seawater or manufacturing them with the help of symbiotic bacteria.

UCLA paleontologist Bruce Runnegar, however, disagrees with Seilacher. Runnegar argues that the fossil known as Ernietta, which resembles a pouch made of wide-wale corduroy, may be some sort of seaweed that generated food through photosynthesis. Charniodiscus, a frond with a disklike base, he classifies as a colonial cnidarian, the phylum that includes jellyfish, sea anemones and sea pens. And Dickinsonia, which appears to have a clearly segmented body, Runnegar tentatively places in an ancestral group that later gave rise to roundworms and arthropods. The Cambrian explosion did not erupt out of the blue, argues Runnegar. "It's the continuation of a process that began long before."

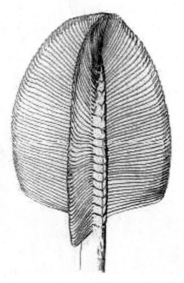

Figure 8.8. Reconstruction of a Precambrian frond.

The debate between Runnegar and Seilacher is about to get even more heated. For, as pictures that accompany the *Science* article reveal, researchers have returned from Namibia with hard evidence that a diverse community of organisms flourished in the oceans at the end of the Vendian, just before nature was gripped by creative frenzy. Runnegar, for instance, is currently studying the fossil of a puzzling conical creature that appears to be an early sponge. M.I.T.'s Beverly Saylor is sorting through sandstones that contain a menagerie of small, shelly things, some shaped like wine goblets, others like miniature curtain rods. And Guy Narbonne of Queen's University in Ontario, Canada, is trying to make sense of Dickinsonia-like creatures found just beneath the layer of rock where the Cambrian officially begins.

What used to be a gap in the fossil record has turned out to be teeming with life, and this single, stunning insight into late-Precambrian ecology, believes Grotzinger, is bound to reframe the old argument over the vendobionts. For whether they are animal ancestors or evolutionary dead ends, says Grotzinger, Dickinsonia and its cousins can no longer be thought of as sideshow freaks. Along with the multitudes of small, shelly organisms and enigmatic burrowers that riddled the sea floor with tunnels and trails, the vendobionts have emerged as important clues to the Cambrian explosion. "We now know," says Grotzinger, "that evolution did not proceed in two unrelated pulses but in two pulses that beat together as one." . . .

Beyond Darwinism

Of course, understanding what made the Cambrian explosion possible doesn't address the larger question of what made it happen so fast. Here scientists delicately slide across data-thin ice, suggesting scenarios that are based on intuition rather than solid evidence. One favorite is the so-called empty barrel, or open spaces, hypothesis, which compares the Cambrian organisms to homesteaders on the prairies. The biosphere in which the Cambrian explosion occurred, in other words, was like the American West, a huge tract of vacant property that suddenly opened up for settlement. After the initial land rush subsided, it became more and more difficult for naive newcomers to establish footholds.

Predation is another popular explanation. Once multicelled grazers appeared, say paleontologists, it was only a matter of time before multicelled predators evolved to eat them. And, right on cue, the first signs of predation appear in the fossil record exactly at the transition between the Vendian and the Cambrian, in the form of bore holes drilled through shelly organisms that resemble stacks of miniature ice-cream cones.

Seilacher, among others, speculates that the appearance of protective shells and hard, sharp parts in the late Precambrian signaled the start of a biological arms race that did in the poor, defenseless vendobionts.

Even more speculative are scientists' attempts to address the flip side of the Cambrian mystery: why this evolutionary burst, so stunning in speed and scope, has never been equaled. With just one possible exception—the Bryozoa, whose first traces turn up shortly after the Cambrian—there is no record of new phyla emerging later on, not even in the wake of the mass extinction that occurred 250 million years ago, at the end of the Permian period.

Why no new phyla? Some scientists suggest that the evolutionary barrel still contained plenty of organisms that could quickly diversify and fill all available ecological niches. Others, however, believe that in the surviving organisms, the genetic software that controls early development had become too inflexible to create new life-forms after the Permian extinction. The intricate networks of developmental genes were not so rigid as to forbid elaborate tinkering with details; otherwise, marvels like winged flight and the human brain could never have arisen. But very early on, some developmental biologists believe, the linkages between multiple genes made it difficult to change important features without lethal effect. "There must be limits to change," says Indiana University developmental biologist Rudolf Raff. "After all, we've had these same old body plans for half a billion years."

The more scientists struggle to explain the Cambrian explosion, the more singular it seems. And just as the peculiar behavior of light forced physicists to conclude that Newton's laws were incomplete, so the Cambrian explosion has caused experts to wonder if the twin Darwinian imperatives of genetic variation and natural selection provide an adequate framework for understanding evolution. "What Darwin described in the *Origin of Species*," observes Queen's University paleontologist Narbonne, "was the steady background kind of evolution. But there also seems to be a non-Darwinian kind of evolution that functions over extremely short time periods—and that's where all the action is."

In a new book, *At Home in the Universe* (Oxford University Press), theoretical biologist Stuart Kauffman of the Santa Fe Institute argues that underlying the creative commotion during the Cambrian are laws that we have only dimly glimpsed—laws that govern not just biological evolution but also the evolution of physical, chemical and technological systems. The fanciful animals that first appeared on nature's sketchpad remind Kauffman of early bicycles, with their odd-size wheels and strangely angled handlebars. "Soon after a major innovation," he writes, "discovery of profoundly different variations is easy. Later innovation is limited to modest improvements on increasingly optimized designs."

Biological evolution, says Kauffman, is just one example of a self-organizing system that teeter-totters on the knife edge between order and chaos, "a grand compromise between structure and surprise." Too much order makes change impossible; too much chaos and there can be no continuity. But since balancing acts are necessarily precarious, even the most adroit tightrope walkers sometimes make one move too many. Mass extinctions, chaos theory suggests, do not require comets or volcanoes to trigger them. They arise naturally from the intrinsic instability of the evolving system, and superior fitness provides no safety net.

In fact, some of prehistory's worst mass extinctions took place during the Cambrian itself, and they probably occurred for no obvious reason. Rather, just as the tiniest touch can cause a steeply angled sand pile to slide, so may a small evolutionary advance that gives one species a temporary advantage over another be enough to bring down an entire ecosystem. "These patterns of speciations and extinctions, avalanching across ecosystems and time," warns Kauffman, are to be found in every chaotic system—human and biological. "We are all part of the same pageant," as he puts it. Thus, even in this technological age, we may have more in common than we care to believe with the weird—and ultimately doomed—wonders that radiated so hopefully out of the Cambrian explosion.

CRITICAL READING

1. Looking at the first three paragraphs, describe how Nash uses an opening encounter to organize and energize some needed background material.

2. Again in the first three paragraphs, Nash uses strong verbs, vivid nouns, alliteration, and parallel constructions to jolt the readers' interest in what could otherwise (apart from the encounter mentioned in question 1) be a necessarily dull outline of paleontological facts. Give examples of all of these and any other rhetorical flourishes that you notice.

3. What was the surprise contained in the rock that Douglas Erwin discovered? (Hint: you must hunt for the answer to this question!) The answer to this question may become more evident if you answer another question first: Is Erwin more likely to be an ally of Seilacher or Runnegar? (See the section "Freaks or Ancestors?")

4. In the section "Freaks or Ancestors?" Nash describes the differing viewpoints of Seilacher and Runnegar. If we view these investigators as continuing the debate between catastrophists and gradualists, which is which, and why?

5. Looking at the same section, explain the issue between seeing Precambrian vendobionts as "animal ancestors or evolutionary dead ends." In chapter 7 ("Background") we saw the importance of being able to redraw the issue map to get past a deadlocked argument. Explain how Grotzinger tries to do that with this issue.

DISCUSSION QUESTIONS

1. Is it really reasonable to describe a 10 million year period as an "explosion"—a "big bang"? What techniques does Nash use to dramatize the surprise of this number? Do you think she is successful?

2. Draw a time line of evolution from information in this article that illustrates the surprise of biology's "Big Bang." Does such an illustration help you grasp the main surprise of the article?

3. At the end of the section "Evolving at Supersonic Speed" Nash says that Bowring likes to ask his biologist friends if they are feeling uncomfortable. This implies an issue between disciplines. What kind of researcher is Bowring—what department of a university would he be in? Why does he expect biologists to feel uncomfortable about his discoveries? Why do you think this gives him pleasure?

4. In the last section of the article, "Beyond Darwinism," the author describes five pictures that try to "fill in the dots" of known facts about species' disappearance and sudden reappearance. Describe all five with the evidence cited to support each. Do you see any potential flaws with the connections between the facts and the theories? Which of these theories seems most likely to you? Why?

WRITING COMMISSION: DINOSAUR EXTINCTION

Back in the newspaper office, your editor has been talking about a new dinosaur exhibit in the City Natural History Museum.

"It's almost a two-hour drive, but you can bet that the kids in town will be pressuring their folks to take them there. The museum had a preview for the press Friday, so I sent some people over to cover it. I

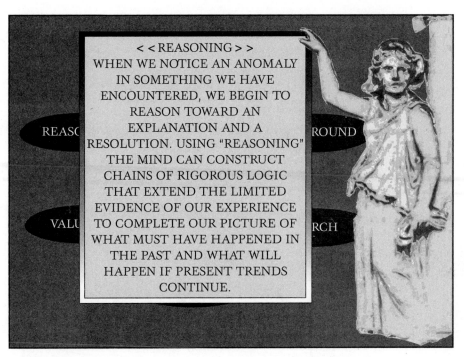

Figure 8.9.

thought it might be fun to have you guys do a piece for the Tuesday kiddie section related to the opening of the exhibit. I thought maybe to give it an educational slant, you could do a bit on that perennial chestnut—Why Did the Dinosaurs Die Out?"

"Whoa!" one of the interns exclaims. "That sounds like a lot of research unless we just blow smoke in the kids' eyes!"

"No, I'd really like to make the little monsters think a bit," your editor replies. "But I know you don't have a lot of time, what with summer picnics and Frisbee contests, so I asked Karen, our legman, to bring back some notes from the museum on this topic. She did a pretty good job, gathering facts from various parts of the museum as well as from the dino exhibit. Did you know that there have been at least 80 different theories advanced for dinosaur extinction among which are that dinosaurs died out because of climatic shifts that occurred when rock that now forms the moon was ripped out of the Pacific basin or that they were overhunted by space aliens? Whew! That reminds me, here are a couple of cartoons about the absurdity of some theories."

THE FAR SIDE   By GARY LARSON

Figure 8.10.   **The real reason dinosaurs became extinct**

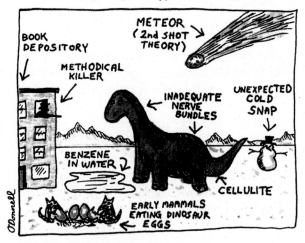

Figure 8.11.

"Anyway, here are the notes Karen brought back. I want you to put them into a form that will give kids the sense that science isn't just a bunch of facts but is an exciting process that uses imagination controlled by logical reasoning. Kind of like putting together a jigsaw puzzle with most of the pieces missing.

"Well, here are a few of those pieces and some guesses at what the whole picture looks like."

Table 8.1.

(a)
Partial Timeline of Geologic Periods and Major Extinction Events

505–438 mya	367 mya	360–245 mya	230 mya
Trilobytes dramatically reduced at beginning of the **Ordovician** period. Near the end, the second largest mass extinction occurred.	Mid-**Devonian** period. Fourth largest extinction ever, particularly of marine invertebrates.	**Carboniferous–Permian** (P) periods.	Triassic (T) period. Largest extinction—90% of all species extinction occurred at the P-T boundary.

208 mya	144 mya	65 mya	
Jurassic period. Extinction of many dinosaurs at both the beginning and the end of the Jurassic period.	**Cretaceous** (K) period.	**Tertiary** (T) period. Dinosaurs became extinct at the K-T boundary 65 mya. The third largest mass extinction included many other animal forms.	

(b)
Animal/Plant Facts

Sea animal groups were hit hardest, especially plankton.

Mammals and small cold-blooded reptiles survived well.

Land plants except ferns died off to a large extent.

25–60% of known species disappeared during the K-T (boundary between the Cretaceous and Tertiary periods) extinction, making it the third most extensive and probably the most "sudden" in history.

(c)
Environmental Facts

There have been four major extinction episodes at intervals of about 200 million years.

During the Devonian there were widespread flooding of continents and worldwide volcanic activity as continents drifted and collided.

Ordovician atmosphere was low in oxygen; ocean levels dropped as a result of increased glacier formation.

Permian had extremes—glaciation near poles, atmospheric warming and desert formation elsewhere.

(Continues)

Table 8.1. (Continued)

A soot layer in the rocks at the P-T boundary may show widespread forest fires.

The Cretaceous period was marked by episodes of high sea level and high average temperatures, resulting in arid climate.

Great supercontinents broke up and moved during the Cretaceous period.

Sea levels (covering 90% of the earth's surface) lowered. The North American inland sea gradually disappeared at the end of the Cretaceous.

There was a lot of volcanic activity during the K-T boundary period.

There is an increase in iridium in K-T boundary layers. Iridium, rare on earth, is known to be prevalent in meteors.

Cracked quartz indicates violent tremors at the K-T boundary.

The earth's north and south magnetic poles were reversed during the K-T period.

There are spherical drops of once-molten rock at the K-T boundary.

Plant life continued with little change across the K-T boundary.

(d)
Extinction Theories

Eruptions of molten rock caused loss of sunlight, reducing plant food source.

A death star hidden companion of the sun that comes near the earth every 26 million years caused loss of sunlight, reducing plant food source.

A nearby supernova—a suddenly exploding star rained radiation on the earth.

Oort Comet Cloud may pass earth's orbit every 26 million years, causing loss of sunlight that reduced plant food source.

An as-yet-undetected planet may circle the sun every 30 million years, perturbing another cloud of comets, which then shower the earth with shading dust.

The impact of a giant asteroid sent up a cloud of dirt that caused loss of sunlight, reducing plant food source.

Magnetic pole reversals may have been caused by intensive radiation from outer space.

Galactic dust caused loss of sunlight, reducing plant food source.

Small-brained stupidity may account for the death of dinosaurs.

Increase of universal entropy made it impossible for life forms to continue.

Some of the new flowering plants may have been poisonous.

Destruction of the ozone layer admitted high levels of radiation that caused fatal mutations.

Worldwide burning of forests caused by lightning, perhaps after a kill-off from asteroid or comet dust, dimmed sunlight, destroying plant food.

There may have been epidemic diseases.

Multiple causes may have acted over longer periods.

In the 1960s, a Russian scientist "discovered" a kind of water that would polymerize and might turn all other water into its own hard, plasticlike form.

Eggshells may have become too thin.

Species may have died out just because they became old and less robust, much as an individual might.

Dinosaurs' habitat may have been lost through increasing forests and decreasing wetlands.

"It seemed like a good idea at the time." How familiar that line is! Our brains are marvelous machines, able to toss up ideas like popcorn when we're faced with explaining an **eye-opener.** Because each of these ideas bursts open in response to the heat of the moment, any of them can be made appetizing with a little rhetorical butter and the salt of argument.

We've seen a few of these popcorn ideas that have been put forward as explanations for the origin and extinction of species. However, when these ideas—often quite plausible and appealing—are put into practice, most of them fail, either immediately, because the causes of the surprising **encounter** were more complicated than we thought, or later, because the consequences of our action produced additional results that we did not foresee—unintended consequences.

The following piece by the popular columnist Mary Schmich is an amusing treatment of this phenomenon, which often has serious and far-reaching consequences.

Unintended Consequences
by Mary Schmich

Sissy stormed into the Inner Self Cafe, a self-help bookstore and cappuccino bar in a Lincoln Park strip mall, screeching like an electrocuted cat.

"Missy, Missy, Missy, what's a girl to do about the outbreak?"

Missy's head jerked up in such alarm that her glass of wheat grass juice splashed across the open pages of her journal.

"Outbreak? Aren't you too old for zits, Sissy? Haven't we graduated to wrinkles?"

"This is no time for jokes," howled Sissy. "Don't you read the news?"

She plopped down in a chair and signaled the barista for a triple cappuccino. He nodded, then foraged through a drawer for a pair of earplugs, preparing for another debate between Sissy and Missy, this space's fictional experts on politics, lies and other people's sex lives.

"Sorry, Sis," said Missy. "I'm on a news diet for my mental health. Since I cut my news consumption, my blood pressure's down and my starving brain has gained 10 pounds."

"So you don't know about the outbreak of unintended consequences?"

"The what?"

"Bob Packwood[2] and the vitamins?"

---

[2] Former Oregon senator, forced from office on charges of sexual harassment and obstructing the Ethics Committee.

"Is that a new band?"

Sissy leaned across the table.

"Unintended consequence *numero uno,* Missy. People like you and me have been so soft on Bill Clinton that Bob Packwood is thinking of running for office again."

"And Happy Easter to him," Missy said." 'Tis the season of redemption. He's been punished sufficiently for his sins."

Sissy hissed. "Bob Packwood is a pig."

"You've never said that about President Romeo, Sissy. What's the difference between him and Bob?"

"The difference? The difference? Bob Packwood is a sexist pig and . . ." Sissy licked the rim of her cappuccino cup. ". . . Bill Clinton is a sexy pig."

Missy snorted. "I see. The difference between a sexist pig and sexy one depends on whether he makes you salivate."

Sissy ran her finger through her cappuccino foam. She giggled. "So?"

"So," said Missy, "in your view, a sexy pig isn't a pig at all. He's just a frisky dog. And you'd be thrilled if Bill were drooling all over you."

"So would you," sniffed Sissy. "You're just too repressed to say so."

She looked earnestly at Missy. "Look, Missy. My views have evolved. I now understand that not all men who make untoward advances to women should be crucified. But when I think that my sophisticated new approach to sexual harassment encourages the likes of Bob Packwood, I'm horrified. Do he and all those other guys really think that women will put up with any old oinker now? Is this the consequence of our tolerance?"

Missy clapped her hands over her ears. "Sorry, Sis, but my new mental health diet bars me from further discussion of sexual harassment. The topic makes my teeth hurt."

"Aching teeth? Sounds like a vitamin D deficiency, Missy. Which brings me to unintended consequence *numero* two."

Sissy held up a recent newspaper. "Do you wear sunscreen?"

"Even in the rain."

"That's why you have a vitamin D deficiency." Sissy tapped the newspaper. "For your body to make vitamin D, you have to absorb sunlight. Researchers have discovered that all that sunscreen is blocking out the sun, ergo the vitamin D. So in pursuit of unlined skin, we're all making brittle bones."

Missy sighed again. "See why I hate the news, Sissy? It's a depressing knot of confusion."

"Precisely," Sissy said and nodded. "Which brings me to unintended consequence number three. Vitamin C."

"Let me guess," said Missy. "Vitamin C causes sexual harassment?"

Sissy cocked her head in thought. "Could be. Anyway." She held up another newspaper. "A bunch of British researchers now tell us as that taking one 500-milligram vitamin C supplement a day could damage your genes. So while we've been popping mega C's to kill our colds, we've been killing off our DNA."

Missy took a final swig of wheat grass juice. "What exactly is your point here? That the only thing more confusing than sexual harassment these days is vitamins?"

"My point," said Sissy, "is that everything we do that's right eventually goes wrong. The newspaper is proof of the plague of unintended consequences."

"And that," said Missy, "is why I've sworn off the news."

CRITICAL READING

1. How does Schmich dramatically delay the central surprise of this encounter?
2. In chapter 6, I proposed that **significance** lies in connections. Sissy connects a number of **eye-opening** encounters that she has come across in newspapers. List these and explain how her general statement of significance can be seen to derive from connecting them.

DISCUSSION QUESTIONS

1. Missy says that discussion of sexual harassment now makes her teeth hurt. What are the policies of your school on this topic? Do they or could they have unintended consequences?
2. How do you feel about using fictional characters to dramatize ideas in a nonfiction setting as Schmich does here?

Exploring the Topic: Unintended Consequences

The collateral damage of a popcorn idea often outweighs its benefits. One spectacular example of the price of unintended consequences was the idea for low-cost high-rise apartments to replace the festering slums of Chicago's South Side, many of which still had outdoor privies in 1955. A few years after they were built, I talked with one of the

Figure 8.12. A beautiful popcorn idea set in concrete: The slum buildings of "Outhouse Alley" being replaced by clean, new 17-story apartment "projects" in 1959.

social workers who had been on the planning commission that recommended the replacement of the densely packed, dilapidated frame tenements with the modern high-rises separated by generous open spaces of lawns, trees, and playgrounds. She said that they believed that the buildings would provide secure and sanitary shelter and that the greenery and light would uplift the morale of the poor.

By the time of my conversation with this penitent social worker in the late 1960s, the disastrous failure of the "projects" was already painfully apparent. The concentration of poor people had proved to be a breeding ground for gang formation; the open spaces provided a dangerous no-man's-land for gun fire; and the elevators and long, dark corridors of the buildings formed treacherous hiding places for muggers and rapists. Now that these notorious vertical ghettos are being torn down, it is hard to believe that no one foresaw the problem.

But in fact good people possessed by a well-intentioned idea often fail to **reason** about possible negative outcomes, whether in the world of social legislation or business. The hapless entrepreneur who

Figure 8.13. Unintended consequences of what seemed a good idea—generations trapped in vertical ghettos.

opens a new video store in the same neighborhood where two others are flourishing looks only at the success of his rivals as an index of his own. The operator fails to focus on the fact that, even if he or she gets enough business to operate, the pie, which might have been enough for two, will now be split in shares too small to be enough for any of the three.

Here is a real-life business example. A large university wanted its professors and staff to use an economical, fixed-cost, bundled long-distance service, but it wanted each department to pay a fair share of the cost based on usage by its professors and staff. So the university divided up each month's bundled costs according to minutes used by each department and billed each department accordingly. To lower their bills, some departments with little usage found they could save money by dialing direct to avoiding having to pay their share of the bundled service. But with fewer departments using the bundled service, the cost of this "economical" service to the remaining departments increased, thus driving more departments to bypass the service, until the long distance costs for the school skyrocketed because everyone was dialing direct. The university hung up the phone on this idea.

And politics is rife with such examples. Because the large population of birds in the Chinese capital of Beijing made the city dirty and perhaps spread disease, the government ordered all the birds in the city killed shortly after World War II. The nuisances committed by the birds were cleaned up, but insects that the birds had eaten began to proliferate, creating more of a nuisance than the birds had. But, as so often happens when people are convinced they are following a good idea, the government refused to backtrack. So, to eliminate the insects, instead of reintroducing birds, the government dug up most of the shrubs and grass of the city where the insects bred. Fine, the insect problem was reduced, but the city became an unpleasant desert, afflicted during the April winds with clouds of Beijing dust added to that blown in from the Gobi, so that now people had to cover their heads with fine mesh bags to avoid breathing the contaminated air.

The point of these examples is to demonstrate the importance of **reasoning.** In the old days, if a doctor told a patient to take a pill, the patient just shrugged and said, "Well, you're the doctor." But after enough people had been treated for the wrong diseases—and after a lot of law suits had been filed—most doctors became much more cautious, telling the patient the probabilities, even the most unlikely ones, of misdiagnosis and potential side effects. No matter how obvious the cause or attractive the solution of a problem may be, you need to use a chess player's imagination to **reason** out the ramifications for yourself and for your reader before you can be satisfied that you see how the endgame will shape up.

WRITING COMMISSION: UNINTENDED CONSEQUENCES

Recall a decision from your local community, from an organization you belonged to, or from your personal life that had unintended consequences. Dramatize this experience in an essay that builds suspense by hinting at the eventual result while laying out all the thinking that went into choosing the course of action. Explain why the unforeseen consequences occurred. If you can come up with another similar encounter, do so. Finally, resolve the piece with advice to the reader about how to avoid such contretemps in the future.

Points to Remember

- The brain tries to create a whole picture of a situation from whatever hard evidence is available. This ability is necessary to grasp the **significance** of our encounters, but it must be used in a disciplined, critical way to avoid big mistakes.

- Computer logic is a good model for this disciplined kind of **reasoning.**

- Faced with incomplete evidence (as we almost always are), we should make ourselves and our readers aware of as many different pictures of a situation as we can think of that account for the facts.

- Most ideas look good on paper, but one of the goals of **reasoning** is to follow out logically the string of consequences that may follow if the idea is implemented. Almost all programs have unintended consequences—sometimes far-reaching and difficult to undo. One job of a writer is to alert people to those consequences.

E-E-R

Encounter

Explain

Resolve

R-S-V-B

Reason

Search

Value

Background

9
Search

Writing emerges from writing. . . . I want to understand these living, breathing, primary sources all around me. . . . These sources speak to me of love and loss, of memory and desire, of the ways in which we come to understand something through differences and opposition. . . . My academic need to find connections sends me to the library. . . . I can walk into source after source, and they will give me insights, but not answers. I have learned, too, that my sources can surprise me. But I must be an inventor if I am to read those sources well, if I am to imagine the connections.

—Nancy Sommers, "I Stand Here Writing"[1]

Opening the Topic: Search and Research

Figure 9.1.

Beware of Dr. Frankenfood!

have screamed headlines in England, Germany, and Russia. And Dr. Frankenfood's monsters are beginning to haunt some Americans as well. The fear—amounting to near hysteria among some people—is of genetic tinkering with everyday food products, like the Flavr-Savr tomato illustrated in Figure 9.1. Mary Shelley, in her famous

---

[1]*College English* (1993) by Nancy Sommers.

233

book, imagined Dr. Frankenstein being able to splice together dismembered parts of human bodies and reactivate them with a bolt of lightning. Modern bioengineers are able to split apart plant chromosomes with enzyme scissors to remove a particular gene or add another at a strategic point. A toxin from a soil bacterium that kills the disastrous corn borer can be spliced into corn seed, for example, to produce a plant that does not need a lot of insecticide spray. In the case of that tomato, an antibiotic gene is spliced in where another of the 20,000 genes is removed. The particular gene that is removed is the one that causes the tomato to soften as it ripens on the vine. As a result, the popular FlavrSavr tomato can be allowed to ripen solidly to full flavor on the vine and still get to the grocery store before it starts to rot.

The idea of fooling around with mother nature reminds some people of Mary Shelley's cautionary tale as a case of unforeseeable consequences—the kind we talked about in chapter 8 ("Reasoning"). England's Prince Charles trumpeted a warning not to meddle in God's realm by tampering with the genetic code of common foods. Headlines have appeared like *Killer Tomatoes; Genetics' Growing Bounty Reaps Fears for Future;* and *Mutant Crops Can Kill You!* It was basically this same fear that Michael Crichton built on when he had his scientists use genetic engineering to recreate the dinosaurs of Jurassic Park. A similar round of near-hysterical concern greeted the fluoridation of city water supplies in the 1950s and still stands in the way of many communities' adding this cavity-preventing treatment to their drinking water. In the 1970s, concern that the use of Freon in spray cans and air conditioners contributed to a growing hole in the protective ozone layer resulted in strong pressure to end its use. There have been other outbreaks of panic over the possibility that radiation from cell phones and high-tension electric lines may cause cancer. The fear of nuclear accidents has put pressure on electric power companies to abandon nuclear power plants altogether. My grandmother, to the end of her rather long life, refused to buy pasteurized milk, fearing that the newfangled science was introducing something harmful into it. Then, of course, there was the Y2K bug scare, during which people stocked up on survival supplies fearing that computers would not work after January 1, 2000, and delivery of everything from power to food and even water would suddenly cease. My daughter-in-law's grandparents considered facing the wintry risks of a New Year's Eve in a woodstove-heated lake cottage in rural North Dakota rather than chance the fancied risks of this doomsday bug.

Some of these fears are unfounded or highly exaggerated, others are not. We are constantly being forced to make choices where some risk is involved. Is it OK to eat this lunch meat that is a week out of date? Can I take megadoses of vitamin C to get over this cold? Is it safer to drive to Columbus, Ohio, or to fly there? Should I go to a chiropractor, an osteopath, an orthopedic surgeon, or a yoga instructor to treat my carpal tunnel syndrome? What are the long-range effects if I, as a parent, spank my children? Or if I leave them all day in a preschool when they are three? Will I be better off living with a partner before marriage or not? Should I prepare for my own retirement or trust Social Security? If I save money in a mutual fund, do I risk losing it if the stock market crashes?

Science continues to show us that some risks and consequences that we used to think were just chance can now be predicted. While this is good in one way, it also makes us shoulder more of the responsibility for bad decisions. "You should have known! ... Why didn't you find out about it first?" How can we, both as individuals and as a society, reasonably evaluate the relative risks of the many decisions we have to make?

The answer is **search.**

The first place we search when faced with a dilemma is our own previous experience. Although I will use airplanes when necessary, I used to prefer to take the train—until I was a passenger in a train accident. But our own **encounters** are not general enough to make secure **resolutions** for the future. So the next day I was eager to **search** for news about the accident in the newspaper to find out why it had happened and the extent of the injuries. There is a need to use elementary, factual **search** to establish the significance even of situations where we have direct, firsthand personal experience. I can reach out farther to find statistics on the relative safety of the various modes of transportation. (But even though I know that planes and trains are safer, that direct encounter outweighs my research, and I usually drive.)

After consulting our own experience we reach out to ask our friends who may have had experience with similar binds. It was this kind of search that Ellen Goodman used to clarify her own experiences with early marriage in the essay "In Love Fornow" (chapter 5, "Resolution"). And we can expand our **search** beyond just our acquaintances by finding polls or surveys that embrace a sampling of everybody in the country. If I go to the Gallup Poll Web site < http://www.gallup.com > right now, shortly after the most recent airline crash, I find a poll that shows that I am not alone in my reluctance to fly. Twenty-three percent of the population has never flown. Of those that do fly, one in five say that they are frightened all or most of the time that they are in the air. This number is one third higher than it was ten years ago when the same question was asked.

If a personal problem requires expertise, we expand our search by consulting with doctors, lawyers, or other specialists. We are helped with this kind of **search** by published interviews with experts or articles or books by them that discuss their **reasoning** and their own firsthand re**search.** These resources, too, are readily available in the library and on the Internet, and they are particularly helpful as we try to map the terrain of issues on which our quandary may lie.

Here is an example of how real-life people with a critical problem interact with these sources to reach a resolution. When my son got leukemia my wife and I knew no one who had been through that ordeal. Fortunately we had good doctors, but when he went out of remission a second time, my wife and I decided we needed to know more facts about the disease to weigh intelligently the treatment he was getting. So I took the next **search** step and went to the library of a university hospital. Even though I had little grasp of the more technical parts of the articles in the medical journals, I gleaned enough to realize that there were several approaches to the treatment of leukemia and that our doctors were following the philosophy that the best course for an incurably fatal disease was a treatment that would give the kid a life that might be a few months shorter than the ultimate possible but would allow him to live that life as normally as possible, avoiding the severest side effects of drugs and radiation. There were other treatment centers, however, that still held out hope for a complete cure through the use of cocktails containing all the drugs that had shown any effectiveness, delivered all at once. This seemed like a good idea at the time, so we determined to travel to a hospital that advocated the more aggressive treatment.

When we returned to our "home" doctors, our son was in remission again, but his white cell counts were dangerously low—one of those unintended consequences of the aggressive treatment. Nevertheless, the determined nature of our search impressed our doctors,

who decided that we were candidates for the then experimental procedure of a bone-marrow transplant, which held out a 50/50 chance
of total cure or imminent death. The resolution was still up to us, but
our pressing search for the facts that lay behind the varying treatment protocols had finally yielded an informed map of the ultimate
risks and benefits.

I tell you this to demonstrate that research is not a simple sortie
into a library (or onto the Internet) in which you hope to bag a few
citations that you can add to the stew of your composition, stir a couple of times, and serve up to your instructor, seasoned with footnotes
and a bibliography. Search is, as the epigraph of this chapter says, an
encounter with living, breathing sources that speak of love and loss.
As the author of that quote, an eminent professor of composition,
also says, these sources do not give final answers. **Search** is only a
part of your rhetorical process; it depends on your inventiveness to
relate it to the other modalities on the way to a **resolution** that your
reader will find **significant.**

In the case of our then fourteen-year-old son, our doctors'
research showed that he was a good candidate and that the University of Minnesota Hospital had done the most thorough scientific
control of this procedure and was having the best success rate with
children. So we resolved to take the risk.

Before the bone-marrow transplant, our son had been an avid
organic gardener, accepting the extreme social agenda of organic gardening magazines that strenuously opposed the use of any chemicals
on food plants. His treatment was about to thrust him to the other
extreme of scientific manipulation of life processes. During treatment he must have felt a little like Dr. Frankenstein's creature. To get
the total body radiation needed to kill off the cancerous blood cells,
he was taken down to the subbasement of the University of Chicago
Hospital, through a couple of thick security doors, and into a dimly lit
room where the place he was to lie was marked on the concrete floor.
Looking up, he saw, fading into the darkness high above, an enormous tubular machine, three stories tall, poised above that spot,
ready to be lowered by hydraulic motors into position directly above
him when he lay down. Inside this Dr. Who–type apparatus was a
continuous belt which would soon be cranked up to full whining
speed to generate the hundreds of thousands of volts necessary to
produce a mutant-cell-killer beam, focused exactly on his spine and
skull. I wondered at his faith in us and in the scientists treating him

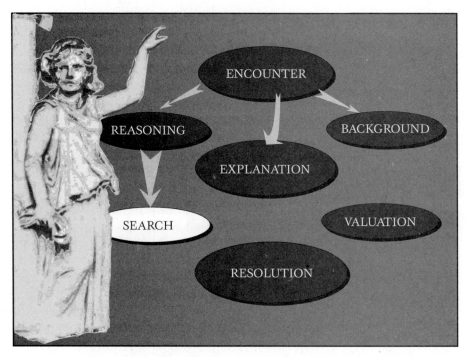

Figure 9.2. Search may range from simply asking a friend for help explaining a problem to a multiyear, multimillion dollar research project—also for help explaining a problem.

as the doors closed on his frail life's isolated encounter with Frankensteinian technology.

I am happy to report that the treatment was completely successful. Our son is now more than twenty years post transplant and a successful computer consultant. When he saw that radical scientific intervention in his own natural processes had saved his life, he became much more open-minded about the beneficial uses of biochemical technology, though he is still wary of the chance of unanticipated consequences in bioengineered food.

My wife and I are immensely grateful for the tireless research by medical scientists that led to the discovery and perfecting of the techniques that saved our son's life. But we also realize that without our own intensive and skilled search program, we might never have discovered that narrow passage that opened from our chaotic world of weltering information into their organized world of tested reasoning.

DEMONSTRATION: USING RESEARCH TO UNDERSTAND PERSONAL EXPERIENCE

To make informed decisions in situations that may have long-range consequences for our lives and the lives of those associated with us, we try as best we can to map the dynamics of the world we live in. But it is often difficult to see the significance of one's place in the crosscurrents of large social movements. If you've ever been in the middle of an emergency, you know how impossible it is to keep track of everything that is going on in front of you, let alone what may be taking place beyond your immediate vicinity. We watch the evening news to evaluate the significance of the protest march or riot we just saw (or were a part of).

There has been some recent retro interest in the decade of the 1960s—an unusually turbulent, exciting, harrowing, uplifting, and confusing time that my wife and I joined in with considerable political gusto. Let's suppose I put myself in that virtual newspaper office that I have been asking you to imagine. The year is 1999, and the editor, aware of renewed interest in the 1960s and of my political activism then, commissions me to write a short article on my experiences. He introduces his request by dropping the Doonesbury cartoon shown in Figure 9.3 on my desk.

I'm going to lay out for you the process I went through in creating this article to demonstrate how research can be—and needs to be—

Doonesbury

BY GARRY TRUDEAU

Figure 9.3. The reference is to the realistic/nostalgic Steven Spielberg movie about World War II, *Saving Private Ryan,* in which Matt Damon played Private Ryan, saved by Oscar nominee Tom Hanks.

used in an essay on a personal experience to discover its surprises and illuminate its significance.

I started my first draft thus:

> In May of 1970, my wife said to me, "We agreed that each of us will do whatever is supremely important to the other. Right? Well, it is extremely important to me to leave the United States in protest against the Vietnam War."
>
> I was horrified. Give up our home? Give up our country? Give up my job? Subject our children to a foreign culture? Give up our dog? Our cat? Was America really that bad? Her suggestion terrified me. But the power of her belief that America was morally wrong in pursuing the war in Vietnam was persuasive. And her logic, that as individuals we were powerless to stop this government that seemed to have gone crazy, was inescapable. So, reluctantly, I agreed. I secured a job teaching in Scotland, and in the summer of 1969 we sold our house, sold our nonessential possessions, took our children, and left the country as expatriates. . . .

True to my teaching, I began my first draft with a firsthand **encounter.** It is a startling personal experience, which is obviously connected with larger social patterns. How, as a writer, was I to broaden my focus from the personal to the social in order to make it **significant** to my readers?

The first instinct was to turn to historical information I already knew. I could proceed in my essay to go back to the Boston Tea Party and other protests leading up to the Revolutionary War. I could cite Henry David Thoreau, who went to jail because he would not pay taxes to support the Mexican War. But the history of protest in the United States is too big a **background** for this short essay. And if I am led to talking about India's Gandhi, who learned civil disobedience from Thoreau, and about the civil rights protests of Martin Luther King Jr., who learned from Gandhi, I am drawn a long way from the specific focus of my family's protest against the Vietnam War.

That kind of common-knowledge history is attractive because it's easy. But to get the kind of needlepoint detail needed to **dramatize** my story, I had to take my **search** to the next step. I had to go to books to look into the historical record of the time. It's a truism that we do not understand the **significance** of the movements we are a part of until they are past and the scorekeepers can add up the statistics of whatever game we were players in. This is as true of decades and eras as it is of football games and train accidents.

Where could I go to find in a hurry the facts I needed? One of the most easily searched sources of facts is an almanac.[2] Consulting the brief histories contained in a couple of these (*The World Almanac, 1989* and *The Universal Almanac, 1990*), I found the following events of those dramatic years:

1964

1. (8/7) Small North Vietnamese boats fired on American destroyers in the Gulf of Tonkin. This gave President Johnson an excuse to demand from Congress a resolution giving him power to do whatever might be necessary to retaliate against this aggression.

1965

2. (1/27–6/30) President Johnson secretly changed the direction of our commitment in Vietnam from that of military advisors and trainers to active participants. He started bombing North Vietnam and increased the troop commitment from 23,000 to 175,000.

1968

3. (1/30) North Vietnam effectively attacked South Vietnam in most major cities, an action called the Tet Offensive.
4. (3/31) President Johnson announced that he would not run for reelection.
5. (4/23) Student war protesters took over the administration building at Columbia University.
6. (4/4) Martin Luther King Jr. was assassinated.
7. (4/10 or 4/23) Peace talks with North Vietnam were begun.
8. (6/5) Presidential candidate Robert Kennedy was assassinated.
9. (August) Antiwar protesters fought with police at the Democratic presidential convention in Chicago.
10. (10/31) President Johnson ended the bombing of North Vietnam.

1969

11. Number of soldiers killed in Vietnam became higher than the number killed in the Korean War.
12. (April) American troop force in Vietnam reached its highest point: 543,400.
13. (7/8) President Nixon began withdrawing troops from Vietnam.
14. (Oct.–Nov.) "Moratorium" protests on the Vietnam War became violent with the Weathermen riots in Chicago.
15. (11/15) Hundreds of thousands of antiwar protesters demonstrated in Washington.
16. (11/16) It was reported that American soldiers had killed 102 civilians in the South Vietnamese town of Mylai.

1970

17. President Nixon increased the bombing of North Vietnam when peace talks seemed to be failing.
18. (4/29) America invaded Cambodia to attack North Vietnamese supply lines; protests occurred all over the United States.
19. (5/4) The Ohio National Guard killed 4 students and wounded 9 others during protests at Kent State University.
20. (12/31) The number of U.S. troops in Vietnam was down to 340,000.

1971

21. (2/8) U.S. troops accompanied South Vietnamese troops into Cambodia to get at North Vietnamese supply lines.
22. (12/26) The number of air attacks on North Vietnam was intensified to the greatest level since 1968.

---

[2] Almanacs were originally calendars with detailed data about the sun, moon, and planets. They were used by farmers for deciding when to plant and harvest, so they came to include weather forecasts and other general advice. Benjamin Franklin published *Poor Richard's Almanack,* which has become famous for its maxims. Modern almanacs have quantities of demographic, historical, geographical, and statistical facts. They are inexpensive; all writers should have them on their desks!

23. (12/31) The number of U.S. troops in Vietnam was down to 139,000.

1972

24. (2/21) President Nixon became the first U.S. President to visit China, demonstrating the lessening of cold war tensions.
25. (3/30) North Vietnam invaded South Vietnam across their border.
26. (4/14) Nixon ordered bombing in Hanoi, North Vietnam, in retaliation.
27. (5/8) Nixon ordered the mining of Haiphong harbor.
28. (5/22) Nixon was the first U.S. President to visit Moscow, demonstrating a lessening of cold war tensions.
29. To help Nixon win reelection, Henry Kissinger, the national security advisor, announced, "Peace is at hand" in Vietnam.
30. (12/18) Nixon ordered more bombing of North Vietnam.
31. There were only 69,000 American troops left in Vietnam.

1973

32. (1/27) U.S. and Vietnam signed the peace agreement that ended the Vietnam War.
33. (1/31) The military draft was ended by President Nixon.
34. (3/29) The last U.S. troops left Vietnam.
35. (4/1) Vietnam released almost 600 U.S. prisoners of war.

But now I feel overwhelmed. One reason facts are more troublesome than generalities is that there are so many of them. In compiling this list, I have already left out scores of events not connected with the war, but there are still so many that they would drown, rather than nourish, the **significance** of our protest. So I have to choose just a very few **eye-opening** ones. It is at this moment that I always remember the advice given by the ballet impresario Sergei Diaghilev to the struggling genius Jean Cocteau[3]: "Astound me." So I compile a list of the facts that stand out as astonishing, the ones that stand out as **eye-openers,** and I take a few notes on them:

(4) The protests against the war caused a president virtually to resign—that was a huge surprise and showed the depth and power of the protest movement.

(11), (12) The fact that we had more than half a million troops in Vietnam and had more killed than in the Korean War was bitterly ironic because the presidents had bypassed the mechanism for declaring war held by the Congress.

(13) The war began to wind down with a new President elected to end it, so it was certainly strange that we left the country a half year later.

---

[3] Cocteau is famous for his ballets, novels, and filmscripts. If you have never seen his 1945 movie *Beauty and the Beast,* do so tonight! If you don't believe me, check out the viewers' comments on the internet at < http://us.imdb.com/search > —a very useful Web site! (*Belle et la Bête* is still so popular that it has also been made available on DVD.)

(14), (15) There were still big war protests after Nixon was elected to end the war. The Weathermen protest in particular was an ugly reminder that a government out of touch with strongly held national anger invited revolution, and it began to appear that such a revolution had a chance of succeeding.

(17), (18), (21) Even though some American troops were being withdrawn, in other ways the war was spreading and intensifying with increased bombing of the North and invasions into Cambodia and Laos.

(19) The most disastrous and the last of the antiwar protests happened at Kent State University, where Ohio National Guard units fired into a mass of students, some of whom were protesting but not threatening anything. This seemed to show that the government was becoming a right-wing militarist one, against all precedent in this country that was supposed to be democratic. It seemed that the government must just be playing games with public opinion when it promised to end the war.

You can see that as I chose the facts that seemed to be the most **dramatic,** I also commented on their **significance.** For there is a huge task of integration yet to be performed. It is awfully tempting at this point for me just to dump the facts out on the table pretty much in the order in which I encountered them in the almanac. I think you can see, by rereading the first two paragraphs and then skipping to the list of selected facts that, even if I artfully tied the facts together with connectives and bridging sentences, I would have an essay that would earn me a disgusted snort from my editor and a demand to stay all night if necessary to whip it into shape.

So I will begin again, using some of those facts for **background** while always trying to keep all them focused on **dramatizing** or **explaining** the main surprise.

And what is that main **eye-opener**? It was not clear in my mind as I started looking through the facts. But, as Nancy Sommers says in the epigraph to this chapter, "my sources can surprise me." As I looked at these sources, indeed, I became so surprised that I had to use a less technical form of **search.** I had to ask my wife about the dates: When did she first think of leaving the country? When did we actually do it? What were the dates? Because it looked as if we left the country after Johnson had renounced the Presidency and after Nixon had already begun to pull troops out of Vietnam. Why did we react so late in the game? Why would an otherwise normal American middle-class family renounce their native land in 1970?

It seems clear from the historical record that the country got hottest after the official tide had already turned, just as the summer gets hottest in the month after the sun has already started to head south. But it was more than just a time lag. Nixon was apparently enacting a promised "secret plan" to end the war, which turned out to involve a wider secret campaign that we were just beginning to get wind of. This administration, like its predecessors, was completely untrustworthy.

At the time of my assignment for this column, the United States was being led by a president (Clinton) of proven mendacity who was bombing people while claiming the highest humanitarian objectives and promising never to commit ground troops while gathering them on Yugoslavia's borders. At this point, as the Doonesbury cartoon suggests, the people were buying into it just as the conservative, love-it-or-leave-it hard hats had bought into Johnson's escalation in the early days of the "police action" in Vietnam.

Again, as Nancy Sommers says, "I must be an inventor if I am to read those sources well, if I am to imagine the connections." The **significant** connection that I discerned between my 1969 **encounter,** my re**search,** and the current **encounter** seemed to be the power-mad leaders of this country violently intervening in the civil wars of countries of whose histories and traditions they had little knowledge and less respect.

It was along this axis of significance that I determined to focus my final draft.

Let me take you through my final draft of this essay, commenting on the process by which I marshaled my modalities, wove together my **searched** facts, and used familiar rhetorical tactics to create a significant reaction to a topical issue.

I realized near the end of my composing process, while searching for a title, that "purple"—the imperial color—alliterates (always a plus in a title) with a lot of words related to my subject (*president, protest, patriotism*), that using it in the title would create a sense of mystery at the beginning, that its symbolism would be central to the significance of the piece (the overweening use of power), and finally that its use in the already-written ending would **close the ring.**

Protesting Purple Patriotism

"We have to leave the country right away!" I heard this from my wife, Marsda, with a rising apprehension and a sinking stomach. You must understand that Marsda is a force of nature. I doubt that the weather bureau has ever used the name Marsda for a hurricane, but they should consider it. My apprehension rose as at the irrationality of

My wife's sudden, radical demand is the initial eye-opening encounter.

a hurricane, and my stomach sank as at its inescapable intensity.

"Give up our home?" I spluttered, logically but helplessly. "Give up our country? Give up my job? Subject our children to a foreign culture? Give up our dog? Our cat? Is America really that bad?"

In 1969 Marsda and I were approaching the middle of our allotted four-score and ten. I was finally settled in a job that gave me satisfaction and a good income, our fourth child had just been born, and we had a spacious house in a beautiful but politically active and interesting suburb. I was hoping at this point to enjoy a little well-earned (as I thought) complacency. But my wife's spirit was vibrating in sympathy with the rising storm of protest throughout the country, protests against the Vietnam War that had grown from an action of 15,000 advisors sent there by President Kennedy to President Johnson's full-scale war of nearly half a million, all without any official declaration by our elected representatives in Congress.

"But Marsda," I said, "President Johnson in effect resigned two years ago—the first time in history a President has done such a thing—just to prove that he was serious about ending the war and to try to calm the winds of protest. Now Nixon is in and pledged to end the war. He has even begun pulling troops out. Isn't this just the wrong time to leave in protest?"

"The Weathermen didn't seem to think so last fall when they went on that rampage here in Chicago. And those hundreds of thousands of people that protested in Washington

---

Sidebar annotations:

Closing **the ring** at strategic points using a pet motif. Here mention of the pets closes the first installment of the personal **encounter**. At this point it stands out only because of its whimsical lack of seriousness.

Tolling **the bell**. Opens the **significant** split in America between the right to protest (good) and the need to protest (bad).

The three paragraphs that link Marsda's spirit and the facts about Johnson's escalation of the war show how a connection can be made between personal experience and searched facts. When it works, it is a powerful combination, adding the interest of firsthand encounters to the authenticity of researched data. In addition, I found an interactive benefit as my writing process continued. The surprise of my experience first pushed me to explore the facts. Then the facts yielded surprises that stimulated me to reflect more deeply on my experience for explanations.

I used a running meteorological metaphor of storms and (serendipitously) Weathermen. But this is just for fun. They may provide a light unifying thread, but there is no strategic significance to their placement.

Searched fact (12).

Searched fact (4).

Searched facts (14) and (15).

Tolling the bell. Emphasizing the split between the destructive idealists and the jingoistic conservatives.

just before Thanksgiving last year seemed to think Nixon needed a little reminding. The country is being torn apart between the radical left and the radical right. It seemed like we had a chance in the early '60s, with all the idealism of the Civil Rights movement, to really make something beautiful happen in the country. But now everybody seems bent on destroying it all."

I remember a long nighttime drive with my father on the eve of our departure during which, almost in tears, he pleaded with me not to leave the country. "You're crazy to leave the country now," he said. "This thing's just starting to wind down."

Searched fact (13).

I dramatized the personal **encounter** by using direct dialogue. I kept the real character of my wife but somewhat fictionalized the character of my father, casting him as a more articulate social conservative than he was. Although this painful conversation between him and me actually took place, the dialogue is almost wholly invented as a convenient way to dramatize the **background** of the highly contentious **issue map** between the flag-wavers and the flag-burners of the time.

"Oh, yeah?" I said, "Do you remember those Weathermen protests last fall? Kids smashing store windows on Michigan Avenue? They seemed to think Nixon needed a little reminding about what he promised. Between the radical left and the radical right, like you, the country is being torn apart. Everybody seems determined to destroy it." (I don't know if my wife has ever realized the respect I pay her ideas after I've finish arguing with her. It's the sincerest kind of respect. I repeat her arguments against people who make my arguments. You see? Of course, I suppose, I have a secret rebel side myself.)

"Besides," I pointed out to my father, "It won't be too many years before your first grandson will be old enough to be drafted. I don't want him to be like the son of our friend who has had to forfeit his citizenship to avoid the draft."

Then came the Kent State massacre: Ohio National Guard units fired into a mass of students, some of whom were protesting but none of whom were armed or threatening. This happened the very month we left the country. It seemed to show

Searched fact (19).

that the government was becoming a right-wing militarist one, against all precedent in this country that was supposed to be democratic. Was Nixon really going to end the war, or had he gotten caught up in the Washington imperial mentality? Was he sincere, or was he just playing the same old media game, trying to manipulate public opinion while he secretly escalated the war by attacking North Vietnamese supply routes in Cambodia?

Searched facts (17), (18), and (21).

Tolling the bell. Protest peaked only after it became clear that the ham-fisted, prevaricating government was counting on the inertia of the democratic process to give its leaders plenty of room to inflict military action before the shining idealism of protest could gather enough momentum to stop it. This **explains** the main surprise—why our **eye-opening** decision to leave occurred **after** the tide seemed to have turned and why the other ultimately effective protests happened so late in the game.

We—I say *we* because by this time I, too, was swept up in the typhoon that might at least scour our private lives clean from all dirty baggage of the past—felt our decision was right, that Washington still had not understood the message of the majority of the country. So having sold our house, crated our dog and cat, packed up our books and dishes, and bundled up the children, we took off for Scotland, where we were welcomed as some of the several thousand idealistic expatriates from that strange but hypnotically fascinating country, America.

As it turned out, the horror of the Kent State massacre seemed to wake everyone up to the fact that the country had started fighting itself. There were no more major protests after that. Although Nixon continued to fight a desperate rearguard action, the number of U.S. servicemen in Vietnam was down to 139,000 by the end of 1971. That was the year when we realized that, with all its faults,

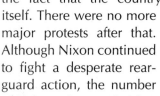

Closing the ring. This paragraph marks the boundary of the **issue mapping background** modality of the preceding several paragraphs by returning to continue the initial personal **encounter.** The pet motif is the reminder to the reader of where we started.

America was the one country that had the vision and the courage to try to solve its problems, even at considerable personal cost. So we crated our dog and cat, packed up our books and dishes, bundled up our children (who now had Scottish brogues), and returned—glad once again to be part of a country where protests like ours could redirect what Pulitzer Prize–winning historian Barbara Tuchman has called its "march of folly."

Closing the ring. The image of the purple robe was suggested by a subconscious link to Julius Caesar who, in Shakespeare's play, thrice puts by the crown offered to him by an adulating but fickle democratic crowd. It seemed apt to symbolize the imperial disease that affects most national leaders. This emphasizes the **significance** of the connection between our private **encounter** and the re**searched** facts.

But what has happened since? Reagan invaded Grenada; Bush invaded Iraq, prompting Saddam Hussein to kill tens of thousands of Kurds; Clinton (who himself was a Vietnam war protester—though at no personal cost) bombed Yugoslavia, saving the Albanians, who promptly started wholesale persecution of Serbs. President after president has taken the threadbare purple robe of imperialism out of the White House closet and led that march right back into folly!

My wife has continued to be troubled by this continuing parade of pompous power and in 1999, was once again looking to put an ocean between ourselves and a bomb-happy country that, by 74%, approved of a president who seemed to be trying to divert attention from his sexual misconduct by conducting a Balkan air war. But like most of the protesters who have seen it all before, my wife's hurricane force has downgraded to a tropical storm. For my part, I still stand in awe of her uncompromising moral energy, but I think of Robinson Jeffers watching America, fifty years ago, "heavily thickening to empire." In his best-known poem "Shine, Perishing Republic," he advised his sons to "keep their distance from the thickening center," but not to leave this shining, though "perishing republic."

Closing the ring with the pet symbolism delimits the final **resolution** and reestablishes the lighter tone after Jeffers's discouraging assessment.

So my wife settles for writing letters to congresspersons and contributing to aid organizations. Besides, as I remind her, our current cat would never survive the necessary uprooting.

I hope that opening a window into the inner workings of one person's writing process may help you see how it is possible to discover the significance of one's personal experience by orienting it within the context of re**searched** facts and to the ongoing dialogue of other writers—what Nancy Sommers calls (in the epigraph of this chapter) those "living, breathing, primary sources all around me. . . . [that] speak to me of love and loss, of memory and desire."

By using the word *search* rather than the more specific *research* I hope to imply that some of these sources come to us by browsing in libraries or by noticing relevant material while reading the newspaper. Other sources, like my quotes from Robinson Jeffers (which I encountered in **my** freshman rhetoric class) and Barbara Tuchman, simply echo from our memory vaults when the impact of jarring events rings a tone of sympathetic vibration. Don't hesitate to use those personally significant echoes found by searching through your own memories, but be sure to identify sources that might not be familiar to all your audience.

INVITATION TO A READING

Now let's see how a professional writer links **search** and personal experience to create a piece of writing of general significance. The author of the following excerpt has devoted much of her journalistic skill to furthering the cause of women's rights, the best-known expression of which was her book *Backlash: The Undeclared War against American Women*. In the 1990s, this "war" became attributed to a crisis of masculinity felt by American males. As a journalist it was part of Susan Faludi's job to investigate firsthand some of the public flare-ups caused by this cultural crisis. What she encountered disturbed her and sent her on a six-year search for an explanation and, she hoped, for a resolution. The bulk of the resulting book, *Stiffed: The Betrayal of the American Man*, describes her firsthand research, interviewing men at those crisis centers. But the book begins with the author's **search** of her own memories, recollections, and journalistic accounts of recent historical events that help her map some disturbing behavior patterns.

The Son, the Moon and the Stars:
The Promise of Postwar Manhood
by Susan Faludi
From Stiffed: The Betrayal of the American Man

When I listen to the sons born after World War II, born to the fathers who won that war, I sometimes find myself in a reverie. I imagine a boy, in bed pretending to sleep, waiting for his father.

The door opens, and the hall light streams in, casting a cutout shadow man across the bedroom floor. A minute later, the boy, wearing his coonskin cap and clutching his flashlight, races after his father along the shadowy upper hallway, down the stairs and out the screen door. The man and the boy kneel on the scratchy wool of the father's old navy peacoat, and the father snaps off the boy's flashlight. The father directs the boy's vision to a faraway glimmer. Its name is Echo. The boy looks up, knowing that the satellite his father is pointing out is more than just an object; it is a paternal gift rocketing him into his future, a miraculous inheritance encased in the transit of an artificial star, infinitesimally tiny, impossibly bright.

I knew this boy. Like everyone else who grew up in the late 1950s and early 1960s, I knew dozens of him. He was Bobby on the corner, who roamed the neighborhood with his cap gun and holster, terrorizing girls and household pets. He was Frankie, who blew off part of his pinkie while trying to ignite a miniature rocket in the schoolyard. Even if he wasn't brought out into the backyard and shown a satellite glinting in the sky, he was introduced to the same promise and the same vision, and by such a father. Many of these fathers were veterans of World War II or Korea, but their bloody paths to virility were not ones they sought to pass on, or usually even discuss. This was to be the era of manhood after victory, when the pilgrimage to masculinity would be guided not by the god of war Mars, but by the dream of a pioneering trip to the planet Mars. The satellite: here was a visible patrimony, a visual marker of vaulting technological power and progress to be claimed in the future by every baby-boom boy. The men of the fathers' generation had "won" the world and now they were giving it to their sons.

Four decades later, as the nation wobbled toward the millennium, its pulse-takers all seemed to agree that a domestic apocalypse was underway: American manhood was under siege. Newspaper editors, legislators, preachers, marketers, no matter where they perched on the political spectrum, had a contribution to make to the chronicles of the "masculinity crisis." Right-wing talk-radio hosts and leftwing men's-movement spokesmen found themselves uncomfortably on common ground. MEN ON TRIAL, the headlines cried, THE TROUBLE WITH BOYS. . . .

If so many concurred in the existence of a male crisis, consensus collapsed as soon as anyone asked the question Why? Everyone proposed a favorite whipping boy or, more often, whipping girl, and blame-seekers on all sides went after their selected culprits with righteous and bitter relish. Feminist mothers, indulgent liberals, videogame makers or testosterone itself all came under attack.

At Ground Zero of the Masculinity Crisis

The search for an answer to that question took me on a six-year odyssey, with stops along the way at a shuttered shipyard in Long Beach, a suburban living room where a Promise Keepers group met, a Cleveland football stadium where fans grieved the loss of their team, a Florida horse farm where a Vietnam vet finally found peace, a grassy field in Waco where militiamen searched for an enemy and a slick magazine office where young male editors contended with a commodified manhood.

But I began investigating this crisis where you might expect a feminist journalist to begin: at the weekly meetings of a domestic-violence group. Wednesday evenings in a beige stucco building a few blocks from the freeway in Long Beach, California, I attended a gathering of men under court order to repent the commission of an act that stands as the emblematic masculine sin of our age. What did I expect to divine about the broader male condition by monitoring a weekly counseling session for batterers? That men are by nature brutes? Or, more optimistically, that the efforts of such a group might point to methods of "curing" such beastliness? Either way, I can see now that I was operating from an assumption both underexamined and dubious: that the male crisis in America was caused by something men were doing unrelated to something being done to them. I had my own favorite whipping boy, suspecting that the crisis of masculinity was caused by masculinity on the rampage. If male violence was the quintessential expression of masculinity run amok, then a domestic-violence therapy group must be at the very heart of this particular darkness. I wasn't alone in such circular reasoning. I was besieged with suggestions along similar lines from journalists, feminists, antifeminists and other willing advisers. Women's rights advocates mailed me news clips about male office stalkers and computer harassers. That I was not ensconced in the courtroom for O.J. Simpson's murder trial struck many of my volunteer helpers as an appalling lapse of judgment. "The perfect case study of an American man who thinks he's entitled to just control everything and everybody," one of them suggested.

But then, I had already been attending the domestic-violence group for several months—the very group O.J. Simpson was, by coincidence, supposed to have attended but avoided with the promise that he would speak by phone to a psychiatrist—and it was already apparent to me that these men's crises did not stem from a preening sense of entitlement and control. Each new member in the group, called Alternatives to Violence, would be asked to describe what he had done to a woman. . . .

A serviceman who had turned to nightclub-bouncer jobs and pastry catering after his military base shut down seemed to confirm the counselors' position one evening shortly before his "graduation" from the group. "I denied it before" he said of the night he pummeled his girlfriend. "I thought I'd blacked out. But looking back at that night, I didn't black out. I was feeling good. I was in power, I was strong, I was in control. I felt like a man." But what struck me most strongly was what he said next: that moment of control had been the only one in his recent life. "That feeling of power," he said, "didn't last long. Only until they put the cuffs on. Then I was feeling again like I was no man at all."

He was typical in this regard. The men I got to know in the group had, without exception, lost their compass in the world. They had lost or were losing jobs, homes, cars, families. They had been labeled outlaws but felt like castoffs. There was something almost absurd about these men struggling, week after week, to recognize themselves as dominators when they were so clearly dominated, done in by the world. . . .

The veterans of World War II were eager to embrace a masculine ideal that revolved around providing rather than dominating. Their most important experiences had centered on the support they had given one another in the war, and it was this that they wished to replicate. As artilleryman Win Stracke told oral historian Studs Terkel in "The Good War," he came home bearing this most cherished memory: "You had 15 guys who for the first time in their lives could help each other without cutting each other's throat or trying to put down somebody else through a boss or whatever. I had realized it was the absence of competition and all those phony standards that created the thing I loved about the army." The fathers who would sire the baby-boom generation would try to pass that experience of manhood on intact to their sons. The grunts who went overseas and liberated the world came home to the expectation that they would liberate the country by quiet industry and caretaking.

The vets threw themselves into their federally funded educations, and later their defense-funded corporate and production-line jobs, and their domestic lives in Veterans Administration–financed tract homes. They hoped their dedication would be in the service of a higher national aim. For their children, the period of soaring expectations that followed the war was truly the era of the boy. It was the culture of "Father Knows Best" and "Leave It to Beaver," of Pop Warner rituals and Westinghouse science scholarships, of BB guns and rocket clubs, of football practice and lettered jackets, of magazine ads where "Dad" seemed always to be beaming down at his scampy, cowboy-suited younger son or proudly handing his older son the keys to a brand new convertible. It was a world where, regardless of the truth that lay behind each garden gate, popular culture led us to believe that fathers were spending every leisure moment in roughhouse play and model-airplane construction with their beloved boys. In the aspiring middle-class sub-urb where I came of age, there was no mistaking the belief in the boy's pre-eminence; it was evident in the solicitous attentions of parents and schoolteachers, in the centrality of Cub Scouts and Little League, in the community life that revolved around boys' championships and boys' scores—as if these outposts of tract-home America had been built mainly as exhibition rings for junior-male achievement, which perhaps they had. . . .

Ultimately, the boy was double-crossed. The fix was in from the start: corporate and cold-war America's promise to continue the World War II GI's wartime experience of belonging, of meaningful engagement in a mission, was never authentic. "The New Frontier" of space turned out to be a void that no man could conquer, let alone colonize. The astronaut was no Daniel Boone; he was just a flattened image for TV viewers to watch—and eventually, to be bored by. Instead of sending its sons to Normandy, the government dispatched them to Vietnam, where the enemy was unclear and the mission remained a tragic mystery. The massive managerial bureaucracies of postwar "white collar" employment, especially the defense contractors fat on government largesse, produced "organization men" who often didn't even know what they were managing—and who suspected they weren't really needed at all. What these corporations offered was a secure job, not a vital role—and not even that secure.

The postwar fathers' submission to the national security state would, after a prosperous period of historically brief duration, be rewarded with pink slips, with massive downsizing, union-breaking and outsourcing. The boy who had been told he was going to be the master of the universe and all that was in it found himself master of nothing. As early as 1957, the boy's diminished future was foreshadowed in a classic sci-fi film. In "The Incredible Shrinking Man," Scott Carey has a good job, a suburban home, a pleasure boat, a pretty wife. And yet, after he passes through a mist of atomic radiation while on a boating vacation in the Pacific, something happens. As he tells his wife in horror, "I'm getting smaller, Lou, every day." As Carey quite literally shrinks, the promises made to him are broken one by one. The employer who was to give him lifetime economic security fires him. He is left with only feminine defenses, to hide in a doll house, to fight a giant spider with a sewing pin. And it turns out that the very source of his diminishment is implicitly an atomic test by his own government. His only hope is to turn himself into a celebrated freak and sell his story to the media. "I'm a big man!" Carey says with bitter sarcasm. "I'm famous! One more joke for the world to laugh at." The more Carey shrinks, the more he strikes out at those around him. "Every day I became more tyrannical," he comments, "more monstrous in my domination of my wife." It's a line that would ring a bell for any visitor to the Alternatives to Violence group and for any observer of the current male scene. As the male role has diminished amid a sea of betrayed promises, many men have been driven to more domineering and some even "monstrous" displays in their frantic quest for a meaningful showdown.

The Ornamental Culture

The more I consider what men have lost—a useful role in public life, a way of earning a decent living, respectful treatment in the culture—the more it seems that men are falling into a status oddly similar to that of women at midcentury. The '50s housewife, stripped of her connections to a wider world and invited to fill the void with shopping and the ornamental display of her ultrafemininity, could be said to have morphed into the '90s man, stripped of his connections to a wider world and invited to fill the void with consumption and a gym-bred display of his ultramasculinity. The empty compensations of a "feminine mystique" are transforming into the empty compensations of a masculine mystique, with a gentlemen's cigar club no more satisfying than a ladies' bake-off. . . .

American men have generally responded well as caretakers in times of crisis, whether that be in wars, depressions or natural disasters. The pre-eminent contemporary example of such a male mobilization also comes on the heels of a crisis: gay men's response to AIDS. Virtually overnight, just as the Depression-era Civilian Conservation Corps built dams and parks and salvaged farmland, so have gay men built a network of clinics, legal and psychological services, fund-raising and political-action brigades, meals on wheels, even laundry assistance. The courage of these caregivers has generated, even in this homophobic nation, a wellspring of admiration and respect. They had a job to do and they did it. Social responsibility is not the special province of masculinity; it's the lifelong work of all citizens in a community where people are knit together by meaningful and mutual concerns. But if husbanding a society is not the exclusive calling of "husbands," all the better for men's future. Because as men struggle to free themselves from their crisis, their task is not, in the end, to figure out how to be masculine—rather, their masculinity lies in figuring out how to be human. The men who worked at the Long Beach Naval Shipyard, where I spent many months, didn't go there and learn their crafts as riggers, welders and boilermakers to be masculine; they were seeking something worthwhile to do. Their sense of their own manhood flowed out of their utility in a society, not the other way around. And so with the mystery of men's nonrebellion comes the glimmer of an opening, a chance for men to forge a rebellion commensurate with women's and, in the course of it, to create a new paradigm for human progress that will open doors for both sexes. That was, and continues to be, feminism's dream, to create a freer, more humane world. It will remain a dream without the strength and courage of men who are today faced with a historic opportunity: to learn to wage a battle against no enemy, to own a frontier of human liberty, to act in the service of a brotherhood that includes us all.

CRITICAL READING

1. Notice the pun in the title. How does that anticipate the **background** Faludi takes as the starting point for the disillusionment that she sees behind the current male crisis? Notice that she

rings the bell of this opening by echoing the word "boy" in the paragraph beginning "Ultimately, the boy was double-crossed." Explain this, and explain how this reversal points to an **explanation** of contemporary male crisis.

2. What were some of the **eye-opening** surprises that launched Faludi's search? She notes that these cried out for **explanation.** What were some of the possible explanations that she and other women conjectured?

3. Faludi adopts two contrasting symbols to embody the **significance** of the modern male experience—the launching of the Echo satellite and the sci-fi movie *The Incredible Shrinking Man.* How do these symbols help her dramatize the **explanation** of male violence?

4. Of the several factual instances that Faludi establishes as trail markers on her background map, which appear to be ones that she would probably have gone to her bookshelves, a library, or the Internet to discover or verify?

5. Faludi's book is an instructive example of the way in which **search,** when conducted with intellectual honesty, can change a writer's preconceptions and result in an original **resolution** that may help the whole society. How did her perception of American masculinity change? What constructive path does she see for men out of their present crisis? How may that help women as well?

DISCUSSION QUESTIONS

1. Drawing on your own experience, do you see any change in the "war between the sexes" from your parents' generation to your own?

2. It is a researchable fact that the U.S. economy has been steadily turning from one based on heavy industry and manufacture to one based on service and finance. Do you think, as Faludi implies, that this change has adversely affected men more than women? Do you think it is harder on a man than on a woman to be "downsized" out of a job?

3. Faludi traces the modern male malaise not to a reaction against the freedoms gained by women but to a society that manipulates masculine imagery while failing to recognize and use men's most productive gifts. Do you agree? Do you think it is possible for men to find an escape from this box by initiating a revolution without an enemy as Faludi envisions?

WRITING COMMISSION: A PERSONAL COLUMN CLARIFIED BY SOME RESEARCH

Your editor is back, this time with a request for a personal column from each of the interns. There has been a furor in the local high school over the poor performance of girls in math classes and the small number of girls enrolling in science classes. The community is divided on the question of whether the school should fund special initiatives in the grade schools to get girls and their parents more interested in science and give them more confidence that girls can perform as well as boys in math.

"A lot of this goes back to the 'nature versus nurture' thing," your editor points out. "And it goes beyond just school work. There is the whole debate about raising boys differently from girls. Are boys genetically programmed to play with trucks and hit each other with them, while girls are genetically programmed to play with dolls and involve other girls in tea parties with them? Or is this something parents unconsciously teach their children as 'correct' social roles?"

"Yeah," one of the female interns interjects. "And even if there are some genetic differences, should parents simply run in a groove dug in the genome right after our ancestors climbed down out of trees? Shouldn't we try to socialize the male animal by bringing him in on the tea parties and show girls how much fun it is to be masters of big machines?"

"Exactly!" responds the editor. "There you go! Now you've all probably had some experience being either girls or boys, and you probably remember seeing how the other kind acts. Some of you have probably had more recent experience as camp counselors, baby sitters, maybe even as aunts, uncles, or parents. So I suggest you start with one of those, or work it in somewhere if you have a better hook.

"But this is an issue that's in the air with pretty strong feelings on both sides. Furthermore it's a complicated issue, and readers will write your column off as a piece of fluff unless you back it up with some actual research and show a pretty strong grasp of all the ins and outs. There is, in fact, quite a bit of scientific research out there, but there are also the charges that research has been strongly biased by feminist or antifeminist political agendas. So even reporting 'scientific' results can be a mine field."

You ask, a little panicked, if this is supposed to be like a research paper.

"Good grief, no!" laughs your editor. "Who would want to read a research paper? But in one way it's harder because you have to select just a couple of facts or instances that provide a clear dialogue with your experience, with each other, and with the issue in our local schools—like a drama of ideas.

"But what you've learned about doing research still applies, even though you're not going to use endnotes or a bibliography.

"For example," the editor continues, "I know that you'll cite your sources for all your facts and tell the readers enough about any expert opinions you quote to make them believe those 'experts' know what they're talking about. Today **everybody's** an expert, especially about sex roles!

"Now as long as we're on the subject of research, I have a handout I always give to my interns. I know most of you have been indoctrinated into library use, probably several times since grade school, and I don't want to beat a dead horse or insult anybody's bibliographic skills, but take this for what it's worth. You may pick up a few pointers from it."

A Quick and Dirty Review of Research Techniques

If you have read one or more books on your subject, it should be easy for you to find appropriate passages in them. If you are looking for new books on the subject, it is harder to find such passages in the short time you will have available for this assignment, but it can be done. The best way that I've found is just to go to the shelves where books on your topic are located. If you know a couple of names of well-known authors on your topic, look first for books by those people. Otherwise, look for newer books by just going down the row. Open the book and glance through it. You can often get a sense of its authenticity—the credibility of the author—just by seeing if it has footnotes, charts, and a bibliography. Indented blocks of paragraphs often indicate case histories that you might find useful. Reading a few lines here and there will give you a sense of the author's sense of audience and warn you if it's too simple minded or too technical for your purposes. If a book seems promising, turn to the table of contents to see if your aspect of the issue is dealt with by name in a chapter. If so, it's probably worth skimming that chapter. If not, try the index. For the purpose of this assignment, a couple of books will do if you can find them. If you try books but come away blank, it's OK. There are other sources.

A section of your library's reference books will contain many statistical abstracts and other fact books, including almanacs, as well as books narrowly targeted to specific topics. These are the quickest way to dig up solid factual information. Your librarian is the best source for discovering which of these compendiums is most likely to have material on your subject.

If your facts are to fulfill their mission of increasing your credibility, they must be credible facts. The way to make them credible is to tell the reader where you got them! Be sure to take careful notes on the titles of your books and articles, the names of the authors, and the dates on which they appeared. If it is a magazine article, also note the name of the magazine. Dates are often important in establishing credibility; all other things being equal, more recent facts are stronger than older ones.

For current issues, magazines are often the best source for facts and reported experiences. Most libraries now have some kind of computer-based periodical indexing system. Get a librarian to show you how yours works. A search by subject will turn up every article from the last few years, so be sure to make your subject narrow enough to avoid a glut of references. Look through the results of your search for likely titles from well-known magazines that are available in your library. Some periodical search services will let you immediately print out the text of the article; with others you have to locate the article on microfilm and use a microfilm projector, some of which will have printing options. Again, ask your librarian how to use the equipment.

The traditional printed index of magazine articles, the familiar huge green volumes of the *Reader's Guide to Periodical Literature,* still has some advantages over computer-based searches. First, you can see all the references at a glance and scan them much more quickly than you can by bringing up screen after screen on a computer. More important, the subject category and subcategory listings and cross-references provided by the editors of this series can often, by themselves, help you clarify your issue map. You may have a friend who was raped, and you want to write on this subject. When you use the *Readers' Guide,* you find that there is a whole subcategory of date rape with its own set of issues of which you might previously have been unaware and which fit the situation of your friend. In addition to shortening your search, this insight can help you focus your topic.

Doing research on the Internet through the World Wide Web is often very rewarding, but it has three serious pitfalls. First, anyone can put anything on the Internet and claim it is fact. To prove this to yourself, check out the safety of Aspartame, the artificial sweetener, on the Internet. It's worth taking a few minutes to amuse yourself by looking at the number of sites trumpeting the dangers of this product. Don't leave before finding at least one site that contradicts the majority and tries to show that it's perfectly safe. You may also have heard the story of Pierre Sallinger's being duped by Internet disinformation about the downing of TWA Flight 800 by accidental U.S. rocket attack. His embarrassment should be a lesson to us all about the unreliability of the Internet.

The second problem is that a typical keyword search on the Web may find 100,000 or more references. Several sites try to help narrow and categorize that search: Excite, Infoseek, LookSmart, Lycos, AskJeeves, and Yahoo are the most popular. It takes careful reading and a lot of practice to sort out the little bit of really helpful information from the mountains of junk on the Internet. But once you've found it, you can usually download it to your own computer and copy it directly into your writing.

Which leads to the third problem—copying sources without credit or permission. The temptation to plagiarize increases when the research is done on the Internet because it is so easy just to download from their file to your file. Columnist Mary Schmich tells the story of a column of hers that became very popular. It was a column of advice to graduates that began "Wear sunscreen." It was copied onto the Internet and soon the attribution changed. It came to be described as a commencement address delivered at MIT by the famous science fiction writer Kurt Vonnegut.

This has two lessons for us. First, although Schmich has laughed off this piracy, it is deeply unfair that the true author did not get the credit (let alone the royalties) she deserved for writing so popular a piece. Second, it reinforces the fact that any information you get from the Internet is suspect. Schmich received nearly a thousand pieces of mail about the incident. One writer asked her, "What is the weirdest e-mail you've received?" She replied, "Several have suggested that there is no Mary Schmich. One claimed Mary Schmich is a character in Kurt Vonnegut's new novel."

Exploring the Topic: Surveys

As I mentioned at the beginning of the chapter, if a puzzle, surprise, or disturbance pushes us beyond the limits of our own data bank of personal encounters and the similar incidents we read about still seem conflicted, the next step is to ask people we know to search **their** personal data banks. Through the science of statistics, it is possible to expand the technique of "asking people" to include not just acquaintances but the entire population of the country.

Which TV programs we get to watch is largely determined by what the mere handful of 1200 Nielsen families watch. Which books we get to read (at least at a discount) and which ones are made into movies is more and more determined by the impressions of those few bookstore owners whom the *New York Times* Best Seller List editor chooses to ask about what's selling well. Which candidates we finally get to vote for is often decided by early, sometimes slapdash polls that encourage or discourage contributors. This is the sometimes tyrannical power of the polls.

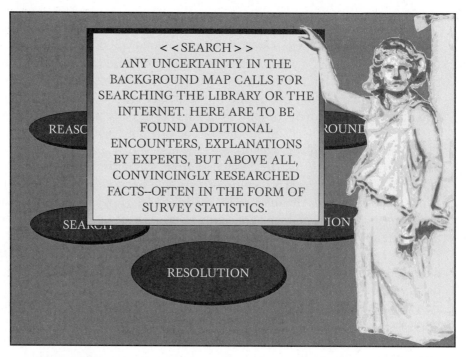

Figure 9.4.

George Gallup, who was for 50 years the most respected name in public opinion polling, fervently believed in the principle that scientific surveys are the voice of the people in a democracy—that through the miracle of statistical sampling, 1,000–2,000 people can be made to represent accurately the will and wishes of the entire population on every subject from motel accommodation preferences to foreign policy and from cola flavors to trends in religious convictions. Although the Gallup Poll and the Harris Survey remain the most widely printed of all, the woods are full of pollsters, and it is the rare piece of nonfiction writing today that does not make use of the results of surveys. To see a broad collection of polls on nearly every subject, visit the Internet site < http://www.pollingreport.com/ > .

Some of the uses of polls are

1. To test the market for a new product
2. To discover how well a product is selling
3. To establish audience size as an index for advertising value
4. To test the appeal of celebrities who endorse products

5. To detect concerns and trends among people
6. To discover important issues that concern people
7. To justify government or company policies
8. To try to prove a point or justify a decision already reached
9. To promote political candidates
10. To select juries sympathetic to defendants

People continue to believe polls, even when some have been spectacularly wrong. *The Literary Digest* went out of business after predicting in 1936 that Alf Landon would beat Franklin Roosevelt; George Gallup survived his prediction in 1948 that Dewey would beat Truman; and the Ford Motor Company lost millions when Albert Sindlinger predicted that they would successfully sell 200,000 Edsels.

How can polls look so scientific and still be subject to such disastrous mistakes?

There are two major problems in getting accurate results from a survey: (1) asking the right number of the right people; and (2) asking the right questions in the right way.

In the early days, pollsters tried to divide up the population according to income, age, ethnic background, education, and geographical area and interview a proportionate number of people from

Figure 9.5. Truman with the news of his "defeat."

Figure 9.6. The Edsel.

each group. Not only was this very cumbersome, but it didn't work well, either. A sample of people simply chosen at random is better. It can also be shown that you only need to interview 2000 randomly chosen people in the whole country to get 95 percent accuracy. Even so, there are some problems getting those people. Some people work two jobs, so they are never home; some people refuse to answer questions; some people live in areas that interviewers will not visit. When your random sample fails to include one of these people, the opinions of all those who are represented by that person are not going to show up in your survey.

Even when you find the people, there may be other problems. Do people understand the question? In the middle of the Vietnam War, for example, when that subject had been in the news for two years, fewer than half the American people could name the capitals of either South or North Vietnam. Discovering how many people supported the mining of Haiphong Harbor, then, without eliminating those who did not know even that it was the port of Hanoi, the capital of North Vietnam, was like asking a Chinese visitor if she preferred baked Alaska or date créme crunch parfait for dessert.

Do people tell the truth to the pollsters? After the Watergate scandal, people were asked whether they had voted for Nixon or McGovern in the 1972 election. So many people refused to admit that they had voted for Nixon, that, according to their responses, McGovern should have won the state of California by 8 percent. (Nixon won every state except Massachusetts and the District of Columbia.) After Kennedy's assassination, almost no one would admit to having voted against him, although he had just barely squeaked by in the election.[4]

Even more of a problem than asking the right number of the right people is asking the right question in the right way. You can really get almost any result you want by how you phrase the question, especially if you allow people only two choices—agree or disagree. Suppose you are making a survey on the question of which parent should get custody of the children in a divorce. Suppose you simply say "Agree or disagree: Mothers should generally be given custody of the children in a divorce." People might generally agree. But what if the mother abuses alcohol or has a new boyfriend every week while the father is a model of sobriety? Some people might feel that, in this case, the father would be a better influence. If you felt like this, how would you answer the question? To say you disagreed would seem to mean that you think fathers are the better single parent; to say you agreed would seem to mean that even a bad mother is better than a good father. The results of such a survey don't really mean much. Let's suppose another pollster asked the question this way: "Agree/disagree: a responsible father should perhaps be given custody of the children in a divorce if the mother is irresponsible." We can imagine that many more people would agree with this statement than would disagree with the first one, thus giving the impression of inconsistency.

Do you think that the results would change if we removed the word "perhaps" from this statement?

These are all things you must keep in mind when you construct a survey to use in your own writing or when you read the results of a survey in a magazine or newspaper.

Is that book you want to read really a best-seller? Michael Wheeler (*Lies, Damn Lies, and Statistics*) tells the story of Chuck Barris, one of the pioneers of TV game shows like "The Dating Game" and "The Gong Show," who "was so dissatisfied about the way his publisher was failing to promote his book *You and Me, Babe,* that he decided to sink tens of thousands of dollars in buying it up in those stores known to be in the *New York Times*' sample. The purchases put

---

[4] *Lies, Damn Lies, and Statistics* (Liveright 1976) by Michael Wheeler.

the book on the best seller list, which then generated enough orders from other stores to get it selling in its own right." Without Barris's fooling the polls in this way, not only would readers never have wanted to read *You and Me, Babe,* they might not even have been able to!

Survey re**search** is a staple of column and article writers on virtually all topics, especially those involving issues. How parents and children should interact—a topic related to Faludi's book and a column you are going to write—was studied in the poll that follows, and those results were interpreted in the *Time* article that follows it.

In 1999, Penn, Schoen and Berland Associates conducted a poll for Nickelodeon, the children's TV channel, and *Time* magazine. In the following list are some of the questions with the results. Because you will soon be constructing your own survey, think about why the pollsters asked these particular questions, why they phrased them as they did, and why they offered just these response options.

Growing Up—The Views of Kids and Their Parents

1. How safe do you feel in your school?

Very safe	49%
Pretty safe	44%
Not safe	5%

2. What is bad about being a kid?

   KIDS SAY

Getting bossed around	17%
School, homework	15%
Can't do everything I want	11%
Chores	9%
Being grounded	9%

   PARENTS SAY

Crime	26%
Youth violence, guns	13%
Peer pressure	13%
Drugs	5%
Homework, chores	4%

3. What are the most important things that kids at your school use to decide who fits in?

    AGES 9–11

Being a good friend	45%
Being good at sports	35%
Popularity	31%
Being funny	31%

    AGES 12–14

Clothes	44%
Popularity	37%
Being good looking	34%
Being a good friend	33%

4. Do you spend more time with your mom, dad, or both about the same?

Mom	47%
Dad	11%
The same	41%

5. How much respect do you think adults have for kids?

	Kids	Parents
A lot	31%	52%
Some	48%	42%
A little	16%	6%
None	5%	0%

6. Of all the people you know or know about, who are the top three you look up to most?

My parents	79%
My grandparents	19%
Athletes	13%

7. Do you believe in God?

Yes	95%

8. Percent who pray

Ages 6–8	73%
Ages 9–11	81%
Ages 12–14	84%

9. How important is it to wait until you are married to have sex?

Very	53%
Somewhat	23%
Not important	22%

10. At what age do you think premarital sex is appropriate?

    Kids—23 years old

    Parents—18 years old

11. Would you like to be President of the United States?
    KIDS SAY
       Yes   36%
       No   62%
12. Would you like your child to be President?
    PARENTS SAY
       Yes   31%
       No   58%
13. Would you rather be Bill Gates or Bill Clinton?
    KIDS SAY
       Bill Gates   67%
       Bill Clinton   21%

Before going on to read the Time article about this survey, discuss with the class what eye-opening surprises you would highlight in these responses if you were going to write about them. (The thirteen questions here have already been selected by the editors to be the most significant from a larger total battery of questions, so you are selecting from a selection!) What significance do you see in those surprises?

Now here is the *Time* article based on the survey results you have just seen. Be particularly aware as you read of what **eye-opening** techniques the author uses to bring those numbers to life.

The Kids Are Alright
by Claudia Wallis with reporting by Harriet Barovick

While parents worry, a new poll by Nickelodeon and TIME shows that youngsters find the world a less scary place—and are in no rush to grow up.

Let's face it, as grownups, it's our job to worry. And for those of us attempting to raise children at the close of this century, there's no shortage of anxieties to gnaw at the nerves and churn the gut. How, we wonder, can our children flourish and stay on course with only a few hours a day of parental devotion? How can kids focus on schoolwork when tempted by a luscious smorgasbord of multimedia junk? Hmm, would Ritalin help? Is Austin Powers too racy for a nine-year-old? How about tube tops and platform shoes? Looming larger is a more ominous concern: Will my child's life end in a burst of gunfire and a pool of blood on the cafeteria's cold linoleum floor?

Surely American kids have never faced a more corrupting, corrosive and threatening environment. Or have they? Given the recent headlines and hand wringing, it is something of a shock to discover that according to a major new kids' survey, children don't see the world that way at all. For them, the mid-century mantra of youth still applies: What, me worry?

From mid-May through June 1, just a few weeks after the Littleton, Colo., shootings, New York–based pollsters Penn, Schoen & Berland Assoc. sat down with 1,172 kids, ages 6 to 14, in 25 U.S. cities. The poll was conducted for Nickelodeon, the children's TV channel, and TIME. Kids from a sample weighted to match U.S. demographics were interviewed one-on-one and without their parents in a venue where most feel at ease: a shopping mall. Pollsters also interviewed 397 parents.

What emerges loud and clear from the study is that kids are very happy to be kids, and they don't view the world as the nasty place their parents perceive it to be. Nine out of 10 say they feel safe in their schools and neighborhoods. While parents list crime, violence and guns as the worst aspects of being a child today, such concerns are way down the list for kids. Their gripes are the timeless laments of childhood: "getting bossed around," homework, chores.

Are kids in a hurry to grow up, as parents presume? No way, say 8 out of 10 of the 6- to 11-year-olds who answered this question. "Because then I'll have to manage my own money and make my own dinner," explained one boy to a pollster. Despite a precocious fondness for R-rated movies (which half the 9- to 11-year-olds and 81% of 12- to 14-year-olds say they've seen), kids are not even eager to become teenagers. Younger kids have more fun, insist 64% of 6- to 11-year-olds. Even in this era of extracurricular overload, most kids (72%) said they have enough time to "just hang around" and do what they please.

As for the much lamented decline of family values, the anarchic influence of such shows as *South Park,* the collapse of parental authority and discipline—well, has anyone mentioned this to kids? Asked whom they admire most, 79% say it's good old Mom and Dad; an additional 19% name their grandparents. Athletes, musicians and movie stars don't even come close.

But God looms large in the life of the younger generation: 95% of the kids surveyed said they were believers. Nearly half claimed to attend religious services every week, and 8 out of 10 say they pray. Sure, they may enjoy dipping into the sultry waters of *Dawson's Creek* on Wednesday nights, but their ideas about sex would cheer William Bennett: 76% of those ages 12 to 14 say it's "somewhat or very important" to wait until marriage before having sex. When the other 24% were asked to name an appropriate age for premarital sex, these pubescent puritans settled on 23. The average age mentioned by parents: 18.

So are adults cultivating gray hairs and worry lines for nothing? Could it be that the kids are alright?[5] For the most part, yes, and don't be so surprised, say several child psychologists consulted by TIME on the poll results.

"Parents remain the most significant people in children's lives, until age 14 or 15, when they have more fully embraced peer culture," says Jean Bailey, coordinator of child and adolescent mental-health services at Lutheran Medical Center in Brooklyn, N.Y. Personal values about religion, sex and obeying authority are primarily shaped by parents right up until the teenage years, when things suddenly shift. While kids may be exposed to sex in the media, "there's a lot of anxiety about what the whole deal of sexual behavior is," says child psychologist Anthony Wolf, author of *Get Out of My Life, but First Could You Drive Me and Cheryl to the Mall?* (1991). Wolf is not surprised that kids are in no rush to become teens: "Teenagers are out there doing all these fast and wild things. Kids see that world as a little scary."

If Americans have the wrong idea about their kids, it may be because of the very disturbed and anomalous kids who make headlines. "We should be very concerned about those kids, but they are a small minority," notes Johns Hopkins sociologist Andrew Cherlin. Adults also tend to read too much into children's superficial gestures. A five-year-old who wants to dress like Posh Spice still wants to be a kid; after all, only kids get to play dress-up! And if kids seem to be growing up faster than they used to, the fault may lie partly with adults, especially some of those in the entertainment business. Says Nickelodeon president Herb Scannell, who commissioned the poll: "One of the problems we have in this industry is we make assumptions: kids don't want to see movies with kids; they want to see movies with teens, movies with aliens. We're not listening to kids."

The kids have taken note of this disregard, and if there's a lesson for parents in the Nickelodeon/TIME poll, it's tune in to your kids and show them some respect. While the majority of parents in the study claim to have great respect for kids, only 31% of kids feel that adults actually do respect them "a lot." This "respect gap" is even more glaring among kids in the 12 to 14 age group: 27% said they get little respect from adults or none at all.

---

[5] This spelling is not yet recognized as correct by most English teachers, although, because a prestigious magazine is using it boldly, even in a title, and because Microsoft Word spell checker accepts it, it is probably on its way to being as accepted as *already* and *altogether.*

"It's true that most adults think they don't have much to learn from children and don't really value their opinions, except on topics like, say, ice cream," says David Elkind, professor of child development at Tufts University and author of *The Hurried Child* (1981). "Kids do have interesting ideas, if you're willing to listen. And I think sometimes adults are not civil enough with kids, saying please, thank you, apologizing for breaking promises."

Sensitive young teens emerge as a particularly interesting group in the poll. The middle school years are perilous. While only 14% of the 9- to 11-year-olds said they had ever tried alcohol, the figure rose to 42% among 12- to 14-year-olds. Drug use rose from zero to 11%; smoking from 11% to 44%.

Peer pressure rears its head in other ways as well. What does it take to "fit in" at school? Kids ages 9 to 11 say it's being a good friend, being good at sports and being funny or popular. But kids in the 12 to 14 group have different criteria: clothes come first, then "being popular" and third, good looks. "This is a little bit sad," observes Wolf, "but it also shows parents what they're up against if they're trying to draw the line on certain clothes." The emphasis on having the right stuff to wear may also help explain why low-income kids in the poll worry the most about fitting in.

The early teens are the years when parents fall off the pedestal. While 57% of 9- to 11-year-olds say they want to be like their parents, only 26% of 12- to 14-year-olds do. "This is the 100% normal, virtually inevitable moment when kids develop an allergy to their parents," says Wolf. "They don't want to breathe the same way their parents do."

Despite all this, 60% of kids ages 12 to 14 say, as most younger kids do, that they would like to spend more time with their parents. The problem, of course, is finding that time, which is at a premium in the increasing number of two-earner households and those headed by single parents. A clear reflection of how families have changed: 41% of the kids sampled said they spend an equal amount of time with both parents. "This is one of our most significant cultural changes," says Dr. Leon Hoffman, who co-directs the Parent Child Center at the New York Psychoanalytic Society. In practice for 30 years, Hoffman has found a "very dramatic difference in the involvement of the father—in everything from caretaking to general decision making around kids' lives." Alas, this change has been slower to reach black children: 76% of black kids surveyed said they spend more time with their mom than their dad.

There are other signs of change. The most worrisome: 1 in 6 kids ages 12 to 14 claims to have seen a gun at school. Other studies have also shown that American kids have easy access to guns. That kids in the survey feel safe at school may be because school shootings remain rare. The study did find, however, that black and Hispanic children are a lot more worried than whites about being crime victims.

On the upside, tolerance for diversity seems to be gathering strength. Most kids support the notion that girls and boys can play on the same sports teams. Nine out of 10 say they have friends of a different race. Four out of 10 say that it's not very important, or not important at all, that a future spouse should be someone of the same race. Most expect to see a black President and a woman President in their lifetime.

As an institution, however, the presidency appears to have suffered: 62% of kids ages 9 to 14 say they do not want to grow up to be President. "It's too much pressure, and everyone is watching you," explained a seventh-grade girl. "I don't want to turn out like Bill and Monica," said an 11-year-old. In fact, 67% of 9- to 14-year-olds said they'd rather be Bill Gates than Bill Clinton.

But mostly, and most reassuringly, kids just want to be kids. What's so great about it? Parents in the poll said the boon for kids today is technology and computers. They just don't get it. The best things about being a kid, say those who really know, are playing, hanging with friends and having fun. Well, duh!

CRITICAL READING

1. Here is an article that does **not** begin with an encounter! What technique does Claudia Wallis use to provoke the interest of her audience?

2. Can you link each of the issues she raises in this list of questions with one of the questions in the survey?

3. What is the modality of the third paragraph ("From mid-May through June 1 . . . ")? Why is it important? Do you think you should have a paragraph like this one when you write about your own or others' surveys?

4. There was a footnote in the original *Time* article, placed after the table of survey questions and results which you examined before reading the article. The footnote reads like this:

> Methodology: Penn, Schoen & Berland conducted 1,172 interviews with children ages 6 to 14 and 397 interviews with parents at 27 shopping malls in 25 cities throughout the U.S. from May 14 to June 1, 1999.
>
> Margins of error: all kids ±2.9%; age categories and parents ±5%.

Looking again at paragraph 3, how does the author make the introduction of this material graceful?

5. Making numbers interesting is a challenge. Give some examples of how Wallis **dramatizes** them.

6. The author (and probably the pollsters) grouped the questions around issues they supposed would be interesting to their readers. Wallis announces at the beginning that she supposes most parents view the growing-up years of their children with alarm. With that in mind, describe the strategy she follows in developing the issue map. What paragraphs mark boundaries on that map where she shifts from supporting one side to showing her awareness of the other?

DISCUSSION QUESTIONS

1. For her **resolution** in the last paragraph, Wallis echoes two statements of **significance** the bells of which have been tolling through the essay: (1) parents are overanxious about the dangers of growing up, and (2) the **explanation** for that is that parents don't listen enough to kids. Do you agree or disagree? Give some specific examples from your experience to support your view.

2. Review the discussion about surveys in the "Exploring the Topic" section. Which of the purposes listed there seems to fit the purposes of this survey best? The statement of methodology quoted in Critical Reading, question 4 talks about the "margin of error." What does that mean? Is it consistent with what you learned in that "Exploring the Topic" discussion? Do you have any concerns about the methodology of the survey after reviewing that discussion?

3. Do any of the questions or their results seem anomalous to you? Can you explain why that might be so? Where and how do you plan to conduct your survey?

COLLABORATIVE WRITING PROJECT: CONSTRUCTING AND WRITING UP A SURVEY

Your virtual newspaper got a lot of response to the columns on whether genetic or cultural differences between boys and girls adversely affect girls in school to the extent that they need special programs in science and math. So the editor has decided that it would be a good idea for you, as a group, to conduct a poll to find out whether people in the community think, first, that there are substantial differences in girls' and boys' school performances, and if so, what those differences are; second, whether people who believe there are such differences think they are cultural or genetic; and finally, whether they think schools should institute compensatory programs for either boys or girls or both and what those programs should be.

"This is going to be a collaborative project. You may already be aware that a lot of the writing that gets done in the business world is group writing. So producing a survey-based column as a team is a good opportunity for you interns to get experience with the collaborative writing process.

"I want you to divide into five teams that will be in competition with each other to produce the best, most interesting, most significant column based on the most reliable survey. Each team will select a coordinator who will be responsible for arranging meetings and seeing to it that every member has a complete list of e-mail addresses and/or phone numbers and for distributing and following up individuals' progress on assignments.

"I would suggest that you proceed something like this:

"Each team should decide what kind of information readers would like to discover and how the agendas of the several community factions lie, including, of course, those of the teachers and the retired taxpayers.

"One or two members can be assigned the task of phrasing suitable questions and responses that will elicit those pieces of information that the group has decided are important. Be careful not to get more questions than your subjects will stand still to answer, but for sure get the demographics—age, gender, education, income, occupation, marital status, number of children. All those could play a role, right?

"One or two members can be assigned to conduct the survey by going around town[6] and getting responses. Another member or two with gifts for math and computer graphics should tabulate the results, do the statistical summaries, and make some graphs.

"Then the group should meet again to discuss the findings and decide what eye-catching surprises lie in the results. I think readers will want to know how these can be explained, and why they're significant.

---

[6] "Town" may be the virtual reality town. If your college is in a small town or suitable neighborhood, this can be the real reality, too. If that is not practical, the campus can be your "town."

"You may find it best to let one hand in each group actually do the rough draft, writing up the results of the survey but of course following the group's intentions regarding the significance of the results.

"After everyone in the group has been furnished with copies, the group should meet to make suggestions for a final revision of the entire piece. Maybe then, too, somebody can come up with a clever title.

"Finally, we can have the showdown. You will all read all the columns and vote for which you think is the best—apart from your own. And we'll print the winner!"

INVITATION TO A READING

Here is a look at how a skilled column writer integrates personal experience, survey information, and research to come up with a somewhat novel resolution in an area closely related to the boy-girl school performance issue.

Clarence Page begins with a personal **encounter** related to a news "hook"—the publication of a book by the Brookings Institution. As a writer who deals with related topics almost daily, he probably needed to go no farther than to his own file of facts to come up with research that significantly connects his personal **encounter** to the **eye-openers** in the book.

In presenting this column, I have called attention to the points at which Page shifts modalities and emphasizes his **explanations** and **resolutions** by "closing the ring" (chapter 6) and "tolling the bell" (chapter 5).

In Praise of Pushy Parents
by Clarence Page

I have just finished talking with my 9-year-old son about a topic more controversial than sex. [1]

It is the question of intelligence. [2]

During one of our nightly discussions about his homework, I brought up the possibility of a perfect report card. I suggested that all A's in all of his subjects was a worthy goal toward which he should aspire. [3]

He went ballistic. "I can't get straight A's," he shouted. [4]

I asked him to calm down and explain to me why he couldn't when we both knew that some of his classmates could. [5]

Head down and pouting, he mumbled, "Some of those other kids have a higher IQ than I do." [6]

Poor kid, I thought. Only 9 years old and already he is convincing himself about what he cannot do. It is heartbreaking to see the toll self-defeating attitudes can take on your own child [7]

[TRANSITION] As an African-American parent, I have been particularly interested lately in self-defeating attitudes. A variety of recent studies are finding such attitudes to be an important factor at the root of the vexing gap that persists in the aptitude test scores of blacks and whites. [8]

[MODALITY SHIFT] As the black middle class has grown since the 1960s, the scoring gap has narrowed somewhat, but, the average black American still scores below 75 percent of whites, according to "The Black-White Test Score Gap," published by Brookings Institution Press. The book is an enlightening collection of findings by 25 experts and was edited by prominent Harvard sociologist Christopher Jencks and Meredith Phillips of UCLA. [9]

The good news is that blacks who manage to score as well as whites often exceed the achievements of whites. For example, Jencks found, blacks are more likely than whites who have the same 12th grade test scores to complete four years of college. It is not hard to imagine how many other racial inequities would vanish if we could close the black-white test score gap. [10]

Unfortunately, the gap has persisted, despite increases in black family income. Even the children of black middle class parents lag far behind their white peers, except, interestingly, black youths who have been raised by white parents. That tends to refute the assertions of innate intelligence differences by race that "The Bell Curve," the controversial 1994 book by Charles Murray and Richard Herrnstein, tried to argue. But it doesn't say much for the way African-American culture has evolved. If genes are not the answer, what is? [11]

Among other findings in Jencks' and Phillips' book: The black-white test score gap appears as early as age 4. We could eliminate half of the gap in the 12th grade by eliminating the gap in pre-school. Academically enriched Head Start and other pre-school programs help, but, without follow-up, the benefits fade in later years. [12]

[MODALITY SHIFT] Sometimes it pays for parents to be pushy. Harvard sociologist Ronald F. Ferguson has found that, when asked to name the lowest grade they could bring home without upsetting their parents, white students usually name a higher grade than blacks. Similarly, Asian-American students whose parents have not completed high school usually name a grade as high as those named by whites whose parents have completed graduate school. [13]

One essay explores negative peer pressure by other black youths, including chastising those who aim for academic achievement as "acting white." Another by Stanford University's Claude Steele, twin brother of conservative essayist Shelby Steele, argues that men and women of all races avoid situations in which they expect others to have negative stereotypes about them, even when they know the stereotypes do not apply. [14]

He found that black and white freshmen chosen at random in an experiment at the University of Michigan and put into an academic program described as "more demanding" actually performed better during and after their freshman year than similar students in a regular or a "remedial" program. [15]

Much of the gap could be closed, some researchers suggest, if parents and educators expected as much from black students as they do from whites. [16]

[MODALITY SHIFT] Armed with this new knowledge, I pulled my son close, as if to share a confidence. "Do you know what IQ is?" I said in a kind, fatherly way. "It is a measure of your ability to take tests." [17]

He looked surprised. He wanted to hear more. [18]

"You can do it," I told him. "You can raise your IQ. All you have to do is prepare yourself." [19]

Apparently it had not occurred to him that his capacity to learn was limitless. [20]

It is. He's a smart kid. He's a lot smarter than I was at his age. He only needs to do what my daddy kept telling me to do: "Apply yourself." [21]

He stopped pouting. His expression brightened. He finished his homework without further complaint. He did a good job, too, and felt proud of himself for doing it. [22]

I was proud of him, too. I was also proud, for that moment at least, to be a pushy parent. [23]

Thanks, Dad. [24]

CRITICAL READING

1. I have marked paragraphs 7, 8, 11, and 13 with bells to indicate that at these points Page **tolls the bell** that repeats (or strongly implies) the most **significant** general idea that **explains** his

encounter with his son. What is the **eye-opener** of that **encounter?** How do the things he has been reading (his search) illuminate the significance of that surprise?

2. Page cites three different kinds of **searched** material: surveys, facts, and expert opinions. Pick out examples of each of these and evaluate the effectiveness of each.

3. Did any of the sources Page found in his **search** specifically identify the explanation that leads to his resolution of his son's behavior? If so, which one? If not, how do you think Page arrived at his conclusion?

4. I marked three modality shifts and a transition paragraph. Explain what is going on in each of these sections. Pay particular attention to the transition, paragraph 8. What does Page accomplish in this brief space in addition to moving from one modality to the next?

5. Page uses a common rhetorical tactic to launch his ending (marked by a ring). We have studied it before. What is it? Are you remembering to try it in your writing?

DISCUSSION QUESTIONS

1. What are some other explanations that are often offered for the gap in scores that Page's sources identify? With other members of your class, map this hotter-than-sex issue. What groups in the column writer's audience would likely hold each of these positions? How do you think Page might respond to them specifically?

2. What other expectations might Page's title evoke? What other kind of pushing do parents often do when their children do not perform well in school?

WRITING COMMISSION: A SEARCH-BASED COLUMN

Your editor is back, and the vociferous mail that your columns have generated is the best response the paper has seen in a long time.

"You guys are turning into really pretty effective writers," the editor starts. "I'm really sorry we could use only one of those survey pieces you did; they were all first rate. But I'm going to make it up to you by letting you each do your own column integrating the research and the surveys you have done on this issue of nature versus nurture and school versus parents in making education equitable for boys and girls.

"Take a look at this column by Clarence Page on somewhat the same issue that is raised by the education of whites versus blacks."

Here the editor hands you the column that is the previous reading.

"It's a pretty good model for the kind of thing I'm looking for here. You can pretty much build on your first column, but you don't have to limit yourself to the issue facing the school board in this town. Think of your findings in terms of the problem faced by every parent and every kid with the possible gender biases at home and at school. Of course you can build on the research you did for the first column, and if you have found a news hook, so much the better. But then weave in the results of your surveys. Notice the way Page identifies his sources. When it comes to your survey, because you are not a famous institution, you will have to describe how and where your group did it so the readers may judge its reliability.

"Please notice that the column, although stimulated partly by his reading the Brookings' report, is clearly Page's column, not theirs. Keep a tight rein on your sources; don't let them overwhelm your writing. It's your name on the byline; it is you making a point with the help of the sources. You are not just a mouthpiece for them.

"Notice, too, that Page doesn't wait to the end to let you know where he's headed. He hits that main point several times—in slightly different words, of course. And he's got a clever title that's provocatively just a little misleading. And—very important—he doesn't forget where he started when he gets to the end.

"You have the tools now to produce a genuinely significant piece with some original surprise to it. Gimme your best shot!"

Points to Remember

- In an information-rich culture, research is not just a textbook exercise for the scholarly minded; it is essential to solving problems in our lives from medical treatment to family life, from diet to work promotions.

- Because our personal experience is usually inadequate to achieve attitudes and decisions confidently in problematic situations, we typically reach out to books and magazines where we can read about others with similar problems, and we reach out to professionals whose jobs are to advise people like us.

- Of course, when we have problems, we ask our friends what their opinions are, and, as a culture, we ask the whole population by means of surveys.

↳ Finally, we may want to have recourse to "hard" data, either from experiments we conduct or from experiments reported by scientists.

↳ Gaining an accurate view of social movements and our place in them requires **search** for both current and historic facts and opinions of people with viewpoints different from our own. Writing based on such research is made most effective by letting the questions, puzzles, surprises, and anomalies direct and select the research.

↳ It is worthwhile spending some time choosing a title that will catch the reader's attention by wordplay, shock, mystery, or excitement.

↳ It is usually not the quantity of **searched** facts that makes them most effective but their appropriateness and authenticity. Research is most likely to modify readers' opinions if you can show that it has modified yours.

↳ Even the most apparently hard-nosed scientific facts may be the result of experiments containing flaws introduced by preconceptions of the experimenters. (And, of course, today's scientific facts will be modified by tomorrow's experiments.)

↳ Research sources should be cited (gracefully), first, to give proper credit to the authors, and second, to increase their credibility with the reader.

↳ Of the many uses of surveys, the ones most important to our purposes are to discover important trends and issues and to map them.

↳ The writing of unbiased questions for surveys that will elicit significant answers is still an art. Preliminary issue-map research is essential to writing questions that will allow people of differing points of view to register their opinions.

↳ Once a survey is completed, the writer's job is to find the significant surprises among all those numbers and dramatize them in ways that will be eye-openers to the readers.

↳ The statistics and facts then must be organized and subordinated to the purpose of your entire piece. It is important to remember with all **searched** material that you are using it to extend background, point toward explanations, map issues, and bolster your own reasoning. You are still the author, and your subject is the **search** for your resolution of whatever surprises generated your interest.

E-E-R

Encounter

Explain

Resolve

R-S-V-B

Reason

Search

Value

Background

10

Valuation

*"You want to use value words. You connect midbrain, subcortical—
you want to hit them down under, in their lizard brains, access their
personal reptiles . . . heh-heh . . . where they don't think—where they
just, y'know, react—with value words." [Said by the pollster in
Senator Stanton's (presumably Clinton's) campaign for the
Presidency.]*

—from *Primary Colors* by Joe Klein

Opening the Topic: Communicating Values

I had just achieved the high point of what I hoped might become a
new career for me as I was careening around the corner of my
midlife crisis. For my final exam in music conducting class, I had just
successfully conducted a small orchestra, chorus, and soloist in a
scene from Gluck's opera *Orfeo el Euridice*. "This," said my forty-
something-year-old brain, "is what I've always really wanted to do!" It
was not that my values were shifting; it was just that I had been
blessed with the opportunity to explore some values other than those
I had been living off of for the past twenty years.

My teacher, a noticeably younger man than I, called me aside for
what I presumed would be effusive congratulations. Indeed, he did
congratulate me on my conducting, but then he added, in an avun-
cular way, "I hope you're not planning to give up your job teaching
English to pursue a musical career."

Shocked, I stammered out, "Oh—ah—no. Of course not." Because,
at my age, I was something of a curiosity pursuing a degree in music
among undergraduates, he knew my story. I was a tenured professor
of English supporting a family of six children. He could probably

guess that my wife was resentful at my spending so much time away from the family pursuing this quixotic dream. But at least one other professor I knew of had become a major opera singer, and I was having some success as a part-time professional. Of course, my teacher was probably aware also of the affinity between the midlife years and the teenage ones and guessed that, like a starry-eyed teenager, I was secretly waiting to be discovered. He wanted to warn me about my chances.

I was discovered, all right, in a most unexpected way. It was by my youngest son, then, I guess, about six years old. Like most kids, he wanted to see where and how his father worked. So when his school had holidays that mine did not, I would let him come to the college and watch me in action. When, soon enough, he got bored with that, he could sit in my office and play with the colored markers, the typewriter, the stapler, and other office paraphernalia. The day after one such visit, I noticed a mailing label stuck to the center drawer of my desk. There, neatly typed, was the blindingly obvious discovery of my central values that only a child could make: "Roger Conner. Teacher and Father."

Because he had also seen me perform as a singer, I thought that this might be a critical comment on that, so I was ready to dock his allowance. But then it hit me that this was an insight into my fundamental values that he had arrived at by simple observation. He had seen through me to what Joe Klein, in the epigraph to this chapter, calls my "lizard brain."

People at midlife often revisit their earlier obsession with the identity question "Who am I?"—which is really a way of asking "What do I value?" And the answer to that question lies hidden in plain sight: You value what you spend time doing. Because teachers do a lot of their work at home on flextime, I had had more than average opportunity to be an active father with our large brood. Parenting and teaching were what I had done for twenty years, and I had done them because, in the inmost fiber of my being, helping young people grow intellectually and emotionally was, apparently, as my son pointed out, what I valued most; music was an avocation.

Of course, valuing this does not exclude valuing that. We can value many things. But time is finite, and once the barest necessities have been met, how we parcel out our remaining time demonstrates the order of our values. So I did not give up my passion for performing; I just scaled it back to an enjoyable amateur level—much to the relief of my wife, my teacher, and, probably, of my erstwhile audiences.

To be effective writers, we must become aware, as my son made me aware, of that lizard brain energy that pushes us to react with a "Yuck!" or a "Yessss!" or a "Well, OK, maybe" to the conflicting, dissonant parts of whatever encounters set us on to write. Unfortunately, just saying "Yuck!" or "Yessss!" will not create in the reader the same reaction that you or I feel as writers. We must connect our lizard brains directly to theirs to transmit the sense of valuation as we wish, subcortically.

As writers we can probably learn something from one group of professionals whose livelihoods depend on making those connections work—advertisers.

We saw in chapter 2 ("The Eye-Opener"), in the article "The Colors of the World in Vivid Black and White," that advertisers have to be critically attuned to the deepest levels of our perception of the world. Just as we saw good ideas creating bad, unintended consequences in chapter 8 ("Reasoning"), so effective, visceral connections can

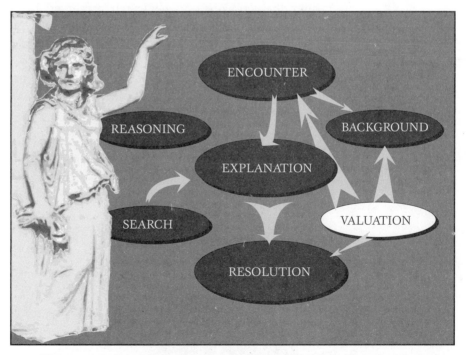

Figure 10.1. It is important to enlist the readers' feelings for or against those aspects of (especially) the encounters and background that you feel strongly about.

create bad, unintended connections. In 1989, the Pepsi-Cola Company, hoping to continue to appeal to the age group that they had dubbed, rather successfully, the "Pepsi generation," sponsored a concert tour by Madonna, then near the peak of her celebrity status. They also contracted with her to do a TV commercial, probably thinking that her flouting of an older generation's mores by flaunting her body would sell well with their target audience. But the hip Pepsi marketers did not realize how deeply her flaunting and apparent flouting of religious symbols offended a large segment of the population. When the news came crashing in on them, they had to withdraw the commercial and their sponsorship of the tour.

At the same time, many of our positive cultural values are energized and distributed through advertising. You may have wondered at Annie Dillard's fear of Santa Claus ("God in the Doorway," chapter 3). How could such a kindly figure inspire fear? Actually the American image of Santa Claus comes to us from Holland by way of the early Dutch settlers of New York. Although Protestant northern Europe had renounced the veneration of the gift-giving sixth-century Saint Nicholas after the Reformation, the Dutch preserved his memory as Sinterklaas—a combination of the venerable saint and a Nordic magician who punished bad little boys and girls while giving gifts to good ones.

What Dillard's neighbor, Miss White, wanted, and what our culture wanted, was an image that celebrated the caring effort of cheerful giving. And that image was just evolving at the time of Dillard's

Figure 10.2. Nast's Santa.

story. The vehicle for this value complex of buying and giving was an ad campaign.

In 1822 Clement C. Moore created a detailed verbal picture of the modern secular Santa Claus with the poem "A Visit from St. Nicholas," also known as " 'Twas the Night before Christmas." In the poem, Santa rides in a miniature sleigh with eight tiny reindeer and is a small man—"A right jolly old elf"—small enough to slip down chimneys. The popular illustrator Thomas Nast began illustrating this poem annually in *Harper's Weekly*. Through the 1850s and 1860s, Nast's Santa grew bigger, until he was a full-size, indeed, oversize man with white hair and bushy beard living at the North Pole with his elfin helpers.

But our modern image of Santa was not fully fleshed out until the 1940s, when Haddon Sundblom started drawing his version of Santa Claus in yearly ads for the D'Arcy Agency, who hired him to persuade people that Coca-Cola was a drink that could be enjoyed in winter as well as summer.

These images seem to have drawn on the power of some subconscious archetype to obliterate both the original Saint Nicholas and the

Figure 10.3. Sundblom's Santa.

not entirely nice magician Sinterklaas, who punished bad girls and boys by leaving them nothing but a lump of coal in their stockings. We can see from this that images, whether visual or verbal, are a powerful way to establish **value**.

WRITING ACTIVITY: SORTING OUT VALUES BEHIND THE LANGUAGE OF ADVERTISING

Just as issue mapping requires an awareness of differing ideas, valuation requires an awareness of how people of different backgrounds feel about things.

In "Home Free?" (chapter 1) Joyce Caruso called herself a "stat." To advertisers, we are all stats, right down to the bottom of our lizard brains. It is here that advertisers have found webs of wants and values that bind us together in cultural groups. A nonprofit research company called SRI International finds it can group all us consumers into just eight categories, the better to expose to our conscious minds the things we really value.

According to James B. Twitchell, in his book *Adcult USA*, SRI divides consumers into eight groups, with "Actualizers" at the top and "Strugglers" at the bottom. (There is little advantage advertising to these groups, because, as far as purchasing is concerned, the latter purchase solely on the basis of necessity and price, and the former have most of what they need and have well-developed, persuasion-proof values of their own.) The remaining six groups are divided into those who are principle oriented, those who are status oriented, and those who are action oriented, as shown in the following list.

Principle Oriented

Fulfilleds Generally older people, often retired. They are comfortably off, looking for things that are practical and will last.

Believers Conservatives. They are religious and patriotic, attending religious services regularly and buying recognized, usually American brands.

Status Oriented

Achievers Hardworking, monetarily successful people. They like to show off the rewards of their hard work and expect others to recognize the symbols of their prestige.

Strivers Yuppies. They are upwardly mobile, trying to become achievers, and like to show their progress and direction by material tokens of their climb and ambition.

Action Oriented

Experiencers Lovers of excitement and activity. They spend a large part of their income on travel, sports, and parties.

Makers Conservative do-it-yourselfers. They like orderliness and focus their energies on improving their private surroundings, often working as professional builders and engineers.

You may notice the analogy between segmenting the audience this way and the way we divided the issue map in chapter 7, "Background". The difference is that an issue map is in the modalities of **background** and **reasoning.** It appeals to people's cerebral logic. The segmenting advertisers talk about is based on appeals to people's lizard brains—the primitive **value** regions that logic cannot readily touch.

Let's see how well this works. The following list contains a selection of famous advertising slogans from the past. See if you can identify the appeal of each of these slogans with one of the six audience segments listed previously.

Write a brief explanation of what it is in the language of each slogan that would have made it appeal to that audience segment. Then note what audience group (it does not have to be one of the six detailed previously) might be turned off by that slogan.

When everyone in the class has done this, it might be fun to compare notes and discuss differences of opinion.

Classic Ad Slogans from the Past

from the book *Soap, Sex, and Cigarettes* by Juliann Sivulka

1. Pepsi, for those who think young.
2. Just do it. (Nike)
3. Nothing outlasts Energizer batteries. They keep going and going.
4. Intel's inside.
5. Find your own road. (Saab)
6. We bring good things to life. (General Electric)
7. It's going to be an Aviance night. (Aviance perfume)
8. All day long. All day strong. (Aleve pain reliever)
9. The real thing. (Coca-Cola)
10. I want my MTV!
11. Give yourself a Dannon body. (Dannon yogurt)
12. Where's the beef? (Wendy's)
13. The ultimate driving machine. (BMW)
14. The heartbeat of America. (Chevrolet)
15. It's finger-lickin' good. (Kentucky Fried Chicken)
16. Put a tiger in your tank. (Esso gasoline)
17. Try it—you'll like it! (Alka-Seltzer)
18. I can't believe I ate the whole thing. (Alka-Seltzer)
17. We try harder. (Avis car rentals)
18. Come to where the flavor is. Come to Marlboro country.
19. You've come a long way, baby! (Virginia Slims cigarettes)
20. When you care enough to send the very best. (Hallmark cards)

The point of this exercise is to dramatize the fact that carefully chosen language can connect so powerfully with the right people's feelings that they will be moved to value what the writer values or find their own values warmly reinforced. This kind of writing can be memorable. And this exercise also dramatizes the fact that locking firmly into one person's value radar may lock the writer out of another's. This fact points up once again how important it is to visualize your particular audience as you write, not only the issue mapping of their cerebral hemispheres but the unconscious polarizations of their lizard brains, as well.

INVITATION TO A READING

Successful advertising depends on touching a common chord in a majority of the target audience. Good writing, on the other hand, needs to surprise, often by introducing dissonance into that common chord. In speaking about paradox in chapter 2 ("The Eye-Opener"), I described a technique of deconstructionism in which the writer takes a pair of polar opposites and reverses the values we normally place on them to surprise a new significance. This kind of invention by inversion is often quite productive. Surprising things can happen when we try reversing the obvious, accepted idea. President Kennedy won the idealism of millions with his inaugural address statement "Ask not what your country can do for you, but what you can do for your country" (echoing Oliver Wendell Holmes). This inversion of values certainly helped in the successful establishment of the Peace Corps that same year. We typically think of the rule of the majority as a good thing, but writers from Plato through Lincoln and onward have pointed out the danger of the tyranny of the majority over the minority. Henry David Thoreau said it most memorably: "A man more right than his neighbors constitutes a majority of one." This reversal of values surprised Thoreau into the realization that the only effective way for a righteous minority to stand up to the tyranny of the majority is through nonviolent resistance. This resolution, taken up by Gandhi to free India from British colonial rule, rebounded to the United States in the practice of Martin Luther King Jr., who led the successful crusade against the democratically embedded racism of the majority.

The author of the following selection achieves his surprise by inverting the usual attitude toward advertising. For the most part, we just take ads for granted as a small, often annoying, sometimes entertaining filigree around the substance of our interaction with the media. But many people see our culture of advertising as a kind of tyranny of the majority. A product—even a superior one—may disappear unless its marketers can maintain a sense that a large number of people favor it, as we saw in the case of the book *You and Me, Babe* in the "Exploring the Topic" section on surveys in chapter 9 ("Search"). Lifestyles that are devalued by our commercial culture may be ostracized by our social culture. Walter Bagehot, an early British sociologist, said, "The real tyranny is the tyranny of your neighbor. . . . Public opinion is a permeating influence, and it exacts obedience to itself; it requires us to think other men's thoughts, to speak other men's words, to follow other men's habits."

But what if we invert this opinion, as the author of the following selection does. Let's try assuming that the discourse of advertising is **central** to our culture instead of peripheral or inimical. If the author can establish such a reversal as even plausible, a number of surprises follow that may help explain the significance of the materialistic American value system.

from *Adcult USA*
by James B. Twitchell

Manufacturing both things and their meanings is what American culture is all about. If Greece gave the world philosophy, Britain gave drama, Austria gave music, Germany gave politics, and Italy gave art, America gave mass-produced objects. "We bring good things to life" is no off-hand claim but the contribution of the last century. And the tag line "Or your money back" is the guarantee. Advertising is how we talk about these things, how we imagine them, how we know their value. [1]

Human beings like things. We buy things. We like to exchange things. We steal things. We donate things. We live through things. We call these things goods as in goods and services. We do not call them bads. This sounds simplistic, but it is crucial to understanding the power of Adcult. Still going strong, the industrial revolution produces more and more things not because production is what machines do, and not because nasty capitalists twist their handlebar mustaches and mutter "More slop for the pigs," but because we are attracted to the world of things. Madonna was not the first material girl. Advertising supercharges some of this power. [2]

This attraction to the inanimate happens all over the world. Berlin Walls fall because people want things, and they want the culture created by things. China opens its doors not so much because it wants to get out but because it wants to get things in. We were not suddenly transformed from customers to consumers by wily manufacturers eager to unload a surplus of crappy products. We have created a surfeit of things because we enjoy the process of getting and spending. The consumption ethic may have started in the early 1900s, but the desire is ancient. Kings and princes once thought they could solve problems by amassing things; we now join them. [3]

The Marxist balderdash of cloistered academics aside, human beings did not suddenly become materialistic. We have always been desirous of things. We have just not had many of them until quite recently, and in a few generations we may return to having fewer and fewer. Still, while they last, we enjoy shopping for things and see both the humor and truth reflected in the aphoristic "Born to shop," "Shop 'til you drop," and "When the going gets tough, the tough go shopping." Department store windows, be they on the city street or inside a mall, did not appear magically. We enjoy looking through them to another world. It is the voyeurism of capitalists. Our love of things is the cause of the industrial revolution, not the consequence. Man (and woman) is not only *homo sapiens,* or *homo ludens,* or *homo faber* but also *homo emptor.* [4]

Mid-twentieth-century American culture is often criticized for being too materialistic. But we are not too materialistic. We are not materialistic enough. If we craved objects and knew what they meant, there would be no need to add meaning through advertising. We would just gather, use, toss out, or hoard indiscriminately. But we don't. First, we don't know what to gather and, second, we like to trade what we have gathered. Third, we need to know how to value objects that have little practical use. What is clear is that most things in and of themselves do not mean enough. In fact, what we crave may not be objects at all but their meaning. For whatever else advertising does, one thing is certain: by adding value to material, by adding meaning to objects, by branding things, advertising performs a role historically associated with religion. The Great Chain of Being,[1] which for centuries located value above the horizon in the World Beyond, has been reforged to settle value on the objects of the here and now. I wax a little impatient here, because most literature on modern culture is downright supercilious about consumption. What do you expect? Most of it comes from a culture professionally hostile to materialism, albeit secretly envious. From Veblen on through Christopher Lasch runs a palpable sense of disapproval as they view the hubbub of commerce from the groves of academe. Concepts of bandwagon consumption, conspicuous consumption, keeping-up-with-the-Joneses, the culture of narcissism, and all the other barely veiled reproofs have limited our serious consideration of Adcult to such relatively minor issues as manipulation and exploitation. People surely can't want—ugh!—things. Or, if they really do want them, they must want them for all the wrong reasons. The idea that advertising creates artificial desires rests on a profound ignorance of human nature, on the hazy feeling that there existed some halcyon era of noble savages with purely natural needs, on

---

[1] The Great Chain of Being is a view of the cosmos as an orderly chain of command from God, through orders of angels, followed by pope and king, through nobles and commoners, to peasants. Each assigned position had its special duty. (See my cultural map following "She Converted" [chapter 7, "Background"]).

romantic claptrap first promulgated by Rousseau[2] and kept alive in institutions well isolated from the marketplace. [5]

Here is a sampling of the affection extended to Adcult by the charitable souls in and around academia. Such critical comments have become so much a part of our common culture that they repeatedly appear in collections of familiar quotations. [6]

> A considerable part of our ability, energy, time and material resources is being spent today on inducing us to find the money for buying material goods that we should never have dreamed of wanting had we been left to ourselves.
>
> —*Arnold Toynbee*

> Few people at the beginning of the nineteenth century needed an adman to tell them what they wanted.
>
> —*John Kenneth Galbraith*

> The modern substitute for argument; its function is to make the worse appear better.
>
> —*George Santayana*

> Advertising is the science of arresting the human intelligence long enough to get money from it.
>
> —*Stephen Leacock*

> Advertising is the rattling of a stick inside a swill bucket.
>
> —*George Orwell*

> Nothing's so apt to undermine your confidence in a product as knowing that the commercial selling it has been approved by the company that makes it.
>
> —*Franklin P. Jones*

> Advertising has done more to cause the social unrest of the twentieth century than any other single factor.
>
> —*Clare Boothe Luce, also attributed to Clive Barnes*

What raises the ire of these pundits is that advertising is stealing their thunder. Commercial speech, not other types of "higher conversation," is defining value for objects. At the human level novelists knew about

---

[2] Jean-Jacques Rousseau was an eighteenth-century French philosopher who popularized the idea that the "noble savages" (i.e., Native Americans and Africans) lived happier and more moral lives than Europeans corrupted by the civilization imposed by the Great Chain of Being.

the defining power of goods before economists did, as the works of Austen, Trollope, Dreiser, James, and Wharton attest. The novel of manners is often the novel of microeconomics. Human gesture is replaced by interaction with manufactured objects. Etiquette becomes subsumed by ownership. Even the smallest objects sometimes assume inordinate value. Many a nineteenth-century novel—especially in America, which had no elaborated history of social and class distinctions—describes at length the display of crockery, the proper machine-woven garb, the giving of a bowl, or the decor of a room. In fact, the drawing room itself was a new venue in which to display the growing collection of self-defining objects. Ralph Lauren and Martha Stewart still trade on these distinctions. [7]

Advertising often achieves these distinctions by "branding." Branding is the central activity of creating differing values for such commonplace objects and services as flour, bottled water, cigarettes, denim jeans, razor blades, domestic beers, batteries, cola drinks, air travel, overnight couriers, and telephone carriers. Giving objects their identity, and thus a perceived value, is advertising's unique power. Think about it: would you spend $100 for a pair of sneakers, $20 for a fifth of vodka, or $30,000 for a car if your friends hadn't heard of the brand? As we will see later, religion is another such branding system—the original branding system. So are politics, education, and . . . art. To use a modern trope: if goods are hardware, meaning is software, and advertising writes most of the software. [8]

Advertising is simply one of a number of attempts to load objects with meaning. It is not a mirror, a lamp, a magnifying glass, a distorted prism, a window, a trompe l'oeil, or a subliminal embed as much as it is an ongoing conversation within a culture about the meanings of objects. It does not follow or lead so much as it interacts. Advertising is neither chicken nor egg. Let's split the difference: it's both. It is language not just about objects to be consumed but about the consumers of objects. It is threads of a web linking us to objects and to each other. [9]

CRITICAL READING

1. The first paragraph contains at least a couple of statements that Twitchell expects to be disturbing eye-openers. What are they and why might they be disturbing?

2. Paragraphs 3 and 5 sketch in some historical **background.** Why does Twitchell think this is necessary, given that he thinks the first paragraph will be disturbing?

3. In paragraphs 2 and 4, Twitchell uses **reasoning** to begin to map the issue of the value of advertising. What techniques does he use to weight the issue so that advertising begins to sound good and the opponents of advertising bad? (Notice how the author weaves back and forth between **background** and **valuation.**)

4. In paragraphs 5, 8, and 9 Twitchell repeats the resolution of the surprising significance of advertising in our culture. Find the sentences in those paragraphs that answer the question "What does advertising do that is so surprisingly significant?" Notice that the repeated resolution rings essentially the same bell each time and is strongly hinted at in the first sentence of the selection.

DISCUSSION QUESTIONS

1. Do you agree that Americans live through **things** and that things are the means by which we symbolize our systems of **value**? Explain and give examples.

2. We saw in chapter 7 ("Background") that convincing people in an argument requires showing that you can sympathize with their viewpoint. This author accomplishes that by quoting several notable writers who have a strong antipathy toward advertising. Where Twitchell sees advertising as a binding cultural force, many of these authors—along with Thoreau (quoted in the "Invitation to a Reading" before Twitchell's selection)—might see it as a tyranny of the majority. Sort out the issue map here, and explain why you agree more with those authors or with Twitchell.

3. What, according to Twitchell, is the difference between brands of "flour, bottled water, cigarettes, denim jeans, razor blades, domestic beers, batteries, cola drinks, air travel, overnight couriers, and telephone carriers"? Give examples of some of these and explain the differences you perceive between brands.

4. Explain what Twitchell means when he says advertising has assumed a role traditionally performed by religion. To what extent do you agree or disagree?

WRITING ACTIVITY: DISCOVERING YOUR OWN VALUES

Option 1

Choose an ad that particularly appeals to you—either in print or on TV—and explore what this ad can tell you about yourself and your relation to our culture.

Start by describing the ad in such a way that the appeal of it is dramatized. Give any necessary background about yourself that will help explain to the reader the appeal of the ad to you. Then explore what **values** the ad embodies and the techniques it uses to do that. Note whether it gets those values across by linking itself with other valued items in the culture or by contrasting with other less-valued items. Now you are ready to analyze yourself both psychologically and sociologically according to your reaction to the value messages of the ad. Try to discover something surprising about yourself in doing this. Finally, reach some resolution that reaches out to the reader.

You can, of course, do the same assignment with an ad that particularly turns you off, but it, too, needs to be a vehicle for revealing something surprising about yourself. This may be a good opportunity to be humorous, but it may equally well be an opportunity to make some penetrating observations about our culture.

Option 2

Take a commonplace idea about what things are good or bad, especially an idea that you think people accept without much reasoning, and turn it inside out. See how far you can get maintaining the opposite of the common **valuation** using examples of your own or others' encounters and any necessary background. From your explanations and reasoning develop a significant resolution that may make your readers more thoughtful about the subject.

Exploring the Topic: Direct and Indirect Verbal Valuation

Direct Valuation

If we look back over the pieces we have read thus far, we can see that in many writings there is a straightforward statement of value. In fact, if you remember, when I was speaking about **resolutions,** I said that there seem to be two main kinds: a **program** for action and an attempt to get readers to change their **attitudes.** Attitudes are feelings based on values. Hence many statements of **resolution** involve a pretty direct statement of **valuation** as well.

☐ Joyce Caruso tells us (chapter 1) that living with parents for a while as an adult can create a valuable bond.

- ☐ Bob Greene (chapter 2) explicitly says that black and white pictures have become valuable because they carry a stronger sense of authenticity than color pictures.
- ☐ Kathleen Parker in "Surviving Marital Miseries" (chapter 4) emphatically states that happiness is not as valuable to marriages as commitment.
- ☐ Thomas Sowell (chapter 7) finds many ways to say that instructions are only valuable if they are written with a clear view of what the user specifically needs to do to use the product.
- ☐ Clarence Page in "In Praise of Pushy Parents" (chapter 9) targets IQ scores as responsible for some kids' negative valuations of themselves.

But the foundation for explicit value statements like these is usually built with less direct subconscious or preconscious devices that sway readers' attitudes more subtly. Although direct statements of value often occupy whole paragraphs, subtle value vectors are often woven throughout a piece of writing. We will examine some of these specific techniques, like connotation, metaphor, and irony in the rest of this chapter.

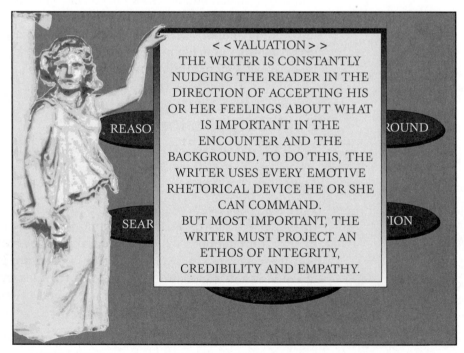

Figure 10.4.

Connotation

Indirect valuation usually seems to depend on side-by-side comparisons ("Why can't you be more like your sister?") or linkages ("This project is a real turkey!"). The columnist Sydney J. Harris periodically put three words side by side to contrast their positive, neutral, and negative connotations. The three words all referred to the same quality, but the contrast in valuation was made clear by applying the best valuation to "myself"—*numero uno,* of course!—the normal one to "you," and the worst one to someone else who wasn't around—"he" or "she." Thus: "I am **careful,** you are **cautious**, he is **compulsive**. I **have a portfolio,** you **buy stocks**, she **plays the market**. I am **faithful,** you are **religious**, he is a **fanatic**. I am **well-read**, you are a **book worm**, she is a **geek**."

I recently received in an e-mail the following unattributed list of paired sentences that illustrate the same idea:

You and Your Boss

When you take a long time, you're slow.

When your boss takes a long time, he's thorough.

When you don't get something done, you're lazy.

When your boss doesn't get something done, he's too busy.

When you make a mistake, you're an idiot.

When your boss makes a mistake, he's only human.

When you do it your own way, you don't do what you're told.

When your boss does it, he's showing creativity.

When you do it on your own, you're overstepping your bounds.

When your boss does it, he's demonstrating initiative.

When you take a stand, you're being bullheaded.

When your boss takes a stand, he's being firm.

When you violate a rule, you're self-centered.

When your boss skips a few rules, he's being original.

When you please your boss, you're brown-nosing.

When your boss pleases his boss, he's being cooperative.

When you help a peer, you're not busy enough.

When your boss does it, he's a team player.

When someone else does your work, you're passing the buck.

When someone else does your boss's work, he's assigning responsibility.

When you're out of the office, you're wandering around.

When your boss is out of the office, he's on business.

When you call in sick, you're going golf-
ing.

When your boss calls in sick, he must be
very ill.

When you apply for leave, you must be
going for an interview.

When your boss applies for leave, it's
because he's overworked.

When you're seen shopping during work
hours, you're a slacker.

When your boss is doing the same, he's
picking up office supplies.

As inheritors of the world's largest language (studies show that
English has three to five times as many words as other languages),
we can make these distinctions among synonyms to twist the
reader's response toward better or toward worse.

*For each of the examples in the following list, tell what connotative
valuation the words or phrases imply toward each subject.*

☐ **"The Informal Essay"** by Baker (chapter 1) I'm sure you
remember the word *prim* applied several times to Mr. Fleagle,
itself a slightly ludicrous name.

☐ **"Home Free?"** by Caruso (chapter 1) The word *bond* is repeated
several times in reference to the relation Caruso has developed
with her mother since returning home temporarily as an adult.
Caruso uses the place names *Kansas* and *New Jersey* for their connotations. *Banana republic,* when first coined, was a statement of
ridicule applied to small South American and Central American
countries newly freed from colonial rule. Now it's a store name
that is widely enough recognized that Caruso can count on its
connotations in this country.

☐ **"Cousin Edwin's Dull Writing"** by Baker (chapter 2) "Mass of
gray print" and "leaden family duty" both suggest something
about Cousin Edwin's writing style.

☐ **"The Colors of the World in Vivid Black and White"** by
Greene (chapter 2) Greene applies the description "dizzyingly
vibrant" to the kinds of illustrations children are able to produce
with computers.

☐ **"Why We Crave Horror Movies"** by King (chapter 4) King says
first that horror films have positive values in letting us test our
resistance to fear, reestablish feelings of normalcy by contrast,
and have fun. But he goes on to posit their main but ambiguous
value thus: Although horror films may not stand high in society's
honor role, they "have a dirty job to do."

☐ **"Asking More from Matrimony"** by Besharov (chapter 4) This
piece by a scientist maintains a nonvaluing objective stance for

most of its duration, but near the end, Besharov uses the phrases "modernized [marriage]" and "obsolete assumptions."

- ☐ **"To Defray Expenses"** by Quindlen (chapter 5) Quindlen uses the place name *South Bronx* to locate the lost boys both in space and in the social value hierarchy. She says that when middle-class and upper-class people look to try to solve the problems of poverty, it is like "look[ing] into this abyss."
- ☐ **"In Love Fornow"** by Goodman (chapter 5) Goodman uses the contrasting connotations of *wholeheartedly* and *halfheartedly*.

"If you're gonna talk the talk, you gotta walk the walk." This wonderful expression (which may or may not still be current talk by the time you read this!) dramatizes the fact that we have a closetful of different vocabulary ensembles that we put on, take off, or change to suit the occasion and the people we're "hanging with" at the moment. The point of the saying is that words are an integral part of behavior, and if you go out wearing a certain ensemble of vocabulary, you'd better be ready to match it with the kind of behavior that it implies. If you talk big, you'd better be ready to deliver. If you use the vocabulary of "forever love," you'd better be ready to commit to marriage. If you use the tough slang of a gang member, you'd better be ready to defend your territory. If you use big words, you'd better know what they mean. The eighteenth-century dramatist Richard Brinsley Sheridan invented the character Mrs. Malaprop, who gave her name to the practice of trying to move in educated circles without the having the necessary background. Misused highfalutin words are still known as *malapropisms*. Here are some famous examples from Sheridan's play *The Rivals*.

- ☐ He is the very pineapple of politeness.
- ☐ [He is] a progeny of learning.
- ☐ 'Tis safest in matrimony to begin with a little aversion.
- ☐ Illiterate him, I say, quite from your memory.
- ☐ As headstrong as an allegory on the banks of the Nile.
- ☐ If I reprehend anything in this world, it is the use of my oracular tongue, and a nice derangement of epitaphs.

If you can figure out what word it was Mrs. Malaprop was trying to use in each of those quotes, congratulations! You are entitled to walk the academic walk!

In other words, a certain style of speaking, like a certain style of dressing, implies a socially recognizable constellation of values. Mixing these messages can create surprisingly powerful reactions of shock, humor, anger, disgust, irony—all of which feelings are the very stuff of valuation.

To drop a slang word into a formal discourse is like wearing a baseball hat (turned 120 degrees toward the back) with a business suit to a meeting. It generates surprise, laughter, perhaps anger, and a demand for an explanation of your fashion statement.

Discuss how the intrusion of the following colloquial or slang words and phrases affects your evaluation of the subject under discussion. Roughly, do you feel more or less positively disposed to it than if a conventional word or phrase had been used? Why?

- [ ] **"Home Free?"** (chapter 1)—dweeb / dissing / weirded out / heloooo / boomerang generation
- [ ] **"Why We Crave Horror Movies"** (chapter 4)—clap you away in the funny farm / rotten little puke of a sister / it keeps them from getting out, man
- [ ] **"Surviving Marital Miseries"** (chapter 4)—you know the script, two years, tops / dadgum I'm happy.
- [ ] **"To Defray Expenses"** (chapter 5)—hanging with his friend
- [ ] **"In Love Fornow"** (chapter 5)—mush quota
- [ ] **"Motherliness"** (chapter 6)—chockablock / seven-five-oh

The lesson for us as writers is to be aware that the words we choose, whether consciously or unconsciously, have value impact and that we can deliberately choose other words that change that impact. Furthermore, when we suddenly change the kind of talk that we're talking, we create a bit of a shock wave in the lizard brain that causes the reader's **value** system to sway.

INVITATION TO A READING

One of the most powerful value connectors is the making of imaginative comparisons using symbolic and metaphorical language.

You have probably at least heard of Rachel Carson's *Silent Spring*, a book that had almost as much impact on the public war on air and water pollution as *Uncle Tom's Cabin* had in stirring up northern sentiment for the Civil War (or War between the States). But you may never have heard of Aldo Leopold, who was the first writer to begin turning the country on to the value of wilderness and wildlife back in the 1930s and 1940s. His books are still widely read and used in planning wildlife management and for the sheer pleasure of his prose.

Although he can be thoroughly cerebral, academic, and technical, Leopold's gentle nudgings for a more appreciative attitude toward all wildlife from weeds to wolves are often achieved through beautifully evocative descriptions, as in this essay containing a dramatic encounter with a wolf that suddenly reversed his feelings on the **value** of one wild animal conventionally thought of as an enemy. But his main conveyance is the imaginative personification of a mountain. By imagining the mountain as a person, he hopes to get us to expand the horizon of our feelings to feel as nature would have us feel.

Thinking Like a Mountain
by Aldo Leopold
from A Sand County Almanac

A deep chesty bawl echoes from rimrock to rimrock, rolls down the mountain, and fades into the far blackness of the night. It is an outburst of wild defiant sorrow, and of contempt for all the adversities of the world.

Every living thing (and perhaps many a dead one as well) pays heed to that call. To the deer it is a reminder of the way of all flesh, to the pine a forecast of midnight scuffles and of blood upon the snow, to the coyote a promise of gleanings to come, to the cowman a threat of red ink at the bank, to the hunter a challenge of fang against bullet. Yet behind these obvious and immediate hopes and fears there lies a deeper meaning, known only to the mountain itself. Only the mountain has lived long enough to listen objectively to the howl of a wolf.

Those unable to decipher the hidden meaning know nevertheless that it is there, for it is felt in all wolf country, and distinguishes that country from all other land. It tingles in the spine of all who hear wolves by night, or who scan their tracks by day. Even without sight or sound of wolf, it is implicit in a hundred small events: the midnight whinny of a pack horse, the rattle of rolling rocks, the bound of a fleeing deer, the way shadows lie under the spruces. Only the ineducable tyro can fail to sense the presence or absence of wolves, or the fact that mountains have a secret opinion about them.

My own conviction on this score dates from the day I saw a wolf die. We were eating lunch on a high rimrock, at the foot of which a turbulent river elbowed its way. We saw what we thought was a doe fording the torrent, her breast awash in white water. When she climbed the bank toward us and shook out her tail, we realized our error: it was a wolf. A half-dozen others, evidently grown pups, sprang from the willows and all joined in a welcoming mélé of wagging tails and playful maulings. What was literally a pile of wolves writhed and tumbled in the center of an open flat at the foot of our rimrock.

In those days we had never heard of passing up a chance to kill a wolf. In a second we were pumping lead into the pack, but with more excitement than accuracy: how to aim a steep downhill shot is always confusing. When our rifles were empty, the old wolf was down, and a pup was dragging a leg into impassable slide-rocks.

We reached the old wolf in time to watch a fierce green fire dying in her eyes. I realized then, and have known ever since, that there was something new to me in those eyes—something known only to her and to the mountain. I was young then, and full of trigger-itch; I thought that because fewer wolves meant more deer, that no wolves would mean hunters' paradise. But after seeing the green fire die, I sensed that neither the wolf nor the mountain agreed with such a view.

Since then I have lived to see state after state extirpate its wolves. I have watched the face of many a newly wolfless mountain, and seen the south-facing slopes wrinkle with a maze of new deer trails. I have seen every edible bush and seedling browsed, first to anaemic desuetude, and then to death. I have seen every edible tree defoliated to the height of a saddlehorn. Such a mountain looks as if someone had given God a new pruning shears, and forbidden Him all other exercise. In the end the starved bones of the hoped-for deer herd, dead of its own too-much, bleach with the bones of the dead sage, or molder under the high-lined junipers.

I now suspect that just as a deer herd lives in mortal fear of its wolves, so does a mountain live in mortal fear of its deer. And perhaps with better cause, for while a buck pulled down by wolves can be replaced in two or three years, a range pulled down by too many deer may fail of replacement in as many decades.

So also with cows. The cowman who cleans his range of wolves does not realize that he is taking over the wolf's job of trimming the herd to fit the range. He has not learned to think like a mountain. Hence we have dustbowls, and rivers washing the future into the sea.

We all strive for safety, prosperity, comfort, long life, and dullness. The deer strives with his supple legs, the cowman with trap and poison, the statesman with pen, the most of us with machines, votes, and dollars, but it all comes to the same thing: peace in our time. A measure of success in this is all well enough and perhaps is a requisite to objective thinking, but too much safety seems to yield only danger in the long run. Perhaps this is behind Thoreau's dictum: In wildness is the salvation of the world. Perhaps this is the hidden meaning in the howl of the wolf, long known among mountains, but seldom perceived among men.

CRITICAL READING

1. Leopold suggests that the howl of the wolf strikes every creature deep in its primordial brain. Then he shows the different **valuations** of that emotional reaction. Describe them.
2. While creatures **evaluate** the wolf's presence on the basis of their own needs, the mountain is objective. What is the mountain's view? Do you agree that it is value neutral?
3. What was young Aldo Leopold's valuation of the wolf? Where had he acquired it? What changed it? Is it now the same as that of the mountain?
4. Look again at the verbal picture of the killing of the wolf. What emotional valuation is built into it? How does Leopold choose his words and select his details to build that feeling into the description?

DISCUSSION QUESTIONS

1. Try rewriting the description of the killing of the wolf to give it the **valuation** that a cowman, deer, or hunter would feel in it. Compare descriptions with other members of the class. How are these three different from one another?
2. Although he was one of the country's first and most dedicated conservationists, Leopold was a skilled and avid fisherman and hunter of wild game. How is it possible to love wildlife and also to love hunting it? Or is Leopold a hypocrite? Discuss other aspects of the animal rights issue from the standpoint of **values**. Do you think the treatment of domestic animals for food is worse than the hunting of wild animals? What about the use of animals to test the safety of products that will ultimately be used by humans?

WRITING COMMISSION: DESIGN A PUBLIC SERVICE AD CAMPAIGN

Your editor feels the newspaper has a civic responsibility to underwrite advertising for nonprofit organizations that support worthy social causes. You interns are a logical choice for this job because, as students, you are likely to be more sympathetic to idealistic causes than some of the wizened veterans of the paper, and, because this is a freebie, it makes economic sense to use low-paid interns!

The assignment is to come up with a complete ad campaign using low-cost media like the newspaper itself, radio, bus ads, and/or leaflets to support the organization of your choice. You will probably want to work collaboratively in groups to produce scripts, text, songs, and illustrations (or descriptions of illustrations). In addition, you should explain for your editor the rationale for each piece of the campaign. Why will it be effective in changing people's attitudes or getting them active in participating in the cause? Your editor will decide whether the presentation of the campaign will be oral with supporting AV material or whether it will be all written.

Exploring the Topic: Metaphorical Language

In the "Opening the Topic" section at the beginning of this chapter, I talked about how communicating values requires connecting the cauldron of primitive emotion in the readers' lizard brains with the rigorous clarity of their evolved logic brains. Words do this most economically through the magic of metaphor. Metaphorical language works because it is precisely an imaginative connection between something a writer has experienced with the conscious, rational brain and an image that the unconscious has tossed up. This combination creates a dreamlike, emotional connection. When these two are thrown together, they hit with a powerful surprise that fuses a similar emotional connection in the reader. We are familiar with this from the image connections made in ads and commercials. A luxury car is shown with a bejeweled woman next to it in an expensive evening gown beneath a columned porte cochere to establish an attitude of luxurious opulence toward a well-disguised functional machine of welded steel run by explosive petroleum products. Or we see a hunking SUV perched a thousand feet above the floor of Monument Valley on top of a great natural sandstone pedestal suggesting victory over untamed wilderness adventure (even though we know it had to be airlifted there by helicopter).

Writers of nonfiction prose use these connections sparingly but occasionally with great effect, as in the following examples that we have seen:

- [ ] Joyce Caruso (**"Home Free?,"** chapter 1) uses New Jersey and Kansas as symbols of banishment from the stimulating social life of New York City.
- [ ] Stephen King (**"Why We Crave Horror Movies,"** chapter 4) likens our subconscious minds to a pit of alligators.
- [ ] Anna Quindlen (**"To Defray Expenses,"** chapter 5) compares the boys of the South Bronx to the fairy-tale Lost Boys of *Peter Pan.*
- [ ] Ellen Goodman (**"In Love Fornow,"** chapter 5) says that modern romance lacks the glue of future hope and is as anemic as a "chocolate heart made of skim milk and Sweet 'n Low."
- [ ] David Brooks (**"She Converted,"** chapter 7) makes an implied comparison of Boomer spiritualism to a butterfly, "always aflight, never settling anywhere."
- [ ] J. Madeleine Nash (**"When Life Exploded,"** chapter 8) says "biologists are teasing apart the genetic toolbox needed to assemble animals," says that some vendobionts resemble air mattresses while others look like corduroy, and explains the empty-barrel hypothesis.
- [ ] When Mary Schmich (**"Unintended Consequences,"** chapter 8) has her fictional character Missy say that the topic of sexual harassment makes her teeth hurt, she is making a metaphorical comparison.
- [ ] Susan Faludi (**"The Son, the Moon and the Stars,"** chapter 9) imagines a boy around 1960 being awakened by his father to see the Echo satellite, which, the boy understands, is an image his father is using—"a paternal gift rocketing him into his future, a miraculous inheritance encased in the transit of an artificial star, infinitesimally tiny, impossibly bright." Faludi also details the movie *The Incredible Shrinking Man,* in which the image of a man actually shrinking in size stands for the social situation of a generation of men. She quotes one such lost man: "I'm like a kite with a broken string, but I'm also holding the tail."
- [ ] In this chapter we have seen James B. Twitchell show how images from advertising work to symbolize meaning, and we have seen Aldo Leopold personify the mountain to provide a perspective on the killing of predators.

For each of the preceding examples, explain how the imaginative comparison works to attach a particular value to the thing being described.

Writers make these connections by means of well-established rhetorical figures that go by various technical names—*simile, synecdoche, symbolism, personification, metonymy*—all of which I am going to lump under *metaphor,* because the process of all is fundamentally the same.

Much of the power of Martin Luther King Jr.'s speech on the steps of the Lincoln Memorial in 1963 derives from metaphorical language.

☐ In a sense we have come to our nation's capital to cash a check. When the architects of our republic wrote the magnificent words of the Constitution and the Declaration of Independence, they were signing a promissory note to which every American was to fall heir. This note was a promise that all men would be guaranteed the inalienable rights of life, liberty, and the pursuit of happiness.

  It is obvious today that America has defaulted on this promissory note insofar as her citizens of color are concerned. Instead of honoring this sacred obligation, America has given the Negro people a bad check which has come back marked "insufficient funds." But we refuse to believe that the bank of justice is bankrupt. We refuse to believe that there are insufficient funds in the great vaults of opportunity of this nation. So we have come to cash this check—a check that will give us upon demand the riches of freedom and the security of justice.

☐ We are not satisfied, and we will not be satisfied until justice rolls down like waters and righteousness like a mighty stream. [In the Biblical Book of Amos, this image is applied to judgment, rather than justice.]

☐ Now is the time to lift our nation from the quicksands of racial injustice to the solid rock of brotherhood.

☐ Let us not seek to satisfy our thirst for freedom by drinking from the cup of bitterness and hatred.

☐ With this faith we will be able to hew out of the mountain of despair a stone of hope. With this faith we will be able to transform the jangling discords of our nation into a beautiful symphony of brotherhood. With this faith we will be able to work together, to pray together, to struggle together, to go to jail together, to stand up for freedom together, knowing that we will be free one day.

For each of these passages, tell what King is trying to describe, what image he attaches to it, and what feeling that image transfers to the subject.

Just as screenwriters and playwrights are the authors who have taught us how to dramatize encounters, so it is poets who teach us most about the indirect infusion of value into our writing by metaphor: the inspiration of setting one experience beside another to illuminate the one with the emotional energy generated by the writer's imaginative connecting of the two.

Explain how this works in the following poem.

The Deer
by Gwenda Conner

I once drove along the highway
And saw there a deer,
Freshly hit,
Scrambling vainly to stand
As it had not yet recognized
The guts on the ground
As its own.
And looking at you now,
At your eyes filled with uneasy fear,
I am reminded of that deer
Like which you, too, insist on living
Despite the relentless blows
Life's dealt you.
But I wonder
As I leave you,
As I did the deer,
Resigned to
My helplessness to assist,
How long you will continue to struggle
Before you succumb.

Discussing your poetry: I'm willing to bet that you have written some poems or song lyrics. Why not try this. Choose an editorial board from among the class members. Let each student anonymously submit one or two of their best pieces to the board. When the board has picked the best of the best, duplicate enough copies for the entire class. Then, as a class, discuss the emotional valuation in each case, how it is achieved, and how successful it is.

If Benjamin Franklin had had his way, we would now have turkeys on our money instead of eagles. When Congress rejected his suggestion for the turkey as a symbol of our country, he wrote to his daughter that the eagle had a "bad moral character." He continued, "I wish the bald eagle had not been chosen as the representative of our country! The turkey is a much more respectable bird, and withal a true original native of America."

As an international symbol of the United States, the Statue of Liberty (originally named "Liberty Enlightening the World") is one that would have been more to Franklin's liking. A gift from France, it was designed by Frédéric-Auguste Bartholdi, who, with others, raised the money to construct it for the centennial of the Franco-American alliance of 1778.

Emma Lazarus, an American author who devoted the last years of her life to the relief of immigrants, especially persecuted European Jews, made the symbolism of the statue explicit in the following sonnet, which appears on a plaque inside the pedestal.

The New Colossus

Not like the brazen giant of Greek fame,
With conquering limbs astride from land to land;
Here at our sea-washed, sunset gates shall stand
A mighty woman with a torch whose flame
Is imprisoned lightning, and her name
Mother of Exiles. From her beacon-hand
Glows world-wide welcome; her mild eyes command
The air-bridged harbor that twin cities frame.
"Keep ancient lands your storied pomp!" cries she with silent
   lips.
"Give me your tired your poor,
Your huddled masses yearning to breathe free,
The wretched refuse of your teeming shore.
Send these, the homeless, tempest-tossed to me,
I lift my lamp beside the golden door!"

In the less familiar opening octave of the sonnet, Lazarus contrasts the accepting feminine qualities of this mild-eyed but mighty woman with the Colossus of Rhodes. That statue, also at the entrance to a famous harbor, was a very masculine one from the third century

Figure 10.5. The Statue of Liberty.

B.C. Standing, head to foot, almost as high as the Statue of Liberty, it was one of the seven wonders of the ancient world.

Symbols can stand for a range of values, so it is up to the author to infuse them with a particular meaning. We do not know exactly what the Colossus of Rhodes looked like; it was felled by an earthquake some 60 years after it was built. At one time it was thought to have straddled the harbor entrance, but it is now believed to have stood beside the harbor and may not have looked all that different from the Statue of Liberty (except for the gender).

It, too, symbolized liberty, and it, too, had a plaque. But the ancient author put a quite different significance into that symbolic image of the Greek God Helios:

> To you, O Sun, the people of Dorian Rhodes set up this bronze statue reaching to Olympus when they had pacified the waves of war and crowned their city with the spoils taken from the enemy. Not only over the seas but also on land did they kindle the lovely torch of freedom.

Explain the difference in valuation of freedom that these authors infuse into the monuments they are celebrating.

Because symbols blazon forth one aspect of the value system of an entire culture, no single artist, like Chares of Lindos, the creator of the Colossus, or Bartholdi or Lazarus can create a symbol unless it represents values that are commonly held throughout the society.

Figure 10.6. Colossus of Rhodes, conjectural illustration.

Prose writers can, however, use their encounters with cultural symbols to reason about and try to clarify or change society's values.

In the following essay, Louise Erdrich, a powerful author of several novels, explores the valuation society places on women and that which women place on themselves through her experiences with the symbol of the veil.

The Veils
by Louise Erdrich
from The Blue Jay's Dance

It has dropped across my face again, the white net, the cloud that at one time or another obscures the features of every woman I have known. It is a snow falling, always, between my face and your face, the shocked expression of social chastity, the charged atoms of social courtesy. Oversimplified emotion, parenthetical dreams, the message is too acute. The veil speaks possession and possessed desire. A violent grace is required, to lift the veil all on your own. By custom, the authority of touch is given to the priest, the husband. The woman's hands are always too heavy, the woman's hands are filled.

The veil is the symbol of the female hymen, and to lift it was once, and often still is, the husband's first marital privilege. The veil is the mist before the woman's face that allows her to limit her vision to the here, the now, the inch beyond her nose. It is an illusion of safety, a flimsy skin of privacy that encourages violation. The message behind the veil is touch me, I'm yours. The purity is fictional, coy. The veil is the invitation to tear it away.

Three photographs

Mary Lefavor, my grandmother—Ojibwa, French, and Scots, perhaps a descendant of the Selkirkers of Rudolph's land—stands beside a fellow first communicant. No more than ten or eleven years old, both are crowned with lilies and carnations, holding Christ's symbol erect. They are captured in the white shadow and the air of their substanceless caves, the veils they wear. My grandmother's face is beautiful, her ankles thick, her eyes too serious. It is as if, in this picture, she knows that she is about to enter a room with many doors, but no windows.

At fourteen she marries, and bears a stillborn child. More children follow—born in a log house raised on allotment land—and other women's children, too, children she loved and raised for others. A reticent woman of profound goodness.

Next photograph:

My mother on her wedding day, so beautiful with her veil thrown back she clouds my father's shy face with happiness. She is adored, the ecstasy is on her, so plain to see. She is leaving the Turtle Mountain Reservation to live with a high school teacher, Ralph Erdrich. She is leaving her mother's house. Home country. Yet there is something in her face of all that is to come—the healthy children, the long marriage, the love that is to bear the weight of conflict through so many decades, a durable look of pleasure.

Last picture:

Me at seven, and that's my mother's wedding veil cut down and tacked onto a lacy headband. I might as well be holding my grandmother's candle, too. It is exactly the same. I have made my first confession. My first sin was lying, the only sin at which I was accomplished. Now, absolved, I wear a new nylon dress that feels like a hair shirt—the bodice is small and the seams scratch underneath my arms. My bangs are curled on rags, my hair reaches down to the small of my back, and I have rehearsed over and over in air and in the mirror the act of tipping my head back, eyes shut and tongue out, receiving Christ.

The precious *no*

To keep my mouth shut. To turn away my face. To walk back down the aisle. To slap the bishop back when he slapped me during Confirmation. To hold the word *no* in my mouth like a gold coin, something valued, something possible. To teach the *no* to our daughters. To value their *no* more than their compliant yes. To celebrate *no.* To grasp the word *no* in your fist and refuse to give it up. To support the boy who says *no* to violence, the girl who will not be violated, the woman who says *no, no, no, I will not.* To love the *no,* to cherish the *no,* which is so often our first word. *No*—the means to transformation.

We are born in cauls and veils, and our lives as women are fierce and individual dances of shedding them. We are stepping higher, higher now, into the thinnest air. It takes about a decade of wild blue dancing to shed just one. If we are lucky and if we dance hard enough, will we be able to look each other in the eye, our faces clear, between us nothing but air!

And what do we do with the nets, the sails that luffed, that tangled around our feet! What do we do with the knowledge and the anger!

I see the veils twisted, knotted between us like sheets for escape. The taut material is strong when pulled and thinned to ropes between us. Primary chords. We can use the means and symbol of our long histories, as women, of emotional and intellectual incarceration. We can remove the flimsy shadows from before our faces and braid them into ropes. We can fasten the ropes between us so that if one of us slips, as we climb, as we live, there are others in the line to stand firm, to bear her up, to be her witnesses and anchors.

We are all bound, we are all in tatters, we are all the shining presence behind the net. We are all the face we're not allowed to touch. We are all in need of the ancient nourishment. And if we walk slowly without losing our connections to one another, if we wait, holding firm to the rock while our daughters approach hand over hand, if we can catch our mothers, if we hold our grandmothers, if we remember that the veil can also be the durable love between women.

CRITICAL READING

1. The first two paragraphs are chockablock with surprises, many of them paradoxical symbols. Point out several of these and explain the conflicted feelings that lie behind them.
2. After the logical **reasoning** paradoxes of the first two sentences, Erdrich presents three **encounters,** which she dramatizes by seeing in them metaphorical meanings of a common symbol— the veil. Explain the symbolism in each case. How do these set the stage for the dramatic, sudden **valuation** of saying "No"?
3. What is accomplished by the metaphor of her grandmother's being about to enter a room with many doors and no windows?
4. Her mother's picture seems to be the happiest of the three. Why?
5. What is the function of the string of *if* clauses that makes up the last sentence? What is the effect of this string of conditionals on the **resolution**?

DISCUSSION QUESTIONS

1. Who or what is most responsible for women's historical "emotional and intellectual" incarceration, according to Erdrich: women themselves, men, a male-dominated society, nature, the church? To what extent do you agree with this view of women's isolated subservience, in the past if not now?
2. What **valuation** do you sense Erdrich puts on marriage, motherhood, career, social reform, friendship, extended family tradition? Do you feel empathetic toward Erdrich's attitudes toward these? What techniques has she used to evoke those feelings in her readers?

Exploring the Topic: Irony

Setting the expected reality beside the real reality with a knowing smile and nod creates a special kind of **valuation** called *irony*. It involves a recognition that, because real reality almost always under-cuts pretension, it is absurd to take anything too seriously, including oneself. Irony seems to create a world without values—unless you count the value of ironic distance: the feeling that author and reader are sharing a quiet joke and a knowing wink at the expense of those who are deeply committed to something (especially if they are proud of their commitment). The following article by Joel Stein illustrates the ironic mode of valuation.

INVITATION TO A READING

In 1999, a 24-year-old graduate of Yale University surprised just about everybody with the success of a small but earnest book about val-ues—specifically about the negative value of the ironic stance that many of the country's intellectual and entertainment taste-makers have, as he believed, adopted.

MANKOFF

"And now a correction: Portions of last night's story on diving mules which were read with an air of ironic detachment should actually have been presented with earnest concern."

Figure 10.7.

The author, Jedediah Purdy, hit a nerve that connected with many readers who felt that moral and cultural relativism had created a culture in which there were no solid, widely accepted values. Purdy observed that anyone, especially in media and academia, who expressed deeply felt ideals was subject to ridicule from sophisticates who put an ironic shield between themselves and anything so naive as convictions. Of course, anyone was free to express their views, even vehemently. But these are understood to be "true **for them**"—a favorite phrase. Any suggestion that there was anything true **for everybody** has been met with an ironic sneer.

A few years before, responding to the same felt need for some bedrock beneath the shifting sands of the cultural desert, former Education Secretary William Bennett had had great success publishing an anthology called *The Book of Virtues.* This contained stories drawn from centuries of Western culture that unapologetically illustrated basic virtues—responsibility, courage, compassion, honesty, friendship, persistence, faith—stories that he hoped families would read together and discuss.

The issue of irony spawned something of a national debate. Early in the primaries of election year 2000, candidate George W. Bush was criticized for his annoying propensity to "raise his chin, lift an

"Whatever."

Figure 10.8.

eyebrow, and curl his lip slightly"—in short, to **smirk.** In the words of one reporter, "We seem to have entered the postironic age. Earnestness is ascendant. Bush simply was caught, mid-smirk, in the middle of a paradigm shift."

The following column, which both defines irony and illustrates it, took flight from the writer's encounter with Purdy's book and with the spate of praise that followed it.

In Defense of Irony
by Joel Stein

For no apparent reason, the media have become very excited about *For Common Things,* a book by a Yale law student named Jedediah Purdy. No one else is reading it, but in my earnest effort to join the media elite and thus get a promotion, I too want to write about this book.

Mostly I want to say that Jedediah Purdy is a funny name. And also that his argument that irony is poisoning our culture is really stupid. That's the kind of argument we ironists use. We also use *idiot* and *scalawag.* But ironically.

I called Purdy's publicist and asked if I could speak to him. Fifteen minutes later, Purdy called. This made me think that earnestness might be a good thing. Then I realized that you have to jump on any media opportunity when you're trying to sell a book called *For Common Things: Irony, Trust, and Commitment in America Today.*

I asked Purdy if the book wasn't just an excuse for not having a sense of humor. He said, "That's a pretty nifty little piece of psychological deductionism." I took that as a yes. Then, to make conversation, I asked him his favorite movie. He paused and said, "I like movies, but I don't orient to them with the same sophistication as a lot of folks."

Now that I've allowed Purdy his equal time as per the National Association of Columnists bylaws, I want to explain why irony is necessary, besides the fact that without it, I'm unemployable. First of all, irony is much more fun than earnestness. Earnestness is thanking God after scoring a touchdown, while irony is having 10,000 spoons when all you need is a knife. Earnestness is what you hide behind when you have nothing to say. Unless you hide behind irony, which is much cooler.

True belief led us to the Cuban missile crisis, while the post-Watergate era allows us to divest emotionally from our government so it can do important work on campaign-finance reform. And skepticism without irony is totally unfun. It leads to folk songs.

By constantly checking ourselves for phoniness, irony forces us either to think more closely about how we feel or to joke honestly about the fact that we feel nothing. I'm worried that in the post-ironic world of Rosie O'Donnell, people suppress so much of their emotions that they believe they love Tom Cruise and peg their audience with Koosh balls.

To argue further for irony, I am going to use Søren Kierkegaard's *The Concept of Irony with Continual Reference to Socrates*. I do this not only because it will make me look smart, but because I get to employ the underutilized ø. Like that crazy Socrates, who made fun of his interlocutors while pretending to compliment them, Kierkegaard uses irony to force his opponents to avoid rehearsed answers and confront their true beliefs. He even wrote under pseudonyms like Hilarius Bookbinder, Nicolaus Notabene and Constantin Constantius. In the world of 19th century Christian philosophy, this is sidesplitting stuff, trust me. In the book, Kierkegaard wrote, "Irony is a disciplinarian feared only by those who do not know it but loved by those who do." When I ran Kierkegaard's argument by Purdy, he said, "Kierkegaard is very neat."

I like that Purdy wants us to consider the consequences of our attitudes. But I think the anti-irony movement is a longing for an innocence that existed only for one moment in Timothy Leary's lab.[3] And if my name were Jedediah, I'd be so ironic, David Letterman would seem caring. Or I'd call myself Jed.

CRITICAL READING

1. In the first paragraph, Stein uses irony to defend himself against the charge that he is betraying an earnest belief in values by engaging Purdy's ideas. Explain how he does this.

2. We have all been put at a loss by people who respond to what we feel was a carefully thought out opinion by saying, emphatically, "That's really **stupid!**" It's infuriating because it forecloses all further discussion; it's a dead end. You may notice that Stein is subtly mocking some of Purdy's responses to his questions. Find a couple of places where Purdy is quoted making equally inane remarks. Stein says that his use of *stupid* and *idiot* are different

---

[3] Timothy Leary established a controversial lab at Harvard in the late 1950s to study the effects of psychedelic drugs to achieve what he believed to be a higher state of consciousness. After being fired from Harvard he became a counterculture cult leader in the 1960s, promoting the (illegal) use of LSD.

because they are **ironic.** What could he mean by that? How does it make a difference?

3. Self-mockery is a key to the ironic attitude. Point out places in the column where Stein makes fun of himself.

DISCUSSION QUESTIONS

1. To what extent do you agree that earnestness can lead to disastrous human suffering and folk music?
2. The ironic attitude is not simply the practice of making fun of everything and everyone. In fact, one might say that Stein is rather earnest about irony. What **value** do you think he sees in it? What danger do you think Purdy sees in the widespread adoption of the ironic attitude?
3. Think of some experiences that you have had that might prompt an ironic response. Think of some where you have been the victim of others' irony.

WRITING COMMISSION: VALUATING A CONTROVERSIAL SYMBOL

The editor of your virtual newspaper has noticed that many of the issues that upset the townsfolk most are symbolic rather than practical ones. So it might make an interesting issue to address a number of these as a group.

"All right, crew. Here is a passel of sore points that pop up in our mail periodically. I want to put out a highly opinionated issue giving you each a byline so that the readers won't blame me. Because they know you are interns and mainly from out of town—some of you even Damyankees!—they may be more tolerant."

Hot Button Issues

☐ This town has a war memorial to the Confederate soldiers who died in the War between the States. Should we tear down this monument to the defenders of slavery?

☐ High school senior girls are required to wear white dresses to the graduation ceremony. Last year the valedictorian refused to make the valedictory address because she insisted on wearing pants and the school wouldn't admit her to the ceremony.

☐ Our county courthouse flies the Confederate flag. Is it possible to separate the traditions of our beloved land from the sin of slavery intertwined in this symbol?

- Some people in the town want to post the Ten Commandments, preferably in schools but otherwise in some prominent public place. Is the ACLU right that this violates the separation of church and state?
- Speaking of the ACLU, can there be a crèche in the town square at Christmastime if there is also a menorah?
- Should George Washington's birthday and Columbus Day be holidays, or is this needlessly offensive to African Americans—some of whom might have ancestors who were slaves of George Washington and whose ancestors would never have been brought here if Columbus had stayed home—and to Native Americans, who might blame Columbus for depriving their ancestors of their native land?

"Because these issues have at least two sides, and because we want to try to present them fairly, I'm going to steal an idea from a pair of columnists on the *Chicago Tribune* staff, Mary Schmich and Eric Zorn. A couple of weeks out of the year, they present a kind of debate column. Mary writes a kind of issue-oriented letter to Eric, Eric responds, usually with a somewhat opposing view, and then Mary gets a quick rejoinder. The next day, they switch.

That's what I want you guys (OK, and gals—pardon me) to do. Find a partner that would like to work with you on one of those issues I listed. Flip a coin to see who writes the first half of the column. That person must make it clear which side his (I mean *their*—no! I won't say that. OK, "his or her") values are on. Then the second person writes a friendly, collegial rebuttal, and the first person gets the last—brief—word.

I have an example here of one of the Zorn-Schmich discussions of how people get upset over the symbolism of labels that we apply to each other. It has to do with the different values we put on calling people names depending on who's doing the calling. You can use this for a model."

Putting Labels Aside May Be the Best Medicine
by Eric Zorn and Mary Schmich

To: Eric Zorn
From: Mary Schmich

I'm feeling ornery today. So I'm going to insult you the worst way I know how:

White man.

Yeah. You heard me, buster. You're a white man.

Ooo. That felt good. So I'm going to kick you even harder: Rich white man.

Sorry. I'm being unreasonable. How could you be rich? You work for a newspaper. So I'll stick to calling you a white man.

Now I want to know—does that wound you? I ask because after I suggested in a recent column that Peter Fitzgerald would be "another rich white man" in the U.S. Senate, some readers complained viciously that the phrase was a sexist, racist slur.

I've been puzzling over which part is the slur. White? Man? Rich? Where I come from, all of those identities confer at least some privilege and power.

But the complaint raises an interesting question about words that deal with race, wealth and gender. Is it really as offensive to refer regretfully to "another rich white man" in the U.S. Senate as it might be to lament the presence of, say, "another poor black woman"?

Few of us like to be described as what we are by people who take issue with what we are. I bristle at being called middle-class, white or feminist by people contemptuous of the middle class, whites or feminists. That doesn't, however, change the fact that I am all those things— though perhaps not the critics' interpretation of them.

Rich white men by any other name are still rich white men. I know and like some. Honest. But—and this was the point about Fitzgerald—I can't pretend to like the fact that the world, including politics, remains dominated by this advantaged minority.

Nevertheless, I concede that for the sake of civilized conversation, it might be wise to forsake such blunt, loaded terms. So, let me ask: What do you think, you middle-class Caucasian male?

To: mschmich@tribune.com
From: (address withheld)

What do I think? I think my mini-van needs an oil change.

And I think you puzzle too much over hostile mail from people who don't really care about your opinions anyway.

But to your point, I think that no one likes to be stereotyped or narrowly categorized because everyone is more complicated and has more dimensions than easy labels suggest. Certain terms and generalizations hurt more than others because of how they're used by those who attempt to marginalize, dehumanize or exclude those over whom they already hold political, social or economic advantage.

I have no patience for anyone who doesn't understand or, more likely, pretends not to understand the difference in throw-weight among various slurs and seeming slurs. It's the historical context, stupid.

Rich white males may not have led perfectly charmed lives, but because they do dominate politics (and industry and finance and law . . .), they don't know the sting of genuine gender or racial bias. So I'm sure our 24-carat achromatic senator-elect never even blinked at your prejudicial remark.

Speaking of money, I'm now persuaded that it's impossible to limit campaign spending without doing great violence to the Constitution, and that the current limits on individual donations serve primarily to confer advantage upon independently wealthy twits who want to buy political viability.

The Twit Anti-defamation League may send their complaints to your address.

To: ericzorn@sensitiveguys.com
From: A Middle-Class White Woman

Your sensitivity has cheered me up. So I'd like to end our week of correspondence on a happy note. This morning I took a cab ride. The driver was a 50ish Greek immigrant. A Republican, he said, when I asked about the election, and happy George Ryan won. Predictable, I thought. Then he stunned me. "But too bad about Carol Moseley-Braun."[4]

"She had experience," he said when I asked why he supported her. "And she was a woman." He went on to say he looked forward to a woman president—maybe that Mrs. Clinton.

It was a good reminder—that political divisions aren't as neat as they sometimes seem, and that all kinds of folks wish for a world run by a more varied group of people.

Points to Remember

♦ Our way of **valuing** experience, shown to the world in what we do, lives in our unconscious mind. As writers we try to get our

---

[4] Braun, from Illinois, was the first African American woman senator. She got in trouble with her personal use of campaign funds and for personal relations with repressive Nigerian leaders and was defeated in 1998.

unconscious "lizard brain" to speak directly to those of our readers, often by linking or contrasting images.

- Because advertisers make their living appealing to people's unconscious value impulses, we can probably learn something about how to do that by studying the techniques advertisers use. One important step is to map the variety of reactions that different readers will have toward your experience and thought.

- Unlike advertisers who try to adapt to the common denominator among their readers' values, writers declare their individuality, often through a surprising twist or inversion of commonly accepted **values**.

- Our minds tend to organize values around concrete images— things or pictures of things. This is another reason it is important to develop the habit of writing highly visual concrete descriptions.

- Judging the goodness and badness of things, because it is largely subconscious, inescapably infuses our writing. However, we often want to put in entire modal sections in which we describe, explain, and even argue for the values we attach to the subject.

- One of the pervasive ways we get values across to readers is through the connotations of the words that we choose to talk about our subject.

- Metaphor is the deliberate attachment of an image from the subconscious to something we want to create an emotional reaction to. Used more by poets than prose writers, it can nevertheless be highly effective in evoking reader response.

- Symbols are a kind of public metaphor that writers often engage to clarify or rebel against common social **values**.

- Whereas metaphor is a way of establishing **value** by linking, irony is a way of establishing value by contrast. The ironist flatters the reader by implying that both share a broader, more sophisticated viewpoint than those whose values she or he is criticizing. Irony also usually has a winsome tone of self-distancing humor that many readers find engaging. But you must note that there can also be a reaction against irony. Many people are turned off by what they see as a smart-aleck stance.

E-E-R

Encounter

Explain

Resolve

R-S-V-B

Reason

Search

Value

Background

11

Integrating the Modalities

A Note from the Author

It's been a long time since the beginning of the term and my talk about Aristotle listening in the corner, watching the Mars launch on different TV channels, what English teachers want, the story of Filippa and the clique, and the writer as juggler. Before reading this chapter, I urge you to go back and reread at least those parts of the Personal Note and chapters 1 and 2. I think you will get a sense of accomplishment from observing how much more meaningful those ideas are now after you have worked with them for many weeks. Progress is gradual, and advancement in a complex skill like writing often seems frustratingly slow. I think, however, that if you go back now and crochet those opening items from this book, you will realize that you have a much better understanding of how the rhetorical playbook can actually work to increase your sense of power and control in communication.

Opening the Topic

OK, I'm tolling the bell, crocheting an item from the beginning of the book, closing the ring. The resolution of this text—which I hope I've repeated enough times—is that good writing opens the reader to its significance by surprise. And then it proceeds to cycle through a series of distinct sections, each with its own manner of writing and its own strategic purpose in leading the reader from an observed disturbance through a convincing explanation to a resolution embodying a new attitude or program or both.

The great eighteenth-century philosopher and mathematician Leibnitz, one of the inventors of the calculus, believed that each individual human soul is encapsulated in what he called a "monad." He got this idea from a common experience we all share of being ultimately isolated from the true core being of other people. Today we might think of these monads as spaceships, each with a single occupant, able to contact each other only through an imperfect system of TV and radio. That is, we never make actual contact but only see and hear each other at a distance through a distorting medium. This would explain why, in human relationships, we often have such trouble communicating. I'm sure you have found, as we all have, that even when we think we're communicating well, it turns out later that we have been talking right past each other, communicating with an image of the other person that was created wholly in our own minds. Writing to other people is in some ways even more difficult, because we do not have cues of sight and sound to help us interpret the immediate reactions of our audience to what we're saying.

But as writers—as human beings—we're most eager to contact other people directly. Believe it or not, it is the techniques of rhetoric that give us a chance to link our spaceships so that we can move into one another's minds. You know what a marvel of engineering it is for two spaceships to be able to dock and latch, each with a hatch that can be opened to allow crewmembers of one ship to enter the other. Rhetoric is just this kind of docking mechanism. It is a system of docking that has been developed over the millennia in our culture so that the receiving ship has a mechanism that matches the author's spaceship. It is complicated. And it must be more than a single probe; it must be a system of hooks and grapples that lock the reader's mind securely enough so that the mental hatch can be opened and true person-to-person contact can be made. This is the ultimate satisfaction both of reading and of writing. It is what ultimately makes the study of these modalities worthwhile. In this chapter we take a last look at the whole system—the whole docking mechanism—that enables us writers to contact another human spaceship.

INVITATION TO A READING

Here is a full-scale article in which a reporter makes an extensive effort to get inside the lives of people in a newly evolving culture. As she tries to convey her experience with them to us, I think you can clearly see the cycling of modalities that she uses to latch us together.

After you've read the whole article, I will demonstrate some of the most important modality sections I see.

Be particularly aware of the eye-opening surprises in each section and of the significance of her moves from one modality to the next.

Goin' Gangsta, Choosin' Cholita
by Nell Bernstein

Her lipstick is dark, the lip liner even darker, nearly black. In baggy pants, a blue plaid Pendleton, her bangs pulled back tight off her forehead, fifteen-year-old April is a perfect cholita, a Mexican gangsta girl. But April Miller is Anglo. "And I don't like it!" she complains, "I'd rather be Mexican." April's father wanders into the family room of their home in San Leandro, California, a suburb near Oakland. "Hey, cholita," he teases. "Go get a suntan. We'll put you in a barrio and see how much you like it."

A large, sandy-haired man with "April" tattooed on one arm and "Kelly"—the name of his older daughter—on the other, Miller spent twenty-one years working in a San Leandro glass factory that shut down and moved to Mexico a couple of years ago. He recently got a job in another factory, but he expects NAFTA to swallow that one, too.

"Sooner or later we'll all get nailed," he says. "Just another stab in the back of the American middle class."

Later, April gets her revenge: "Hey, Mr. White Man's Last Stand," she teases. "Wait till you see how well I manage my welfare check. You'll be asking me for money!"

A once almost exclusively white, now increasingly Latin and black working-class suburb, San Leandro borders on predominantly black East Oakland. For decades, the boundary was strictly policed and practically impenetrable.

In 1970 April Miller's hometown was 97 percent white. By 1990 San Leandro was 65 percent white, 6 percent black, 15 percent Hispanic, and 13 percent Asian or Pacific Islander. With minorities moving into suburbs in growing numbers and cities becoming ever more diverse, the boundary between city and suburb is dissolving, and suburban teenagers are changing with the times. In April's bedroom, her past and present selves lie in layers, the pink walls of girlhood almost obscured, Guns N' Roses and Pearl Jam posters overlaid by rappers Paris and Ice Cube. "I don't have a big enough attitude to be a black girl," says April, explaining her current choice of ethnic identification.

What matters is that she thinks the choice is hers. For April and her friends, identity is not a matter of where you come from, what you were born into, what color your skin is. It's what you wear, the music you listen to, the words you use—everything to which you pledge allegiance, no matter how fleetingly.

The hybridization of American teens has become talk show fodder, with "wiggers"—white kids who dress and talk "black"—appearing on TV in full gangsta regalia. In Indiana a group of white high school girls raised a national stir when they triggered an imitation race war at their virtually all white high school last fall simply by dressing "black." In many parts of the country, it's television and radio, not neighbors, that introduce teens to the allure of ethnic difference. But in California, which demographers predict will be the first state with no racial majority by the year 2000, the influences are more immediate. The California public schools are the most diverse in the country: 42 percent white, 36 percent Hispanic, 9 percent black, 8 percent Asian.

Sometimes young people fight over their differences. Students at virtually any school in the Bay Area can recount the details of at least one "race riot" in which a conflict between individuals escalated into a battle between their clans. More often, though, teens would rather join than fight. Adolescence, after all, is the period when you're most inclined to mimic the power closest at hand, from stealing your older sister's clothes to copying the ruling clique at school.

White skaters and Mexican would-be gangbangers listen to gangsta rap and call each other "nigga" as a term of endearment; white girls sometimes affect Spanish accents; blond cheerleaders claim Cherokee ancestors.

"Claiming" is the central concept here. A Vietnamese teen in Hayward, another Oakland suburb, "claims" Oakland—and by implication blackness—because he lived there as a child. A law-abiding white kid "claims" a Mexican gang he says he hangs with. A brown-skinned girl with a Mexican father and a white mother "claims" her Mexican side, while her fair-skinned sister "claims" white. The word comes up over and over, as if identity were territory, the self a kind of turf.

At a restaurant in a minimall in Hayward, Nicole Huffstutler, thirteen, sits with her friends and describes herself as "Indian, German, French, Welsh, and, um . . . American": "If somebody says anything like 'Yeah, you're just a peckerwood,' I'll walk up and I'll say 'white pride!' Cause I'm proud of my race, and I wouldn't wanna be any other."

"Claiming" white has become a matter of principle for Heather, too, who says she's "sick of the majority looking at us like we're less than them." (Haywood schools were 51 percent white in 1990, down from 77 percent in 1980, and whites are now the minority in many schools.)

Asked if she knows that nonwhites have not traditionally been referred to as "the majority" in America, Heather gets exasperated: "I hear that all the time, every day. They say, 'Well, you guys controlled us for many years, and it's time for us to control you.' Every day."

When Jennifer Vargas—a small, brown-skinned girl in purple jeans who quietly eats her salad while Heather talks—softly announces that she's "mostly Mexican," she gets in trouble with her friends.

"No, you're not!" scolds Heather.

"I'm mostly Indian and Mexican," Jennifer continues flatly. "I'm very little . . . I'm mostly . . ."

"Your mom's white!" Nicole reminds her sharply. "She has blond hair."

"That's what I mean," Nicole adds. "People think that white is a bad thing. They think that white is a bad race. So she's trying to claim more Mexican than white."

"I have very little white in me," Jennifer repeats. "I have mostly my dad's side, 'cause I look like him and stuff. And most of my friends think that me and my brother and sister aren't related, 'cause they look more like my mom."

"But you guys are all the same race, you just look different," Nicole insists. She stops eating and frowns. "OK, you're half and half each what your parents have. So you're equal as your brother and sister, you just look different. And you should be proud of what you are—every little piece and bit of what you are. Even if you were Afghan or whatever, you should be proud of it."

Will Mosley, Heather's seventeen-year-old brother, says he and his friends listen to rap groups like Compton's Most Wanted, NWA, and Above the Law because they "sing about life"—that is, what happens in Oakland, Los Angeles, anyplace but where Will is sitting today, an empty Round Table Pizza in a minimall.

"No matter what race you are," Will says, "if you live like we do, then that's the kind of music you like."

And how do they live?

"We don't live bad or anything," Will admits. "We live in a pretty good neighborhood, there's no violence or crime. I was just . . . we're just city people, I guess."

Will and his friend Adolfo Garcia, sixteen, say they've outgrown trying to be something they're not. "When I was eleven or twelve," Will says, "I thought I was becoming a big gangsta and stuff. Because I liked that music, and thought it was the coolest, I wanted to become that. I wore big clothes, like you wear in jail. But then I kind of woke up. I looked at myself and thought, 'Who am I trying to be?' "

They may have outgrown blatant mimicry, but Will and his friends remain convinced that they can live in a suburban tract house with a well-kept lawn on a tree-lined street in "not a bad neighborhood" and still call themselves "city" people on the basis of musical tastes. "City" for these young people means crime, graffiti, drugs. The kids are law-abiding, but these activities connote what Will admiringly calls "action." With pride in his voice, Will predicts that "in a couple of years, Hayward will be like Oakland. It's starting to get more known, because of crime and things. I think it'll be bigger, more things happening, more crime, more graffiti, stealing cars."

"That's good," chimes in fifteen-year-old Matt Jenkins, whose new beeper—an item that once connoted gangsta chic but now means little more than an active social life—goes off periodically. "More fun."

The three young men imagine with disdain life in a gangsta-free zone. "Too bland, too boring," Adolfo says. "You have to have something going on. You can't just have everyday life."

"Mowing your lawn," Matt sneers.

"Like Beaver Cleaver's house," Adolfo adds. "It's too clean out here."

Not only white kids believe that identity is a matter of choice or taste, or that the power of "claiming" can transcend ethnicity. The Manor Park Locos—a group of mostly Mexican-Americans who hang out in San Leandro's Manor Park—say they descend from the Manor Lords, tough white guys who ruled the neighborhood a generation ago.

They "are like our . . . uncles and dads, the older generation," says Jesse Martinez, fourteen. "We're what they were when they were around, except we're Mexican."

"There's three generations," says Oso, Jesse's younger brother. "There's Manor Lords, Manor Park Locos, and Manor Park Pee Wees." The Pee Wees consist mainly of the Locos' younger brothers, eager kids who circle the older boys on bikes and brag about "punking people."

Unlike Will Mosley, the Locos find little glamour in city life. They survey the changing suburban landscape and see not "action" or "more fun" but frightening decline. Though most of them are not yet eighteen, the Locos are already nostalgic, longing for a Beaver Cleaver past that white kids who mimic them would scoff at.

Walking through nearly empty Manor Park, with its eucalyptus stands, its softball diamond and tennis courts, Jesse's friend Alex, the only Asian in the group, waves his arms in a gesture of futility. "A few years ago, every bench was filled," he says. "Now no one comes here. I guess it's because of everything that's going on. My parents paid a lot for this house, and I want it to be nice for them. I just hope this doesn't turn into Oakland."

Glancing across the park at April Miller's street, Jesse says he knows what the white cholitas are about. "It's not a racial thing," he explains. "It's just all the most popular people out here are Mexican. We're just the gangstas that everyone knows. I guess those girls wanna be known."

Not every young Californian embraces the new racial hybridism. Andrea Jones, twenty, an African American who grew up in the Bay Area suburbs of Union City and Hayward, is unimpressed by what she sees mainly as shallow mimicry. "It's full of posers out here," she says. "When *Boyz N the Hood* came out on video, it was sold out for weeks. The boys all wanna be black, the girls all wanna be Mexican. It's the glamour."

Driving down the quiet, shaded streets of her old neighborhood in Union City, Andrea spots two white preteen boys in Raiders jackets and hugely baggy pants strutting erratically down the empty sidewalk. "Look at them," she says. "Dislocated."

She knows why. "In a lot of these schools out here, it's hard being white," she says. "I don't think these kids were prepared for the backlash that is going on, all the pride now in people of color's ethnicity, and our boldness with it. They have nothing like that, no identity, nothing they can say they're proud of.

"So they latch onto their great-grandmother who's a Cherokee, or they take on the most stereotypical aspects of being black or Mexican. It's beautiful to appreciate different aspects of other people's culture—that's like the dream of what the twenty-first century should be. But to garnish yourself with pop culture stereotypes just to blend—that's really sad."

Roland Krevocheza, eighteen, graduated last year from Arroyo High School in San Leandro. He is Mexican on his mother's side, Eastern European on his father's. In the new hierarchies, it may be mixed kids like Roland who have the hardest time finding their place, even as their numbers grow. (One in five marriages in California is between people of different races.) They can always be called "wannabes," no matter what they claim.

"I'll state all my nationalities," Roland says. But he takes a greater interest in his father's side, his Ukrainian, Romanian, and Czech ancestors. "It's more unique," he explains. "Mexican culture is all around me. We eat Mexican food all the time. I hear stories from my grandmother. I see the low-riders and stuff. I'm already part of it. I'm not trying to be; I am."

His darker-skinned brother "says he's not proud to be white," Roland adds. "He calls me 'Mr. Nazi.' " In the room the two share, the American flags and the reproduction of the Bill of Rights are Roland's; the Public Enemy poster belongs to his brother.

Roland has good reason to mistrust gangsta attitudes. In his junior year in high school, he was one of several Arroyo students who were beaten up outside the school at lunchtime by a group of Samoans who came in cars from Oakland. Roland wound up with a split lip, a concussion, and a broken tailbone. Later he was told that the assault was "gang-related"—that the Samoans were beating up anyone wearing red.

"Rappers, I don't like them," Roland says. "I think they're a bad influence on kids. It makes kids think they're all tough and bad."

Those who, like Roland, dismiss the gangsta and cholo styles as affectations can point to the fact that several companies market overpriced knockoffs of "ghetto wear" targeted at teens.

But there's also something going on out here that transcends adolescent faddishness and pop culture exoticism. When white kids call their parents "racist" for nagging them about their baggy pants; when they learn Spanish to talk to their boyfriends; when Mexican American boys feel themselves descended in spirit from white "uncles"; when children of mixed marriages insist that they are whatever race they say they are, all of them are more than just confused.

They're inching toward what Andrea Jones calls "the dream of what the twenty-first century should be." In the ever more diverse communities of Northern California, they're also facing the complicated reality of what their twenty-first century will be.

Meanwhile, in the living room of the Miller family's San Leandro home, the argument continues unabated. "You don't know what you are," April's father has told her more than once. But she just keeps on telling him he doesn't know what time it is.

CRITICAL READING

1. Search for some library and Internet sources that enable you to compare Nell Bernstein's statistics about the ethnic makeup of California schools with those of the rest of the country. List the sources you found. How does California compare with the rest of the country? Have there been changes since 1994 when this was written?

2. Bernstein organizes this article through a series of interviews that take her to different venues around suburban Oakland. Trace the progress of her extended **encounter**. Do you think she described

these in the order they happened, or do you see a rhetorically strategic reason for her shaping them as she did?

3. Formulate the main issue that Bernstein maps in response to her observations. Which side of that issue would you say she is on? Give evidence for your answer.

4. Is Bernstein's **resolution** one of trying to change her readers' attitudes or of trying to instigate a program? Make a close-fitting paraphrase of her resolution.

5. How does Bernstein crochet the ending? Explain how April's criticism of her father has gained significance through all the intervening experiences.

DISCUSSION QUESTIONS

1. Explain the background of Mr. Miller's belief that he lost his job because of NAFTA. Do you think he is probably justified in his belief? Could NAFTA have affected the whole community? (If necessary, do some research before answering.)

2. Why do you think there is a desire on the part of some teens from "good" families to be, or affect to be, "bad"? What role do or should adults play in this phenomenon? Give some examples to illustrate your points.

3. Have you ever lived in a multiethnic community? If so, compare the interactions you witnessed with those described in the article. Use specific events and quotations to illustrate the comparison. If not, describe advantages and disadvantages of living in a homogeneous community. Illustrate with specific examples.

4. Do you come from a multiethnic family, or do you have relatives or friends who have married across ethnic lines? If so, compare their experiences with those in this article. Use specific events and quotations to illustrate the comparison. If not, have you ever dated or had a close friend of a different ethnic background? Describe interesting surprises, both positive and negative, and assess the significance of each in terms of the issues of this article. If not, would you consider such a relationship? Why or why not?

DEMONSTRATION: MODALITIES IN "GOIN' GANGSTA, CHOOSIN' CHOLITA"

Here is a chance to check your observations about the modalities in "Goin' Gangsta, Choosin' Cholita" with mine. I have done a sampling of the modality shifts; at the end I will ask you what others you found. You will notice also that I have highlighted what I feel is the **surprise** in each example and the **significance** of it. Although surprise is most evident in encounters, reader interest needs to be fed by surprises in the other modalities as well.

Encounter

Her lipstick is dark, the lip liner even darker, nearly black. In baggy pants, a blue plaid Pendleton, her bangs pulled back tight off her forehead, fifteen-year-old April is a perfect cholita, a Mexican gangsta girl. But April Miller is Anglo. "And I don't like it!" she complains, "I'd rather be Mexican." April's father wanders into the family room of their home in San Leandro, California, a suburb near Oakland. "Hey, cholita," he teases. "Go get a suntan. We'll put you in a barrio and see how much you like it." [1]

> Although the research for this article probably took several days, Bernstein's choice of topic was probably inspired by encountering Caucasian cholitas in and around San Francisco. So she begins with a particular encounter—an interview—with one of them.

The Surprise

> The author **encounters** a girl who rejects her birthright of membership in what (up to now) has been the country's dominant culture.

A large, sandy-haired man with "April" tattooed on one arm and "Kelly"—the name of his older daughter—on the other, Miller spent twenty-one years working in a San Leandro glass factory that shut down and moved to Mexico a couple of years ago. He recently got a job in another factory, but he expects NAFTA to swallow that one, too. [2]

Background

"Sooner or later we'll all get nailed," he says. "Just another stab in the back of the American middle class." [3]

Later, April gets her revenge: "Hey, Mr. White Man's Last Stand," she teases. "Wait till you see how well I manage my welfare check. You'll be asking me for money!" [4]

A once almost exclusively white, now increasingly Latin and black working-class suburb, San Leandro borders on predominantly black East Oakland. For decades, the boundary was strictly policed and practically impenetrable. [5]

> April's **background** was a segregated, working-class suburb. As jobs are lost (ironically to Mexico), the area becomes poorer, and disadvantaged groups can afford to enter.

The Surprise

Search

In 1970 April Miller's hometown was 97 percent white. By 1990 San Leandro was 65 percent white, 6 percent black, 15 percent Hispanic, and 13 percent Asian or Pacific Islander.

The Surprise

With minorities moving into suburbs in growing numbers and cities becoming ever more diverse, the boundary between city and suburb is dissolving, and

The author's re**search** found that the change in ethnic makeup of the suburb had been pretty drastic over the last 20 years.

suburban teenagers are changing with the times. In April's bedroom, her past and present selves lie in layers, the pink walls of girlhood almost obscured, Guns N' Roses and Pearl Jam posters overlaid by rappers Paris and Ice Cube. "I don't have a big enough attitude to be a black girl," says April, explaining her current choice of ethnic identification. [6]

Reasoning

What matters is that she thinks the choice is hers. For April and her friends, identity is not a matter of where you come from, what you were born into, what color your skin is. It's what you wear, the music you listen to, the words you use—every-

The author **reasons** that "choosing" your heritage implies a wholly new meaning of the word *ethnicity*.

thing to which you pledge allegiance, no matter how fleetingly. [7]

The hybridization of American teens has become talk show fodder, with "wiggers"—white kids who dress and talk "black"—appearing on TV in full gangsta regalia. In Indiana a group of white high school girls raised a national stir when they triggered an imitation race war at their virtually all white high school last fall simply by dressing "black." In many parts of the country, it's television and radio, not neighbors, that introduce teens to the allure of ethnic difference. But in California, which demographers predict will be the first state with no racial majority by the year 2000, the influences are more immediate. The California public schools are the most diverse in the country: 42 percent white, 36 percent Hispanic, 9 percent black, 8 percent Asian. [8]

Sometimes young people fight over their differences. Students at virtually any school in the Bay Area can recount the details of at least one "race riot" in which a conflict between individuals escalated into a battle between their clans. More often, though, teens would rather join than fight. Adolescence, after all, is the period when you're most inclined to mimic the power closest at hand, from stealing your older sister's clothes to copying the ruling clique at school. [9]

White skaters and Mexican would-be gangbangers listen to gangsta rap and call each other "nigga" as a term of endearment; white girls sometimes affect Spanish accents; blond cheerleaders claim Cherokee ancestors. [10]

"Claiming" is the central concept here. A Vietnamese teen in Hayward, another Oakland suburb, "claims" Oakland—and by implication blackness—because he lived there as a child. A law-abiding white kid "claims" a Mexican gang he says he hangs with. A brown-skinned girl with a Mexican father and a white mother "claims" her Mexican side, while her fair-skinned sister "claims" white. The word comes up over and over, as if identity were territory, the self a kind of turf. [11]

At a restaurant in a minimall in Hayward, Nicole Huffstutler, thirteen, sits with her friends and describes herself as "Indian, German, French, Welsh, and, um . . . American": "If somebody says anything like 'Yeah, you're just a *peckerwood*,' I'll walk up and I'll say '*white pride*!' Cause I'm *proud* of my race, and I wouldn't wanna be any other." [12]

Valuation

"Claiming" white has become a matter of *principle* for Heather, too, who says she's "sick of the majority looking at us like we're less than them." (Haywood schools were 51 percent white in 1990, down from 77 percent in 1980, and whites are now the minority in many schools.) [13]

The Surprise

Surprises are to get attention. Valuation is a consolidation that goes on constantly. Although the author **encounters** teens who are proud of their adoptive cultures, the underlined words show she **values** those who are true to their authentic heritage.

Asked if she knows that nonwhites have not traditionally been referred to as "the majority" in America, Heather gets exasperated: "I hear that all the time, every day. They say, 'Well, you guys controlled us for many years, and it's time for us to control you.' Every day."[14]

When Jennifer Vargas—a small, brown-skinned girl in purple jeans who quietly eats her salad while Heather talks—softly announces that she's "mostly Mexican," she gets in trouble with her friends. [15]

"No, you're not!" scolds Heather. [16]

"I'm mostly Indian and Mexican," Jennifer continues flatly. "I'm very little . . . I'm mostly . . ." [17]

"Your mom's white!" Nicole reminds her sharply. "She has blond hair. [18]

"That's what I mean," Nicole adds. "People think that white is a bad thing. They think that white is a bad race. So she's trying to claim more Mexican than white." [19]

"I have very little white in me," Jennifer repeats. "I have mostly my dad's side, 'cause I look like him and stuff. And most of my friends think that me and my brother and sister aren't related, 'cause they look more like my mom." [20]

"But you guys are all the same race, you just look different," Nicole insists. She stops eating and frowns. "OK, you're half and half each what your parents have. So you're equal as your brother and sister, you just look different. And you should be proud of what you are—every little piece and bit of what you are. Even if you were Afghan or whatever, you should be proud of it." [21]

Will Mosley, Heather's seventeen-year-old brother, says he and his friends listen to rap groups like Compton's Most Wanted, NWA, and Above the Law because they "sing about life"—that is, what happens in Oakland, Los Angeles, anyplace but where Will is sitting today, an empty Round Table Pizza in a minimall. [22]

"No matter what race you are," Will says, "if you live like we do, then that's the kind of music you like." [23]

And how do they live? [24]

"We don't live bad or anything," Will admits. "We live in a pretty good neighborhood, there's no violence or crime. I was just . . . we're just city people, I guess." [25]

Will and his friend Adolfo Garcia, sixteen, say they've outgrown trying to be something they're not. "When I was eleven or twelve," Will says, "I thought I was becoming a big gangsta and stuff. Because I liked that music, and thought it was the coolest, I wanted to become that. I wore big clothes, like you wear in jail. But then I kind of woke up. I looked at myself and thought, 'Who am I trying to be?' " [26]

They may have outgrown blatant mimicry, but Will and his friends remain convinced that they can live in a suburban tract house with a well-kept lawn on a tree-lined street in "not a bad neighborhood" and still call themselves "city" people on the basis of musical tastes. "City" for these young people means crime, graffiti, drugs. The kids are law-abiding, but these activities connote what Will admiringly calls "action." With pride in his voice, Will predicts that "in a couple of years, Hayward will be like Oakland. It's starting to get more known, because of crime and things. I think it'll be bigger, more things happening, more crime, more graffiti, stealing cars." [27]

"That's good," chimes in fifteen-year-old Matt Jenkins, whose new beeper—an item that once connoted gangsta chic but now means little more than an active social life—goes off periodically. "More fun." [28]

The three young men imagine with disdain life in a gangsta-free zone. "Too bland, too boring," Adolfo says. "You have to have something going on. You can't just have everyday life." [29]

"Mowing your lawn," Matt sneers. [30]

"Like Beaver Cleaver's house," Adolfo adds. "It's too clean out here." [31]

Not only white kids believe that identity is a matter of choice or taste, or that the power of "claiming" can transcend ethnicity. The Manor Park Locos—a group of mostly Mexican-Americans who hang out in San Leandro's Manor Park—say they descend from the Manor Lords, tough white guys who ruled the neighborhood a generation ago. [32]

They "are like our . . . uncles and dads, the older generation," says Jesse Martinez, fourteen. "We're what they were when they were around, except we're Mexican." [33]

"There's three generations," says Oso, Jesse's younger brother. "There's Manor Lords, Manor Park Locos, and Manor Park Pee Wees." The Pee Wees consist mainly of the Locos' younger brothers, eager kids who circle the older boys on bikes and brag about "punking people." [34]

Unlike Will Mosley, the Locos find little glamour in city life. They survey the changing suburban landscape and see not "action" or "more fun" but frightening decline. Though most of them are not yet eighteen, the Locos are already nostalgic, longing for a Beaver Cleaver past that white kids who mimic them would scoff at. [35]

Walking through nearly empty Manor Park, with its eucalyptus stands, its softball diamond and tennis courts, Jesse's friend Alex, the only Asian in the group, waves his arms in a gesture of futility. "A few years ago, every bench was filled," he says. "Now no one comes here. I guess it's because of everything that's going on. My parents paid a lot for this house, and I want it to be nice for them. I just hope this doesn't turn into Oakland." [36]

Glancing across the park at April Miller's street, Jesse says he knows what the white cholitas are about. "It's not a racial thing," he explains. "It's just all the most popular people out here are Mexican. We're just the gangstas that everyone knows. I guess those girls wanna be known." [37]

Not every young Californian embraces the new racial *hybridism*. Andrea Jones, twenty, an African American who grew up in the Bay Area suburbs of Union City and Hayward, is unimpressed by what she sees mainly as shallow mimicry. "It's full of posers out here," she says. "When *Boyz N the Hood* came out on video, it was sold out for weeks. The boys all wanna be black, the girls all wanna be Mexican. It's the glamour." [38]

VALUATION Experienced writers know how to nudge the reader toward the values they are going to conclude with. This is often done with words of positive or negative connotation. *Hybridism* is a good word at 4H clubs but otherwise suggests bringing things together that don't belong.

Driving down the quiet, shaded streets of her old neighborhood in Union City, Andrea spots two white preteen boys in Raiders jackets and hugely baggy pants strutting erratically down the empty sidewalk. "Look at them," she says. "Dislocated." [39]

She knows why. "In a lot of these schools out here, it's hard being white," she says. "I don't think these kids were prepared for the backlash that is going on, all the pride now in people of color's ethnicity, and our boldness with it. They have nothing like that, no identity, nothing they can say they're proud of. [40]

Explanation

"So they latch onto their great-grandmother who's a Cherokee, or they take on the most stereotypical aspects of being black or Mexican. It's beautiful to appreciate different aspects of other people's culture—that's like the dream of what the twenty-first century should be. But to garnish yourself with pop culture stereotypes just to blend—that's really sad." [41]

The Surprise

The author lets the **reasoning** of a girl she **encounters** offer the **explanation** for Anglos choosing to be Mexicans. And that explanation is based on the rapid change in the **background** of the community—Anglos are not used to minority status.

Note how the author begins to tie modalities together toward the final **resolution. Explanation** and **resolution** should flow naturally from the other modalities.

Roland Krevocheza, eighteen, graduated last year from Arroyo High School in San Leandro. He is Mexican on his mother's side, Eastern European on his father's. In the new hierarchies, it may be mixed kids like Roland who have the hardest time finding their place, even as their numbers grow. (One in five marriages in California is between people of different races.) They can always be called "wannabes," no matter what they claim. [42]

"I'll state all my nationalities," Roland says. But he takes a greater interest in his father's side, his Ukrainian, Romanian, and Czech ancestors. "It's more unique," he explains. "Mexican culture is all around me. We eat Mexican food all the time. I hear stories from my grandmother. I see the low-riders and stuff. I'm already part of it. I'm not trying to be; I am." [43]

His darker-skinned brother "says he's not proud to be white," Roland adds. "He calls me 'Mr. Nazi.' " In the room the two share, the American flags and the reproduction of the Bill of Rights are Roland's; the Public Enemy poster belongs to his brother. [44]

Roland has good reason to mistrust gangsta attitudes. In his junior year in high school, he was one of several Arroyo students who were beaten up outside the school at lunchtime by a group of Samoans who came in cars from Oakland. Roland wound up with a split lip, a concussion, and a broken tailbone. Later he was told that the assault was "gang-related"—that the Samoans were beating up anyone wearing red. [45]

"Rappers, I don't like them," Roland says. "I think they're a bad influence on kids. It makes kids think they're all tough and bad." [46]

Those who, like Roland, dismiss the gangsta and cholo styles as *affectations* can point to the fact that several companies market *overpriced* knockoffs of "ghetto wear" *targeted* at teens. [47]

> **VALUATION** The negatively charged words here imply that the author agrees with Roland's values and that the commercialism of the ethnic crossover styles cheapens the whole movement.

But there's also something going on out here that transcends adolescent faddishness and pop culture exoticism. When white kids call their parents "racist" for nagging them about their baggy pants; when they learn Spanish to talk to their boyfriends; when Mexican American boys feel themselves descended in spirit from white "uncles"; when children of mixed marriages insist that they are whatever race they say they are, all of them are more than just confused. [48]

> Beginning a paragraph with *But* is always an important signal that an entire modality is changing direction. The author may be finding a way out of the negative valuations.

Resolution

> Preparing for the **resolution**. Professional writers nearly always pick up one or more of the earlier encounters to launch their conclusions, because it gives the reader a feeling of completeness and closure. It is an excellent device for apprentice writers also, because looking back to the first encounter helps to ensure that the resolution you are about to synthesize has indeed evolved from your starting point and is not a mutant intruder of some ancestry unknown to this essay.

The Surprise

They're inching toward what Andrea Jones calls "the dream of what the twenty-first century should be." In the ever more diverse communities of Northern California, they're also facing the complicated reality of what their twenty-first century will be. [49]

Drawing again from Andrea's **reasoning** and the demographic **background,** the author tries to reach a new, synthesized, higher **resolution** of the problem from the wider perspective of the larger society—The way to the desired all-American melting pot is surprisingly more difficult than most of us had imagined.

CRITICAL READING

Go thorough the parts of the article that I skipped and map the modality movements, noting when Bernstein shifts from one to another. (You can use paragraph numbers for identification.) You will probably find that in many cases more than one modality is operating in a paragraph. For each major modality shift, justify your identification. Tell, in other words,

- ☐ Who is **encountering** whom
- ☐ What is being **explained**
- ☐ What **valuation** is applied to what
- ☐ How you know that Bernstein must have **searched** out this information
- ☐ What need in the reader requires this **background**
- ☐ What **reasoning** the author is doing to justify her opinion or perception
- ☐ How the issue is being **resolved** and whether the issue is being resolved by a change of attitude or a program

Finally, explain the significance of each modal section.

INVITATION TO A READING

Here is a final, and I think very moving example, of the power of skillful writing to help us "dock" with another human space ship and enter a life, some parts of which will seem quite alien to most of us. Once inside, this writer may succeed in tuning our values to a more harmonious pitch by surprising us with the significance of an extraordinary encounter.

In his book *On the Rez* Ian Frazier describes his visits to the Pine Ridge Indian Reservation in South Dakota where his Oglala friend Le

War Lance lives. (The Sioux, whose own name for themselves was *Lakota*—a name which they still use—are divided into many branches, one of which is the Oglala.) In the course of describing life on the reservation and some of the history of the Indians' experience with the U.S. government and non-Indian Americans, Frazier celebrates the spirit of heroic freedom that he believes Europeans learned in large part from the Indians. It is a spirit he believes that most of us are losing today even while it continues to persist undimmed in Indian culture. In particular, on one of his visits to the Pine Ridge Reservation, Frazier learned of a girl athlete, SuAnne Big Crow. Before her tragic death in an auto accident at the age of eighteen, she had, through her intense dedication to basketball and to people, come close to fulfilling a medicine man's prophecy. The medicine man had told SuAnne's mother, Leatrice "Chick" Big Crow, that SuAnne had been the spirit of a former chief Big Crow come back to reunite the people of the tribe.

I have put numbers at junctures where I sense the author has shifted gears from one modality to another—or sometimes from one mix of modalities to another mix. As you are reading, see if you can identify the one or two modalities that seem to be operating in each section. Feel free to make other divisions if you sense other shifts.

from *On the Rez*
by Ian Frazier

[1] One afternoon Le and I were driving on Highway 18 in Pine Ridge when I noticed a single-story factorystyle building across a weedy field. It had some lettering and a mural of a landscape on the front. A sign by the highway said it was the SuAnne Big Crow Health and Recreation Center, and below that were the words "Happytown, USA." I asked Le if he knew who SuAnne Big Crow was. He said, "She was a basketball star for Pine Ridge High School who helped 'em win the state championship and died in a car wreck a few years back. It was when I was living in New York, though, so that's about all I know."

A day or two later, I drove up to the building and parked in the dirt parking lot out front. Up close, I could see that the mural painted on the building's wall of corrugated steel depicted Sioux country from the Black Hills to the prairie and Pine Ridge. The tops of the letters of "SuAnne" in the center's name were lost in the white clouds over the Hills. A chunk of cinder block propped open the green steel front door. I went in. First to greet me was the smell of hamburgers frying. In the many times I would return, that frying smell would always be there. I would bring it away with me in my clothes and even in the pages of my notebooks, and when I happened to meet it in other places, I would always think of the SuAnne Big Crow Center. I had never much liked hamburgers or their smell before, but now it is a happy and inspiring aroma in my mind.

The entry hall had fluorescent lights above and a banner that said WELCOME TO HAPPYTOWN, USA. The images in the hall were a temporarily confusing combination of Oglala pride and 1950s-revival style. The words for "Boys" and "Girls" on the restroom doors on my left were in Sioux. On a table in a corner was a highly polished pair of brown-and-white saddle shoes. Above them hung the flag of the Oglala nation, and next to the flag was a large framed portrait of a young Elvis Presley—a more Indian-looking Elvis, it seemed to me, with a darker complexion and blacker, straighter hair. Framed photographs of a teenage girl smiling in a basketball warm-up jacket, making a shot in a basketball game, looking serious in a formal dress next to a boy in a tuxedo, gave the place the additional aura of a shrine.

The hall led, on the left, to a cafe in a big room with a lunch counter and tables and booths. The back end of a 1955 Packard affixed to one wall held potato and macaroni salads in its open trunk. A few late lunch customers were eating burgers at the booths or helping themselves to salad. A loud jukebox played fifties and sixties songs. Old-time Pepsi-Cola memorabilia decorated the walls, along with black-and-white photo portraits of John F. Kennedy and Martin Luther King, and several more portraits of Elvis. Kids of junior high age and younger were hanging out—eating ice-cream cones, playing video games.

At the end of the hallway on the right was a smaller room with glass trophy cases along the walls. The trophies all were from the athletic career of SuAnne Big Crow, the teenage girl in the photos, the person for whom the center was named. I looked at the trophies, I watched a short video playing on a VCR in the room, I read some framed news stories
[2] about SuAnne Big Crow, and a sense of discovery came over me. Here was a hero—not a folk hero, a sports hero, a tribal hero, or an American hero, but a combination of all these. I had thought that Oglala heroes existed mostly in the past. But a true Oglala hero appeared in the late 1980s, while the rest of the world was looking the other way, in suffering Pine Ridge, right under everyone's noses: SuAnne Big Crow.

. . .

[3] By the time SuAnne was in eighth grade, she had grown to five feet, five inches tall ("but she played six foot," Zimiga said); she was long-limbed,

well-muscled, and quick. She had high cheekbones, a prominent, arched upper lip that lined up with the basket when she aimed the ball, and short hair that she wore in no particular style. She could have played every game for the varsity when she was in eighth grade, but Coach Zimiga, who took over girls' varsity basketball that year, wanted to keep peace among older players who had waited for their chance to be on the team. He kept SuAnne on the junior varsity during the regular season. The varsity team had a good year, and when it advanced to the district playoffs, Zimiga brought SuAnne up from the JVs for the play-off games. Several times she got into foul trouble; the referees rule strictly in tournament games, and SuAnne was used to a more headlong style of play. She and her cousin Doni De Cory, a 5'10" junior, combined for many long-break baskets, with Doni throwing downcourt passes to SuAnne on the scoring end. In the district play-off against the team from Red Cloud, SuAnne scored thirty-one points. In the regional play-off game, Pine Ridge beat a good Todd County team, but in the state tournament they lost all three games and finished eighth.

[4] Some people who live in the cities and towns near reservations treat their Indian neighbors decently; some don't. In cities like Denver and Minneapolis and Rapid City, police have been known to harass Indian teenagers and rough up Indian drunks and needlessly stop and search Indian cars. Local banks whose deposits include millions in tribal funds sometimes charge Indians higher loan interest rates than they charge whites. Gift shops near reservations sell junky caricature Indian pictures and dolls, and until not long ago, beer coolers had signs on them that said, INDIAN POWER. In a big discount store in a reservation border town, a white clerk observes a lot of Indians waiting at the checkout and remarks, "Oh, they're Indians—they're used to standing in line." Some people in South Dakota hate Indians, unapologetically, and will tell you why; in their voices you can hear a particular American meanness that is centuries old.

When teams from Pine Ridge play non-Indian teams, the question of race is always there. When Pine Ridge is the visiting team, usually their hosts are courteous, and the players and fans have a good time. But Pine Ridge coaches know that occasionally at away games their kids will be insulted, their fans will not feel welcome, the host gym will be dense with hostility, and the referees will call fouls on Indian players every chance they get. Sometimes in a game between Indian and non-Indian teams, the difference in race becomes an important and distracting part of the event.

[5] One place where Pine Ridge teams used to get harassed regularly was in the high school gymnasium in Lead, South Dakota. Lead is a town of

about 3,200 northwest of the reservation, in the Black Hills. It is laid out among the mines that are its main industry, and low, wooded mountains hedge it round. The brick high school building is set into a hillside. The school's only gym in those days was small, with tiers of gray-painted concrete on which the spectator benches descended from just below the steelbeamed roof to the very edge of the basketball court—an arrangement that greatly magnified the interior noise.

[6] In the fall of 1988, the Pine Ridge Lady Thorpes went to Lead to play a basketball game. SuAnne was a full member of the team by then. She was a freshman, fourteen years old. Getting ready in the locker room, the Pine Ridge girls could hear the din from the fans. They were yelling fake-Indian war cries, a "woo-woo-woo" sound. The usual plan for the pre-game warm-up was for the visiting team to run onto the court in a line, take a lap or two around the floor, shoot some baskets, and then go to their bench at courtside. After that, the home team would come out and do the same, and then the game would begin. Usually the Thorpes lined up for their entry more or less according to height, which meant that senior Doni De Cory, one of the tallest, went first. As the team waited in the hallway leading from the locker room, the heckling got louder. The Lead fans were yelling epithets like "squaw" and "gut-eater." Some were waving food stamps, a reference to the reservation's receiving federal aid. Others yelled, "Where's the cheese?"—the joke being that if Indians were lining up, it must be to get commodity cheese. The Lead high school band had joined in, with fake-Indian drumming and a fake-Indian tune. Doni De Cory looked out the door and told her teammates, "I can't handle this." SuAnne quickly offered to go first in her place. She was so eager that Doni became suspicious. "Don't embarrass us," Doni told her. SuAnne said, "I won't. I won't embarrass you." Doni gave her the ball, and SuAnne stood first in line.

She came running onto the court dribbling the basketball, with her teammates running behind. On the court, the noise was deafeningly loud. SuAnne went right down the middle; but instead of running a full lap, she suddenly stopped when she got to center court. Her teammates were taken by surprise, and some bumped into one another. Coach Zimiga at the rear of the line did not know why they had stopped. SuAnne turned to Doni De Cory and tossed her the ball. Then she stepped into the jump-ball circle at center court, in front of the Lead fans. She unbuttoned her warm-up jacket, took it off, draped it over her shoulders, and began to do the Lakota shawl dance. SuAnne knew all the traditional dances—she had competed in many powwows as a little girl—and the dance she chose is a young woman's dance, graceful and modest and show-offy all at the same time. "I couldn't believe it—she was powwowin', like, 'get down!'" Doni De Cory recalled. "And then she started to sing." SuAnne began to sing in Lakota, swaying back and forth in the jump-ball circle, doing the shawl dance, using her warm-up jacket for a shawl. The crowd went completely silent. "All that stuff the Lead fans were yelling—it was like she reversed it somehow," a team-mate said. In the sudden quiet, all you could hear was her Lakota song. SuAnne stood up, dropped her jacket, took the ball from Doni De Cory, and ran a lap around the court dribbling expertly and fast. The fans began to cheer and applaud. She sprinted to the basket, went up in the air, and laid the ball through the hoop, with the fans cheering loudly now. Of course, Pine Ridge went on to win the game.

Because this is one of the coolest and bravest deeds I ever heard of, I want to stop and consider it from a larger perspective that includes the town of Lead, all the Black Hills, and 125 years of history:

[7] Lead, the town, does not get its name from the metal. The lead the name refers to is a mining term for a gold-bearing deposit, or vein, running through surrounding rock. The word, pronounced with a long *e*, is related to the word "lode." During the Black Hills gold rush of the 1870s, prospectors found a rich lead in what would become the town of Lead. In April 1876, Fred and Moses Manuel staked a claim to a mine they called the Homestake. Their lead led eventually to gold and more gold—a small mountain of gold—whose value may be guessed by the size of the hole its extraction has left in the middle of present-day Lead. In 1877, a mining engineer from San Francisco named George Hearst came to the Hills, investigated the Manuels' mine, and advised his big-city partners to buy it. The price was $70,000. At the time of Hearst's negotiations, the illegal act of Congress which would take this land from the Sioux had only recently passed. The partners followed Hearst's advice, and the Homestake Mine paid off its purchase price four times over in dividends alone within three years. When George Hearst's only son, William Randolph, was kicked out of Harvard for giving his instruc-tors chamber pots with their names inscribed on the inside, George Hearst suggested that he come West and take over his (George's) share in the Homestake Mine. William Randolph Hearst chose to run the San Francisco *Examiner* instead. His father gave him a blank check to keep it going for two years; gold from Lead helped start the Hearst newspaper empire. Since the Homestake Mine was discovered, it has produced at least $10 billion in gold. It is one of the richest gold mines in the world.

Almost from the moment of the Custer expedition's entry into the Black Hills in 1874, there was no way the Sioux were going to be allowed to keep this land. By 1875, the Dakota Territorial Legislature had already divided the Black Hills land into counties; Custer County, in the southern Hills, was named in that general's honor while he was still alive, and while the land still clearly belonged to the Sioux. Many people in government and elsewhere knew at the time that taking this land was wrong. At first, the Army even made halfhearted attempts to keep the prospectors out. A high-ranking treaty negotiator told President Grant that the Custer expedition was "a violation of the national honor." One of the commissioners who worked on the "agreement" that gave paper legitimacy to the theft said that Custer should not have gone into the Hills in the first place; he and the other commissioners reminded the government that it was making the Sioux homeless and that it owed them protection and care. The taking of the Black Hills proceeded inexorably all the same.

. . .

[8] Inescapably, this history is present when an Oglala team goes to Lead to play a basketball game. It may even explain why the fans in Lead were so mean: fear that you might perhaps be in the wrong can make you ornerier sometimes. In all the accounts of this land grab and its aftermath, and among the many greedy and driven men who had a part, I cannot find evidence of a single act as elegant, as generous, or as transcendent as SuAnne's dance at center court in the gym at Lead.

[9] For the Oglala, what SuAnne did that day almost immediately took on the stature of myth. People from Pine Ridge who witnessed it still describe it in terms of awe and disbelief. Amazement swept through the younger kids when they heard. "I was, like, 'What did she just do?' " recalled her cousin Angie Big Crow, an eighth-grader at the time. All over the reservation, people told and retold the story of SuAnne at Lead. Any time the subject of SuAnne came up when I was talking to people on Pine Ridge, I would always ask if they had heard about what she did at Lead, and always the answer was a smile and a nod—"Yeah, I was there," or "Yeah, I heard about that." To the unnumbered big and small slights of local racism which the Oglala have known all their lives, SuAnne's exploit made an emphatic reply.

[10] Back in the days when Lakota war parties still fought battles against other tribes and the Army, no deed of war was more honored than the act of counting coup. To count coup means to touch an armed enemy in full possession of his powers with a special stick called a coup stick, or

with the hand. The touch is not a blow, and only serves to indicate how close to the enemy you came. As an act of bravery, counting coup was regarded as greater than killing an enemy in single combat, greater than taking a scalp or horses or any prize. Counting coup was an act of almost abstract courage, of pure playfulness taken to the most daring extreme. Very likely, to do it and survive brought an exhilaration to which nothing could compare. In an ancient sense which her Oglala kin could recognize, SuAnne counted coup on the fans of Lead.

[11]   And yet this coup was an act not of war but of peace. SuAnne's coup strike was an offering, an invitation. It took the hecklers at the best interpretation, as if their silly mocking chants were meant only in goodwill. It showed that their fake Indian songs were just that—fake—and that the real thing was better, as real things usually are. We Lakota have been dancing like this for centuries, the dance said; we've been doing the shawl dance since long before you came, before you had gotten on the boat in Glasgow or Bremerhaven, before you stole this land, and we're still doing it today; and isn't it pretty, when you see how it's supposed to be done? Because finally what SuAnne proposed was to invite us—us onlookers in the stands, which is the non-Lakota rest of this country—to dance, too. She was in the Lead gym to play, and she invited us all to play. The symbol she used to include us was the warm-up jacket. Everyone in America has a warm-up jacket. I've got one, probably so do you, so did (no doubt) many of the fans at Lead. By using the warm-up jacket as a shawl in her impromptu shawl dance, she made Lakota relatives of us all.

"It was funny," Doni De Cory said, "but after that game the relationship between Lead and us was tremendous. When we played Lead again, the games were really good, and we got to know some of the girls on the team. Later, when we went to a tournament and Lead was there, we were hanging out with the Lead girls and eating pizza with them. We got to know some of their parents, too. What SuAnne did made a lasting impression and changed the whole situation with us and Lead. We found out there are some really good people in Lead."

[12]   America is a leap of the imagination. From its beginning, people had only a persistent idea of what a good country should be. The idea involved freedom, equality, justice, and the pursuit of happiness; nowadays most of us probably could not describe it a lot more clearly than that. The truth is, it always has been a bit of a guess. No one has ever known for sure whether a country based on such an idea is really possible, but again and again, we have leaped toward the idea and hoped.

What SuAnne Big Crow demonstrated in the Lead high school gym is that making the leap is the whole point. The idea does not truly live unless it is expressed by an act; the country does not live unless we make the leap from our tribe or focus group or gated community or demographic, and land on the shaky platform of that idea of a good country which all kinds of different people share.

This leap is made in public, and it's made for free. It's not a product or a service that anyone will pay you for. You do it for reasons unexplainable by economics—for ambition, out of conviction, for the heck of it, in playfulness, for love. It's done in public spaces, face-to-face, where anyone is free to go. It's not done on television, on the Internet, or over the telephone; our electronic systems can only tell us if the leap made elsewhere has succeeded or failed. The places you'll see it are high school gyms, city sidewalks, the subway, bus stations, public parks, parking lots, and wherever people gather during natural disasters. In those places and others like them, the leaps that continue to invent and knit the country continue to be made. When the leap fails, it looks like the L.A. riots, or Sherman's March through Georgia. When it succeeds, it looks like the New York City Bicentennial Celebration in July 1976, or the Civil Rights March on Washington in 1963. On that scale, whether it succeeds or fails, it's always something to see. The leap requires physical presence and physical risk. But the payoff—in terms of dreams realized, of understanding, of people getting along—can be so glorious as to make the risk seem minuscule.

[13] I find all this hopefulness, and more, in SuAnne's dance at center court in the gym in Lead. My high school football coach used to show us films of our previous game every Monday after practice, and whenever he liked a particular play, he would run it over and over again. If I had a film of SuAnne at Lead (as far as I know, no such film or video exists), I would study it in slow motion frame by frame. There's a magic in what she did, along with the promise that public acts of courage are still alive out there somewhere. Mostly, I would run the film of SuAnne again and again for my own braveheart[1] song. I refer to her, as I do to Crazy Horse, for proof that it's a public service to be brave.

---

[1] A reference to the1995 Mel Gibson movie about a 13th Century Scot, William Wallace, who led his people to a victory over the English invaders. Although Braveheart was executed in London, his spirit led to independence for Scotland with ultimate reconciliation .

CRITICAL READING

1. How did you identify each of the sections as to its modality or modalities?
2. In section 4, Ian Frazier begins a bit of triangulation, introducing the subject of race prejudice without an immediate transition. When do we find out where it is leading? Is the technique successful in piquing your curiosity? Do you see another place where the author uses triangulation? Explain how it works.
3. There are a number of eye-openers in several different modality sections. Specify the ones that seem most striking to you.
4. What technique does Frazier use to dramatize the encounters he describes?
5. Describe the issue map that Frazier lays out in this selection. In chapter 6 (Background), I described how conflicts can sometimes be resolved by redrawing the issue map. In the epigraph of that chapter I quoted Matthew Miller: "Politicians escape this kind of dead end when . . . leaders emerge with fresh ways of framing the issues." Can SuAnne's success in bringing a measure of racial harmony to the Black Hills be attributed to her ability to shift the issue map? If so, describe how it worked. If not, how was it that she succeeded?
6. This is a strongly value-centered piece. Point out some specific techniques by which Mr. Frazier communicates emotionally the value he sees in Indian culture.

DISCUSSION QUESTIONS

1. Would you have felt differently about this piece if it had been written by an Indian? Explain.
2. Many people would argue that it is politically incorrect to refer to "Native Americans" as "Indians." But in the entire book from which this excerpt is taken, neither Frazier nor his Indian friends on the reservation use the term *Native Americans*; when they want to refer generally to people from a variety of tribes, they use the word *Indian.* How do you feel about this?
3. Frazier is not an Indian (although he is enough of an admirer of the Indian values of freedom and heroism that one of his Indian friends calls him a "wannabe"). Would your reaction to the credibility of the author have been different if he had been an Indian? Does his **not** being an Indian have an impact on your reaction to the article?

WRITING COMMISSION

Both the pieces in this chapter, as well as "She Converted" in chapter 7 ("Background"), deal with a surprising new feature of a culture that is increasingly more ethnically diverse—the ability, maybe even the necessity of choosing one's own ethnicity. This was brought to national focus during the census of 2000. One was able to check as many boxes as one thought applied, including 4 varieties of Hispanic and 11 varieties of Asian, in addition to White, Black, or American Indian. The census help Web page gave an example of a person who might consider himself or herself "white black Korean." This might lead some people to say "Ethnicity doesn't matter as much any more," or, as we saw in the three essays noted here, others might say that, indeed, it matters more, but it becomes a matter of choice.

The author of "On the Rez" says, earlier in the book from which we read an excerpt,

> I am a middle-aged non-Indian who wears his hair in a thinning ponytail copied originally from the traditional-style long hair of the leaders of the American Indian Movement of the 1970s, because I thought it looked cool. When I'm driving across a field near the town of Oglala, on the Pine Ridge Reservation, and I see my friend Floyd John walking across it the other way, I stop, and he comes over to the car and leans in the window and smiles a big-tooth grin and says, "How ya' doin', wannabe?" I kind of resent the term "wannabe"—what's wrong with wanting to be something, anyway?—but in my case there's some truth to it. . . . That [Indian] self-possessed sense of freedom is closer to what I want.

In some sense he is "choosin' " Oglala.

The editor of your virtual newspaper has noticed this trend as your period of virtual internship draws to a close. In celebration of the diversity that your presence on the staff has brought to this town, the editor would like you to use these three articles ("She Converted . . .," "Goin' Gangsta, Choosin' Cholita," and "On the Rez") as the focus for an article on "Choosing your Ethnicity."

You have probably seen in newspapers book reviews comparing and contrasting two or three books on a single topic that happen to come out at the same time. That's the idea your editor has here with these three articles. Because your readers will not have read these articles, you will have to introduce them, summarize them, compare the values each writer has discovered in this brave new world.

"In addition to mapping the issue of whether society does or should let people decide their own ethnicity, I expect you to search your own experience in the light of these articles," your editor says. "It is, after all, the diversity you bring to this town that we are celebrating. If you have options in selecting among ancestors, lay out the values of the different groups as you see them and reason out the consequences of the various choices."

"Nonethnicity is still a choice, right?" someone says.

"Sure," the editor replies, "but you have to show why it's a better option, personally and socially, than the back-to-the-roots-of-my-choice movement."

"It's been an interesting summer, Chief! With the healing power of time, we'll probably be able to look back on this and chuckle!" one of you says.

"Well, in spite of the sleepless nights I've had to spend cleaning up your prose, I'm kind of proud of your growth, and I don't suppose us editors can take **all** the credit for that."

"**We** editors, Chief," you point out.

"Aw, g'wan. Git outta here!"

Points to Remember

- Good writing can overcome the naturally isolated human condition by providing a docking mechanism between writer and reader of well-tested rhetorical devices.
- A writer shifts modalities in strategic cycles so as best to engage the reader's mind and emotions.
- The cycles return to a progressively revealed resolution of the surprise that first started the writer's search for an explanation.
- The purpose of writing is, through the benefit of your experience and effort, to help a reader better understand and better deal with other people, the cultures those people create, and the natural universe we all share on this spaceship, Earth.

Literary Credits

Joel Agee
"Cruelty" from TWELVE YEARS by Joel Agee.

Shana Alexander
"Motherliness" from TALKING WOMAN by Shana Alexander. Copyright © 1976 by Shana Alexander.

Russell Baker
Excerpts from GROWING UP by Russell Baker. Copyright © 1982 by Russell Baker.

Sandy Banks
"Reflections on the State of the Union" by Sandy Banks from LOS ANGELES TIMES, July 11, 1999. Copyright © 1999. Reprinted by permission of The Los Angeles Times Syndicate.

Nell Bernstein
"Goin' Gangsta, Choosin' Cholita" by Nell Bernstein from WEST Magazine, November 13, 1994. Reprinted by permisison of the author.

Douglas Besharov
"Asking More From Matrimony" by Douglas Besharov from THE NEW YORK TIMES, July 14, 1999. Copyright © 1999 by The The New York Times Co. Reprinted by permission.

David Brooks
"Living Room Crusaders" by David Brooks from NEWSWEEK, December 15, 1997. Copyright © 1997 by Newsweek, Inc. All rights reserved. Reprinted by permission.

Photo Credits

Cartoon and Drawing Credits

Index